RICHARD HOLMES is Professor of Military and Security Studies at Cranfield University and the Royal Military College of Science. He has written over a dozen books on military history, and his bestsellers include *The Western Front* and *Wellington: The Iron Duke*. He has presented several television series for BBC 2, including both series of *War Walks*. For over thirty years he served as a Territorial infantry officer, rising to the rank of brigadier.

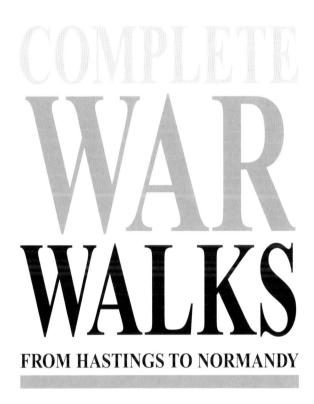

COMPLETE
WAR
WALKS

FROM HASTINGS TO NORMANDY

Richard Holmes

This edition was first published as two separate volumes: *War Walks* in 1996 (hardback) and 1997 (paperback), and *War Walks 2* in 1997 (hardback) and 1998 (paperback) These books were published to accompany the television series entitled *War Walks* The first series was first broadcast in 1996 Series Producer Mark Fielder · Series Producer/Director Steven Clarke The second series was first broadcast in 1997 Executive Producer Grant Mansfield · Series Producer Mark Fielder Producer/Directors Rachel Bell, Steven Clarke, Mark Fielder and Keith Sheather

Published by BBC Worldwide Limited
80 Wood Lane, London W12 0TT

War Walks was first published in hardback 1996 and in paperback 1997
War Walks 2 was first published in hardback 1997 and in paperback 1998
This edition, *Complete War Walks*, was first published in paperback in 2003
© Richard Holmes 2003
The moral right of the author has been asserted

ISBN 0 563 48717 8

Commissioning editors: Sheila Ableman and Sally Potter
Project editor for this edition: Warren Albers
Art director: Linda Blakemore
Designer: Annette Peppis
Maps: Line and Line
Picture research: Anne-Marie Ehrlich, Deirdre O'Day and Charlotte Lochhead
Production controller: Arlene Alexander

Set in Times New Roman
Printed and bound in Great Britain by Butler and Tanner Ltd, Frome

Contents

Introduction

If you want a book about strategy then you have already read too far, for this is a book about men, most of them very ordinary, and the ground they fought on. In a sense this is an unfashionable book, for historiography has long moved away from 'scraps and chaps'. Yet battles and the men who fought them are important: more so than we might wish to admit in an age when war's credibility as a means of pursuing political aims is increasingly questioned.

This book is intended to work at two levels. At one, it is narrative military history, slanted towards the view of regimental officers and men, and intended for the general reader in armchair, train compartment or airline seat. At another, it is aimed at travellers who intend to view the fields themselves. It is not a guidebook in the strict sense, for it will neither suggest where you might eat or sleep, nor attempt comprehensive coverage of the cemeteries and monuments. Instead it identifies those pieces of ground best able to take us, like Dr Who's tardis, from the present to the past. Some can be reached by car but others cannot and, in any event, the texture of a battlefield is best felt by walking the ground, if only for a mile or two. The formula inevitably varies from place to place: the Somme, which lasted for four months, offers a far greater range of walks than Agincourt, which was over in a couple of October hours. The scale of the Blitz and subsequent urban regeneration limit the field experience of this battle, which is perhaps best captured in a London's Imperial War Museum. In contrast, the forest of Mormal, between the battlefields of Mons and Le Cateau, is a beautiful setting for a quiet hour or two.

Each chapter is laid out in three parts, with an introduction which sets the campaign into political and military context, a second, larger section of narrative describing the campaign and battle, and the third, 'a view of the field', suggesting ways in which visitors to the battlefield can see the viewing-points – 'stands', as battlefield visitors often call them – and imagine the events that unrolled across them.

Choosing the Battles
This book focuses on a selection of battles, six fought in Britain – or rather, in one case, struggle that straddled the Channel. A further six are set in a few hundred square miles of northern France and southern Belgium, a space so confined that a single day's drive could take us across most of our battlefields. Choosing the battles from a long list of potential candidates was far from easy, but a certain logic prevails. Battles that had far-reaching consequences, historically and politically, were brought to the forefront of the possible choices. In some cases, because of a battle's importance, it entered part of an enduring mythology that demands attention. There were other obvious considerations that favoured certain battles over others: battles that were particularly decisive, or ones that were well documented, or have battlefields that remain striking today. I shied away from some battles that had already been described so well, in print or on film, that I felt there was nothing new to add. In the end, the list was narrowed down to twelve battles, ranging from medieval Britain to twentieth-century France: Hastings, Agincourt, Bosworth, Naseby, the Boyne, Waterloo, Mons and Le Cateau, the Somme, Arras, Dunkirk, the Blitz and Operation Goodwood.

The Changing Weaponry of War
So much for space. In time we march from Hastings in 1066 and Agincourt in 1415, fought with weapons which might not have dismayed the Romans, to the break-out from Normandy in 1944, whose veterans still enrich Remembrance Day. In the process we touch many of the developments that have shaped the face of war. Cannons were first used in Europe during the Hundred Years War, and in the First World War the inhabitants of Crécy and Azincourt (as Agincourt is now known) heard creeping barrages and lightning bombardments which would have horrified a medieval gunner as much as his smelly and unreliable cannon shocked the men of his own day.

For the men of Hastings, battle centred on muscle-power, applied to bowstring or sword-hilt, for this, like Agincourt, was war in its first age. Waterloo saw war in its second age. Although raw muscle still played its part – cavalrymen hewed one another through steel and bone with a desperation that would not have surprised a medieval warrior – the real killer was flying iron or lead, impelled by gunpowder from the products of the

Industrial Revolution. The process accelerated in the First World War. We might see the Somme as a contest of machine-minders, with gunners busy at their work stations on the giant assembly line that converted metal and chemicals into torn earth and dead soldiers, and the infantry part of their raw material. It was this unequal contest between flesh and metal that so impressed contemporaries. 'Somehow it makes one feel so helpless,' reflected a veteran. 'There is no chance of reprisal for the individual man. The advantage is all with the shell, and you have no comeback.'

The machinery of war grew more complex on the Somme. Tanks made their first halting entry on to the stage there on 15 September 1916, and in May 1940 they burst across it, heading westwards this time, to change the way men thought about war. In August 1914 the aircraft made its first real contribution to major war when an aviator from the Paris garrison saw that the Germans had turned in front of the French capital: the out-flanking wheel of the Schlieffen plan had failed. A generation later, gull-winged Stukas provided German armour with flying artillery, while the preparation for Operation Goodwood in 1944 used strategic bombers to transform the landscape, up-end Tiger tanks, and transform languid Norman countryside into a latter-day version of the Somme.

The Changing Style of Command
It was not simply the tools of killing that changed. Styles of command and the technology on which they depend are rarely as eye-catching as weapons, but they are every bit as important. At Operation Goodwood we can glimpse the dawn of the war's third age, as information technology began to dominate steel, just as that steel had supplanted raw muscle. Our first battles show generalship in its heroic guise: William, Duke of Normandy, and King Harold, a clash of the Titans at Hastings; Henry V, who led his men heroically at Agincourt; and the Duke of Wellington, British commander at the height of his powers as a very 'hands-on' commander at Waterloo. All would have agreed that command in battle meant personal intervention, and that personal intervention meant personal risk. Indeed, the nature of their armies and the weapons they used gave them little choice.

Heroic generalship never ran smoothly: what might have happened had the French sword which lopped off part of Henry's crown bitten deeper, or if one of the bullets which decimated Wellington's staff had hit the duke himself? It was damaged beyond repair by the increase in the size of armies that came with the perfection of conscription in the late nineteenth century. When Henry shouted, 'Advance banners!' he could see his whole host move off across the muddy plough at Agincourt.

Although Wellington's army was much larger, he could gallop across the whole Waterloo position in a few minutes, and his knack of finding the battle's balance meant that he was always on hand to stiffen a shaky square or unleash those volleys that sent the Imperial Guard ebbing back down the slope.

In 1914 this old machine broke down at last. In that first year of the war it was difficult for a commander to be sure where he ought to be. Moltke, German commander-in-chief, was too distant from the battle, and isolation and responsibility imposed on his flawed character a burden it could never sustain. Joffre, his French opponent, was altogether more robust, and had taken the wise precaution of conscripting one of France's leading racing drivers who spun him between subordinate headquarters at a speed which Napoleon – no sluggard when it came to covering ground – would have envied.

As the First World War went on, many senior officers felt compelled to stay back at their headquarters to command rather than to go forward to lead. And after all, what meaningful personal contribution could they make by scrambling about in the trenches? Nonetheless, many generals displayed courage denied them by popular mythology and, in doing so, paid the supreme penalty. Of the first seven British divisional commanders who went to France in 1914, three were killed in action and one was wounded. Only one British divisional commander was killed on the Somme, and the battle's character was in part determined by a more remote style of command. It may be unfair to call it château generalship, but it was certainly command by telephone and typewriter. Technology and military logic alike conspired to draw generals into the rear, almost a foreign country to the glum heroes up the line, where they lost the demonstrative, risk-taking and risk-sharing quality which had hitherto been a matter of honour.

There were still times, even during the Second World War, when heroic leadership tilted the balance. Henry V or Wellington might have had little in common with Major-General Erwin Rommel, commanding 7th Panzer Division at Arras in 1940. Yet they could scarcely have disapproved of his instinct, as British tanks ploughed deep into his division, to position himself at the crucial point, animating a defence which might not have proved successful without his leadership – a quality ancient even when Agincourt was fought.

Crucial Campaigns
The battles we visit in this book differ almost as much in size or significance as they do in weapons or tactics. Some, like Agincourt, Waterloo,

Naseby and the Blitz, shunted history in a particular direction. A victory for the attacker might have had results that we can only guess at: indeed, we have only to look at Hastings, and the far-reaching changes it initiated, to see just how decisive some battles could be. Mons and Le Cateau were tiny by comparison with many other First World War battles, but it is hard to see how the British could have lost them and still won the war. A decisive Allied victory on the Somme might not have ended the war at a stroke, but it could scarcely have failed to alter its complexion. Churchill was right to observe that 'wars are not won by evacuations'. Without the successful extraction of so much of the BEF at Dunkirk his efforts to continue the war would have been fatally undermined. The Blitz was not a battle in the same sense as the others discussed in these pages, but morale was fundamental to it: there was no wholesale collapse of popular resolve in Britain's battered cities. The British counter-attack at Arras and the attack in Operation Goodwood had more modest implications, but each helped to shape a crucial campaign.

Private and Official Accounts of War
Our journey across most of these battlefields is based on a rich mixture of source material. Wellington remarked that it was as difficult to write the history of a battle as of a ball: participants did different things at the same time, with subjective views of events and often no yardstick against which their own recollections might be measured. Nevertheless, if we are to see battles through the eyes of participants, we must start by listening to what they have to tell us. The personal accounts of twentieth-century combat stretch down the whole chain of command. Officers had long kept diaries and written to family and friends. One consequence of the rise in literacy, the availability of writing materials and the arrival of a cross-section of male population in the army was that the keeping of diaries spread throughout the ranks.

The more I work on the First World War the more I am struck by the quality of many of the accounts written by men serving in the ranks. In some cases this ought to be no surprise. Frederic Manning, author of *The Middle Parts of Fortune* and its expurgated version *Her Privates We*, was a poet and essayist who served in the ranks by choice. Ernest Shephard, on the other hand, left school at fourteen and went to sea before enlisting into the Dorset Regiment in 1909 at the age of seventeen. He fought in France as a sergeant and company sergeant-major and was killed as a second lieutenant in January 1917. He recorded his experiences in eighteen small pocket-books, clearly and descriptively written, and illustrated by sketch-maps of trenches. John Lucy was a corporal in 1914 but, as his memoir *There's a Devil in the Drum* demonstrates, was anything but the bone-headed NCO so beloved of scriptwriters. Shephard's diaries and Lucy's account have both been published, but there are hundreds of unpublished personal accounts (an increasing number on audio tapes) in private hands and public collections.

Armies generate paperwork in quantities which sometimes stun even those who ought to be inured to their bureaucratic methods, and a lot finds its way back to archives. The Public Record Office at Kew is an essential port of call for the military historian. In both world wars, units kept daily diaries and these generally survive at Kew. They are of mixed value. If a unit was in the thick of action, its adjutant or chief clerk, upon whom the writing of the diary usually devolved, might have his mind on other things. The important rubs shoulders with the commonplace: a battery diary might tell us how many shells it fired – but not what their targets were.

Official historians have a larger canvas to paint. The official histories of both wars are divided into volumes covering given theatres of war: the red-jacketed First World War series for France and Belgium consists of several volumes for each year, together with associated tomes of maps and annexes. Most were the work of Brigadier-General Sir James Edmonds, whose objectivity remains a matter of debate amongst historians who harbour deep-seated suspicions of the Establishment. Thus even if an official history can devote space to telling the truth, it may not always tell us the whole truth. However, if you plan to visit a First World War battlefield you put yourself at a disadvantage by not consulting the first-rate maps in the official histories.

Finding the truth becomes harder the further we retreat from the twentieth century. Waterloo is an exception, recognized as such even in its day. Contemporaries found it so obviously climactic that it inspired unprecedented interest, and it is no accident that the British struck a medal for soldiers of all ranks who fought there, although campaign medals were not generally granted at that time. Captain William Siborne assembled several hundred letters written in response to his appeal for help in constructing his massive Waterloo Model, and these were later published by his son. Moreover, the battle features in dozens of recollections, published and unpublished, which cover the Napoleonic period, and as far as this book is concerned Waterloo ranks alongside the Somme for the availability of detailed accounts.

Our study of Agincourt is supported by better contemporary accounts than is the case with the most medieval and early modern battles but, even so, sources are tantalizingly thin and we cannot be sure of facts which would present no problems in any of our later battles. How were the English drawn up? Did the archers fight on the flanks of blocks of men-at-arms, between, or even in front of them? It is small wonder that Lieutenant-Colonel Alfred Burne developed the expression 'inherent military probability' when studying battles of the period, for there are moments when scholarship can inch its way no further and must take a leap of educated judgement. Bosworth, although a more recent clash, presents us with an even more serious problem. It is impossible to be genuinely certain where it happened. There is a fine visitors' centre on one possible field; I suggest the another possible site, and there are other suggestions in currency. How wonderful it would be to have the sort of archaelogical help that we now have at Naseby, where painstaking work on musket-ball scatters suggests that King Charles's tough infantry (with Wales as well represented in its ranks as it had been amongst Henry's archers at Agincourt) fought harder, against all the odds, than I had once believed.

Whatever our deductions about the way Hastings, Agincourt and Bosworth were fought, we still lack that view from the past that illuminates our other battles. Ensign Gronow tells us what it felt like to be in a square at Waterloo, Corporal Ashurst gives us a snapshot of the sunken road at Beaumont-Hamel on the Somme, and Major Hans von Luck describes defending Cagny against onrushing British armour. We have no answering voice from Harold's stout axemen; Davy Gam or Lewis Robbesard Esquire, or Henry Tudor's knights: the sands of time have choked them, and we must let the ground they fought on and the weapons they bore speak for them.

Visiting the Battlefields
The maps in this book are intended to enable the reader to make sense of the narrative and to locate individual stands or viewing-points; they are not designed for navigation across Shakespeare's 'vasty fields of France'. For this purpose it is hard to beat the 1:200,000 Michelin maps of the Continent. Agincourt and the Somme lie on Sheet 52, Waterloo and Mons on Sheet 51, Le Cateau and Arras on Sheet 53 and Operation Goodwood on Sheet 54. The Commonwealth War Graves Commission (2 Marlow Road, Maidenhead, Berkshire SL6 7DX, tel. 01628 634 221, website www.cwgc.org) produces the Michelin series overprinted with the location of its cemeteries. The Commission will provide information on the place of burial of servicemen who have known graves, as well as on the Memorials to the Missing which commemorate those who do not. The Institut Géographique National 1:50,000 maps are considerably more

detailed, and commend themselves to those who intend close study of a single battlefield.

In England, the Ordnance Survey Landranger 1:50,000 scale, or the rather better Pathfinder 1:25,000 are ideal companions to a battlefield tour. Ordnance Survey Ireland has produced a series of Discovery 1:50,000 maps, and County Meath (covering the Boyne battlefield) is available on sheets 34 and 35. A compass is always a help, for north can sometimes seem elusive without one.

The stands described here can be reached along roads or tracks that, at the time of writing, offer public access, although I cannot guarantee that this will remain the case. Visitors to battlefields do well to remember that one man's historical site is another's livelihood, and a little common sense often turns away a good deal of wrath. Finally, almost any visit to a twentieth-century battle site can confirm the fact that the products of the munitions factories and of the superpowers of their day were fired into it. Tons of unexploded shells and mortar bombs are ploughed up each year – my friend Colonel Henri d'Evry, late of the Spahis, lost the back of his plough to a shell ten years ago – and are left in piles where farm tracks meet the road. There is almost always such a pile where the track turns off the Serre road to Sheffield Memorial Park on the Somme. Other items turn up on ground that thousands of feet must have crossed: I found a live Hales rifle-grenade, dating from the First World War, in the Durhams' assembly area up on Vimy Ridge. Leave such things well alone, for mustard gas corrodes the lungs as fatally in 2003 as it did in 1916, and high-explosive, even old high-explosive, is a killer.

Notable Museums

Although most chapters give specific recommendations for museums, several deserve early mention. A visit to the Royal Armouries, now in its splendid new accommodation at Leeds, will bring helmet and hauberk, matchlock and flintlock, bill and baldric to life, and its painstaking re-enactments give a good idea of the skills required by the men of iron whose footsteps we follow. The National Army Museum, Royal Hospital Road, Chelsea, now includes a gallery whose life-size figures could easily have swaggered or slouched away from Bosworth, Naseby or the Boyne. I am particularly fond of that doughty cavalier, Captain Richard Atkyns of Prince Maurice's Regiment of Horse. The Imperial War Museum, south of the River Thames in Lambeth, is concerned with the two world wars and post-war campaigns: both it and its satellite, on the old airfield at Duxford near Cambridge, richly repay a visit. In France, the museum at Agincourt has been substantially improved since I wrote about the battle, and the museum in the old air-raid shelters at Albert on the Somme is no less transformed: I visit both with pleasure.

The Preservation of Battlefields

Britain has not been good at preserving battlefields or providing visitors with help in their interpretation: the visitors' centre at Bosworth is one of the few honourable exceptions. There may be a Victorian memorial, but it is often in the wrong place and sometimes vandalized. Worse still, new roads dissect haunted acres, and brick and concrete mask vital ground. It is rarely easy to combine progress with preservation, but battlefields have often fared badly. I applaud the efforts of the Battlefields Trust, which has helped English Heritage to compile a register of battlefields and does its best to ensure that they are not ravaged in the cause of progress. The Trust is always eager for more members, and its co-ordinator is Michael Rayner, Meadow Cottage, 33 High Green, Brooke, Norwich NR15 1HR.

KEY
Military Symbols used on Maps

☐ Allied/British troops

■ Enemy/French or German troops (depending on which troops are the enemy in the battle referred to)

Formation Symbols

☐ Army

☐ Corps

☐ Division

☐ Brigade

☐ Regiment

☐ Battalion

☐ Company

Types of Units

⊠ Infantry (so an Allied Infantry Battalion is represented thus ⊠ with an Enemy Infantry Battalion represented thus ⊠)

◿ Cavalry (so a Cavalry Brigade is represented thus ◿ with an Enemy Cavalry Brigade represented thus ◤)

⬭ Armour (so an Armoured Division is represented thus ⬭ with an Enemy Armoured Division represented thus ⬬)

⊠ Mechanised Infantry

⦸ Armoured Reconnaissance

COMPLETE WAR WALKS
BATTLE SITES

1 Hastings 1066
2 Agincourt 1415
3 Bosworth 1485
4 Naseby 1645
5 The Boyne 1690
6 Waterloo 1815
7 Mons and Le Cateau 1914
8 The Somme 1916
9 Arras 1940
10 Dunkirk 1940
11 The Blitz 1940-41 *
12 Operation Goodwood 1944

* Although London was most
heavily bombed, other cities and
towns were also attacked.

North Sea

NETHERLANDS

R. Rhine

Dover

Strait of Dover

Dunkirk

BELGIUM

Calais

10

■ BRUSSELS

Hastings

Lille

R. Scheldt

6 ● Waterloo

● Liège

2 Agincourt

R. Canche

Mons

● Charleroi

R. Scarpe

9 ● Arras

7

Crécy

R. Authie

Cambrai ● ● Le Cateau

Abbeville

Bapaume

LUXEMBOURG ■

Albert ●

8 ● Péronne

R. Bresle

Amiens

R. Somme

R. Béthune

Sedan

R. Meuse

R. Moselle

● Rouen

R. Aisne

● Rheims

● Metz

R. Oise

R. Marne

Verdun

R. Seine

● Pontoise

R. Eure

■ PARIS

Châlons-sur-Marne

R. Moselle

CE

R. Seine

CHAPTER I

Hastings
1066

Background

Hastings was a clash of Titans. William the Bastard, Duke of Normandy, was at the height of his powers. He was about 38 years old, 5 feet 10 inches (178 cm) tall, with a stockiness that would turn to corpulence in later life, red hair cropped at back and sides in the Norman fashion and fleshy face smooth-shaven. So physically tough that he could carry another man's armour as well as his own, he was harsh to the point of brutality. In 1051 citizens of Alençon had waved cow hides from the walls of their besieged town to remind William of his humble origins (his mother was the daughter of a tanner). William, to retaliate, had some of the citizens skinned when he took the place.

Harold Godwinson, King of England, was about 45. Tall and handsome, with the long hair and moustaches in the Saxon style 'he stood before the people as another Judas Maccabeus'. Like his rival he was an experienced soldier, with a reputation for dash and quick decision. When the two met on a sandy Sussex ridge that bright October day, beneath the leopards of Normandy and the dragon of Wessex, it was a fight to the death.

Yet Hastings was more than an epic struggle between two towering personalities. It was that rare event, an utterly decisive battle. One side defeated the other – and killed its leader into the bargain – in a clash which decided the war. The long-term political, social and economic changes that flowed from it were nothing short of revolutionary. It was the end of the Saxon England of ale-bench and bright mead, folk-moot, earl and churl, of monarchs who were sometimes little more, and occasionally rather less, than first amongst equals. In their place came a king who

The Bayeux Tapestry shows how, at
the height of the battle, William pushed
back his helmet to show his shaken troops
that he was still alive. Count Eustace
of Boulogne, who has seized the papal
banner, points to the Duke, helping him
rally the army. William carries a wooden
club, a symbol of his authority rather
than a practical weapon. The knight on
the left wields a cruciform-hilted sword,
similar to that in the centre photograph.
At the bottom right is a great axe, swung
two-handed, with deadly effect, by many
of Harold's men.

affirmed that he ruled the land, and that his nobles, no matter how mighty, held territory as his tenants and owed him counsel and support.

One of the Conqueror's biographers summed him up as 'admirable; unlovable; dominant; distinct'. He may have been a hero to the Normans, but the English and their Scandinavian kinsmen lamented that:

> Cold heart and bloody hand
> Now rule the English land.

It is small wonder that the echoes of 1066 reverberated for centuries. Nearly six hundred years later, at the time of the Civil War, the Levellers complained of the 'Norman Yoke' and looked back to an imagined Eden when every man was as good as his fellow. Sir Walter Scott's *Ivanhoe,* pitting cruel Normans against brave if sometimes muddle-headed Saxons, was part of a wider perception which cast the Norman as part-villain, part fall-guy. And when W. J. Sellar and R. J. Yeatman wrote their wonderful spoof history almost seventy years ago they fastened on one of the only two dates they thought every schoolboy would know, and called it *1066 and All That.*

Hastings is extraordinarily well-documented for a battle of the period. History has a tendency to be written by the victors, and Hastings is, by and large, no exception. William of Poitiers and William of Jumièges wrote contemporary accounts from the Norman point of view, and Guy, Bishop of Amiens, probable author of the *Carmen de Hastingae Proelio,* identified with William's French–Flemish allies. Ordericus Vitalis and Robert Wace, wrote, slightly later, from the Norman standpoint. Three versions of *The Anglo-Saxon Chronicle*, together with the monks William of Malmesbury and Florence of Worcester, tell the Saxon side of the story. All vary in style and reliability. William of Poitiers, for instance, cast Duke William as a classical hero for an audience who expected as much entertainment as history, while *The Anglo-Saxon Chronicle* simply catalogued those events which seemed, to its monkish authors, to be important.

Finally, the Bayeux tapestry provides another invaluable source. It is an embroidered scroll 20 inches (51 cm) high and 230 feet (70 m) long, and was made, possibly at the instigation of William's half-brother Odo of Bayeux, shortly after the battle. Its cartoon-style combination of pictures and captions is extraordinarily detailed, but its interpretation is steadfastly pro-Norman, and there are areas where it is tantalizingly ambivalent. In studying the battle we must pick our way with care through this litter of source material, much of it incomplete and sometimes conflicting. But enough of scrolls and chronicles: let us move on to the events leading to the battle itself.

The Causes of the Norman Invasion

The Norman invasion of England in 1066 was the immediate result of the death of King Edward the Confessor. The King was childless, and it had seemed for some time that a disputed succession would follow his death. The rules governing succession were flexible: being designated as heir by the reigning monarch, coming from the royal family and being acclaimed by the leading nobles all counted for much.

England had not been a kingdom for long. After the departure of the Romans, waves of Germanic Anglo-Saxon invaders had pushed the native Celts into Cornwall, Wales and Scotland. There were Viking raids in the ninth and tenth centuries, and Scandinavians had settled in the area north of the Wash, known as the Danelaw. Until the ninth century Britain was divided into several kingdoms, although those south of the Humber came under the unified authority of the *Bretwalda,* 'ruler of Britain'. In the tenth century the Saxon kings of Wessex recaptured the Danelaw, establishing a united kingdom.

Edward the Confessor came from the old Saxon line of kings. He was the son of Ethelred II – known as Ethelread the Unready, though this sobriquet is a corruption of 'Unraed', or 'Bad counsel'. A new wave of Viking attacks encouraged Ethelred to send Edward and his brother Alfred to safety in Normandy, whose ruler, Duke Richard, was the brother of Ethelred's wife Emma. Edward's half-brother Edmund Ironside ruled England briefly, but was followed by the Dane Cnut (Canute to the English), who married Ethelred's widow Emma and was succeeded by his sons Harold and Harthacnut.

Edward accepted the crown in 1042, but it brought him little pleasure. Some Scandinavian princes had a strong claim to the throne, so trouble from the Vikings could be expected. His realm was divided between earls who enjoyed enormous power. Chief among them was Earl Godwin of Wessex, who held southern England from Cornwall to Kent. One of his sons, Sweyn, held part of the West Midlands, and another son, Harold, held East Anglia. Edward's brother Alfred had been blinded, probably at Godwin's behest, on a visit to England in 1036 and had died as a result. Nevertheless the King was forced to marry Godwin's daughter Edith.

Though Edward did his best to build up his own party, encouraging Normans to settle in England, he could do little against Godwin. Yet when, in 1051, Godwin broke into open revolt, the King was supported by

Earl Siward of Northumbria and Earl Leofric of the Midland earldom of Mercia: Godwin was exiled, Edith was repudiated as Edward's queen, and William, Duke of Normandy, was nominated Edward's heir.

William had been born in Falaise in 1027 or 1028, the illegitimate son of Robert, sixth Duke of Normandy, and Herleve, a tanner's daughter. Herleve was soon married off to Herluin of Conteville, and bore him Odo, later Bishop of Bayeux, and Robert of Mortain, who became one of the largest landowners in eleventh-century England. William was never legitimized, nor initially had he much reason to think of himself as heir to the dukedom. But when Duke Robert died on pilgrimage to the Holy Land in 1035 William was his natural successor, though it took him till 1060 to make his position secure.

The duchy of Normandy had been settled in the early tenth century by Vikings, mainly of Norwegian stock, and their leader Rollo had come to an agreement with Charles the Simple of France which gave him possession of the duchy. There were close links between England and Normandy. Both were Christian, though both retained strong threads of Scandinavian culture interwoven with elements of old religions.

By the time of William's birth Normandy was, as the Conqueror's biographer David C. Douglas writes, 'French in its speech, in its culture, and in its political ideas.' The duchy was thickly populated and well-cultivated, and its ports, especially Caen, enjoyed rich trade, much of it with Scandinavia. William strengthened the Duke's authority, dispossessing awkward noblemen: in 1055 Werlenc, Count of Mortain, was replaced by William's half-brother Robert. 'The Norman conquest of England,' declares Douglas, 'was made possible by the growth of Norman power during the earlier half of the eleventh century, and by the consolidation of the Duchy under the rule of Duke William.'

Edward's links with Normandy made William a perfectly proper choice for his heir. Yet no sooner had the decision been made than it was overturned. In 1052 Godwin and his sons re-established themselves by force of arms. King Edward's Norman allies were expelled – the Norman archbishop of Canterbury was replaced by the Saxon Stigand, a cleric of doubtful reputation who was promptly excommunicated by the Pope – and the King was compelled to reinstate Godwin's daughter Edith as his Queen. Godwin died in 1053, and his sons prospered. Tostig had already become Earl of Northumbria, and Harold, Godwin's eldest surviving son, succeeded his father as Earl of Wessex. Another brother, Gyrth, ruled East Anglia, and a fourth, Leofwine, had an earldom stretching from Buckinghamshire to Kent. In 1064 a chronicler called Harold 'subregulus' – under-king – and well he might.

Harold was by no means certain to succeed Edward. William had a claim to the throne, and so too, in their ways, did Walter of the Vexin, Ethelred's grandson; Eustace of Boulogne, Edward's brother-in-law; and Harald Hardrada, King of Norway. In 1064 Edward sent Harold to Normandy, possibly to confirm William's succession. His ship was blown off course and landed near the mouth of the Somme: the local count threw him into prison but released him at William's request. According to both William of Poitiers and the Bayeux tapestry, Harold swore an oath of fealty to William, undertaking to represent him at Edward's court and support his succession. We cannot be sure if Harold took the oath under duress, was tricked, or hoped that he might gain from the arrangement. He went campaigning with William in Brittany, and then returned to England laden with gifts. On his return the family's position deteriorated further. Tostig's subjects rebelled against him: Tostig fled abroad, as yet another claimant to the throne, and his earldom was given to Morcar, bother of Earl Edwin of Mercia.

Edward died on 5 January 1066, having, on his death-bed, nominated Harold as his successor, though whether the King was aware of his actions in his last moments with Harold and his supporters at the bedside must remain doubtful. Harold was immediately accepted as king by the *witanagemot*, the council of magnates, and the next day he was crowned in Westminster Abbey.

As soon as he heard the news, William took counsel with his own magnates. Encouraged, notably by William fitzOsbern, to believe that an invasion of England was practicable, he took pains to foster support in Normandy and beyond. Emissaries were sent to the Pope, who supported his claim: the Duke was to fight at Hastings beneath a papal banner. While William's diplomatic activity helped secure his position in Europe, his military preparations went on apace and he began to assemble an invasion fleet at the mouth of the River Dives.

Changes in Fighting Tactics
William's assault came at a time when military institutions were in the process of far-reaching change. Some military historians have seen Hastings as the classic example of a clash between infantry and cavalry armies: as those last long-haired axemen crumpled around the corpse of their king, they suggested, there dawned an age in which the armoured knight rode supreme over his opponents. The Saxons, Sir Charles Oman declared, simply applied 'the stationary tactics of a phalanx of axemen', and Major-General J. F. C. Fuller saw Hastings as 'the final great infantry fight'.

It was not that simple. That the armoured horseman was gaining steadily in importance there can be little doubt. But the process which legally linked land tenure to an obligation to provide a set number of knights for a given period, usually 40 days – known in historical short-hand as feudalism – was far less advanced in eleventh-century Normandy than historians used to believe. Indeed, it is possible that only after such feudal obligations had been imposed on conquered England was the system generally applied in Normandy. Nevertheless, if it was rare for great landowners, lay and ecclesiastical, to be expected to produce a fixed quota of knights, most of William's Norman troops were raised by his magnates, many of them his own relatives. Some knights lived in their lord's hall at his expense; others had holdings on his estates; and wealth-ier knights would themselves maintain warriors who lived with them or were settled on their land.

William's knights fought on horseback at Hastings. But this was not inevitable: at the battles of Tinchebray (1106) and the Standard (1138) Norman knights fought on foot. Their weapons and equipment were not notably different from those of the well-equipped foot-soldier.

Armour and Weaponry
In the Bayeux tapestry Norman knights and Harold's thegns and house-carls are almost identically clad and armed. A mail shirt (hauberk), made from interlocked iron rings hammered or riveted together, was the main defensive garment. The short mail corselet, reaching just below the waist, was old-fashioned by 1066, though some were worn in both armies. Knights wore knee-length hauberks, split front and rear for riding, often provided with an integral mail hood.

Some figures on the Bayeux tapestry have long mail sleeves, while others have short sleeves with leather strapping to protect their forearms. The hauberk, worn over a thick tunic, was heavy and uncomfortable, and was donned only when battle was imminent. Hauberks were expensive, and there were never enough to go round: the tapestry suggests that while fighting was in progress the dead were stripped of their hauberks so that the unarmoured living could put them to good use.

The conical iron helmet, with a nasal to protect the nose, was the common form of Viking military headdress in both England and Normandy. Some helmets were hammered from a single piece of iron, but most were made of segments riveted together. A lining of leather or padded cloth helped cushion the head against blows. A helmeted warrior had a grim, impersonal appearance: when it was rumoured that William had been killed he pushed his helmet back so that his face was clearly identifiable.

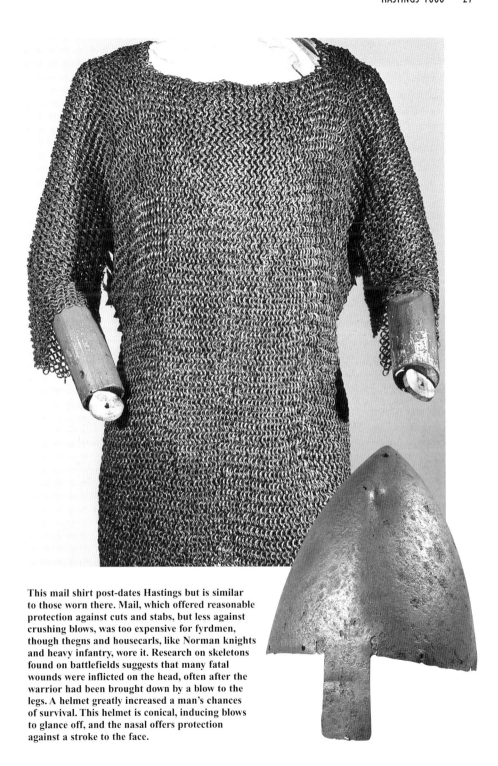

This mail shirt post-dates Hastings but is similar
to those worn there. Mail, which offered reasonable
protection against cuts and stabs, but less against
crushing blows, was too expensive for fyrdmen,
though thegns and housecarls, like Norman knights
and heavy infantry, wore it. Research on skeletons
found on battlefields suggests that many fatal
wounds were inflicted on the head, often after the
warrior had been brought down by a blow to the
legs. A helmet greatly increased a man's chances
of survival. This helmet is conical, inducing blows
to glance off, and the nasal offers protection
against a stroke to the face.

Norman knights carried both sword and spear. Their swords were long, straight, double-edged weapons with a cruciform hilt. While a sword's edge would be defeated by mail, a heavy blow could break bones beneath the mail, and the garments of humbler foot-soldiers offered little protection against the sword. Spears were of two distinct types. Javelins, which usually had slender heads, were thrown; and other spears, often fitted with broader heads, were used for thrusting.

The Bayeux tapestry suggests that these stabbing-spears were used for over-arm thrusts, or couched beneath the arm so that the weapon would strike with the full impetus of man and horse. This was a new tactic, of which knights in succeeding centuries were to make much use. Saddles had high pommels and cantles to front and rear, and stirrups – a relatively recent arrival from the East – were worn on long leathers, so that the knight, legs straight, was almost standing in them.

Horsemen and most foot-soldiers carried a shield. All of those being carried by knights in the tapestry are kite-shaped, though some infantry had the older round or oblong version. Shields were made of wood, often lime, the 'war-linden' of Norse sagas, sometimes with metal rims to prevent them being split by a blow to the edge. Circular shields had a central metal boss which covered the hole in which the warrior's hand grasped an iron grip, and probably had a leather strap through which the forearm passed. Another strap enabled the shield to be slung from the warrior's shoulder on the march or allowed him to use a weapon with both hands.

Kite-shaped shields were more convenient than round shields for a mounted man, and offered protection to the side of his body and his upper leg. They too had straps for hand and forearm, and a longer strap to permit the use of both hands. Shields bore a variety of symbols: these were not, as they would later become, heraldic devices.

A few knights carried maces, metal clubs with flanged or knobbed heads. These delivered lethal blows to unprotected skulls and could even defeat a helmet. Both William and his half-brother Odo are shown in the tapestry carrying smaller wooden clubs. These are symbols of command, rather like the vine-staff of Roman centurions and the batons carried by senior officers in later centuries.

The majority of William's men were infantry. Most of his heavy infantry wore mail hauberks and conical helmets, protected themselves with shields, and bore spears and swords. He also had archers, some of whom carried bows and others crossbows. The bow was shorter and less powerful than the longbow which was to become a characteristic weapon of English armies during the Hundred Years War (1337–1453). The tapestry shows it being drawn to the chest, but it is more likely that it was drawn to the face. Arrows were carried in quivers slung from shoulder or waist-belt, or in larger containers which stood on the ground. Recent evidence suggests that at least some arrow-heads resembled the bodkin point used by English and Welsh archers in the Hundred Years War. These narrow heads were effective against mail at close range. However they could not penetrate shields, and the tapestry depicts English shields bristling with arrows.

Although the tapestry shows no crossbows, it is likely that William had crossbowmen, for both William of Poitiers and the *Carmen* refer to them. Crossbows shot stubby bolts with iron heads and parchment quills which could penetrate mail at close range. The crossbows themselves were less powerful than later types, which required a winch or lever to draw the string back: William's crossbowmen simply placed their feet on the bow and drew the string with their hands. One hauberked archer appears in the tapestry, but the great majority of Norman archers wore little protective clothing: a fortunate few might have had helmets or padded coats.

The Fighting Man
Robert Wace affirms that William had little difficulty in obtaining promises of more men than he required for the campaign. Magnates were induced to take part by more than loyalty or obligation, for there was every prospect that there would be rich pickings in a conquered kingdom. The Norman contingent numbered about 4000 men under William himself, and included not only leading noblemen, like his half-brothers Odo of Bayeux and Robert of Mortain, but also a sprinkling of younger sons who had everything to gain from a successful campaign. Robert, son of Roger of Beaumont, for instance, fought well in command of a detachment on William's right during the battle, and was created Earl of Leicester.

There were two substantial allied contingents. Count Eustace of Boulogne led a Franco-Flemish contingent of about 1500 men, and there were perhaps 2000 Bretons, probably under Alan Fergant, cousin of their ruling count and William's son-in-law. Once again the prospect of profit was a major attraction, and the fact that the Pope had blessed the enterprise must have helped. It is difficult to be precise about numbers, but William had about 2000 cavalry, 4000 heavy infantry and 1500 archers under his command.

Harold's army reflected the administrative and social structure of Saxon England. The earls were effectively viceroys in their earldoms. These were made up of shires, which were themselves divided into hundreds. The sheriff (shire-reeve) administered the king's estates within his shire and had a host of other legal and administrative functions, summoning and commanding the fyrd, the military levy of the shire, amongst them.

Saxon society had three tiers: thegns, churls and slaves. Men might rise and fall: a merchant who made three successful voyages became a thegn, and a thegn who failed in his duty to the king might become a slave. Social status was bound up with land – at this time a thegn had to hold at least five hides of land, a hide (between 60 and 120 acres, depending on locality) being assessed on the land's worth.

The Danish kings of England had adopted the practice of retaining household troops called housecarls, and the earls followed suit, keeping warriors at their own expense or settling them on estates. Harold was to be handicapped in 1066 by fighting two campaigns in rapid succession, the first against his brother Tostig and Harald Hardrada in the north, and the second against William in the south. When the losses of the northern campaign are taken into account, Harold and his brothers Gyrth and Leofwine may have brought 1000 housecarls to Hastings.

While housecarls were, as Warren Hollister called them, 'a unique, closely-knit organization of professional warriors who served the kings of England from Canute to Harold Godwineson [sic] and became the spearhead of the English army,' they were more than mere mercenaries. They were paid by their lords, but, as Richard Abels has suggested, 'their obligation to fight did not arise from the cash nexus but from the bonds of lordship.' The Anglo-Saxon vernacular poem *The Battle of Maldon*, describing the unsuccessful struggle of Earl Byrthnoth and the East Anglian fyrd against Vikings in 991, makes much of the housecarl's duty not to leave the field if his lord has fallen. After the Earl's death, one of his men declares:

> Steadfast warriors around Sturmere will have no cause
> to taunt me with words, now my beloved one is dead,
> that I travelled home lordless,
> turned away from the fight, but a weapon must take me...

We cannot assume that poetic imagination is historical fact, but *The Battle of Maldon* described a heroic ideal and, as we shall see at Hastings, it was a code the housecarls lived and died by: they were not men who intended to journey home lordless.

If housecarls were professional warriors, the members of the fyrd were not. We cannot be sure of the precise relationship between land tenure and military service across the whole of Saxon England, but in Berkshire, whose record survives, one man was required to serve for every five hides of land. King's thegns, landowners on a large scale, were required to produce one man for each of their five hides, and towns were assessed on a similar basis.

Fines were imposed for failing to appear at muster when summoned, and a king's thegn could lose his land if he declined to do service. If the king was present in person with the army desertion was punishable by death. But if a warrior fell in battle at his lord's side, his heirs could succeed to his land without paying the customary heriot (death duty). Similar obligations, increasingly commuted for monetary payment, applied to provide men for service at sea. Regional groupings called 'ship-sokes', usually three hundreds, were each responsible for paying for a vessel. The sea ports of Kent and Sussex supplied ships and warriors of their own, financing them from the profits of their courts, which would otherwise have been paid to the king.

The fyrd could be called up for a period of two months, and this summons could be repeated if required, though morale, agriculture and trade would suffer. Fyrdmen were liable for service anywhere within the realm, or even overseas. In an acute emergency the king could summon the general fyrd – every able-bodied freeman – to serve within the borders of his shire. The militia thus raised was little use in open field, but it could garrison towns or watch the coasts.

In many respects Harold's army looked like William's. Housecarls and thegns wore byrnies – hauberks – and conical helmets, protected themselves with shields, and fought with sword and spear. Fyrdmen were less well-equipped. Robert Wace described them as 'a great gathering of *vilainaille*, of men in everyday clothes', but this is an over-simplification. In 1108 *The Anglo-Saxon Chronicle* notes that the King ordered that a helmet and byrnie should be produced from every eight hides of land in England. Many fyrdmen would have worn iron helmets or leather caps, and some would have followed the Viking practice of wearing tough hide coats, almost as good as mail for warding off point or edge.

The axe was widely used by Harold's men. Small axes could be swung or thrown single-handed. But the broad or bearded axe was the Saxon warrior's most formidable weapon. Its massive head was mounted on an ash shaft about 3 feet long (1 m) long; swung two-handed, with the force of battle-frenzy behind it, it could split a horse's skull.

The tapestry shows only one Saxon archer, and the small size of the figure implies that he might be a boy. The apparent absence of archers in Harold's army has caused historians some difficulties. It is clear that a missile exchange, in which arrows were shot, stones slung or cast, and javelins thrown, was the usual preliminary to battle: *The Battle of Maldon* describes an early stage of the fight when 'bows were busy'. In the saga *Heimskringla* Snorri Sturluson describes the English making good use of archers at Stamford Bridge. However, Snorri is so clearly wrong on so many matters that his evidence is generally regarded as untrustworthy.

There is, though, abundant evidence of archery in England in the immediate aftermath of the Conquest, leading Richard Glover to deduce that 'bows were as common as dogs in the England ruled by the Conqueror's son.' He goes on to point out that Harold took the fyrd of southern and central England to Stamford Bridge with him. Having won the battle, he heard of William's landing on 1 October: he lay dead on the field of Hastings, 250 miles (400 km) away, on 14 October. The infantry of the day would have had no chance of covering this distance in a dozen days: the only men to fight in both battles would have been housecarls and thegns who made the journey on horseback. Glover concludes that there were indeed archers in the English army in 1066, but they had gone to Stamford Bridge with Harold and were not available to him at Hastings. In this respect, as in many others, the Duke should perhaps be known, as John Gillingham has suggested, as William the Lucky Bastard.

Glover also argues that the *Heimskringla*'s suggestion that the English fought on horseback at Stamford Bridge may not be as absurd as is usually thought. Anglo-Saxons and Vikings alike had used horses for transport off the battlefield. The question of whether or not the Anglo-Saxons of this period fought mounted is too complex to resolve here, but the weight of evidence suggests that they sometimes did so. In her study of the medieval warhorse, Ann Hyland points out that horses frequently formed part of the heriot paid by Anglo-Saxon noblemen. From their description these are no shaggy ponies or ambling palfreys, but warhorses. This said, there is no doubt that Harold's men fought on foot at Hastings, as their ancestors had at Ashdown in 871: 'Shield to shield, and shoulder to shoulder.'

'The cohesion of the shield-wall,' writes Nicholas Brooks, 'was the fundamental principle of Anglo-Saxon battle tactics.' Poets wrote of the 'battle-hedge' and the 'shield-fort'; and breaking the line, through cowardice, to plunder, or in misplaced zeal, could be fatal. Men formed up so that their shields presented an unbroken front: William of Poitiers tells us that at Hastings the English were packed together so densely that the dead could not fall and the wounded could not leave the ranks. There was probably one man for every 2 feet (60 cm) of the front rank, with another ten ranks behind. It was not simply a matter of jamming warriors

The Bayeux Tapestry shows the English shield-wall under attack. These warriors are well-equipped thegns or housecarls, whose overlapping shields offer good protection. Some of them are using stabbing-spears, and others have bundles of javelins. There is an archer; a mace (top left) is amongst the missiles hurled at the oncoming knights. The small pennants (gonfanons) may designate individual contingents.

together, for a man needed room to use his weapons. The broad axe demanded space, because its user swung it back across his shoulder, leaving himself, so Wace assures us, vulnerable to a frontal thrust.

Both armies had distinctive banners and war-cries. Harold's men fought beneath the dragon of Wessex, rather like a wind-sock, and the king's own banner, an embroidered figure of a fighting man. The Norman banner bore the leopards of Normandy, and, in addition, William had been given a consecrated banner by the Pope. Many warriors on both sides had small pennants, gonfanons, fluttering from their spears: these may have denoted the leaders of small units. The Norman war-cry was '*Dex Aie*' – 'God's Aid'. Wace describes the English war-cries as 'Olicrosse' and 'Godemite' – his rendering of 'Holy Cross' and 'God Almighty'. The fyrd barked its defiance in an older, simpler form: 'Out, out'. Harold had about 7000 men at Hastings, and the sight of their phalanx, bristling with spears and axes and reverberating to the roar of 'Out, out' and the clatter of weapons striking shields, must have been formidable.

Campaign and Battle

Harold spent Easter 1066 at Westminster, where he would have marvelled at what *The Anglo-Saxon Chronicle* calls 'the long-haired star' (in fact Halley's comet, widely regarded as a portent of great trouble). As if on cue, his brother Tostig, who had wintered in Flanders, raided the south coast with a fleet of 60 ships. Harold assembled what the *Chronicle* calls 'a naval force and a land force larger than any king had assembled before in this country', and Tostig sailed off northwards, rebuffed by Earls Edwin and Morcar when he tried to land. Many of his sailors deserted, and he eventually reached Scotland with only 12 small ships. Tostig seems to have contacted William, with a view to forming some sort of alliance, without success. By the summer, however, he had come to terms with Harald Hardrada, another claimant to the throne.

William Prepares to Invade
While Harold was preparing to deal with his recalcitrant brother, William's preparations went on. His fleet assembled in the Dives estuary, north-east of Caen. The coastline has changed, but the marshes east of Dives-sur-Mer – which helped form a hard shoulder on the British left when the Allies landed in Normandy in 1944 – mark what was once a substantial estuary.

Wace declared that William had 696 ships, for his father had told him so, but he admits that nobody was really sure of the number. In a study of the naval logistics of the campaign, C. M. Gillmor concludes that, while it is impossible to be certain, Wace's is a fair estimate. Both the limited time available and the amount of timber required – 74 trees were needed to build a Viking ship of the period – suggest that some vessels must already have existed. There was a small Norman navy, and some ships were hired from Flanders: Flemish mercenaries had manned most of Tostig's ships. Even so, the work required, and its impact on the forests of Normandy, must have been prodigious. Most of William's ships were clinker-built transports, broader in the beam than fighting vessels, relying upon a single square-rigged sail and using auxiliary oars to get out into open sea or to move when becalmed.

The activity inland was scarcely less intense. Adding non-combatants, like armourers, butchers, cooks and servants to soldiers and sailors, William would have had more than 10,000 men encamped around Dives-sur-Mer. It speaks volumes for his abilities as both disciplinarian and logistician that this concentration of personnel was sustained without the starvation, disease or indiscipline which frequently attended such ventures.

Some of the time was spent training. Medieval armies, with their complex cross-currents of loyalty, were often no better than armed mobs. Individual knights, bred to the use of arms, were usually skilled and courageous. Small groups of mounted warriors, known as conroys, organised in multiples of five men and following the gonfanon – banner – of their leader, were accustomed to working together. Combining disparate conroys from different lordships – Norman, Breton and Flemish – was another matter altogether. We cannot be sure of the state of collective training in William's army, and this uncertainty lies behind one of the central questions at Hastings: was the retreat of the Norman army, which drew the English down in pursuit, real or feigned?

That summer Harold kept the southern fyrd assembled to face an invasion, first by Tostig and then by William, and he eventually gathered together a fleet of 700 ships. He himself embarked and lay off the Isle of Wight: *The Anglo-Saxon Chronicle* says that he then considered setting out in search of the Norman fleet. In early September his army ran out of supplies and had to be disbanded. 'When the Nativity of St Mary came, the men's provisions were finished,' laments the *Chronicle*, 'and no one could keep them there any longer.' Harold sent his fleet to London – some vessels foundered en route – and he set off for his capital on horseback.

With the English fleet out of his way, William was able to move his own armada along the coast to St-Valéry-sur-Somme. He too lost some ships, and the bodies of passengers and crew were buried at night so as not to dishearten the rest of the force. The horses were probably sent overland, following a similar route to that used by Henry V in the early stages of the Agincourt campaign in 1415. Once at St Valéry William was much closer to the coast of southern England, clear of the difficult currents in the Bay of the Seine, and better able to profit from the southerly wind for which he waited impatiently.

The Battle of Stamford Bridge

Having lost the first round of the campaign, Harold found himself facing a new peril. In the first week of September Harald Hardrada unfurled his raven banner 'Land-Ravager' and crossed the North Sea with perhaps 300 ships. He was joined in the Tyne by Tostig and his own little fleet, and together they moved down the coast, raiding as they went. In mid-September they entered the Ouse and reached Riccal, 10 miles (16 km) from York. On 20 September Earls Edwin and Morcar met them at Gate Fulford, just outside the city, and after a hard-fought battle the earls were beaten: York surrendered at once.

HASTINGS
1066: The Two Campaigns

 Harold, King of England's
movements

Harold Hardrada's and
Tostig's movements

William of Normandy's
movements

| 0 | 20 | 40 | 60 Miles |
| 0 | 20 40 60 | 80 | 100 Kms |

The Sussex Coast in 1066

Andredsweald

•Hastings

•*Pevensey
Castle*

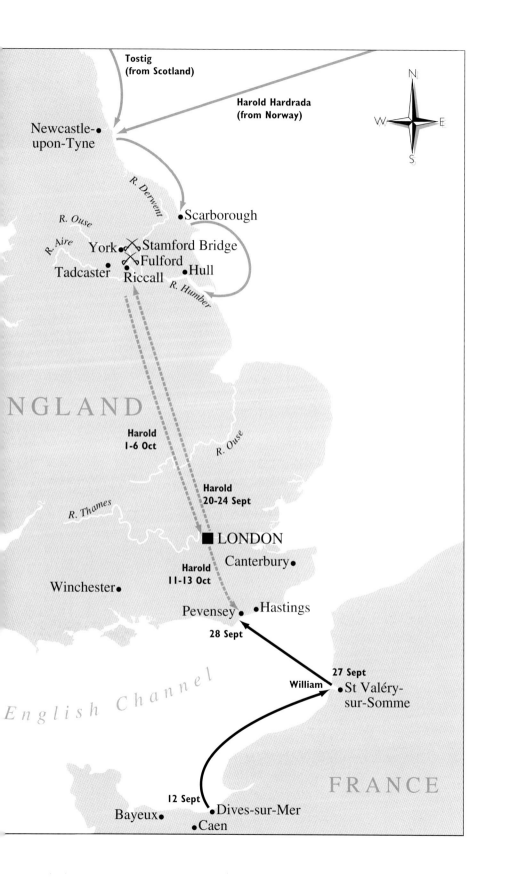

Harold heard of the Norwegian invasion shortly after disbanding his army. He summoned the fyrd, spent a fortnight gathering troops, and set off north up the old Roman road. As Denis Butler observes, the march was 'without parallel or precedent in its own time.' Harold covered 190 miles (306 km) in five days – an astonishing achievement for the fyrdmen – to reach Tadcaster on 24 September. Troops from the Midland shires joined the King on his march, and he was also met by some of the survivors from Gate Fulford. On 25 September he reached York, discovered that his enemies seemed to have no idea of his presence, and marched on towards them at Stamford Bridge on the River Derwent, 8 miles (13 km) away.

About two-thirds of the invaders were at Stamford Bridge, awaiting the arrival of local leaders who were to formally assent to Hardrada's rule. Although they had helmets, shields and personal weapons with them, most had left their byrnies with the ships at Riccal, guarded by the remainder of the force, under the nominal command of Hardrada's son Olaf with his brother-in-law Eystein Orre, known as the gorcock (red grouse) and other experienced warriors to advise him.

The sudden arrival of Harold's army was a tremendous shock: Snorri wrote that, as it appeared through a dust cloud on the York road, the flash of armour and weapons looked like the glint of sunlight on broken ice. Hardrada asked Tostig for advice, and the Earl recommended falling back to the ships. This would have been difficult, for, although the armies were separated by the Derwent, the invaders would have had to cross at Kexby to reach their ships, and the English were likely to reach the crossing first. Hardrada decided to accept battle, sent gallopers to Riccal ordering the remainder of his army to join him, and set up Land-Ravager on what are now called Battle Flats.

The Norsemen had been dispersed when Harold appeared: some had wandered down to the river or begun to round up cattle on the water-meadows. Those caught on the east bank sold their lives dearly, buying time for their comrades to form their shield-wall around Land-Ravager. One axeman, who had worn his byrnie on the march up from Riccal, held the narrow bridge, hewing down more than forty assailants, until an Englishman in a small boat or swill-tub manoeuvred himself under the bridge and thrust his spear through a gap in the planks and up, under the man's armour.

Hardrada rode round his army on a black horse. It stumbled on the uneven ground, throwing him, but he quipped that a fall was luck for a traveller. Snorri says that a group of horsemen approached the Vikings and hailed Tostig, offering him his old earldom and a third of the kingdom if he submitted. When Tostig asked what Hardrada would receive, he was told: 'Seven feet of English ground, or as much more as he may be taller than other men.'

This may be more poetic imagination than fact, for Snorri goes on to say that the English then charged on horseback, which is improbable if for no other reason than the state of the horses after the long march. It is more likely that this was like Maldon writ large: first an exchange of arrows, javelins and stones, and then a brutal hand-to-hand fight as shield-wall met shield-wall. It was an unequal contest, for the Norsemen were unarmoured. Hardrada was mortally wounded in the neck by an arrow, and the battle flowed fast against his men. Harold may have sent messengers to offer his brother quarter, but the surviving Norsemen 'called out all of them together that they would rather fall, one across the other, than accept quarter from the Englishmen.' Tostig died soon afterwards, hit by an arrow as he stood beside Land-Ravager.

The black raven banner still fluttered over the carnage when Eystein Orre and his men arrived from Riccal. Although they were tired after their march in armour, the impact of their assault was so fierce that 'ever since in England "gorcock's storm" is used to mean great peril of men', and they cut their way through to Land-Ravager. Many threw off their armour to fight unencumbered, and offered easy targets. At last the gorcock was killed and Land-Ravager was taken: 'darkness fell before the slaughter was altogether ended.' Harold allowed Olaf Haraldson and the survivors to sail home, taking Hardrada's body with them. The slaughter had been so great that they needed only 24 of their 300 ships.

Stamford Bridge would be better-remembered were it not obscured by Hastings. It ended the last of the great Viking invasions, and was the ultimate revenge for years of burnt farmsteads and butchered peasants. The battle, and the campaign which led up to it had shown Harold Godwinson at his best: whatever the twists and turns on his path to the throne, he had proved himself a decisive leader. But he had little time for self-congratulation, he may even have been enjoying his victory feast when, on or just after 1 October, a messenger brought word that William had landed.

The Arrival of the Normans
William had grown so frustrated waiting for a southerly wind at St Valéry that he had had the saint's relics paraded around the town. The wind obediently changed direction, and it was probably on the afternoon of 27 September that the Normans embarked, sailing before dusk. William led the way in his own ship, the *Mora*, a gift from his wife. A lantern at the masthead was intended to help the fleet keep direction,

but dawn found *Mora* on her own. Mindful of his men's morale, William enjoyed an ostentatiously good breakfast while he waited for the rest of his fleet. Soon there was 'a forest of masts' with *Mora*: two ships lost their way and probably landed at Old Romney, where their crews were killed.

It was about 9 a.m. on 28 September that the first of William's ships entered Pevensey Bay, 56 miles (90 km) from St Valéry. The coastline of the area was markedly different then. Pevensey Bay was larger, with a tidal lagoon behind it, protected by a narrow spit of land, with the ruined Roman fort of Anderida at its tip. To the east was the Hastings peninsula, all but cut off by the Brede to the east and Bulverhythe lagoon to the west. Inland, the brooding forest of the Andredsweald stretched away northwards.

The fleet approached land prepared for resistance, but it was soon clear that the coastline was undefended. As William landed he slipped on the shingle, threw out his hands to protect himself as he fell, and scratched his face. There was a flicker of alarm, but William fitzOsbern shouted that the omen was good: the Duke had grasped England with both hands, and meant to guarantee it to his successors with his blood. Pioneers protected the landing place by adding a ditch and some timber to the Roman fort – William had brought wood for prefabricated forts with him – and patrols scouted inland.

William moved army and fleet to Hastings either later on the same day or the following day, erecting his remaining prefabricated forts, probably in the old Roman castle, and camping on Baldslow Ridge above the town. The peninsular was large enough to form a secure base for his army, and was easily defended. The move to Hastings suggests that William intended taking the road to Dover and thence to London, rather than the single road through the Andredsweald to London, where his horsemen would have been at a disadvantage in close country.

William's initial caution stemmed, at least in part, from the fact that he had no recent news of Harold's whereabouts. Indeed, it was only when a messenger from Robert fitzWymarc, a kinsman who held land in England, brought news of Stamford Bridge that he knew just how fortuitous that south wind had been. Time was not on his side. Harold might hold the neck of the peninsula and, at the same time, blockade Hastings with his fleet, forcing William to starve or fight. There was everything to be gained by provoking Harold into attacking, and William's patrols ravaged the surrounding villages, gathering supplies which would be useful if Hastings was blockaded and deliberately insulting Harold, in whose old earldom Sussex lay.

Preparing for Battle

Harold himself had taken only five days to reach London, where he once again summoned troops (no easy task in view of the demands already placed upon the fyrd). A monk was sent with a formal message to William, a Norman monk returned, rejecting Edward's nomination of Harold, and offering to resolve the dispute in court or by single combat. Wace suggests that Gyrth, Harold's brother, advised the King not to risk battle but to devastate the countryside round Hastings, starve the Normans out, and to allow him to command the army. Harold refused: he did not wish to ravage his own territory, and was determined to lead his army himself. It is clear that Harold left London before his army was complete.

William of Jumièges wrote that the king 'rejected caution', and Florence of Worcester believed that 'one half of his army had not arrived'. Harold set off on 11 October and marched through the Andredsweald, reaching Caldbec Hill, a mile from the forest edge, on the evening of 13 October. The hill was crowned by a prominent hoar-apple tree which served as a rallying-point, and the nearby forest road met the roads to Chichester and Dover: Hastings itself was 7 miles (11 km) south.

It is likely that Harold hoped to catch the Normans unawares and attack at once, as he had at Stamford Bridge, though suggestions of a night attack are fanciful. It is possible that he simply hoped to confine his enemies in Hastings while his own army grew stronger. But the initiative was no longer his. William's scouts reported the arrival of the English, and the Duke called in his foragers and kept his men under arms all night. Wace maintains, with some wonderfully misspelt Saxon toasts, that the English spent the night drinking and dancing: '*Bublie*, they cried and *weissel*, and *laticome* and *dricheheil*…' The Normans, in contrast 'made confession of their sins…'

Communal drinking was certainly part of the process of male bonding in Anglo-Saxon society – as in so many others. A warrior in *The Battle of Maldon* had exhorted his comrades to 'remember the times that we often made speeches over mead…about fierce encounters.' However, we may doubt whether Harold's men were much inclined to carouse after an exhausting march and with the prospect of imminent battle.

William heard mass and took the sacrament before dawn on Saturday 14 October. At some stage he addressed his troops, perhaps haranguing their leaders so that his exhortation could be passed on, or simply speaking to those around him. His message was clear. 'You fight not merely for victory but also for survival,' according to William of Poitiers. He hung round his neck the sacred relics on which Harold had sworn his oath in

1064, and at about 6 a.m. moved off northwards along the Roman road. The Bretons, with detachments from Anjou, Maine and Poitou, led the way, followed by the Franco-Flemings under William fitzOsbern and Eustace of Boulogne. The Normans, led by William on his black charger, brought up the rear. Each contingent had both infantry and cavalry, and at this stage the horsemen were probably on foot, their hauberks laid across their saddles.

About an hour later the head of the column reached Blackhorse Hill, the highest point of the long ridge of Telham Hill. Here William's men prepared for action, donning their hauberks. About 1000 yards (900 m) away the English army had formed up on Senlac Hill, a ridge running squarely east-east across the road. Small streams with marshy banks flowed away from both its ends, and the ground immediately to the south-west was boggy. Both flanks were steep (about 1 in 12) and covered with trees and undergrowth. The southern face of the ridge had a gentler gradient, 1 in 15 near the road and 1 in 33 at the ridge's western end. South-west of Senlac the road crossed a saddle, with two more brooks running off to the west.

Harold's standards flew from the highest point of the ridge, and his army extended for about 400 yards (365 m) on either side. It is impossible to be certain of its exact disposition, but it is possible that the King's brothers, Gyrth and Leofwine, were on either flank, and that the first few ranks of the array consisted of housecarls and thegns, with the less well-armed fyrdmen behind them. A bodyguard protected Harold and the standards. The Bayeux tapestry shows a fyrdman arriving at the last moment, yet more evidence that Harold's army was incomplete.

Its arming finished, William's army probably continued along the road and crossed the saddle, only then shaking out into battle order, with the Bretons on the left, the Franco-Flemish on the right and the Normans in the centre. To have deployed earlier would have presented difficulties because of the brooks and boggy ground, and although William was now very close to the English, he probably calculated that they would not come down from their commanding position to attack him.

Each division formed up with its archers and slingers to the front. Then came the heavy infantry with spears, and lastly the cavalry. William planned to disorganize the English phalanx with missile weapons, then use heavy infantry to make gaps in the shield-wall, and finally unleash the knights to shatter the defence and pursue any survivors. The Duke himself was probably on the high ground behind the centre of his line, with a bodyguard and the leopard standard carried by Turstin, son of Rollo.

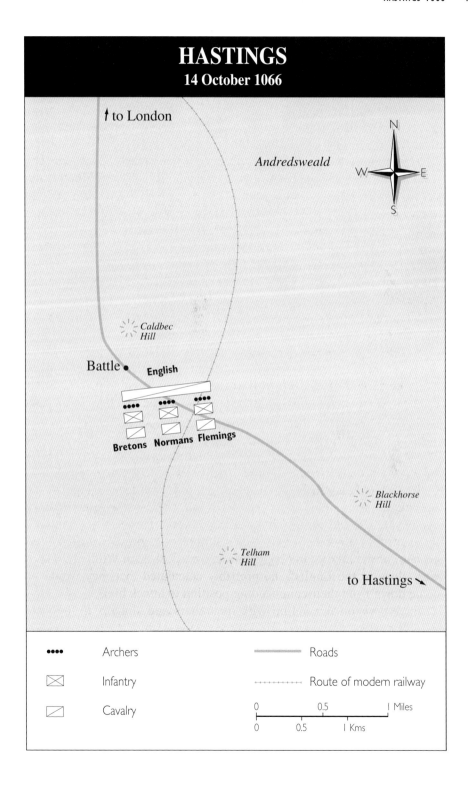

HASTINGS
14 October 1066

to London

Andredsweald

N
W — E
S

Caldbec Hill

Battle •   English

Bretons Normans Flemings

Blackhorse Hill

Telham Hill

to Hastings

•••• Archers

⊠ Infantry

▱ Cavalry

Roads

·········· Route of modern railway

0   0.5   1 Miles
0   0.5   1 Kms

The Battle Begins

Guy of Amiens tells how the minstrel Taillefer, who had ridden forward singing the epic *Song of Roland* and juggling with his sword, asked William for permission to strike the first blow. He rode forward, attacked a group of Englishmen and killed two, but was soon cut down. The battle proper began at about 9 a.m. with a terrible braying of trumpets on both sides. William's archers and crossbowmen moved forward and engaged the English line. They were shooting uphill, and their arrows were either caught on the shield-wall or passed over the English altogether. As Harold had few archers there were almost no arrows to pick up and re-use, and ammunition would soon have run short. The missile attack had been a failure, and the English line was scarcely touched.

William now committed his heavy infantry, who toiled up the slope to be met first by a few arrows, javelins, stones, throwing-axes – even, if the tapestry is to be believed, maces – and then the great expanse of the shield-wall. This was the sort of fighting with which housecarls and thegns were grimly familiar, and the attackers made little progress. Even when William sent in his cavalry they were unable to break the shield-wall. The English profited from the slope, their close cohesion and the effectiveness of their weapons. Horsemen were felled by spear or axe as they sought an opportunity to thrust where the shield-wall wavered or where an axeman left his chest uncovered as he drew his weapon back to strike; and knights throwing javelins were themselves hit by missiles.

It may be that the Breton horsemen, who attacked where the slope was most gentle, collided with the shield-wall before their allies to the right and bore the strain of fighting longer. In any event they were the first to break, and poured down the slope, their panic infecting other contingents. 'Almost the whole of the Duke's army yielded,' admits William of Poitiers. Even the Normans began to fall back, in their case not in 'shameful flight, but a sorrowful withdrawal' because they believed William had fallen.

William rose to meet the crisis. He galloped in front of the fugitives, striking some and threatening others with his lance, pushing his helmet back so that his features could be seen and shouting; 'Look at me! I am alive, and will be the victor, with God's help! What madness induces you to flee? What avenue of retreat is open to you?' He rallied enough knights to turn on a party of Englishmen who had followed the Bretons down the hill, and cut them to pieces as they made a stand on a hillock at the foot of the ridge. The tapestry, which shows unarmoured figures falling to Norman swords, suggests that they were probably ill-disciplined fyrdmen, but some scholars have suggested that the counter-attack was led by Harold's brothers, both of whom were killed at about this time.

This reverse weakened Harold's right – he would probably have thinned the rest of his line in order to make good the losses – but it left his overall position intact. William's men renewed the attack, and William of Poitiers pays particular tribute to the Normans, who fought 'with a courage beyond compare'. However, 'realising that they could not overcome an enemy so numerous and standing so firm without great loss to themselves, [they] retreated, deliberately feigning flight.' All the contemporary sources refer to this stratagem, which Poitiers suggests was repeated three times, and William of Malmesbury makes it the chief reason for the Norman victory. Every time the Normans retreated the English pursued, and, in doing so, were cut down as the knights spurred back into battle.

The flight, real or feigned, has spilt scarcely less ink over the past nine centuries than it did blood that October day. Weighty authorities, Sir Charles Oman prominent amongst them, have suggested that medieval cavalry was so inherently poorly disciplined that a manoeuvre of this subtlety would have been beyond it, and Colonel Charles Lemmon pointed out that it was difficult for well-trained modern troops to carry out such a manoeuvre in a military tournament. On the other hand, both Bernard Bachrach and R. Allen Brown point out that the feigned retreat was described in contemporary histories and military textbooks, and had been used by the Normans at Arques in 1053 and Messina in 1060.

The truth is that there are too many ifs and buts to be certain. We know neither how much collective training had gone on at Dives and St Valéry, nor how well-disciplined William's knights, and, no less to the point, their chargers, really were. On the one hand it is improbable that the whole of William's cavalry would have pretended to flee. Given the primitive arrangements for command and control, it would have been impossible to tell all the riders when, where and how far to retreat. On the other, it is likely that individual detachments, conroys or their multiples, could have wheeled to follow their leader's gonfanon down the slope and then rallied on it, drawing some battle-maddened defenders down in unwise pursuit. During this phase of the battle, grinding on into the short October after-noon, we should perhaps see the solidarity of the shield-wall being eroded all along its length by local feigned retreats and counter-charges.

Whether as a result of feigned retreats or simply hours of savage fighting, the English army was much-reduced by early afternoon, though it remained, as Poitiers tells us, 'a formidable force and difficult to surround'. His use of the word 'surround' suggests that the Normans had still not established themselves on the ridge, and even if casualties had thinned its ranks, with fyrdmen stepping forward to replace fallen house-carls and thegns, Harold's battle-line retained its original length.

The Bayeux Tapestry tells its story like a comic strip. *Above:* On the left we see the Bretons, their horses in difficulties on the boggy ground near the hillock to the right front of Harold's line. The unarmoured fyrdmen, plying shield and spear, who had followed up the fleeing Bretons are shown making their stand on a hillock. All of them were killed when William's men rallied and returned to the attack. *Left:* Although it is not possible to be absolutely sure how Harold died, most scholars now agree that he was wounded by an arrow in the eye and then cut down by a Norman knight. William of Malmesbury's version of his death, which accords with what we see in the tapestry, is that Harold's thigh was hacked after he had fallen: the knight who struck the blow was expelled from the army for his ignoble deed.

The Last Hours of the Battle

It was about 3 p.m., with daylight beginning to fade, when William again threw his army up the trampled and slippery slope, littered with the debris of earlier attacks. There would have been little momentum to this final assault, for men were exhausted and horses blown. The three divisions had become one: many knights had lost their horses and were fighting on foot, and William himself, Poitiers assures us, had had three horses killed under him.

It is often assumed that William paved the way for this last attack by ordering his archers to shoot into the air so that their arrows fell behind the shield-wall. Robert Wace makes much of this, but contemporary accounts do not mention it, and, although the tapestry shows some archers with their bows at a higher than usual angle, it is inconclusive evidence. What is certain is that, by this late stage in the battle, the shield-wall would have been far less cohesive than it had been in the morning, and many of the men in its front rank would by now have been poorly armed, so archery was more likely to be effective.

Harold has traditionally been regarded as the most illustrious victim of the Norman bowmen, though the section of tapestry that seems to show him hit in the eye by an arrow is enigmatic and there are several different accounts of his death. Beneath the caption 'here King Harold is killed' we see one figure, equipped with shield and spear, struggling to pull an arrow from its eye, and another, with axe and banded leggings, falling to a horseman's sword-cut. The weight of scholarly opinion now tends to favour the old interpretation: Harold, wounded by an arrow in or above the eye, was killed by a knight.

The English position was already crumbling badly when Harold fell, and his death no doubt encouraged numerous fyrdmen to slip away. Retreat was not an honourable option for surviving members of his body-guard, who, with most of the housecarls and thegns, formed a shrinking circle around the banners of the dragon and the fighting man, and the body of their king. Eventually the dragon was beaten down and the fighting man taken, to be sent to the Pope in return for his own gift of a banner. Then the last of the English on the field, 'few in number', says William of Malmesbury, 'but brave in the extreme,' – died fighting.

The Aftermath

By this time many fyrdmen and, no doubt, a few housecarls and thegns too, had left the field. Some took horses tethered in the rear and made off on them. 'Many died in the depth of the forest:' wrote Poitiers, 'their pursuers found corpses all along the roads.' He goes on to say that the pursuit was hampered by poor light and difficult ground, and that some of those escaping made a stand near 'a deep valley and numerous ditches'. There is even less unanimity amongst the chroniclers about this, the so-called Malfosse (evil ditch) incident, than about most other aspects of the battle. Inconclusive though the sources are, it is not unlikely that some of the survivors did indeed turn on their pursuers in the half-light of that dreadful day, for the Saxons, as Poitiers acknowledges, 'were always ready to cross swords'.

William returned to the battlefield from the pursuit, and 'could not gaze without pity on the carnage'. The next morning the victors began the enormous task of separating friend from foe amongst the corpses, perhaps as many as 4000 in all. The Normans were buried, and the families or friends of dead Englishmen were allowed to take them away for inter-ment. The remainder were probably left where they fell, like the Norsemen who died at Stamford Bridge: Ordericus Vitalis saw their whitened bones there 70 years later. Although the bodies of Gyrth and Leofwine were found, Harold himself could not be recognized. His mis-tress Edith Swan-Neck is said to have waited near the battlefield and was able to identify the King's mutilated body. William of Malmesbury claims that a knight was expelled from the army for having cut Harold's hands off after death. Harold's mother Gytha offered William her son's weight in gold for his body. William, unwilling to grant burial in hallowed ground to a man whose ambition had caused so much grief, refused. The body was probably buried beneath a pile of stones on unconsecrated ground but, according to a strong tradition, was later moved to Waltham Abbey in Essex.

William Seals His Victory

Complete though William's victory at Hastings was, it did not end the war at a stroke. After waiting five days in his camp above Hastings, resting his army and hoping in vain that the English would send a delegation, William marched, via Tenterden and Lympne, to Dover, where his army was afflicted by an outbreak of dysentery. William himself pushed on to accept the surrender of Canterbury, where he too was overtaken by sickness. A strong detachment made for London, fired Southwark, but found London Bridge firmly defended and was unable to take the city by surprise.

William's main force continued westwards, through Guildford, and on to Winchester, the ancient capital of Wessex, which surrendered. Parties of mounted men fanned out across Hampshire and Berkshire, laying waste to the countryside to obtain food and intimidate the Londoners. Archbishop Stigand submitted at Wallingford, and other English leaders came in to surrender at Little Berkhamsted in Hertfordshire. Encouraged by his own army and by these magnates, who believed that William's assumption of the throne would bring the stability they desired, the Duke advanced on London. Recent evidence suggests that there was a sharp battle with hostile Londoners near St Paul's, but the army that had won Hastings was not to be thwarted by this sort of resistance, and William was crowned king in Westminster Abbey on Christmas Day 1066.

A View of the Field

Despite a shifting coastline and over nine centuries of building, the key events of October 1066 are easy to trace on the ground. Pevensey Castle is a good starting-point, though it is important to remember my caution-ary words about the changed outline of the coast in this part of Sussex. The low-lying Pevensey Levels, north of the town, are in fact the silted-up lagoon, and the A259 to Bexhill runs across the narrow neck which once joined it to the sea.

The Romans built Anderida, one of the Saxon shore forts, on a spit of land then open to the sea on three sides. In 491 it was besieged and taken by Aelle, King of the South Saxons, who massacred every man, woman and child in it: 'there was not even one Briton left there,' laments *The Anglo-Saxon Chronicle*. When William landed there he made prepara-tions for hasty defence, and later the site was strengthened by his half-brother Robert of Mortain, who built a keep in the south-east corner of the Roman fort. The castle was besieged several times, notably by Simon de Montfort's son in 1264-5, but was never taken by assault. As the sea receded it gradually lost importance, though it was briefly fortified during the Spanish invasion scare of 1587-8, and during the Second World War machine-gun positions were built into its ancient walls. Pevensey Castle is open daily from 10 a.m. to 6 p.m.

Hastings

We cannot be sure whether, after his first landing at Pevensey, William moved to Hastings by land, or accompanied his fleet. Local tradition suggests the latter, for the massive Conqueror's Stone, on the seafront near the pier, is said to have served as table for his first meal in England. The castle on the hill above the old town was begun in 1067 or 1078 to replace the wooden structure put up immediately after the landing. There are substantial remains, including parts of the north and east walls, a gatehouse and a tower, although the steady advance of the cliff-edge has claimed the southern part of the castle. It is open daily between 10 a.m.

and 4.30 p.m., and the Battle of Hastings Experience is repeated every half-hour. The Town Hall contains the Hastings embroidery, a 243 foot (74 m) long tapestry depicting events in British history since 1066, made by the Royal School of Needlework to commemorate the nine hundredth anniversary of the Conquest.

Battle
The town of Battle, where the battle of Hastings took place, is 7 miles (11 km) from Hastings on the A2100. This partly follows the route of the old road, and, approaching the battlefield as the Conqueror would have done, the traveller crosses Blackhorse Hill, where William's men halted to don their hauberks. Then, further north, the track to Telham Court leads to a spot on the old road from which William might first have caught sight of his opponents on Senlac Hill, although trees now obscure his view.

William crossed the saddle in the area between the lodge of Battle Abbey Park and Battle station, and deployed for battle on both sides of the road. The site of Harold's position is now dominated by the ruins of Battle Abbey. William ordered that a church should be build on Senlac Hill to commemorate his victory, and its high altar was traditionally placed on the spot where Harold fell. Bendictine monks later built St Martin's Abbey nearby, and its fourteenth-century gatehouse, dormitory and refectory survive. The building of the abbey and subsequent work in the sixteenth century altered the slope of the hill, which is gentler now than it was in 1066.

Much of the battlefield is now sensitively administered by English Heritage, and is entered from a car park at the bottom of Battle High Street. A public car park stands directly in front of the gatehouse, now the entrance to Battle Abbey School, and the battlefield car park is a little further on, to the right. There is an introductory video, and vistors can then use hand-held audio wands to take a 30- or 45-minute battlefield tour. Route maps are provided for those who prefer not to take the audio tour.

Although the west range of abbey buildings forms part of Battle Abbey School and can only be visited during the school's summer holiday, the greater part of the abbey, including church, cloister, common room and novice's room, is open to the public. The position of the high altar of the Norman church is marked by a stone, erected in 1903 to mark the place where Harold fell, and there is a smaller stone nearby giving a more modern suggestion for the spot. The site is still very atmospheric, and there are open grassy slopes south-east of the abbey, where much of the fighting took place.

Harold's battle-line ran to east and west across ground which later bore the abbey buildings. With the twin towers of Princess Elizabeth's Lodging

The twin towers of Princess Elizabeth's Lodging, part of the complex of buildings, Battle Abbey and Battle Abbey School, which are now on the site of Harold's position. Here they are seen from the slope up which the Normans attacked. In 1066 this ground was open and the slope was steeper. The English shield-wall ran along the ridge, its front roughly following the line of this fence.

behind us we can see, off to our right front, the hillock where the English who pursued the fleeing Bretons made their last stand. Beyond it the stream, which helped make the ground so boggy in 1066, was later dammed to make fish ponds for the abbey. Harold's right probably stretched some 250 yards (230 m) beyond Princess Elizabeth's Lodgings. A broad track along the ridge-top, past the children's activity area, leads to a wooded area where the ground falls away sharply and marks the right end of Harold's line. His left probably ended about 50 yards (45 m) south of the primary school in Battle itself.

Harold's army approached the position along the line of the modern High Street, and Whatlington Road which swings right at its northern end. About 500 yards (460 m) along it, a white windmill, now a private house, stands on the position of the hoar-apple tree on Caldbec Hill. Kingsmead Open Space, just behind the mill, is probably where Harold and so many of his men spent their last night on earth.

CHAPTER 2

Agincourt
1415

Background

The young king rode a white horse. Like his men Henry V had passed an anxious night but, if the grey morning weighed as heavily on his spirits as it did on theirs, he did not show it. He rode along the front of his little army, telling his soldiers what they needed to hear. Their cause was just; the penalty of failure would be unthinkable; and he would fight alongside them to the end. He must have seen what a sorry spectacle his host, as a medieval army is properly termed, presented. There was rust on armour and mud on silken surcoats. The going was so heavy that many of his archers, who had long since discarded their breeches after repeated bouts of dysentery, were marching barefoot to keep their footing. After a long and dispiriting wait the French declined to attack but remained drawn up, rank on rank, at the far end of the field. The king ordered: 'Banners advance! In the name of Jesus, Mary and St George!' His men knelt, kissed the earth which they could soon expect to cover them, and stepped off across the plough.

The Hundred Years War (which lasted from 1337 to 1453) was an intermittent struggle between nations whose identity solidified as it went on; a coalition war, with the English often supported by Burgundians and Gascons, and even a civil war, whose combatants looked back to a heritage that was partly shared. Conflict between England and Scotland played much the same part in forming the English army of the Hundred Years War as the Boer War did for the British army of 1914.

We cannot be certain that this is an accurate likeness of Henry V, but the face radiates the cold determination which characterised him. The pudding-basin haircut was popular with knights who spent much of their time cooped up in helmets like this basinet. The cruciform-hilted broadsword was the classic knightly weapon.

Edward I (1239–1307) was known as 'the hammer of the Scots' and his experience in Wales and Scotland encouraged him to change the way English armies were raised. He disliked levying troops as an obligation of land tenure, when men who held estates from the Crown were bidden to appear with their followers for forty days' unpaid service. Often too few reported for duty, the end of their service might not coincide with that of the campaign, and their weapons and equipment might not be up to the task in hand. Edward began to raise soldiers by indentures or contracts, whereby a commander was paid to furnish specified troops for a set time at agreed rates of pay. In practice both systems co-existed for a time, and even when the indenture system was widespread a magnate, serving for pay, would ride to war with many of his feudal underlings behind him.

Fighting Tactics

The dominant military instrument of the age was the man-at-arms, a warrior armoured from head to foot and trained to fight on horseback, known in popular shorthand as a knight. He might actually have been a knight, who had the standing to be eligible for knighthood and had undergone the formal ceremony. But he was as likely to be an esquire, a rank below the knight, or a man with no social pretensions but the ability to obtain and use arms and armour. The charge of the mounted knight was often decisive, but it had acute limitations where ground did not favour massed cavalry or where infantry was prepared to stand and fight. It was a blunt weapon, yet its appeal to a knightly class, bred to fight on horseback and despise spurless peasantry on foot, was enormous.

English kings found it hard to recruit knights and use them well. It was difficult to find men whose wealth enabled them to serve with horse, armour and attendants, while geography and opponents limited the effectiveness of those who did serve. Their charge sometimes succeeded in Edward I's forays against the Scots, as it did at Dunbar in 1296. At Falkirk two years later cavalry broke up the 'schiltroms' – close-packed masses – of Scots spearmen only after their ranks had been thinned by archery.

Edward II had not grasped the importance of combined arms tactics when he met the Scots on the Bannock Burn near Stirling in June 1314. He squandered his cavalry against four great schiltroms, masking the fire of his archers in the process. When the archers moved off to a flank and opened fire they were caught by the Scots cavalry and ridden down. The schiltroms then pushed on into the English infantry, left shaky by the retirement of the horse. As Scots reinforcements came into view, the English broke and fled.

Bannockburn helped to change English tactics, and early results were encouraging: when Sir Andrew Harclay's royalists beat the rebellious Duke of Lancaster at Boroughbridge in 1322 they fought on foot in the Scots manner. At Dupplin Moor in 1332 and Halidon Hill the following year, dismounted English men-at-arms and archers proved too much for even Scots spearmen, and the Earl of Northampton, supporting a contender for the Duchy of Brittany, saw off a larger French force at Morlaix in 1342.

The English learned other lessons in the north. A host crawled slowly across the landscape, trailing provision carts and baggage wagons. It took the field in the summer, when food for men and horses might be found on its march. As long as it moved it could bring fresh sources of supply within reach of foraging parties, but when it halted the most energetic 'purveyors', as its quartermasters were called, might find it impossible to match dwindling supply to ravenous demand.

The Scots, in contrast, were adept at staging raids which lived off plunder and supplies carried on pack-horses, and the English developed similar techniques which formed the basis for that important component of medieval strategy, the *chevauchée*. This large-scale raid sought to avoid battle but to inflict damage on the areas it passed through, weakening an enemy's economic base and moral authority. A *chevauchée* might be forced to fight, and the greatest English victories of the period – Crécy, Poitiers and Agincourt – took place when *chevauchées* were caught by superior French forces. Battles did not ensure that territory passed from vanquished to victor. To secure territory, a commander needed to take the key towns in it, and this usually demanded sieges which were costly in lives and time, and demanded specialist knowledge and equipment.

As a *chevauchée* moved through enemy territory there were great opportunities for profit. Michael Prestwich has identified 'patriotism, desire for chivalric renown, and hope of financial gain' as motives which led men to fight for Edward III, and points out that 'the hope of gaining wealth through plunder was a major incentive'. The chronicler Thomas Walsingham affirmed that 'there were few women who did not have something from Caen, Calais and other overseas towns; clothing, furs, bedcovers, cutlery. Tablecloths and linen, bowls in wood and silver were to be seen in every English house.' If humble men could feather their nests, their commanders did even better: ransoms paid to redeem captured noblemen enabled the brave or lucky to make a fortune at a stroke. Sir Walter Manny obtained £8000 for the prisoners he took in 1340, and the enormous ransom of £500 000 paid to free John II of France, captured at Poitiers in 1356, cemented English royal finances for a generation.

The Fighting Men

Royal preference for recruiting well-paid volunteers and the profit made from campaigning in France helped to change the character of English infantry. Most of Edward I's spearmen and archers were pressed men, recruited by commissioners of array who were not averse to accepting bribes to leave a man at home. By the time of Crécy in 1346 there were still pressed men aplenty: in 1347 one Robert White was released from prison, after his committal for 'homicides, felonies, robberies, rapes of women and trespasses', to serve at the siege of Calais. But alongside the likes of Robert White marched men of a very different stamp. Archers, first recruited in Nottinghamshire and Derbyshire, and then increasingly in Wales, Cheshire and Lancashire, had played an important part in the wars of Edward I.

By the time of Edward III growing numbers of archers were mounted, using horses for mobility on campaign and dismounting to fight on foot. Archers became men of recognized status, lower than knights but higher than ordinary foot soldiers. This was not enough to ensure that they would be captured rather than killed out of hand, for they ranked below the level at which the medieval laws of war offered theoretical protection. There was little point in keeping an archer prisoner because his family could not buy his release. So he might be killed, or so mutilated as to be militarily useless. The derisive gesture of waving two fingers at an opponent dates from this period, for the French would sometimes cut the forefingers off captured archers so they could not draw a bow. The defiant wave, made as an archer scampered for safety, showed that he was still in fighting trim and would be back with a bow in his hand and arrows in his belt. It was a gesture which typified the cockiness of someone who knew that across 100 yards (90 metres) of turf he was the equal of any knight in the land.

The longbow, source of this confidence, was a 6-foot (1.8-metre) stave, ideally of yew, although elm or ash would do, fashioned so that its belly, which faced the archer, was rounded and its back was flat. The bow tapered to the knocks, where the bowstring was attached. It was carried unstrung, and a knowing archer would keep his bowstring somewhere dry: in a pouch for long journeys, or under his hat or helmet if there was a sudden shower before battle. The 30-inch (75-cm) 'cloth-yard' arrow was made from a variety of woods, although ash was a favourite because its weight increased impetus. Barbed broadheads were effective against unarmoured men or horses, but for penetrating armour there was nothing to equal the unbarbed bodkin point. Arrows were usually fletched with goose feathers.

As many as four dozen arrows were carried in a quiver or tucked into the waist belt, and once an archer had taken up position he might stick arrows in the ground to aid speedy reloading. He could dispose of ten or twelve a minute, shooting to a maximum effective range of some 300 yards (270 metres). At this distance he might risk a 'roving shaft' at an individual target, although he would be lucky to hit it. It was never wise to take risks: when the English besieged Caen in 1346 some of the garrison bared their buttocks from the walls (a doubly offensive gesture at the time, because Englishmen were widely believed to have tails) and were killed by the shafts that followed. Long-range arrows were directed into the thick of the enemy's formation, archers shooting, as the chronicler Froissart wrote, 'so thick and fast that it seemed like snow'. It was not until the range was much closer that the archer would aim straight at his chosen target, the heavy war-arrow with its bodkin point smashing through most of the armour it hit.

The medieval archer drew to the side of his head, not the front of the face like a modern bowman. The power required to draw a bow varied from 80–160 lb (36–72 kg). And it was not a matter of brute force but of technique and strength combined, the result of long practice at the butts which developed arms and upper body. While a man could be easily taught to use a crossbow, by no means a contemptible weapon even though it was fragile and slow to reload, he had to be bred to the longbow.

The Causes of the Hundred Years War
Although in theory the Hundred Years War sprang from Edward III's claim to the throne of France, on the grounds that his mother was a daughter of the French royal house of Capet, it had wider causes. The English Crown held large possessions in south-west France, and each monarch had to pay homage to the French king for them, which resulted in regular legal wrangling. The great towns of Flanders were natural customers for English wool, and looked to England for aid against France. The Scots, conversely, expected French support against England. Edward loved pageantry and knightly accomplishments, and saw foreign war as an opportunity to strengthen a throne undermined by years of factional strife.

Fighting broke out in 1337, but it was not until July 1346 that Edward landed in Normandy to mount a *chevauchée* to join his Flemish allies in the north. The French blocked his path and although Edward managed to cross the Somme at Blanchetaque, between Abbeville and St Valéry, he was brought to battle at Crécy on 26 August. Genoese crossbowmen in French service were the first to taste the goose feather. As they faltered under the blizzard of arrows, wave after wave of knights spurred forward against the English. By nightfall the French had lost, by one estimate, 1500 knights and 10,000 foot soldiers. Edward marched on to take Calais, which became the chief English base in northern France.

Over the next few years the French experimented with attacks by men-at-arms, dismounted so that horses would not be maddened by arrows, combined with flanking thrusts by mounted men. In 1356 they caught a *chevauchée* under Edward III's son, the Black Prince, near Poitiers, but were badly beaten. Their king, John II, a prisoner in English hands, agreed to concede territory and pay a huge ransom, but his son had to be brought to heel by a *chevauchée* which encouraged him to conclude the Peace of Brétigny in 1340, confirming Edward's possession of much of south-west France. John died, still a prisoner, before his ransom had been fully paid, leaving his kingdom in the hands of his weak and sickly son Charles V. In 1369 war bubbled up again. This time the French avoided battle and instead used tactics developed by Bertrand du Guesclin, snatching a town here and a castle there, all the time eroding English territory. *Chevauchées* were destructive but inconclusive, and although the Peace of Paris, signed in 1396, rationalized the *status quo* it left long-term issues unresolved.

The political balance had changed when fighting resumed in 1415. The Black Prince had died before ascending the throne and his son, Richard II, was deposed by Henry Bolingbroke, grandson of Edward III, who ruled as Henry IV. The first years of Henry's reign were not easy, with trouble from Scots, Welsh and English rebels, and when the twenty-five-year-old Henry V came to the throne in 1413 his hold on power was far from secure. However, he displayed what his biographer Desmond Seward calls 'extraordinary self-confidence in governing', based on his experience as Commander-in-Chief against the Welsh leader Owain Glyn Dŵr and sharpened by uncompromising piety. When he was Prince of Wales he supervised the burning of a Lollard, John Badby. As Badby began to scream, Henry had him taken from the barrel in which he was being burnt and offered him a pension if he would recant. Badby refused, and Henry sent him back to his barrel.

Henry's belief in the justice of his claim to the throne of France, his intention of uniting France and England under a single crown, and his long-term hope of freeing Jerusalem from the infidel, helped to move him inexorably along the road to war. The condition of France can only have encouraged him. There was civil war between the Armagnacs, who supported Charles VI's younger brother the Duke of Orleans, and the Burgundians, adherents of John, Duke of Burgundy. In addition, Charles swung between sanity and madness. Henry's emissaries negotiated for territory, for the hand of Charles's daughter Catherine, and for a substantial dowry, although it was unlikely that Henry was serious in his quest for a negotiated peace. He had been steadily preparing for war, maximizing royal revenue and borrowing money from Englishmen and foreigners alike. In July 1415 he formally declared war on France and began a campaign he had been preparing for over two years.

Campaign and Battle

Henry assembled 2500 men-at-arms and 8000 archers at Southampton. All were recruited by indenture, their captains contracted to produce men at set rates of pay. Retinues varied in size. The king's brother Humphrey, Duke of Gloucester, agreed to supply 200 lances and 600 mounted archers. The duke reported with two men-at-arms short: his brother punished him by giving him no pay for a year, so he had to find the money for his retinue himself. At the other end of the scale, Lewis Robbesard Esquire turned out with three foot archers. Some of Henry's followers had fought against him in the past. Amongst the substantial Welsh contingent was Davy Gam Daffyd ap Llywellyn, once a follower of Owain Glyn Dŵr.

The word 'lance' included not only the warrior himself, but also his servants and a number of horses which reflected his rank. Dukes provided fifty horses and drew 13s 4d a day, knights served with six horses and received 2s a day, while archers, about half of them mounted, drew 6d a day. Given that a well-to-do knight would expect to live on £208 a year, a minor gentleman or merchant from £15 to £19 and a ploughman £4, this was good pay, and there was every expectation of ransom or plunder as a bonus.

There were farriers to tend to the 10,000 horses, miners and a mass of siege equipment, four Dutch master-gunners and sixty-five gunners manning 'The King's Daughter', 'London', 'Messenger' and other firearms from Bristol and the Tower of London. There was also a small army of armourers, bowyers, fletchers, masons, shoemakers, carters, cooks and chaplains. The host embarked on 1500 vessels: Henry aboard the *Trinity Royal*, at 500 tons (508 tonnes) the largest ship in the armada.

The Siege of Harfleur
The fleet set sail on 11 August, and two days later it anchored in the Seine estuary, 3 miles (5 km) from Harfleur. On the following day the army landed, toiling ashore across mud flats under a blazing sun to besiege Harfleur, an excellent base from which to overrun Normandy or

Route of English Army

Route of French
Main Army

Route of French
Advance Guard

Frontier

0   10   20   30 Miles

0   10   20   30   40   50 Kms

ENGLAND

Hythe•

Romney•
•Rye
Winchelsea•
•Hastings

English Channel

Dieppe •
•
Arques
11 Oct

Fécamp
9 Oct •

Harfleur•
8 Oct
Honfleur •

Caudebec •
8 Oct
R. Seine
Rouen •

•Lisieux

Evreux •

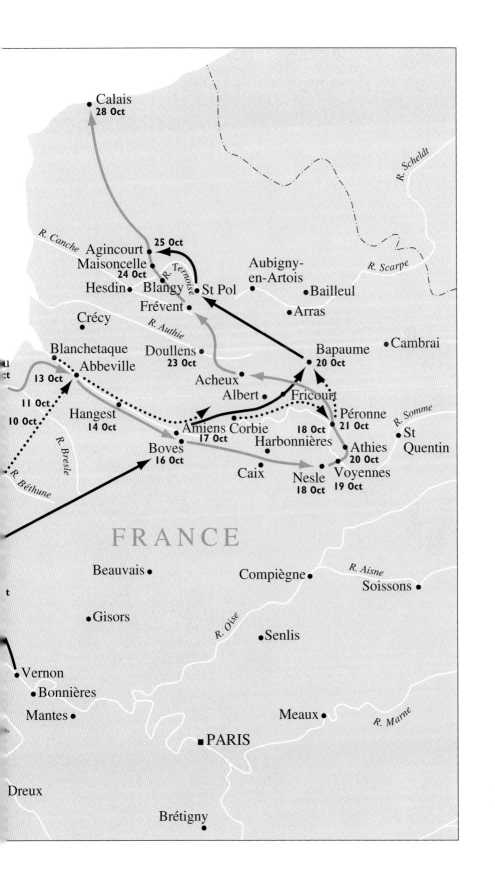

Calais
28 Oct

R. Canche

Agincourt **25 Oct**
Maisoncelle
24 Oct
Hesdin   Blangy   St Pol
Frévent

R. Ternoise

Aubigny-
en-Artois   Bailleul

R. Scarpe

Arras

Crécy

R. Authie

Blanchetaque
Abbeville
13 Oct

Doullens
23 Oct

Acheux

Albert   Fricourt

Bapaume
20 Oct

Cambrai

R. Somme

Péronne
21 Oct

St
Quentin

11 Oct
10 Oct

Hangest
14 Oct

R. Bresle

Amiens   Corbie
17 Oct

Harbonnières

Athies
20 Oct

R. Béthune

Boves
16 Oct

Caix

Nesle
18 Oct

18 Oct

Voyennes
19 Oct

FRANCE

Beauvais

Compiègne

R. Aisne

Soissons

Gisors

R. Oise

Senlis

Vernon
Bonnières

Mantes

Meaux

R. Marne

■ PARIS

Dreux

Brétigny

threaten Paris. Its strong walls were surmounted by twenty-six towers, and barbicans of earth and timber reinforced its three gates. The defenders, 100 men-at-arms under John d'Estuteville, were well supported by the inhabitants, and had opened the sluices so as to allow the rivers Eure and Lezade to flood all but the eastern front of the town.

Henry set up his camp before the Leure Gate on the town's southwestern edge, while his brother Thomas, Duke of Clarence, established himself on Mont Cabert opposite the north-eastern walls. It took two days to finish unloading, and meanwhile Henry showed that he was bent on recovering lands that were rightfully his by announcing that looting churches and arson were forbidden. Women and priests were not to be molested, harlots were not allowed in camp, and all his men were to identify themselves by wearing the red cross of St George. Those who broke these rules were to be hanged.

The English had surrounded Harfleur with a stockade by 19 August, but before the ring was closed a local nobleman, Raoul de Gaucourt, slipped in with 300 men-at-arms. The siege went slowly. It was impossible to undermine the walls because the defenders dug counter-mines, trenches were easily flooded, and French crossbowmen and gunners kept up a destructive fire. Eventually Henry's twelve heavy guns were lugged into position and opened fire from behind wooden screens. Their 'gunstones' wrecked buildings, but the defenders repaired breaches in the walls with stakes and baskets of earth. Henry supervised the bombardment in person, and on 3 September felt confident enough to suggest that it would only take another week to reduce the place.

He was seriously wrong. Although the French made no real attempt to relieve the town, dysentery, brought on by local shellfish, foul water and contaminated food, broke out in the besiegers' cramped and filthy lines. The Duke of Clarence and the Earls of March and Nottingham were amongst the noblemen invalided home, and the Earls of Arundel and Suffolk, and Thomas Courtenay, Bishop of Norwich and one of the king's most trusted advisers, died. Perhaps 2000 Englishmen perished, and as many again were so ill that they had to be shipped home.

The fighting at the south-western gate proved decisive. On 15 September a French sortie burnt the siege tower facing the gate, but the next day Sir John Holland – son of the Earl of Huntingdon who had been killed in a rebellion against Henry IV in 1400 – led an assault which captured the gate's main bastion, already badly damaged by cannon fire. Garrison and townsmen alike knew that if the town was taken by storm, carnage would inevitably ensue. De Gaucourt offered to surrender if no help came by midday on Sunday 22 September and Henry agreed.

The inhabitants of Harfleur escaped with their lives but little else. The gentlemen amongst the garrison were freed on parole, with orders to present themselves in November at Calais. The richer townsmen were sent to England at once, and would remain there until ransoms were paid. The poorer citizens were expelled, although Henry gave them a little money to make the process marginally less unpleasant. They were replaced by Englishmen. Proclamations were made in the cities of England offering cash subsidies to artisans and merchants who would settle in Harfleur: about 10,000 took advantage of the offer.

Henry first planned to develop his campaign either by marching on Paris or by mounting a *chevauchée* south of Bordeaux. However, losses at Harfleur and the need to garrison the town (with 500 men-at-arms and 1000 archers under the Earl of Dorset) left him so badly depleted that neither option was now feasible. In the meantime, Henry sent a message challenging the dauphin to single combat for the throne of France. The plump and lethargic Louis predictably declined. Henry waited a week for the answer, and then embarked on a scheme which dismayed his council of war and was destined to bring his army to the verge of destruction. He would march straight to Calais.

It is impossible to explain this decision from a twentieth-century standpoint. The French were gathering in unknown strength. The River Somme and a dozen lesser watercourses flowed between Henry and his objective. He would have to move so fast that there would be little opportunity for plunder; even if he reached Calais he would have gained nothing that he did not already have at Harfleur; and many of his men had not recovered from dysentery contracted during the siege. But when Henry told his council that he did not intend to allow the French 'to rejoice in misdeeds, nor, unjustly against God, to possess my goods,' he meant exactly that. He would march on Calais in the hope that God would demonstrate the justice of his claim to the crown of France.

Henry set out on 8 October with about 900 men-at-arms and 5000 archers marching parallel with the coast in the customary three 'battles'. Sir Gilbert Umfraville and Sir John Cornwall, Henry's uncle by marriage and a soldier of twenty-five years' experience, led the advance guard; the king, the Duke of Gloucester and Sir John Holland rode with the main battle; while the king's uncle, the Duke of York, commanded the rearguard with the Earl of Oxford. There were no cannon or wagons, and provisions for eight days were carried on pack-horses. Henry made for the Somme, intending to march eastwards along it to the ford at Blanchetaque, and had already sent orders for the Calais garrison to dispatch a force to secure the northern bank.

The French Host

Amongst the French, military discord mirrored political friction. Charles VI hoped to lead his army in person but was in his usual delicate state of health, and the ancient Duke of Berry, leader of the Armagnacs and a veteran of Poitiers, was unwilling to risk his death or capture. 'It is better to lose a battle,' he remarked knowingly, 'than a king and a battle.' The dauphin, as unfit for high command as he was for single combat with Henry V, could not be denied the opportunity to tinker with part of the French host. That seasoned campaigner John the Fearless, Duke of Burgundy, was an obvious candidate for command but was unacceptable to the Armagnacs and, denied high command, chose not to serve.

It was decided that three royal dukes – Charles of Orleans, John of Bourbon and John of Alençon – would command, in co-operation with the senior military officials of the royal household, the constable, John d'Albret, and the marshal, John le Maingre, known as Boucicault. Amongst the dukes only Bourbon had any military success to his credit: he had beaten an Anglo-Gascon force at Soubise in 1413. The two professionals, in contrast, were accomplished soldiers, and Boucicault's fighting reputation made him, as Matthew Bennett observes, 'a legend in his own lifetime'.

Cautious deployment matched divided command. The more experienced French leaders wished to contain the English rather than fight them, and mid-September saw the dauphin with the main force at Vernon, on the northern border of Normandy, keeping track of events at Harfleur but doing little to prevent their progress. What was to become the French advanced guard was in two parts, with Boucicault at Caudebec, on the Seine north-west of Harfleur, and d'Albret at Honfleur, across the Seine estuary from the beleaguered town. As the English moved off, Boucicault followed them, and then joined d'Albret who marched up through Rouen to hold the crossings of the Somme.

Henry's March to Calais

The English advanced in the harsh style of the *chevauchée*. French chroniclers maintain that Fécamp abbey was burned and women who had taken refuge there were raped. The castellan of Arques, on the River Béthune, tried to deny the English supplies but gave way when Henry threatened to burn the town, and the same happened at Eu on the River Bresle. When Henry approached Blanchetaque on 13 October, his scouts took a prisoner who admitted that d'Albret was at Abbeville with 6000 men and Guichard Dauphin, Lord of Jaligny, had blocked the ford with stakes and held it in strength. The Calais garrison had sent a force to Blanchetaque but it had been intercepted and driven off.

The English had no choice but to march eastwards in the hope of discovering an unguarded crossing or, as gloomier souls prophesied, of reaching the river's headwaters where they could cross easily. Finding the bridge at Pont Remy held against him, Henry passed the night of the 13th at Bailleul. The following day was spent in a further fruitless search for crossings, and the army halted in and around Hangest. On the 15th Henry approached Amiens – he could not take it without artillery – and spent the night at Pont de Metz.

The next day's march took him on to Boves, whose garrison supplied bread and wine knowing that the town would be burned otherwise. When the soldiers asked to be allowed to fill their bottles with the wine Henry declared that they would 'make bottles of their bellies' and get out of hand. He was right to be on his guard against drunkenness, for soldiers across the centuries have found alcohol a relief from the shock of battle and the rigours of campaigning. German troops attacking only a few miles to the north in the March offensive of 1918 drank their way through gallons of captured alcohol: one officer complained that his men were held up not by a lack of German fighting spirit but by an abundance of Scottish drinking spirit.

There seems to have been no desertion from Henry's host, probably because fugitives would have received short shrift from the peasantry. Some inhabitants unwisely showed their sympathies for the French by hanging red clothes or blankets from their windows to symbolize the Oriflamme, the sacred red banner which signified war to the death and was kept in the royal abbey of St Denis and taken into the field at the beginning of the campaign. Henry had their houses burned, and his army left a wake of scorched timbers and empty storehouses behind it. The king showed determination to keep a firm grip on discipline by hanging a man caught stealing from a church. However, there was little cause for satisfaction, and a chaplain whose *Gesta Henrici Quinti* is one of our best sources for the campaign, summed up the army's opinion: 'We then expected nothing else, but that after having finished our week's provisions and consumed our food, the enemy by craftily hastening on ahead and laying waste the country before us, would weaken us by famine … and overthrow us who were so very few, and wearied with much fatigue, and weak with lack of food.'

On 17 October Henry swung northwards and threatened Corbie on the Somme, giving its garrison a bloody nose when it sallied out to meet him. He may have been trying to force a crossing, to raise his men's morale by letting them fight, or to persuade the French that he intended to follow the course of the river as it curls up towards Péronne. In fact he

French prisoners, wearing armour and with the visors of their helmets still lowered, are led off after surrender. Henry's decision to kill his prisoners during Agincourt was based on the fact that these men had only to pick up discarded weapons to become dangerous once again.

marched straight across the open end of the loop, and 18 October found him at Nesle, only a couple of miles from the Somme. His scouts reported that there were passable fords ahead at Voyennes and Bethencourt, and on the 19th the army splashed across two narrow causeways, both damaged by the French and patched up with bundles of sticks, straw and timber torn from nearby houses. The army marched on to Athies and, as the chaplain recorded, 'spent a joyful night in the nearby hamlets'.

The Progress of the French
Although we cannot be sure of French movements, Matthew Bennett's judicious reconstruction offers the best explanation. The French advance guard, perhaps equal in numbers to the English and under the command of d'Albret and Boucicault, mirrored Henry's movements on the north bank of the Somme. It lost time by marching on the outer edge of the river's loop while the English cut straight across, and was at Péronne when Henry crossed, too far away to oppose him in strength. Once Henry was safely across the weakness of this force, the caution of its commanders and the imminent arrival of the French main body encouraged avoidance of battle until the host was united.

The French main body, which may have numbered 50,000 men including all its camp followers, did not reach Amiens until 17 October.

Bennett points out that the riverside route taken by the advance guard was unsuitable for a force this size, especially in a rainy October, and that the French probably marched to Bapaume, on the uplands north of the river. Here they were well placed to block Henry's advance on Calais, for the French had little doubt where he was bound. On 20 October three French heralds visited him to declare that 'many of our lords are assembled to defend their rights, and they inform you by us that before you come to Calais they will meet with you and fight with you and be revenged of your conduct.' When asked what road he would take, Henry replied:

Straight to Calais, and if our enemies try to disturb us in our journey, it will not be without the utmost peril. We do not intend to seek them out, but neither shall we go in fear of them either more slowly or more quickly than we wish to do. We advise them again not to interrupt our journey, nor to seek what would in consequence be a great shedding of Christian blood.

Preparing for Battle
The English marched northwards on the 21st, leaving Péronne on their left, and crossing the tracks of what the chaplain termed 'an unimaginable host'. That night was passed at Mametz and Fricourt, on ground that was to be bitterly contested in July 1916 during the battle of the Somme, and on the 22nd Henry marched on through Albert to Acheux and Forceville. The French were moving on a parallel route, and on the 24th the English crossed the little Ternoise river at Blangy to find 'hateful swarms of Frenchmen' drawn up for battle just to the north. The French edged away to Azincourt and Ruisseauville, and took up a position blocking the Calais road where it ran between two woods. Henry halted for the night at Maisoncelle, barely 1 mile (1.6 km) to the south-east.

It was, by all accounts, a ghastly night. The English had covered about 300 miles (480 km) in sixteen days, the last of them in the teeth of rain blowing in from the west. There had been little to eat, although many could not stomach food and the army's path was smeared with the bloody flux of dysentery. The king and some nobles found shelter in the hovels of Maisoncelle, with men-at-arms and archers huddled up under hedges or in orchards. As the rain sluiced down even Henry wavered. He released his prisoners and sent a message to the French offering to return Harfleur and pay compensation in return for safe passage to Calais. Yet when Sir Walter Hungerford suggested that another 10,000 archers would help, the king rounded on him and declared that all they had were God's people. A French esquire wrote that the English played music to revive their spirits, but this is at best uncertain. We know that Henry ordered the army to keep silent: noisy gentlemen would lose horse and armour, while ranks below yeoman would forfeit their right ear. What sound there was in the English camp was chiefly the low murmur of men making their peace with God – if the queues for priests were too long, soldiers confessed to their comrades – and the furtive scraping of stone on steel as edges were put on swords and daggers.

The French camp, in contrast, was lit by fires and filled with the noise of grooms and servants preparing for the morrow. Some of the more extreme chroniclers' suggestions – that the French had a painted cart ready for the captive Henry and that their lords diced for the Englishmen they expected to capture (an archer was the worthless blank face of a dice) – owe more to subsequent propaganda than four-in-the-morning reality. An English army, even in this desperate state, was still deadly and few French knights would have wished to go into battle sleepless and hungover.

Agincourt has myth wrapped around myth like the layers of an onion. Shakespeare's 'little touch of Harry in the night' had little to do with warnings about the loss of ears, and Laurence Olivier's film compounded the felony by depicting a French mounted charge as the battle's climax. In his masterly work *The Face of Battle*, John Keegan caught the battle's bloody glint, telling us that it is:

> … a school outing to the Old Vic, Shakespeare is fun, *son et lumière*, blank verse, Laurence Olivier in battle armour; it is an episode to quicken the interest of any schoolboy ever bored by a history lesson, a set-piece demonstration of English moral superiority and a cherished ingredient of a fading national myth. It is also a story of slaughter-yard behaviour and of outright atrocity.

This warning is especially apposite in a book of this sort. It is easy to cast all the English archers as hardy yeoman led by brave and generous gentlemen, forerunners of the men who stood in square at Waterloo and those footsore warriors whose rifle-fire at Mons was the twentieth-century's answer to the arrow-storm. The truth is a good deal less romantic.

As Henry's host prepared for battle at dawn on 25 October 1415 it was full of inconsistencies which still perplex us and which, in their way, are the real thread linking the men of Agincourt with later generations. There was a courage born of desperation, stiffened by tension between social classes and within small groups, as men strove to secure the respect of others – comrades, leaders or subordinates – whose judgement they valued. There was a powerful sense of national identity and a general belief in the rightness of the king's cause, although few would have been able to evaluate the merits of his claim to the throne of France.

Few men felt deep hatred for their enemy – although archers might experience a frisson of pleasure when killing social superiors – but most displayed callous disregard for an opponent who was simply different. They came from an environment where Lollards were roasted to death before large crowds, and traitors were partly strangled before being castrated and disembowelled. The profit motive was never far away, and if an enemy did not give up his purse a knife in the belly would stop his bleatings. Heroic leadership helped to keep men to their task, and there was a whiff of the main chance even in this: John Holland was fighting to redeem the family honour – and the family earldom. And in the last analysis there was simply nowhere else to go: time had run out.

Henry heard Mass and took Communion before arming for battle. Like his men-at-arms he wore full armour, its articulated plates covering his whole body, although instead of donning the visored basinet popular on both sides he opted for the heavier great helm with a crown around it. Over his armour went a silken surcoat decorated with his arms, leopards quartered with lilies. Since men-at-arms dressed alike the surcoat was a useful aid to identification, although we may doubt just how many combatants were able to tell friend from foe by heraldry alone. War-cries were more helpful: the English yelled 'St George!' and the French '*Montjoie! St Denis!*' Henry carried the heavy knightly broadsword with its cruciform hilt, and on his right hip was a dagger, known as the misericord for it slipped between the plates of armour to let the life out of a wounded enemy. Some men-at-arms would have trusted to their swords, but others carried maces or the murderous pole-axe, a combined spear and axe about 5 feet (1.5 metres) long.

An archer was more lightly clad. A leather 'jack' or a brigandine interleaved with steel plates protected his body, and on his head he wore an open-faced helmet, a wicker cap reinforced with iron, or an aventail – a chain-mail hood. A leather bracer protected his left arm from the whip of the bowstring, and leather tabs shielded his shooting fingers. In addition to bow and arrows he bore a short sword and a dagger, the latter often what Victorians bowdlerized into 'ballock' dagger, although the two balls which formed its guard leave us in no doubt as to what archers called it. Some carried mallets, as useful for driving in the pointed stakes which they carried to protect themselves from cavalry as they were for braining an opponent.

For years it was believed that the men-at-arms formed up in three battles with wedges of archers between them and at the ends of the line. This interpretation stems from Froissart's use of the word *herce* to describe the English formation at Crécy and was elaborated by Alfred Burne and others into what Michael Prestwich sums up as 'a standard battle formation … with each battalion of dismounted men-at-arms

This battle painting *(above)* is idealized, but it does show the castle of Agincourt, and British and French are identifiable by their banners. Archers, in the foreground, repel the French cavalry. The mêlée in the centre was in fact fought by dismounted men-at-arms. Part of an original muster-roll *(right)* lists detachments of archers and men-at-arms which made up the English army.

flanked by wings of archers.' More recently Jim Bradbury has argued that there is no justification for assuming that Froissart intended *herce* to mean harrow (the basis of the Burne deduction) rather than an alternative interpretation, and his painstaking examination of the sources suggests that 'the archers were placed on the wings, forward and fanning out-wards, so that when the enemy attacked against the main body in the centre, the archers were able to close in on them from the flanks.'

We are unlikely to be absolutely certain of the truth, but two points

are worth noting. The first is that the archers were mobile. Their stakes did not form a continuous palisade but rather a hedge within which the defenders, fighting in loose order several men deep, could easily move around. They could run forward to shoot, scuttle back into the stakes, and re-emerge to take on tired men-at-arms. Secondly, the question of numbers must give us pause for thought. Henry had only 900 men-at-arms and less than 5000 archers. Breaking up these men-at-arms into three distinct bodies separated by archers would have made for a very brittle formation, with the men-at-arms unable to offer mutual support to their fellows in another division.

I prefer to see the English forming up with men-at-arms in the centre and archers on the flanks before Henry rode out to address his men, reminding them of the justice of his claim, warning that the French had sworn to mutilate captured archers and affirming that he would fight to the end and not seek ransom. The king dismounted – he was wearing no spurs, which showed that he intended to fight on foot – and a long pause followed. Henry hoped that the French would attack him, but they seemed to have no intention of doing so, and eventually he ordered his banners to advance, and the line moved off towards the French, drawn up in the gap between the woods of Agincourt, on the English left, and Tramecourt, on their right. Despite the heartening sound of trumpet and tabor the English made slow progress across slippery ground, and there were several halts to ensure that all kept up.

As the English advanced the gap between the woods narrowed, and at the outermost flanks some archers found themselves amongst the trees: this was probably the origin of a claim that archers were sent into Tramecourt Wood to lie in ambush. At a long bowshot from the enemy the English halted. The archers hammered in their stakes and all eyes turned to Sir Thomas Erpingham, the fifty-eight-year-old veteran in overall command of the archers. His was the responsibility of deciding the moment of opening fire, and he was to give the signal by throwing his baton into the air.

The French Plan of Battle

Although d'Albret and Boucicault were cautious in their approach to battle, it is clear from a document in the British Library that, earlier in the campaign, they had devised a plan for launching a combined arms attack designed to neutralize the archers. They intended to station four bodies of men-at-arms side by side in the centre, with all the available archers and crossbowmen ahead of either wing. Mounted detachments would hook round into the English flanks or rear in an effort to catch the archers unawares. It was an intelligent scheme, although it had two signal failings. The ground on which the French elected to fight was so narrow that dismounted battles could not deploy side by side and flank attacks were rendered impossible by the woods. And in the French army of 1415 making a plan was one thing: persuading a rabble of gentility to carry it out was quite another.

The French drew up in a formation which bore a passing resemblance to the plan. Most of their 25,000 or so fighting men were men in three battles, one behind the other. Enguerrand de Monstrelet, who fought that day, recalled that there were 8000 men-at-arms, 4000 archers and 1500 crossbowmen in the first line under the command of the constable, accompanied by the Dukes of Orleans and Bourbon. The Count of Vendôme was meant to command 1600 mounted men on the left flank and Clignet de Brébant 800 on the right, but both had rather less. The second battle, under the Dukes of Bar and Alençon, was composed of up to 6000 men-at-arms and armed servants. It is possible that the archers and crossbowmen who should have been in the first battle had been literally elbowed into the second, for one disgusted French chronicler complained that not one of them fired a shot. The third division contained perhaps 8–10,000 mounted men-at-arms.

Battle and Massacre

When Sir Thomas Erpingham's baton spun into the air the first arrows thrummed off into the leading French battle. There were few formal commands. The captains nearest Sir Thomas would have seen the baton, and orders to draw and loose would have rippled down the line. A French chronicler tells us that his countrymen heard the command '*nestroque*': 'now stretch', perhaps, as goose feathers were drawn back to the head. It is likely that the French archers and crossbowmen shot a shaft or two and then drew back, as well they might in view of the terrifying disparity of fire effect.

The cavalry on each wing was weaker than it should have been, probably, as one French source laments, because men-at-arms had wandered off during the long wait. But those who remained, perhaps 150 on each flank, charged immediately the archers began to shoot. It was a hopeless venture. The ground was already churned into mud where French horses had been exercised the night before, and the woods meant that these were not flank attacks, merely frontal assaults at the ends of the English line. William de Saveuse, on the French right, bravely led a handful of men right in amongst the stakes. One caught his horse in the chest, and the knight was pitched over its head, to be knifed as he lay helpless on the ground. The fact that some of the stakes were not securely embedded enabled many of his followers to escape. The left wing did no better, and archers shot hard at the fleeing horsemen, panicking their steeds and sending them crashing into the leading battle, causing widening ripples of disorder in this close-packed formation.

Despite the chaos caused by the retreating cavalry, the first battle set off for the English line. The ground was heavy going for men in full armour carrying shortened lances or pole-axes. It would have been evident to the archers that this was the moment for their maximum effort, and they would have stepped up their rate of fire so that there may have been 80,000 arrows a minute hitting the advancing French. There would have been little in the way of formal orders. We should steer clear of novelists' inventions which have captains bellowing 'Shoot wholly together', but we can expect the experienced to have set a heartening example and to have offered the advice which old soldiers give, unasked, to young.

Boucicault and his comrades made for the English centre, defined by its forest of silk: Henry stood beneath his own standard and the banners of the Trinity, St George and St Edward. The enemy men-at-arms, their own social equals, were their real target. Secondly, they would instinctively have shifted away from those arrows plunging in from the flanks. Paradoxically, those in the centre would have been safest, because as the range closed the archers would have found it hard to engage knights who were at an acute angle to them, and would probably have concentrated on more obvious targets on the flanks of the great crocodile squelching onwards.

It speaks volumes for the courage of the French knightly class that any of the first battle pressed on to engage the English men-at-arms. But so slow was their pace and so painful their progress that they had little impact. The mêlée which ensued is best described as bloody murder. This was no place for elegant swordplay: men hacked at one another for the minutes that their strength lasted, trying to beat in an opponent's helmet, hew his legs from under him or shove a lance through his visor. Fatigue or a missed footing often meant death, for once a man was down he was

This impression of Agincourt, from a French manuscript, mixes truth and fiction. The archers would have been much more lightly-equipped, and it is unlikely that the French archers and crossbowmen engaged in this sort of contest. However, at the very start of the campaign Henry had indeed ordered his men to wear red crosses on white surcoats to help them distinguish friend from foe and to emphasise that his was a holy war.

easily finished off. Henry spent part of the battle standing astride the wounded Earl of Oxford and in doing so almost certainly saved his life. The Duke of York died, probably not killed, as is often suggested, by being suffocated under a pile of the dead, but by having his head smashed in. His nephew came close to sharing his fate. A group of French esquires had sworn to kill Henry and one of them, or possibly the Duke of Alençon, lopped a gold fleuret off his crown. The archers, with little to shoot at, joined the mêlée, moving more nimbly than exhausted men-at-arms and plying sword, dagger and mallet to deadly effect.

Historians are right to question whether there could have been piles of bodies as high as a man, but there were certainly heaps of dead and wounded (Boucicault was dragged from beneath one when the fighting ended) and the mêlée was more suggestive of slaughterhouse than tournament. Alençon lost his fight with the king, sank to his knees (probably with sheer exhaustion) and removed his helmet. This was an unmistakable gesture of surrender because he had made himself indefensible, but he was brained with an axe by a berserk Englishman. If it was not easy for a French knight to surrender to an English one, coming to terms with an archer presented particular problems. Few of them spoke French: many of the Welsh spoke no English. Trying to assure Owain ap Llywellyn as he bounded up in sweaty brigandine that you were a gentleman of fair estate was often a fruitless task.

This ghastly scrum eddied back into the second battle, but instead of reinforcing the survivors of the first battle this simply increased the pressure of jammed bodies: 'more were dead through press than our men might have killed,' claimed one Englishman. The struggle had now been going on for perhaps two hours, and the men-at-arms in the third battle were beginning to make off, joined by survivors of the first two battles. The English were extracting prisoners from the carnage and sending them to the rear, no doubt calculating their worth in ransom as they did so. Then two events occurred which were to turn the battle, already bloody enough, into sheer massacre.

A local lord, Isambart d'Agincourt, raided the lightly guarded English camp with a handful of men-at-arms and 600 peasants and carried off some items of value. At about the same time the Counts of Marle and Fauquembergues managed to persuade several hundred French men-at-arms to follow them in a mounted charge which foundered in a fresh storm of arrows. We cannot be sure how news of the attack on his camp was presented to Henry, who probably thought the raid indicated that a more substantial rear attack was under way, possibly in co-ordination with the charge by Marle and Fauquembergues. Victory was not fully secured, and the French prisoners, disarmed but still armoured, easily outnumbered their captors. The field was littered with discarded weapons, and if the prisoners re-armed themselves they could change the battle's outcome.

Henry ordered that the prisoners should be killed: only the most prominent, like the Dukes of Orleans and Bourbon, were to be spared. The order was doubly horrifying. It went against the laws of war to massacre, in cold blood, unarmed noblemen who had surrendered, and it represented a huge financial loss for the English who counted on ransoms to boost the profits of the campaign. Henry warned that he would hang anyone who refused to obey but, recognizing that even he might not exact compliance from his affronted nobility, gave the butcher's task to an esquire with 200 archers. One eyewitness said that the prisoners were 'cut in pieces, heads and faces' as daggers were thrust through their visors, and a French survivor saw some burnt to death when the hut they were confined in was fired.

The battle and the slaughter which followed may have cost the French as many as 10 000 dead, including the Dukes of Alençon, Bar and Brabant, 9 counts, 92 barons and at least 600 knights and many more gentlemen. The Dukes of Bourbon and Orleans, the Counts of Eu, Richemont and Vendôme and 1500 knights and gentlemen were taken prisoner, figures which suggest that the massacre was less than comprehensive, partly because the business of murder must have taken some time and the crisis would have been passed before all the prisoners were dead. These losses were politically as well as militarily damaging: a French historian has calculated that one-third of the monarch's supporters perished. The English lost the Duke of York, the young Earl of Suffolk, whose father had died at Harfleur, and a handful of men of note, including Davy Gam Esquire and his sons-in-law Walter Lloyd and Roger Vaughan. We do not know how many archers died: no knightly chronicler would be much concerned with the fate of these artisans of battle.

The English spent the rest of the day finding overlooked prisoners, collecting arms, armour and valuables, and cutting the throats of the wounded who were beyond help. The latter would have been numerous, for depressed fractures of the skull and penetrating wounds of the abdomen, injuries typical of this sort of fighting, would baffle medical science for another 500 years. The English dead were collected in a barn at Maisoncelle. The building was stuffed with faggots, fired and burnt

Overleaf: **In the foreground of this medieval siege, archers have stuck arrows in the ground to shoot more rapidly, and a crossbowman is using a small winch, a moulinet, to draw back his bowstring. On the left archers and handgunners exchange missiles with the defenders, protected by wooden screens.**

well on into the night while Henry's noblest captives served him at dinner on bended knee.

Withdrawal and Departure

The rain began again next morning, and the English army trudged to Calais, heavily laden with spoils and still short of food. It was not welcomed enthusiastically when it arrived, and soldiers found that they had to pay extortionate prices – or barter prisoners and captured armour – for food and lodging. Henry stayed in the nearby castle at Guisnes, and left for England on 16 November during a storm. It was typical of his confident piety that although two of his vessels sank Henry was unperturbed by an experience which French prisoners found worse than Agincourt.

Agincourt did not end the war, and bitter fighting followed until the Treaty of Troyes was signed in 1420. On the death of Charles VI the crowns of England and France were to be united in the person of Henry or his successor, although the French were to be allowed to retain their language and customs. Henry married the Princess Catherine shortly afterwards, and expressed the hope that 'perpetual peace' was now assured. He was wrong, for not all Frenchmen were prepared to accept the verdict of Troyes, and Henry was campaigning south of Paris when he fell ill, probably with dysentery, in August 1422. He was taken back to the castle at Vincennes where he died, at the age of thirty-five and just six weeks before Charles VI: he never became King of France.

A View of the Field

It is hard to comprehend the Hundred Years War without an idea of how the men who fought in it were armed and equipped; a visit to a museum with a good collection of arms and armour is a useful prelude to walking the field. British readers cannot do better than visit the Royal Armouries Museum in its new home in Leeds. There are arms and armour on display, and the Agincourt cinema shows a documentary-style re-enactment of the battle.

The longbow did not survive well. Once it was old or broken it was of no value save as firewood, and it was not until the raising of Henry VIII's warship *Mary Rose* that we were really able to see what bows looked like. We cannot be certain that the longbows are the same size as their medieval forbears but they are 6 feet (1.8 metres) long, carved from the heartwood and sapwood of yew. Their arrows, made from poplar, are 30 inches (75 cm) long without their heads, which have rusted away, and would have had 6 inches (15 cm) of spiral fletching. Some bows and arrows remain in the *Mary Rose* museum in Portsmouth and others are in the Royal Armouries. Amongst the skeletons found when the vessel was raised were two identified as archers. One had a thickened left forearm, and both had spinal deformities caused by constantly drawing a heavy bow while the body was twisted. The archer's craft followed him to the grave.

Henry's Route to Agincourt
The route of the Agincourt campaign covers too much ground, some of it now too built-up or scarred by autoroutes to be comfortably walkable, although it is easy to drive in a long weekend by landing at Le Havre and leaving through Calais, as Henry did after the battle was over. Le Havre, originally called Havre de Grâce, was begun on the orders of Francis 1 in 1514 to replace the silted-up town of Harfleur, which in Henry V's time was reached by a channel running through salt marshes to the Seine estuary. Although it is now effectively a suburb of the rather unprepossessing Le Havre, the centre of Harfleur is attractive, with several well-preserved old buildings. Substantial remains of the barbican which protected the Rouen Gate survive amongst blocks of flats south of the Place d'armes, which is now the town's main car-park and covers the site of the medieval harbour. St Martin's church is our first real contact with Henry V, for he walked barefoot to the badly damaged building on 23 September 1415 to give thanks for his capture of the town. A plaque on an outside wall informs us that the English were driven out in 1435: a statue to one of the heroes of the episode presides over the roundabout where the N15 enters the town. The little Musée du Prieuré, a short walk from the church, contains stone balls thrown by siege-engines, and a model of the siege, on the first floor, reminds us that the English used mangonels and trebuchets as well as primitive cannon.

Henry's march to the Seine took him to Fécamp, whose splendid Norman Gothic church was almost complete following the rebuilding rendered necessary by a fire caused by a lightning strike. The abbey was to become the home of the liqueur Bénédictine, and a museum in the more recent abbey buildings contains both works of art and information on the liqueur. What was Arques in Henry's day is now Arques-la-Bataille, named in honour of the Protestant victory over the Catholic League on 21 September 1589. This battle, with that fought at Ivry the following year, established the Protestant leader Henry of Navarre as Henry IV, first monarch of the Bourbon dynasty. The substantial remains of the castle, whose governor agreed to supply Henry V's troops with provisions, still dominates the town. It had been rebuilt by Henry I, William the Conqueror's youngest son, in 1123, although its massive earthworks were begun by the Conqueror's uncle, William d'Arques. During the 1589 battle the castle provided a firm base for Henry of Navarre's artillery, and a stone relief of Henry himself can be seen above the third of the fortified gates. The castle at Eu, Henry V's next port of call, is, alas, a more recent replacement: the fortress of his day was demolished in 1475.

The River Somme and its Surroundings
The River Somme has been much changed by canalization, a fact which affects Blanchetaque and Henry's crossing points further upstream. The Somme was fordable at Blanchetaque, where there was a layer of bedrock just below its surface. It was hard to identify even when Edward III crossed there on his way to Crécy in 1346 and he relied on a local guide to show him where it was. At the time the Somme was tidal and its valley marshy and liable to flooding: canalization of the river in the nineteenth century has changed all this. The ford was approached from the northern end of the village of Saigneville and although the ford itself has long since disappeared it is possible to reach its site: the northernmost of the three minor roads shown disappearing towards the Somme Canal on the Michelin map is the one to take, and ends at a pleasant picnic site on the bank.

Some fragments connect us with Henry V along his route south of the Somme. At Boves, where the king was concerned about the drinking habits of his men, the ruins of the twelfth-century castle give an impressive view towards Amiens. However, they are far less impressive than those at Arques and are approached, with some difficulty, via the D167. At Voyennes and Bethencourt, where the English crossed the Somme, the river now flows just east of the Somme Canal, and much of what was marshy ground in 1415 is now garrisoned by fishermen's huts and allotments and has little to tell us. Péronne, the base of the French advanced guard on the day Henry crossed, has been altered by the construction of subsequent fortifications, bombardment in 1870, and damage during the First World War. The town lay in the path of invading armies, and in 1536 an attack by the Holy Roman Emperor Charles V was beaten off when the townswoman Marie Foure animated the defence. Its castle, built in the thirteenth century, was reinforced by a seventeenth-century brick bastion, and more recently modified to accommodate the Historial de la Grande Guerre.

The next stage of Henry's march takes us across the battlefields of the Somme, and it is not until we reach the River Ternoise at Blangy that the Middle Ages again rise to meet us. We cannot be certain whether or not

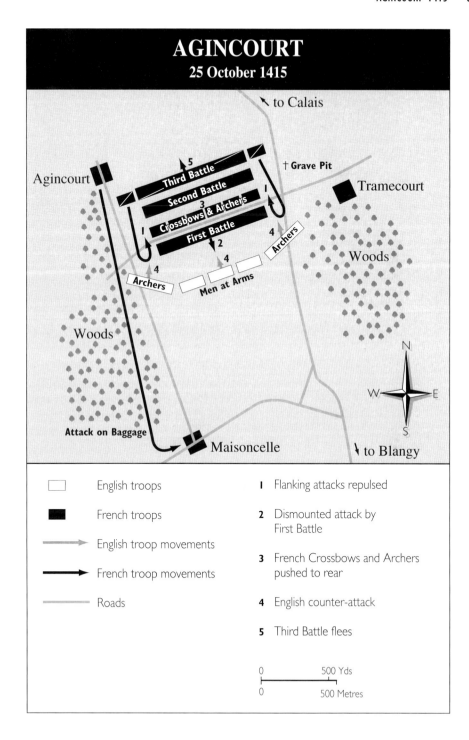

AGINCOURT
25 October 1415

↖ to Calais

† Grave Pit

Agincourt

Tramecourt

Third Battle

Second Battle

3
Crossbows & Archers

First Battle

Archers

Woods

5

1

4

2

4

4

Archers

Men at Arms

Woods

N

W — E

S

Attack on Baggage

Maisoncelle

↘ to Blangy

☐ English troops	**1** Flanking attacks repulsed
■ French troops	**2** Dismounted attack by First Battle
→ English troop movements	**3** French Crossbows and Archers pushed to rear
→ French troop movements	**4** English counter-attack
— Roads	**5** Third Battle flees

0   500 Yds

0   500 Metres

the English had to fight for the bridge at Blangy, but we do know that it was from the village that they first glimpsed the French host and recognized the full dimensions of their task.

The field of Agincourt is largely unspoiled. It lies where the D104 winds up from the Ternoise to slip through the woods between Tramecourt to the east of the road and Azincourt (as the village is now spelt) to its west. There is a small but pleasant museum in Azincourt, maintained with cordial enthusiasm by Claude and Michelle Delcusse. The castle, which could be glimpsed through the trees from the battlefield in 1415, has long since disappeared, but there are some tiles from its floor in the museum. Maisoncelle, where the English camped before and after the battle, lies south-west of Azincourt.

The Battlefield of Agincourt
It is not often that we can trace the events of a medieval battle on the ground with as much confidence as at Agincourt. It is best to approach the field, as Henry's men would have done, from the south-east. The English formed up along the little road which connects Maisoncelle with what was then the Calais road and is now the D104. There is a monument at the corner, as well as an orientation table which is less than helpful because part of the battlefield is hidden from view. It is better to stand on the high ground where the road enters Maisoncelle, and to look north-west: Azincourt church can be seen to the left, and a prominent café stands at the junction of the Calais and Azincourt–Tramecourt roads. The French drew up on the high ground on the far side of this latter road.

As one moves up this tongue of open country it is important to remember that the woods on both flanks were thicker and came closer to the road than they do now: there was little space between the Calais road and the edge of the Tramecourt wood on your right. The French position blocked the gap but gave no room to deploy, and there was no realistic possibility of flanking cavalry moving through the woods. It is a short walk, and a shorter drive, to the Azincourt–Tramecourt road. By turning left at the junction, walking about 100 yards (90 metres) towards Azincourt and then turning to face his original direction of advance, the visitor is in the epicentre of the field. The initial French cavalry charges would have come in along the wood edges to left and right – always remembering that these were closer then than they are now – and the French men-at-arms would have made their way on foot straight across the field in front to cross the road and hit the English line a little behind it. The mêlée then moved slightly towards the initial English position and then back along the French line of advance. It is easy, looking at the ground, to imagine the dreadful shambles that resulted from tens of thousands of French men-at-arms being compressed into such a tiny space, first riddled with arrows, and then compelled to fight not only men-at-arms but also far nimbler archers.

A crucifix surrounded by trees on the Calais road, to the viewer's right front, marks one of the grave-pits where the French dead were buried: the sites of the others have now been lost, but we may surmise that they are in the field between the present pit and Azincourt. Some of the dead were taken further afield. The Duke of York's body was boiled to strip the flesh from his bones, which were sent back to England. His entrails are believed to be buried in the church at Fressin, across the D928 west of Azincourt. On the edge of the D154, in the woods just south of Fressin, stand substantial remains of a castle built in the fifteenth century by Jean de Créquy, chamberlain to King Philip the Fair. Several of the French noblemen killed in the battle were buried in the abbey church of St-Georges at Auchy-les-Hesdin, on the Ternoise north-east of Hesdin itself, and some are commemorated on a plaque to the right of the door. One of them, Gallois de Fougières, Provost-Marshal to the Marshal of France and as such an ancestor of a modern gendarmerie officer, was moved to the national police cemetery earlier this century.

Calais
Henry left France from Calais, an English city from 1347 until it was retaken by Francis, Duke of Guise, in 1558: when she heard what had happened, Mary I of England lamented that the name of Calais would be found engraved on her heart. Part of the scruffy Fort Risban, which defends the western entrance to the harbour, is of English construction, and would have seen Henry's ship leave port on 16 November 1415. Rodin's statue *The Burghers of Calais*, which stands between the *hôtel de ville* and the Parc St-Pierre, celebrates Eustache de St-Pierre who led five fellow citizens to surrender the town to Edward III in 1347. They were barefoot, stripped to their shirts and had the hangman's rope about their necks. Edward, enraged by the town's long resistance, would have strung them up but his wife, Philippa of Hainault, begged him to spare them.

It is typical of the vagaries of Calais' fortune that an old German blockhouse, within sight of Rodin's statue, contains a small museum which deals with the town's occupation during the Second World War and the activities of the local Resistance. As we conclude our *chevauchée* it is chastening to remember that the Channel, now so easily crossed, has shielded Britain from things which, in their way, were as ghastly as the aftermath of Agincourt.

CHAPTER 3

Bosworth
1485

Background

It was the last hurrah of English chivalry. Richard III, in full armour, gold crown around his helmet, led a handful of his closest adherents down the hill. He had already declined a captain's suggestion that he should flee, replying: 'This day I will die as a king or win.' His target was the knot of knights surrounding his rival, Henry Tudor, and so great was his impact that he killed Henry's standard-bearer, William Brandon, and knocked down John Cheney, a man 'of surpassing bravery'.

It could not last. Some of Richard's supposed supporters turned against him, and his little band was encircled and outnumbered. However gallant his last charge, there was nothing romantic about his last moments. His horse stuck fast in a swamp, and he was dragged from its back by foot-soldiers and finished off as he writhed on the ground. Then his mangled body was stripped and thrown across a horse, 'hair hanging as one would bear a sheep.'

Bosworth marked a change of direction for the monarchy which had been initiated, nearly four centuries before, after another English king had died in battle. William the Conqueror's coronation on Christmas Day 1066 had not secured Norman rule. William faced repeated uprisings, and his stern response culminated in his systematic ravaging of the North in 1069: he could not bend the Saxons, so broke them instead.

The Conquest was much more than a change of dynasties. As John Gillingham has observed: 'England received not just a new royal family but also a new ruling class, a new culture and language.' In 1066 there were some 4000 thegns. When the *Domesday Book* completed its survey 20 years later only two significant English lords remained: fewer than 200 Norman barons now

Gothic armour *(top)* was popular at the time of Bosworth. Well-fitting armour was less cumbersome than it appears, and a man-at-arms could mount and dismount in armour. Although horses could be partly protected, and would bite and kick in self-defence, they were vulnerable to an infantryman who ducked beneath them. The halberd *(bottom)* was a popular infantry weapon: it could be used for cutting and stabbing, and sometimes had a hook to pull a horseman from his charger.

held the land. The castles which are still a feature of our landscape bear witness to the fact that the Conqueror's was a garrison state.

The extent to which Norman rule permeated English society has divided historians, though most agree that if the Conquest brought profound change, it did not sever strong threads of continuity. At one level, French language and culture were dominant: at another, as D. M. Stenton observed, 'the slow routines of the agricultural year remained the basic facts of life, and Englishmen pursued them as they had done for centuries before Hastings was fought and lost'.

The Plantaganets
William's sons, William Rufus (reigned 1087–1100) and Henry I (reigned 1100–1135), clashed with their elder brother Robert, who had inherited Normandy. With Robert's defeat at Tinchebray in 1106 kingdom and duchy were again united. Henry's heir was his daughter Matilda, married to Geoffrey Plantaganet, son of Count Fulk of Anjou. But Henry's nephew Stephen also laid claim to the throne, and in 1153, after a bitter civil war, it was agreed that Stephen would reign for life, and that on his death Matilda's son Henry Plantaganet would succeed. The name Plantaganet derives from the Angevin emblem of *planta genista* – broom plant – and the memorial marking the spot where Richard III is believed to have fallen at Bosworth observes that he was the last of the Plantaganet kings.

Henry II (reigned 1154–1189) inherited an empire running from the Pyrenees to the Scottish border. He spent two-thirds of his reign on the Continent, holding his possessions together, and determined to partition them between his three eldest sons. In the event, Richard I (reigned 1189–1199) inherited most of his father's domains and spent little time in England. He died childless, and although his brother John (reigned 1199–1216) took over most of the Angevin Empire he could not hold it.

In England, a baronial revolt forced John to accept limitations on royal power embodied in Magna Carta (1215). Attempts to implement it led to more clashes, and the barons offered the throne to the French Prince Louis. The supporters of John's son Henry III (reigned 1216–1272) defeated Louis, but Henry proved less successful on the Continent, giving up most of the Angevin Empire and doing homage to the French king for Gascony. He too found himself in difficulties with his barons, but the defeat of Simon de Montfort at Evesham in 1265 enabled him to pass on a stable kingdom to his son Edward.

Edward I (reigned 1272–1307) spent much of his rule at war. Between 1276 and 1284 he subdued Wales, though, despite his nickname 'the hammer of the Scots', he was less successful in Scotland. His son Edward II (reigned 1307–27) was defeated by Robert Bruce at Bannockburn in 1314, a victory which helped Scotland win recognition as an independent nation.

Edward was no more successful at home, and was imprisoned and murdered in 1327. His son Edward III (reigned 1327–1377) continued to fight the Scots but was never able to make his victories conclusive. He campaigned in France on an even greater scale, claiming the French throne by right of his mother, Isabella, a princess of the French royal house. Although he won Crécy (1346), the first land battle of the Hundred Years War, and his son the Black Prince went on to win Poitiers (1356), decisive victory eluded him in France as it had in Scotland.

The Wars of the Roses
Edward's death saw the first stirrings of another conflict. Its title, 'The Wars of the Roses', has irritated some historians, who have pointed out that red and white roses were only two of the many badges used by the Houses of Lancaster and York. Instead of a long-running dynastic struggle, John Gillingham identifies three distinct wars. The first was caused by Henry VI's failure as king, the second by the discontent of the Earl of Warwick and the third by Richard III's seizure of the throne. These conflicts all occurred within a single society and the space of one gener-ation. They were largely wars within the political nation, and much of the country's social, economic and religious life went on around them.

Edward III's fourth son, John of Gaunt, Duke of Lancaster, an enor-mously wealthy man, dominated the government under the last years of Edward. He was opposed by his elder brother the Black Prince, and by Edmund Mortimer, Earl of March, who enjoyed wide influence in Wales and the Marches and was married to Edward's grand-daughter. In as much as the Wars of the Roses were about dynastic rivalry, the warring dynasties were founded by John of Gaunt and Edmund Mortimer.

King Edward outlived the Black Prince, whose ten-year-old son Richard II succeeded to the throne in 1377. During his minority, war went badly in France, Spain and the Scottish Borders, and in 1381 the growing burden of taxes sparked off the Peasants' Revolt. The young king behaved with great courage, and the rebels dispersed, encouraged by charters abol-ishing serfdom and trade restrictions. After the rising the ruling class reasserted itself. 'Villeins ye are still,' Richard told a delegation of peasants, 'and villeins ye shall remain.'

The King was less fortunate with his noble opponents, who resented his attempts to bring the Continental war to an end. In 1397 their

'Merciless' Parliament executed, imprisoned or exiled most of his supporters. Richard took pains to rebuild his own authority, and in 1398 served his opponents the same way. Determined to snuff out all sources of resistance, he exiled John of Gaunt's son, Henry Bolingbroke, Duke of Lancaster.

It was a fatal mistake. Richard misjudged his own power and alienated much of the political nation, for if a duke could be exiled without reason, whose property was safe? Bolingbroke speedily returned with an army at his back: Richard was captured and 'agreed' to abdicate. Bolingbroke claimed the throne by descent, conquest and the need for better rule, and became Henry IV.

'The consequences of the usurpation of 1399,' wrote A. R. Myers, 'dogged the Lancastrian dynasty like a Nemesis which in the long run it could not escape.' Henry's rule depended on might, not right, and the men who had helped him to the throne had to be rewarded. There was a conspiracy in early 1400, which narrowly failed to kill Henry but sealed the fate of Richard II, who died in Pontefract Castle soon afterwards. Owain Glyndwr led a rising in Wales, and in the North the powerful Percys allied themselves to the Scots and marched south to join him. Henry defeated them at Shrewsbury, but it was not until 1408 that the Earl of Northumberland, head of the Percys, was killed. Although the last five years of Henry's reign were relatively peaceful, the country was prey to tensions which the crown's dependence on the magnates prevented it from checking.

Henry V, who came to the throne in 1413, was a pious, self-confident young man who had gained experience in his father's wars. He asserted his claim to the throne of a France weakened by factional strife. Though Henry was sincere, his claim also made good political sense, for the war offered noblemen and humble soldiers alike the prospect of personal profit, and success would demonstrate that his father's seizure of the throne had divine approval. His victory at Agincourt that October eclipsed even Crécy and Poitiers, but it was not until 1420 that Henry was able to conclude a treaty which would give him the French throne on the death of its holder.

Henry died early, however, in 1422, and was succeeded by his two-year-old son, Henry VI. During the first years of the new king's minority power was in the hands of a council, its factions led by Henry's uncle Humphrey, Duke of Gloucester and Henry Beaufort, Bishop of Winchester. Another uncle, John, Duke of Bedford, was Regent of France, and it was thanks to his skill that England retained a tenuous grasp on her continental possessions. The war went badly, and its cost promoted resentment in Parliament and encouraged the Beaufort faction to seek terms with France. The young king's marriage to a French princess, Margaret of Anjou, brought a two-year truce. When the war flared up again in 1449 the French over-ran the whole of Normandy and went on, in 1453, to destroy the last English army at Castillon in Gascony, leaving only Calais in English hands.

The loss of Normandy provoked violent reaction. The King's chief minister, the Duke of Suffolk, was impeached in Parliament and fled, only to be captured by mutinous sailors and summarily beheaded, and Jack Cade led a Kentish rising which briefly occupied London. The gentle and devout Henry VI was never robust and now suffered a complete collapse. Richard, Duke of York, Edmund Mortimer's great-grandson and, since Duke Humphrey's death in 1447, leader of the opposition to the Beauforts, was declared Protector of the Realm during the King's illness. Queen Margaret bore a son in October 1453, and although York was swift to recognize him as heir to the throne, the Queen's fears for the child's safety made her an implacable enemy of York's. The scene was set for the first round of open war.

In May 1455 the Yorkists advanced on London, and at the first Battle of St Albans, Edmund Beaufort, Duke of Somerset, was killed and King Henry captured. Fighting broke out afresh in 1459, and in December 1460 York, who had now claimed the throne, was defeated and killed at Wakefield. Margaret then marched south and beat the Yorkist Richard Neville, Earl of Warwick, at the second Battle of St Albans, but her husband dissuaded her from taking London. Instead, it was York's eldest son Edward, a youth of 19, who entered the capital, where he was proclaimed Edward IV.

Edward and Warwick marched north against the Lancastrians, and on Palm Sunday 1461 the armies met at Towton, 6 miles (10 km) north of Ferrybridge in Yorkshire. The battle was fought in a driving snowstorm, and Lord Fauconberg, commanding the Yorkist vanguard, ordered his archers to shoot a volley of arrows which, with the gale behind them, hit the Lancastrians. The Lancastrians shot back, but to little effect as their arrows fell short. When the armies came to hand-strokes the battle was pursued with unusual ferocity. The turning-point came when the Duke of Norfolk arrived on the Lancastrian left flank with Yorkist reinforcements, and as night fell the Lancastrians broke. The survivors had to cross the River Cock as they made for Tadcaster, and many died under the swords of the pursuing cavalry. Contemporary estimates of 28,000 killed are probably too high, but Towton was the largest battle of the Wars of the Roses and the bloodiest ever fought on English soil.

Many leading Lancastrians were slain in the battle, and other notable captives were killed shortly afterwards. The Bishop of Exeter was among the many who hoped that this carnage signalled the end of the blood-letting. 'After so much sorrow and tribulation,' he mused, 'I hope that grateful tranquillity and quiet will ensue, and that after so many clouds we shall have a clear sky.'

The good bishop was to be disappointed, and the reason for this lay in the characters of two of the architects of Yorkist victory, Edward IV and his cousin Richard, Earl of Warwick. The young king was affable and pleasure-loving, and left the affairs of the kingdom to Warwick. In 1464, after a long campaign in the north, the Earl defeated Queen Margaret, and captured her hapless spouse the following year. Warwick was in the process of negotiating a peace with France, which would have been sealed by a marriage between Edward and a French princess, when he was told that the King had already wed a pretty Lancastrian widow, Elizabeth Woodville. Royal favours were showered upon the Woodvilles, and Warwick, stung to the quick, began to shift his allegiance, coming to an agreement with the King's brother, George, Duke of Clarence, to whom he married his daughter.

In the spring of 1469 there were risings in Yorkshire in which Robin of Redesdale – probably Sir William Conyers, a Neville supporter – played a leading part. But Warwick first pretended to be an honest intermediary, pressing the King to meet the rebels' demands for reform, but on 26 July 1469 he beat the royal army at Edgecote, executing its captured leaders. Edward himself was taken shortly afterwards and kept in honourable cap-tivity. But Warwick could not exploit his success. He did not wish to restore Henry VI, and could not govern through Edward IV, who was soon released and swiftly reasserted his authority.

Early in 1470 Warwick and Clarence began another rising, but it was nipped in the bud by Edward's victory at Lose-cote Field near Stamford in Lincolnshire, so called because of the speed with which the rebels jettisoned their armour. Edward declared Warwick and Clarence traitors, and they fled to France where, under pressure from Louis XI, they were reconciled with the exiled Queen Margaret.

In September 1470 England was invaded by Warwick and Clarence with Lancastrian support. King Edward fled to Burgundy, and Henry IV, wits quite gone, was removed from the Tower of London and reinstalled on the throne. The Duke of Burgundy supported his royal guest, and in March 1471 Edward landed at Ravenspur on the Humber. Most Yorkists rallied to him, and even Clarence changed sides, realizing that the associ-ation between Margaret and Warwick would be fatal to his own ambitions.

Edward entered London unopposed, and on 13 April moved north to meet Warwick who was approaching with a larger army.

The battle of Barnet was fought on Easter Sunday, 14 April 1471, in a fog so thick that the armies were not quite aligned, and the right wing of each overlapped the other's left. The Lancastrian right beat the Yorkist left and vice versa, but when the victorious Lancastrians returned to the field they were fired on by their own side and fled in panic. Although both sides suffered heavy losses, the battle was a Yorkist victory, for Warwick himself perished.

Queen Margaret had not accompanied Warwick to England, depriving him of the aid of Lancastrians who might have risen against Edward IV. She landed at Weymouth, with her son Edward, Prince of Wales, the day Warwick died at Barnet, and found much support in the West Country. King Edward left Windsor with a hastily assembled force on 24 April, and on 3 May he caught up with the Lancastrians at Tewkesbury. The Duke of Somerset, the Lancastrian commander, took up a strong natural position south of Tewkesbury Abbey, but appears to have been provoked into attacking by the superior firepower of the leading Yorkist division, under Edward IV's brother Richard, Duke of Gloucester. The armies were locked in battle when a small force of Yorkist spearmen, posted in Tewkesbury Park on Edward's left, swung in and crumpled Somerset's right flank. The Lancastrian army broke, and its casualties were heavy: Queen Margaret's son, young Prince Edward, was amongst the slain. Somerset and other surviving nobles took refuge in Tewkesbury Abbey but were hauled out and beheaded the following day.

There were risings elsewhere, only one of them serious. Thomas Fauconberg, an illegitimate son of William Neville, Lord Fauconberg, and a cousin of Warwick's, led a force of seamen, soldiers from the Calais garrison, and disaffected men from Kent and Essex in an assault on London. It had been dealt with by citizens and loyal noblemen before King Edward returned to the capital on 21 May.

He quickly set the seal on his victories. Margaret, captured after Tewkesbury, was imprisoned and then exiled to France. The captive Henry VI died 'of pure displeasure and melancholy', though it would not be unfair to see Edward's hand behind his demise. The Lancastrian nobility had been decimated by death in battle and execution after it, although modern research has shown that the damage done to the nobility by the Wars of the Roses was not as great as contemporaries opined. One of the two remaining Lancastrian peers, John de Vere, Earl of Oxford, was captured in 1474 after a siege in St Michael's Mount off the Cornish coast. He was packed off to prison at Hammes Castle, near Calais.

The dynasty seemed secure. Edward IV had two sons, Edward, born in 1470, and Richard, born three years later. The crown's chronic financial weakness was being remedied by the enormous wealth of the house of York, confiscations from defeated Lancastrians, and a subsidy paid by the French as the price of ending a brief war in 1475. The troublesome North was in the capable hands of the King's brother, Richard of Gloucester. Clarence, forgiven for his earlier lapse, took to intriguing again and was killed – he may, as legend suggests, have been drowned in a tub of Malmsey wine. There was some bickering at court, but when was there not? Whatever the failings of Shakespeare's *Richard III* as history, its opening lines (a pun on the family's *rose-en-soleil* badge) deftly captures this apotheosis of the royal house:

> Now is the winter of our discontent
> Made glorious summer by this sun of York
> And all the clouds that lour'd upon our house
> In the deep bosom of the ocean buried.

Changes in Weaponry and Armour
While combat in the Wars of the Roses would not have shocked the men who fought at Hastings, war had moved on. The bad-egg stink of black powder was now laced into the familiar battlefield stench of blood, sweat and ordure, human and equine. Gunpowder had been known in China in the eleventh century, and primitive cannon were in use in Europe early in the fourteenth, but it was another century before they were widespread. Iron cannon tended to be fragile, so most guns were cast in brass.

Though standardization of calibres was still more than a century away, cannon came in several general types. At the lower end of the scale were close-range weapons like the orgue, a group of gun-barrels fastened to a frame so that all could be fired at once (the ancestor, in its clumsy way, of the machine-gun). Larger cannon, like the serpentine, provided the armies of the period with the closest they came to field artillery. Although these might throw iron or stone balls 1000 yards (900 m), their crews would be fortunate to get off ten shots an hour and more fortunate still to hit what they aimed at. Many battles began with a cannonade, but few rounds were fired before the opposing armies were at work with sword and axe.

If cannon had a limited effect on battles in open field, they were devastating against castle walls. Sieges, which might once have lasted for months as engineers tried to undermine fortifications, or cost many lives as infantry assaulted up scaling-ladders or from siege towers, could now be over in days: in 1405 Berwick surrendered after a single shot had been fired.

Engineers responded by building fortifications lower and putting sloping earth, not rising stonework, in the way of the cannon ball. At the very end of the fifteenth century the bastion, an arrow-head gun-platform thrust forward from the walls of a fortress, made its first appearance, and soon became the quintessential item of artillery fortification. Although there are some examples in the British Isles, artillery fortification never speckled the British landscape as it did the continental.

Gunpowder also contributed to infantry firepower. By 1485 primitive 'hand-gonnes' had been replaced by weapons which were beginning to resemble the musket of later generations. These had a wooden butt and, in some cases, a mechanism which brought a smouldering cord down to the touch-hole when the firer pressed its trigger.

Hand-guns could kill men and terrify horses, but for range, accuracy and rate of fire they were eclipsed by the longbow: in 1549 insurgents under the Norfolk landowner Robert Kett outshot German mercenary hand-gunners sent against them. The longbow's origins remain disputed, though the Welsh were certainly making good use of it as early as 1150, when Gerald de Barri observed that Welsh archers sent arrows through an oak door four fingers thick. In 1252 the royal Assize of Arms decreed that all Englishmen who owned land worth more than 40 shillings or chattels worth 9 marks were to provide themselves with sword, dagger, bow and arrows.

The bow's use had been developed during Edward I's Scottish and Welsh wars, and it was the characteristic English infantry weapon of the Hundred Years War. In the Wars of the Roses the archers on both sides often cancelled one another out. It was only when one side gained a clear advantage – like the Yorkists at Towton – or was unable to bring its bowmen into play – like the Yorkists at Edgecote – that the bow proved a battle-winner. Plate armour was now so well developed as to keep out most arrows save at close range, though areas protected only by mail were always vulnerable.

It is almost true to say that archers were born, not made, for it took years of practice for a man to achieve the upper body strength to use a war-bow with a draw-weight of over 100lb (45 kg). Dominic Mancini, an Italian priest who visited England in 1482–3 told his bishop:

Their bows and arrows are thicker and longer than those used by other nations just as their arms are stronger than other people's, for they seem to have hands and arms of iron. As a result their bows have as long a range as our crossbows.

Battlefield losses made inroads into the stock of trained archers. Sixteenth-century complaints that the bow was falling into disuse doubtless had much to do, as contemporaries suspected, with the rise of football and other 'lewd games', but the casualties of the century's bloodier battles also played their part.

If the longbow had developed since Hastings, so too had its cousin the crossbow. Many fifteenth-century crossbows had steel or composite staves, and their increased power meant that they had to be drawn by a windlass or pulley. Their stubby bolts could crack plate armour if they struck it squarely, and a well-trained crossbowman could shoot four or five times a minute.

Some infantrymen bore staff weapons. The long-bladed English bill was popular throughout the period. The halberd, with an axe-blade one side and a point on the other, was equally effective. Mercenaries from the Low Countries served on both sides, and often used the pike, with a shaft up to 18 feet (5.5 m) long.

The pike had an awesome reputation on the Continent, and Swiss pikemen inflicted catastrophic defeats on feudal cavalry. In Flemish hands, too, it was a weapon to be reckoned with, but in the Wars of the Roses it never assumed the same importance, possibly because wedges of pikemen were vulnerable to bowmen at a distance and to billmen once their shorter weapon was inside the pike's reach. Much of the conflict between Scots and English centred around the interplay between tough Scottish spearmen, who drew up in masses called *schiltroms,* and English archers and billmen.

The man-at-arms was still king of the battlefield. He was the descendant of William's horsemen, though his appearance had changed since the days of the conical helmet and mail hauberk. Plate armour arrived to reinforce mail in the thirteenth century, full plate was in use at the beginning of the fifteenth, and over the next hundred years it reached a peak of sophistication. Armour was subject to the vagaries of fashion and the impact of technology. Curved surfaces induced blows to glance off, and articulated joints assisted movement. Surfaces might be gilded or engraved, or blued, browned or painted to protect them from rust.

Some armour was English-made, but much came from Flanders, South Germany and North Italy. A wealthy man could afford a suit in the latest fashion – the flamboyant Gothic style was popular at the time of Bosworth – but there was mixing and matching as old but serviceable armour was retained in use. The term man-at-arms includes any warrior

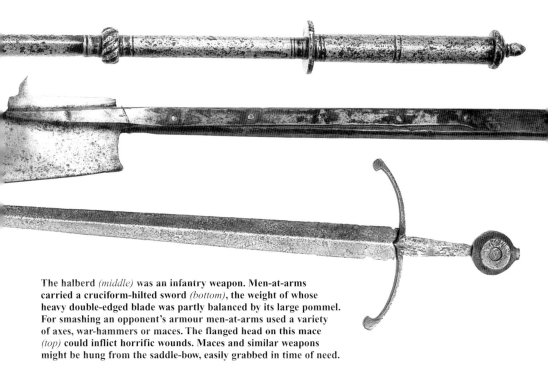

The halberd *(middle)* was an infantry weapon. Men-at-arms
carried a cruciform-hilted sword *(bottom)*, the weight of whose
heavy double-edged blade was partly balanced by its large pommel.
For smashing an opponent's armour men-at-arms used a variety
of axes, war-hammers or maces. The flanged head on this mace
(top) could inflict horrific wounds. Maces and similar weapons
might be hung from the saddle-bow, easily grabbed in time of need.

fighting in full armour – knight, esquire, gentleman or mounted sergeant.
The latter, derived from the Latin *serviens*, servant, denoted a warrior
below the rank of gentleman but above that of common soldier.

Not all men-at-arms wore full armour. Some could not afford it, and
others, especially if fighting on foot, abandoned breast- and back-plate in
favour of a brigandine, a jerkin made of several layers of cloth or leather
with small iron plates sandwiched between. A knight's brigandine might
be covered in rich material and finished with gilded rivets, while a lower-
ranking man-at-arms or infantryman would have been content with something less decorative. Simpler still was the jack, a quilted canvas jacket or
jerkin stuffed with padding, worn by many infantrymen. Brigandines and
jacks were worn over mail, if the soldier had it, and might be reinforced
by plate armour, for instance in the form of arm or leg defences.

The straight cruciform-hilted sword was the classic knightly weapon,
but other arms were often more appropriate. The lance was invaluable in
the first impact of a charge. War-hammers and maces could combine
blades, spikes and hammerheads to pierce or smash armour. The pole-axe,
with a spiked or bladed head on a shaft 3–4 feet (90–120 cm) long, was a
favourite weapon for men-at-arms on foot. At Edgecote the Yorkist Sir

William Herbert 'valiantly acquitted himself in that, on foot and with his pole-axe in his hand, he twice by main force passed through the battle of his adversaries and without any mortal wound returned.' Soldiers carried a knife of some sort, from the knightly misericorde (so called because it slipped between plates of armour to ease the life out of a crippled opponent) to the 'ballock' dagger, with its distinctive two-globed guard, favoured by foot-soldiers.

Although some foot-soldiers plied a small one-handed buckler, shields went out of general use in the middle of the fifteenth century. They had been a convenient way of displaying heraldic devices which aided recognition in battle, but these could still be shown on tabards worn over armour. Contingents raised by individuals or towns usually wore coloured livery tunics, with a badge on chest or shoulder, over their jacks or brigandines: Warwick's men wore red jackets with his badge of bear and ragged staff in white. Badges like this were simpler than coats of arms. Richard III used his white boar, Henry Tudor a red dragon, and the Earl of Oxford a white star: Lord Welles, with a rather weak pun, favoured a bucket and chain.

Military Organization

Liveries and badges reflected military organization. The Norman conquest saw the establishment of feudalism in England: great noblemen, the king's tenants-in-chief, held their land in return for providing agreed numbers of knights for a set period; and they in turn granted land to knights who would serve when required. Other knights might form part of their lord's household, or simply be hired.

The process was never entirely satisfactory for the monarch, who risked seeing knights melt away as their term of service expired, or who might simply find them inappropriate for the task in hand. Magnates and retainers, who faced the disruption arising from a call to arms, found the arrangement no more appealing. Increasingly, feudal service was commuted into payment called scutage – from the Latin *scutum* (shield) which offered greater flexibility. Infantry were often recuited by means of a commission of array, which appointed commissioners – usually men of military experience – to supervise levies raised by local communities.

Edward III tried to revive feudal obligations, insisting that a man worth £40 in land was obliged to provide two men-at-arms. Successes in the Scots War restrained the outcry caused by such demands, but in 1352 he conceded that they would be made only with Parliament's agreement. Thereafter he developed the practice of contracting with leaders, who, in return for pay, agreed to provide a force of a specified size at a given date.

These contractors tended to be noblemen, who used the bonds of loyalty which already existed around their estates as the basis for their contingents. Great landowners maintained knights and squires who were paid annuities or given land-holdings to retain their loyalty, and who acted as sub-contractors by turning out with retinues of their own. Some archers served full-time in the household of a nobleman, but others were recruited only in time of war.

The contract system worked well enough during the Hundred Years War, when soldiers might expect rich pickings in France. After the war England was awash with unemployed soldiers, many of whom found employment in the retinues of great nobles. When royal authority was weak, noblemen with armed bands grew increasingly powerful, encouraging lesser men to put themselves under their protection and, in return, to provide military service, wearing the lord's badge and livery.

Though there was no standing army in the late Middle Ages, the royal household provided the kernel for raising an army. Kings maintained bodyguards of knights and men-at-arms: Edward IV had his own archers, and soon after his accession Henry VII founded the Yeomen of the Guard. Calais was an English-held enclave in France, with castles like Hammes and Guines protecting it. Its garrison was composed of professional soldiers, and the post of Captain of Calais was a powerful one. English kings had frequently recruited foreign mercenaries, who were often more reliable than Englishmen in civil wars, provided their wages were paid. Finally, most monarchs had a regional power base and family affiliations which made it easier for them to raise troops on home ground.

Yet the fact remains that, to raise a large army, a king relied heavily on the support of great nobles, and much of the manoeuvring of the age was intended to encourage loyalty by means of dynastic links, and grants of money, land or titles. Disloyalty was punished not simply by death – beheading for noblemen and hanging, drawing and quartering for lesser men – but by attainder, which deprived the condemned man of lands, title and possessions, leaving his family paupers.

Campaign and Battle

'Between 1483 and 1485,' writes Michael Bennett, 'it is tempting to see all roads leading to Bosworth. This quiet market centre, in the heart of *champion* England, seems almost to have exercised a gravitational pull on the actors in the tragedy of Richard III.' And tragedy it was, for in two short years the sun of York burned out for ever, scorching many who came close to it.

BOSWORTH
1485: The Campaign

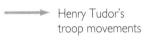 Henry Tudor's
troop movements

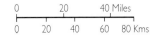 Richard III's
troop movements

0		20		40 Miles

0	20	40	60	80 Kms

Irish Sea

Welshpoo

● Machynlleth

Henry Tudor

● Haverfordwest

● Milford Haven

7 Aug

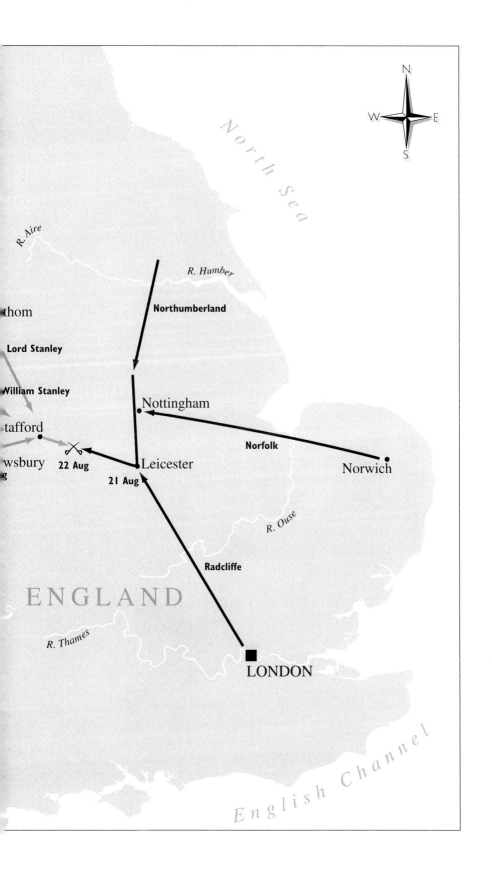

The Protectorate

Edward IV unexpectedly fell ill at Easter 1483 and died on 9 April. On his death-bed he exhorted his counsellors to make peace with one another, and nominated his brother Richard as Protector, chairman of the council which would govern in his son's minority. No sooner was the King dead than Queen Elizabeth and her relatives, notably her brother Earl Rivers and Thomas Grey, Marquess of Dorset, her son by her first marriage, sought to bring the thirteen-year-old young King Edward down from Ludlow with a Woodville escort and have him crowned as soon as possible. Richard was away in the North, probably at his castle at Middleham, but saw the risks he ran. Not only would his influence count for little in a Woodville-dominated court, but his personal safety could hardly be guaranteed.

Others found the Queen's faction equally threatening. Edward IV's chief counsellor Lord Hastings feared that 'if power slipped into the grasp of the Queen's relatives they would avenge the injuries they claimed he had done them – for between him and them there was a feud of long standing.' Hastings was Captain of Calais, and warned the Queen's kinsmen that if they made Edward V's escort too large he would flee to Calais – whence, in collaboration with the French or Burgundian courts, he could make their lives difficult. They agreed that the escort should not exceed 2000 men. The powerful Henry Stafford, Duke of Buckingham, had been married off at the age of 11 to one of the Queen's sisters, but resented the match and regarded his in-laws as arrivistes: he too was not anxious to see the Woodvilles triumphant.

On 29 April Gloucester met Buckingham at Northampton, and the Dukes were not pleased to find that the young King Edward and his escort had already passed on their way to London. When Earl Rivers and his nephew Sir Richard Grey rode back to welcome the Dukes they were arrested. Gloucester and Buckingham then rode on to Stony Stratford where they took charge of the King, seizing more of his entourage and sending them off to castles in the North. The Queen took sanctuary in Westminster Abbey when she heard the news, taking with her Richard, Duke of York, her younger son and the Marquess of Dorset.

The Dukes entered London on 4 May, announcing that they had rescued the King from evil counsellors and parading cartloads of weapons bearing the Woodville badge as proof that the Queen's kinsmen had intended to rule by force. The Queen's brother Sir Edward Woodville was in command of the fleet, but it was persuaded to rally to the Protector. Richard's government seemed evenly balanced. The Queen's relatives were ousted, but Hastings remained Lord Chamberlain and Captain of Calais, and even Archbishop Rotherham and Bishop Morton, who had supported the Woodvilles, were allowed to remain on the council.

Thus far Richard's behaviour had not been unreasonable, and it is easy to argue, as his supporters still do, that he was simply acting in self-defence and seeking to promote stability. The events of the weeks that followed make that justification harder to uphold but, with so little evidence at our disposal, it is difficult to be sure of his real motives. Certainly, Shakespeare's characterization of Richard as a man bent on securing the crown at all costs cannot be sustained. He had been conspicuously loyal to Edward IV, and immediately after the King's death threw his weight behind Edward V, though he pressed his claim to be Protector.

This may well have been the full extent of his ambition until the first week of June 1483, but thereafter it is clear that he was indeed determined to pluck down the crown. We cannot be sure whether he was spurred on by personal ambition, had come to the conclusion that only decisive action on his part could end the risk of anarchy, or, as seems most likely, had allowed these motives to become blurred.

There were risks in inaction. Richard's powers as Protector were limited and would eventually end. The council was unwilling to arraign the Queen's relatives for treason. Some historians have argued that Hastings, Morton and other council members were conducting secret negotiations with the Queen through Jane Shore, an ex-mistress of Edward IV who had also been involved with Hastings and Dorset.

Richard Claims the Crown

Early in June Richard began to order his supporters in the North to assemble soldiers, who were to muster at Pontefract on 18 June and then march south under the Earl of Northumberland. In the event he struck without their aid. On 13 June hostile members of the council were arrested while sitting at the Tower of London: Hastings was dragged outside and beheaded on the spot. It is possible that he had been sounded out on Richard's next proposed step, and death was his penalty for demurring. On 16 June soldiers surrounded Westminster Abbey, and the Archbishop of Canterbury persuaded the Queen to hand over the Duke of York, who was lodged with his brother in the state apartments in the Tower.

The coup was pressed ruthlessly. On 22 June the Lord Mayor's brother, Dr Ralph Shaa, preached a sermon in St Paul's, suggesting that Edward IV and Elizabeth Woodville had not been properly married. As the princes in the Tower were illegitimate they could not succeed to the throne, and the Duke of Gloucester was invited to do so instead. The Woodvilles seized in April were executed, while Thomas Howard and Thomas Berkeley (who had backed Richard) became Duke of Norfolk and Earl of

Nottingham. The Earl of Northumberland duly entered London with his army and Richard was crowned on 6 July.

Richard continued to reward his followers, many of them northerners. Viscount Lovell became Lord Chamberlain and Sir Robert Brackenbury Constable of the Tower. Both were appointed to the king's council, as were Lord Scrope, Sir Richard Radcliffe, Sir James Tyrell and Sir Richard FitzHugh. These new appointments, which reflected a shift towards the Nevilles – Richard's wife Anne was a Neville – caused some dissatisfaction, not least amongst traditional Yorkist supporters. The fate of the princes in the Tower of London also tweaked tender sensibilities. The surviving evidence would not convict Richard of complicity in their death, and there is some reason to suspect that they were murdered on Buckingham's orders in late July, but it was obvious that Richard stood to gain from the demise of his nephews.

Shortly after his coronation Richard travelled slowly to his old stamping ground in the North, received a warm welcome in York, and went on to see his son Edward invested as Prince of Wales. On 11 September he was passing through Lincoln on his way back to London when he heard that rebellion had broken out across the South, and that no less a man than Buckingham was implicated in it.

The autumn rising included not only Woodville supporters – Dorset had escaped from Westminster Abbey – but also close adherents of the late Edward IV and some prominent Lancastrians. Buckingham may have joined the rebellion because he felt that it was bound to succeed, and it certainly attracted widespread support across the South.

The Emergence of Henry Tudor
One of the strengths of the rising was the participation of Henry Tudor. His grandfather Owen, scion of a proud but undistinguished family of Welsh gentry, had been a member of Henry V's household and after the King's death had secretly married his widow, Catherine of Valois, who bore him two sons. When news of the union emerged Owen was imprisoned and Catherine sent off to a nunnery, but Henry VI soon warmed to his half-brothers, creating the elder, Jasper, Earl of Pembroke and the younger, Edmund, Earl of Richmond. Edmund married Margaret Beaufort, daughter and heir of John Beaufort, Duke of Somerset. The Beauforts were the result of an irregular union between Edward III's son John of Gaunt and Catherine Swynford. Although they had subsequently been legitimized, the Beauforts had also been barred from the succession. In 1456 Edmund died young, but not before begetting a son named in honour of Henry VI.

Henry Tudor, Earl of Richmond, had spent his life tossed on the stormy seas of politics. He was looked after by his uncle Jasper until 1461, when the Yorkist Lord Herbert was rewarded with Jasper's earldom of Pembroke and Henry became Lord Herbert's ward. Henry may have been presented at court in 1470 when Jasper helped restore Henry VI, but the following year he and his uncle fled abroad after the Yorkist triumph.

The fugitives were making for France but landed on the coast of Brittany, where they became pawns in the power-play between the Duke of Brittany, the King of France and the King of England. However, in mid-1483 the Duke of Brittany was prepared to give Henry military support. The fact that his formidable mother Margaret had married Lord Stanley, Steward of the King's Household, can have done him no harm. Moreover, Margaret and Elizabeth Woodville were in contact, and discussed the possibility of a marriage between Henry and the former Queen's daughter Elizabeth of York.

Henry's first intervention in English politics failed miserably. The 1483 rising lacked central direction, while Richard and his allies acted with determination. The King summoned troops to Leicester, whence he offered a free pardon to commoners caught up in the rebellion and put a price on their leaders' heads, while Norfolk moved down to protect the capital and deal with rebels in the South-East. Unseasonably bad weather made Buckingham's advance from South Wales particularly dispiriting. The Duke was betrayed and taken in chains to Salisbury, and when Richard arrived on 2 November Buckingham was executed.

Henry Tudor put in briefly at Plymouth, heard that the rebellion had collapsed, and returned to Brittany. Michael Bennett is right to observe that it was in a spirit of defiance rather than optimism that, before a gathering of exiles in Rennes Cathedral on Christmas Day 1483, Henry formally laid claim to the crown of England, though his title to it was weak indeed, and promised to marry Elizabeth of York as soon as he was king.

Richard Loses Support

Richard had reason to believe that the collapse of the rising left him secure, and many foreign observers agreed with him. They were not, on the face of things, wrong to do so, for the new King had many sterling qualities. He had administered the North efficiently, and shown himself a capable commander. He was genuinely pious, and proved a generous patron of the Church. If lack of stature robbed him of his brother's commanding presence, it obscured neither his regal bearing nor his Plantaganet features. He took a well-informed interest in the law, and prized good and equitable government.

But as king he was a failure. There had always been a streak of ruthlessness within him, and as he tried to tighten his grip on power he seemed out of sympathy with the mood of the land and reliant on a small group of advisers, notably Lovell, Radcliffe and Sir William Catesby. A piece of contemporary doggerel linked them to the King's white boar badge:

The Rat, the Cat, and Lovell the Dog
Do rule all England, under the Hog.

The 1484 Parliament, with Catesby as its Speaker, passed an unprecedented 100 acts of attainder in a single session: there had been 140 for the whole of Edward IV's reign.

The death that year of Richard's only legitimate son, Edward of Middleham, was a crushing blow. It is indicative of popular mistrust that, although the King came to an accommodation with Elizabeth Woodville, enabling her to leave sanctuary, it was widely believed that he had done this only in order to marry her daughter Elizabeth of York. Worse, it was said that he poisoned his wife Anne, who died in 1485, to be free to do so. The middle of the year found him at Nottingham, well aware that an invasion was likely, and anxious for it to come, not merely to end the uncertainty but to give him the chance to seek God's judgement in battle.

As Richard's position deteriorated so Henry's improved. In 1485 he left the Breton court and moved to that of Charles VIII of France. He had not been there long when he was joined by the Earl of Oxford, released from Hammes Castle by its disaffected governor. Richard recaptured Hammes and in 1485 appointed his own illegitimate son, John of Gloucester, Captain of Calais, effectively taking it into his own hands. His trusted henchman Sir James Tyrell was installed as Captain of Guines, but in the process lost his grip on Glamorgan, for which he was also responsible. It was not, as events were to show, a fair exchange.

Henry's chances of success hinged on undercutting Richard's support, for, unless he did so, any invasion force would be swamped by a larger royal army. John Howard, Duke of Norfolk, was head of a new noble family, and had gained his dukedom, the earldom of Surrey for his son Thomas, and much confiscated land to boot, as a reward for backing Richard. The Howards had played a notable part in putting down the 1483 rising, and, although they preferred their mighty castle of Framlingham to the royal court, they had much to lose from a change of regime.

In contrast Henry Percy, Earl of Northumberland, was head of a great house which was much older. The Percys had been attainted after the Yorkist victory in 1461 and saw the family earldom given to a Neville, brother of Warwick, but were restored to favour when Warwick rebelled in 1470. Henry Percy formed a good working relationship with Richard when the latter had been King Edward's Viceroy in the North, but by 1484 he found his retainers slipping away into royal service. He was sounded out by Henry Tudor's representatives, and cannot have found it easy to choose where his loyalties should lie.

Thomas, Lord Stanley, was in an even more ambivalent position. His great-grandfather had been a soldier of fortune under Richard II, and since then the family had risen, through deft political moves and good governance of their estates, to form a solid regional power base in Lancashire and Cheshire. Stanley's father was ennobled in 1456 and died soon afterwards, but his son showed all the family flair for backing the winning side. If, from one viewpoint, this was sheer dynastic self-interest, from another it was a refusal to allow the oscillations of national politics to affect the lives of ordinary folk in the family's domains.

Lord Stanley's eldest son George had married the daughter and heiress of Lord Strange, thereby inheriting that title, and his brother Sir William Stanley had done almost as well for himself by marrying the widowed Countess of Worcester. The Stanleys had supported Richard during the autumn rising of 1483 and prospered by it, with grants of lands and offices. But by the summer of 1485, even if the King was unaware of just how deeply Lord Stanley's wife, Margaret Beaufort, was involved in Henry Tudor's preparations, he knew that the family had divided loyalties. When Stanley was sent off to raise troops his son, Lord Strange, was retained at court as a hostage.

Preparations for War
Richard had kept court in Westminster over the winter of 1484–5, and in the spring moved, by way of Windsor and Kenilworth, to Nottingham. Although the King was fond of hunting in nearby Sherwood Forest, he was drawn to Nottingham for excellent strategic reasons. He had improved its already strong castle, which was within easy distance of his own power base north of the Trent, and from it he hoped to dominate the Midlands. The Duke of Norfolk controlled East Anglia, Brackenbury's men garrisoned the Tower of London, and Lovell, at Southampton, watched the south coast. South Wales, an obvious source of Tudor support, was the responsibility of the King's brother-in-law, the Earl of Huntingdon, who had done his best to rally the local gentry.

A manuscript illustration of the Yorkist victory at Tewksbury (1471). In the foreground are the rival archers, wearing helmets and quilted jacks: some have placed spare arrows on the ground to help them shoot more rapidly. Behind them are the armoured men-at-arms. The lance, couched under the arm, was effective in the first impact of a charge: thereafter horsemen used sword, mace or battle-axe.

In June, sensing that invasion was imminent, Richard declared that the former Earls of Oxford and Richmond – deprived of their titles as attainted traitors – had allied themselves with the French. He went to issue commissions of array, ordering his officers to muster men and collect money for their pay. Knights, esquires and gentlemen were to hold themselves in readiness to support the King 'upon peril of losing their lives, lands and goods'.

Details of Henry Tudor's final preparations are obscure, but it is likely that he began to assemble arms, supplies and ships at Rouen in the spring. His army was built round a solid core of perhaps five hundred exiles, many of them, like his brother the Earl of Pembroke, the Earl of Oxford and Sir Edward Woodville, men of military experience. The bulk of Henry's army consisted of foreign troops, some provided by Charles VIII of France and others serving for pay – or, in the case of some Frenchmen, simply to get out of prison. One mercenary captain, Philibert de Chandee, was on good terms with Henry and remained in England after Bosworth; and strong tradition suggests that Bernard Stuart and Alexander Bruce led a contingent of Scotsmen in French service.

This modest force would be insufficient to defeat Richard, and Henry knew that he would have to attract support as soon as he landed. He had been in close contact with his English backers, had reason to expect that his arrival would inspire risings in many parts of the country, and knew, from messages from his mother, that the Stanleys were likely to throw their weight behind him. Yet the venture was still very risky. Richard was an accomplished soldier, and at Nottingham he was well placed, like a spider on his web, to react promptly to a landing. Henry could not afford an early reverse, which would dissuade potential supporters from declaring for him and push the undecided into Richard's arms.

The invasion fleet sailed on 1 August, and on Sunday 7 August Henry landed, just before nightfall, at Milford Haven in South Wales. His choice of Wales should come as no surprise. Although the country had lost its independence, national sentiment remained powerful. Proud and stubborn minor gentry had fought with distinction in the English armies of the Hundred Years War. Welsh soldiers had played their part in the Wars of the Roses, and a Welsh contingent, after a heroic struggle, suffered at Warwick's hands at Edgecote.

Henry and his uncle knew South Wales well, and although the Herberts, the dominant family, supported Richard, there had been widespread promises of support. We cannot be sure whether Henry actually spoke Welsh, but his years in exile at a Breton court which took pride in its Celtic culture can only have strengthened Henry's consciousness of his

Welsh roots. His appearance fanned a flame already kindled by bards who sang of a national revival:

> We are looking forward to the coming of Henry:
> Our nation puts its trust in him.

Shortly after landing, Henry knighted a select group of his companions, and marched through Haverfordwest and Llanbadarn to Machynlleth. Parties of gentlemen and yeomen rallied to him as he went, but there was disturbing news that Rhys ap Thomas and William Herbert, with their own retinues and levies from South Wales, were moving parallel with the rebels. This shadow-boxing may have been designed to persuade Richard that the landing had already been contained, to buy more time for a decision by ascertaining that Henry was in earnest, or simply to demonstrate the worth of those two contingents when they at last joined Henry at or near Welshpool. More Welshmen trooped in to a muster on Long Mountain, outside the town, and on 15 August Henry demanded the surrender of Shrewsbury. The town capitulated after a brief show of resistance, but only the next few days would show whether the rebellion, so strong in Wales, could be exported into England.

Richard received news of the landing on 11 August at his hunting lodge at Beskwood, near Nottingham. The *Croyland Chronicle* declares that 'the king rejoiced, or at least seemed to rejoice, writing to his adherents in every quarter that now the long wished-for day had arrived.' Fresh summonses were sent out to commissioners of array, noblemen and gentlemen, and the King's committed followers called out their own adherents. The Duke of Norfolk wrote to his 'well-beloved friend John Paston', head of a family of Norfolk gentry:

Wherefore I pray that you meet with me at Bury [St Edmunds], for, by the grace of God, I purpose to lie at Bury as upon Tuesday night [16 August] and that you bring with you such company of tall men as you may goodly make at my cost and charge, besides that which you have promised the king; and, I pray you, ordain them with jackets of my livery, and I shall content you at your meeting with me.

Paston's response is an index of the difficulties facing Richard. There is no evidence that he brought any men badged with the white lion of the Norfolks to the muster, and the fact that he became Sheriff of Norfolk two months later was fair reward for judging the mood of the country so well. Even gentlemen already on their way to the King at Leicester were not to be trusted. Brackenbury brought a contingent of southern gentlemen up from London, but both Sir Thomas Bourchier and Sir Walter Hungerford slipped away at Stony Stratford to join the rebels.

Richard was confident enough to celebrate the Feast of the Assumption of the Blessed Virgin Mary in some style on 15 August, but soon afterwards he heard first of mass defections in Wales, and then of the fall of Shrewsbury. A party of his closest adherents, including Lovell, Catesby and Radcliffe, had already joined him, and it was clear that Norfolk was levying men as ordered. The Earl of Northumberland was proving less prompt, and a royal summons for troops from York, issued on 16 August, may reflect the fact that Northumberland was not raising the North as Richard had hoped.

The Stanleys were even more ambivalent. As soon as he heard of the landing, Richard had summoned Stanley to Nottingham, but the peer replied that he had sweating sickness and could not come. Stanley's son, Lord Strange, tried to escape, but was caught and interrogated. He admitted that his uncle Sir William Stanley and a family henchman Sir John Savage had conspired with Henry, but swore that his father was loyal. He wrote, no doubt with Richard's encouragement, to tell his father of his plight and to urge him to join the King with all his forces.

Henry could have struck straight from Shrewsbury to London, but instead marched eastwards, drawing closer to the Stanleys and keeping open a line of retreat into Wales. At Newport he was joined by Sir Gilbert Talbot, a landowner of some importance and uncle to the Earl of Shrewsbury, with 500 men. This was Henry's first substantial English contingent, and it must have been most welcome.

At Stafford Sir William Stanley rode in for a brief meeting. He had marched down from Holt on the Welsh border, while his brother, who had set off from Lathom in Lancashire, was moving on a converging course further to the east. We do not know what was said, but it is likely that Sir William pointed out that his brother could not declare for Henry till the last possible minute without condemning Lord Strange to death. Lord Stanley's force probably reached Lichfield on 17 August and then moved eastwards, falling back in front of Henry and giving the impression that it was making for Richard's muster at Leicester.

Henry's advance persuaded the King to leave Nottingham on 20 August, although his army was still incomplete. Other contingents joined him at Leicester, to produce what the *Croyland Chronicle* exaggeratedly calls 'a number of warriors…greater than had ever been seen before in England collected together on behalf of one person.' The Duke of Norfolk and the Earls of Northumberland, Surrey, Lincoln and Shrewsbury were present, as well as several other peers.

We cannot be sure if this portrait of Richard III by an unknown artist, probably painted after his death, is an accurate likeness. Its close resemblance to a contemporary portrait suggests that it is. Richard was a good soldier and an accomplished administrator. His 'book of hours', a private book of devotions for daily use, has survived, and suggests that he was devout in a solid and unflamboyant way. He was certainly not the hunchbacked monster created by Shakespeare, but the circumstances of his accession and the fate of the princes in the Tower help make him one of the most controversial of English kings.

Henry Tudor's claim to the throne was not strong, but he was able to profit from French
assistance, strong support in Wales, and existing divisions within the political nation to defeat
Richard III at Bosworth and become Henry VII. The support of the powerful Stanley family
was crucial though, interestingly, one of the Stanleys was subsequently executed for treason
to Henry. He was not the warrior prince of Shakespearean mythology, but a painstaking
administrator: this portrait hints at the sharp and unemotional brain behind the austere face.
Henry was feared rather than loved, and there was popular rejoicing when he died.

On Sunday 21 August – 'the Lord's Day before the feast of Bartholomew the Apostle' – Richard led his host across the old Bow Bridge out of Leicester towards Atherstone. He marched through Peckleton and Kirkby Mallory to Sutton Cheney whence, hearing from his scouts that Henry was moving towards White Moors, he pushed on up to the commanding ground of Ambion Hill, west of Sutton Cheney.

Henry had made a formal entry into Lichfield on 20 August with as much show as he could muster. He seems to have spent that night between Lichfield and Tamworth, accidentally separated from his army, which was mightily relieved to see him when he rode into its camp next morning. On 21 August he was near Atherstone, possibly at Merevale Abbey: three months later he repaid the villages of Atherstone, Fenny Drayton, Mancetter and Witherley for corn taken by his men.

He met Lord Stanley some time on 21 August. Again, we cannot be sure what passed between the two men. A Scot, Robert Lindsay of Pitscottie, writing almost a century later but drawing on oral tradition, maintains that Stanley was bribed. It is safe to say that Stanley was assured that Henry would not be niggardly in rewarding him, and it is likely that Henry offered battle the following day confident that the Stanleys would support him. That night more men slipped away from Richard's army: Sir John Savage the younger, Sir Simon Digby and Sir Brian Sandford all brought their detachments to join Henry.

Shakespeare, writing with Henry's grand-daughter on the throne, had good reason to paint Richard's last hours as dark as possible. But other near-contemporary accounts also testify that the King had a poor night's sleep, and the *Croyland Chronicle* adds that his camp was so badly organized that he was unable to take communion. A strong local tradition suggests that he breakfasted on fresh water from a spring now called King Richard's Well. Desertions over the past weeks and his doubts about the Stanleys, and perhaps Northumberland too, cannot have lifted his spirits. However, his army, at least 10,000 strong and perhaps as large as 15,000, outnumbered the 5000 under Henry's direct command, and even if the Stanleys' 5000 men fought against him he probably still had the edge.

The Battlefield

It is rarely easy to be absolutely sure of the location of medieval battles – Hastings is a happy exception. In the case of Bosworth, although contemporary accounts speak of a battle in Redmoor Plain, and of Richard being killed at Sandeford, neither placename now survives. John Gillingham observes that the most one can say for certain is that the action took place between the villages of Market Bosworth to the north, Sutton Cheney to the east, Stoke Golding to the south and Upton to the west. Attempts to produce detailed maps are, he warns, 'quite worthless'.

The Bosworth Battlefield Visitor Centre disagrees, and sets out the traditionally accepted site of the field between Ambion Hill and the village of Shenton. D. T. Williams' booklet *The Battle of Bosworth Field* confirms this siting and Michael Bennett's comprehensive *The Battle of Bosworth* follows suit, although its author notes, in a postscript, his suspicion that the traditional site is wrong.

In 1985 Colin Richmond suggested that the battle was fought closer to Dadlington and Stoke Golding than was generally thought, noting that the church wardens of Dadlington had received royal permission to collect money 'for the building of a chapel of St James, standing upon a parcel of the ground where Bosworth field, otherwise called Dadlington field…was done'. Many skeletons were found in 1868 and about 1950 when graves were being dug in Dadlington churchyard. These may of course have been the remains of those killed following the battle, but, as we shall see, the death of Richard ended the fighting relatively swiftly, leaving little reason for pursuit and slaughter. It is clear that a marsh featured in the battle, and Peter J. Foss has argued, in *The Field of Redemore*, that this is most likely to have been west of Dadlington and north of Stoke Golding, where 'there is a band of alluvial flatland subject to periodic flooding'. Crown Hill, where Henry was traditionally crowned after the battle, is on the edge of Stoke Golding. Lastly, although the term Redmoor or Redemore has vanished from modern maps, the first-ever Ordnance survey map, printed in 1834, calls the area between Ambion Hill and Dadlington 'Radmore Plain'.

It is safe to say that Richard's army spent the night on Ambion Hill, and then descended into a plain to give battle, finding a marsh partly screening the enemy front. I favour placing the battlefield just north-west of Dadlington, but acknowledge that this is far from certain. We can be no more positive about the dispositions of the rival armies. Sunrise that morning was at 5.15, and Richard would have wished to move his army off Ambion Hill (too confined a field for such a great force) as soon as he could. Polydore Vergil, who based his version of the battle on eyewitness accounts, describes how Richard 'drew his whole army out of their encampments, and arrayed his battle-line, extended at such a wonderful length…'

It is likely that Richard followed the custom of the age and formed three divisions, or 'battles'. The evidence suggests that Norfolk commanded the leading and Northumberland the rearward battle, very possibly with Brackenbury in the centre. The fact that Northumberland took little part in the action has persuaded some commentators that the battles were intended to form up one behind the other. Given the numbers at Richard's disposal it is more likely that he would have wished to deploy his divisions side by side to make best use of his superiority. Northumberland's battle, arguably destined for his left flank, may have halted short of its intended location for a number of reasons. Perhaps it had not had time to deploy before fighting broke out, or perhaps Northumberland was treasonably cautious. Richard himself, with 'a select force of soldiers', doubtless from his own household, was on the slopes behind Norfolk.

As his own army prepared for battle, Henry sent a messenger asking Lord Stanley to join him, perhaps in accordance with plans agreed the previous day. Polydore Vergil tells us that Stanley replied that his step-son should deploy first, and he would then 'be at hand with his army in proper array', a response which can scarcely have cheered Henry. There is as much doubt surrounding the location of the two Stanley contingents as there is over other details of the battle. Lord Stanley seems to have spent the night near Higham on the Hill, just north of Nuneaton, and to have been on the march north-westwards when he received Henry's request: he probably halted near Dadlington. This line of march would be fully in accordance with Stanley's double game: he would appear to be joining Richard, but would be well placed to support Henry if he chose to do so. Some sources place his brother north of the battlefield, but it is unlikely that the Stanleys would have wished to fight separately – if, indeed, they were to fight at all. Sir William Stanley, described in one ballad as 'hindmost at the outsetting' is most likely to have been just south of his brother, perhaps near Stoke Golding.

The Fighting Begins
Henry wisely gave command of his main battle to the experienced Earl of Oxford. Polydore Vergil declares that there were two smaller flanking battles, under Sir John Savage the younger to the left and Sir Gilbert Talbot to the right. Henry himself, with a handful of horsemen and some infantry, was a good distance behind Oxford's battle.

Vergil tells us that there was a marsh between the armies 'which Henry deliberately left on his right, to serve his men as a defensive wall'. Jean Molinet, a Burgundian court historian, writes that Richard's artillery engaged the front of Henry's army, causing it to edge round to its left and come up towards Richard's right. The King's men gave 'a great shout' as battle was joined, and the archers on both sides let fly. Oxford's change of direction had given him the advantage of the prevailing wind, which blew from the south-west, and meant that his men did not have the sun in their eyes: his bowmen may consequently have been a good deal more effective than Norfolk's. But there was little time for an archery contest before the two vanguards were at hand-strokes.

The Duke of Norfolk's men, with the slope behind them, must have hit the Earl of Oxford's line hard, but the Earl had expected this and ordered his men to close up and not shift more than 10 feet (3 m) from their standards which were planted in the earth. After the failure of their initial attack, Norfolk's men 'broke off from fighting for a little while', and there are suggestions that some of them, their hearts never really in the battle, began to slip away.

As Norfolk's line wavered, Oxford's pushed forward, supported by Savage and Talbot, and there was a period of vicious hand-to hand fighting. We cannot tell how long it lasted – Vergil says the whole battle took only two hours – nor discern much of its detail. However, it was during this phase of the battle that most of the individual combats that were to pass into legend seem to have taken place, and these often reflected pre-existing animosity between combatants. For example, Oxford had beaten Norfolk's division at Barnet, only to be captured because the other flank had collapsed, and while Oxford was a prisoner Norfolk had secured most of his land. Molinet reports that Norfolk was captured at Bosworth and sent to Oxford, who had him killed, but it is more likely that the Duke fell as his men were pushed back, the less committed breaking first, leaving only Richard's most confirmed supporters and their immediate entourages fighting against worsening odds.

Northumberland's division was not engaged. The *Croyland Chronicle* records that 'no engagement could be discerned, and no battle blows given or received'. This may be because Northumberland had deliberately decided not to fight, or may reflect the fact that, hampered by the lengthy deployment of Richard's army from Ambion Hill, he was still too far back to be able to engage. The latter is more likely for, although Northumberland had probably been less than wholehearted in his support for Richard, he spent some time in prison after Henry's victory – scarcely a fair reward for calculated inaction.

From his vantage-point Richard would have seen Norfolk's division beginning to crumple. Some of his companions urged him to flee, and Salazar, a Spaniard in his service, said: 'Sire, take steps to put your person in safety, without expecting to have victory in today's battle, owing to the manifest treason in your following.' But Richard would have none of it. If he could kill Henry he might yet win: he quickly assembled a group of knights and gentlemen and led them 'from the other side,

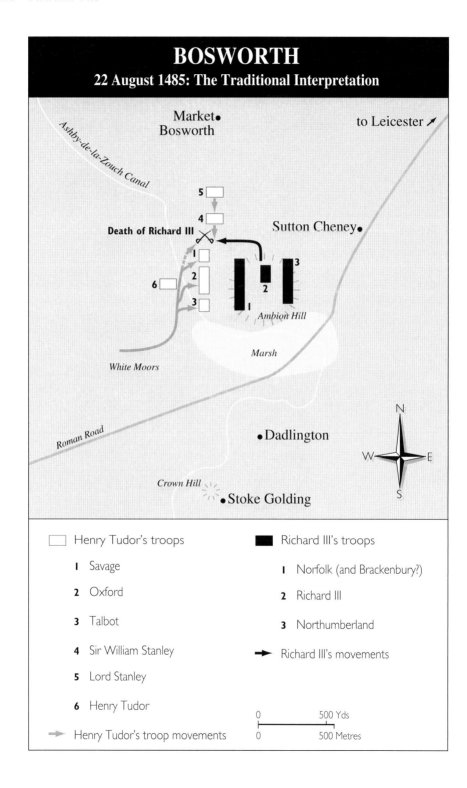

BOSWORTH
22 August 1485: The Traditional Interpretation

Market•
Bosworth

to Leicester ↗

Ashby-de-la-Zouch Canal

5

4

Death of Richard III ✕

Sutton Cheney•

1

6

2

3

3

2

1

Ambion Hill

White Moors

Marsh

Roman Road

•Dadlington

N
W——E
S

Crown Hill

•Stoke Golding

☐ Henry Tudor's troops

1 Savage

2 Oxford

3 Talbot

4 Sir William Stanley

5 Lord Stanley

6 Henry Tudor

➡ Henry Tudor's troop movements

■ Richard III's troops

1 Norfolk (and Brackenbury?)

2 Richard III

3 Northumberland

➡ Richard III's movements

0   500 Yds

0   500 Metres

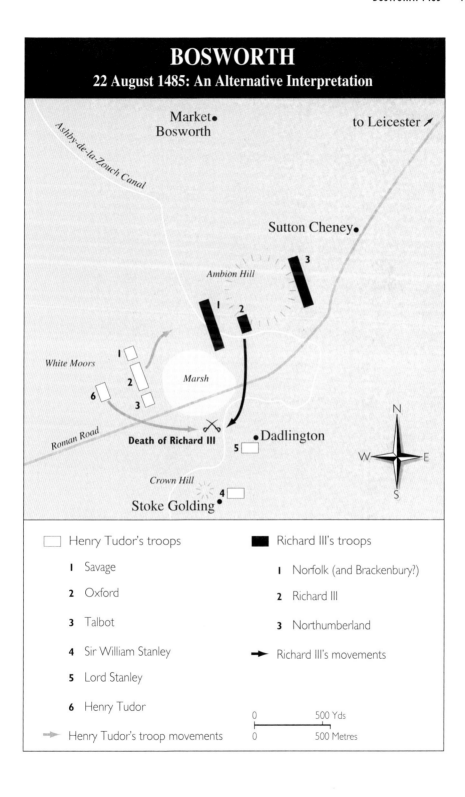

BOSWORTH
22 August 1485: An Alternative Interpretation

Market• Bosworth

to Leicester ↗

Ashby-de-la-Zouch Canal

Sutton Cheney•

Ambion Hill

3

1

2

White Moors

1

2

6

3

Marsh

Roman Road

Death of Richard III

5

•Dadlington

N
W—E
S

Crown Hill

4

Stoke Golding•

☐ Henry Tudor's troops

1 Savage

2 Oxford

3 Talbot

4 Sir William Stanley

5 Lord Stanley

6 Henry Tudor

→ Henry Tudor's troop movements

■ Richard III's troops

1 Norfolk (and Brackenbury?)

2 Richard III

3 Northumberland

➡ Richard III's movements

0   500 Yds
0   500 Metres

beyond the battle-line' against the knot of men surrounding his rival. The fact that Richard's horse became stuck in a bog makes it likely that this charge took place around the battle's southern flank, and that the King stumbled upon the marsh which had protected Oxford's right flank.

The Death of Richard

Even those who had no love for Richard, or were writing when Henry or his descendants were on the throne, cannot deny Richard the honour of his last moments. He killed Henry's standard-bearer and hacked his way towards the pretender with sword or axe. His henchmen fought and died beside him, most dragged from their horses by foot-soldiers: Sir Percival Thirlwall, holding the royal standard, had his legs hewn from beneath him. Richard and his knights may even have managed to reach Henry had Sir William Stanley not chosen this moment to intervene. His force had probably edged in towards Henry's right rear once the fighting began, and when Richard charged it was well placed to deliver what was in effect the battle's deciding blow. Richard and his supporters had no chance against these fresh troops. The Warwickshire priest John Rous, who wrote about the battle not long afterwards, described Richard as 'cruel beyond measure'. But he went on to say: 'though small in body and feeble of limb, he bore himself like a gallant knight and acted with distinction as his own champion until his death, shouting oftentimes that he was betrayed, and crying "Treason! Treason! Treason!".'

Richard's death put an end to the fighting. Some of his men made off, while others, Northumberland amongst them, surrendered on the field. Casualties had been relatively small: Molinet suggests 300 on either side, and Vergil writes that about a thousand of Richard's men had fallen to scarcely a hundred of Henry's. Norfolk, Brackenbury and Radcliffe were amongst the dead, while Brandon was the only notable fatality in Henry's army.

After the battle Henry withdrew to what Vergil calls 'the nearest hill', by tradition Crown Hill near Stoke Golding. It was said that Richard's crown, which had slipped from his helmet during his last struggle, was found beneath a thorn-bush. Henry was crowned by Sir William Stanley or his brother, and the assembled throng bellowed 'God save King Henry! God save King Henry!'

Previous pages: **The view from Ambion Hill, looking north across the traditional battlefield, towards the high ground from which the Stanleys may have attacked. The field is well laid out, with explanatory signboards and banners marking the positions of various contingents.**
Inset: **Sutton Cheney church, where Richard is believed to have heard mass before the battle.**

A View of the Field

We can still find traces of Richard, although his last resting-place is unknown. His naked body was slung across a horse, taken back to Leicester and exposed for two days in the church of St Mary of the Annunciation in the Newarke, to make it clear that Richard had indeed been killed, before being buried unceremoniously in the monastery of the Grey Friars near St Martin's Church. It has been said that the King's bones were thrown into the River Soar at the time of the dissolution of the monasteries, but it is more likely that they lie in Leicester in the vicinity of Grey Friars Street. A fine bronze statue of the King stands in Castle Gardens, looking towards Bow Bridge.

Legend affirms that when Richard rode out across Bow Bridge the day before the battle his spur clipped a stone pillar. A wise woman declared that where his spur struck his head should be broken, and when the King's body was carried across the bridge after the battle his head hit the same stone. The old bridge was demolished in 1861 and the plaques commemorating this incident were added to its less than elegant replacement. A plaque in nearby Castle Street marks the five hundredth anniversary of the battle.

Middleham Castle, in North Yorkshire, was known as 'the Windsor of the North'. Once owned by the Nevilles, it was acquired by Richard in 1471: its chapel and gatehouse survive. The nearby market cross with a double flight of steps bears Richard's boar badge. Richard's only legitimate son, Edward, was born at Middleham, and is buried, beneath a crowned effigy, at Sheriff Hutton, about 12 miles (19 km) north of York. Richard was a frequent visitor to Raby Castle, which had also belonged to the Nevilles: it is still inhabited and can be visited on summer afternoons. Barnard Castle is now a spectacular ruin above the River Tees, but the oriel window in the great chamber has Richard's white boar carved above it.

The Bosworth Visitor Centre
The Bosworth Visitor Centre is at Ambion Hill, Sutton Cheney, 2 miles (3.2 km) south of Market Bosworth and 16 miles (26 km) south-west of Leicester. There is an exhibition hall, film theatre, cafeteria and bookshop. The latter is especially well-stocked, and usually has copies of Peter J. Foss's *The Field of Redemore,* the best analysis of the debate on the battlefield's location, which has the merits of not only being cheap but also of fitting comfortably into a jacket pocket.

There is a Battle Trail which is helpfully laid out with information boards and banners marking the positions of the various contingents. The

Visitor Centre favours the traditional interpretation of the battlefield, with which I happen to disagree, but it is eminently worth a visit: its well-made models give a good impression of the men who fought at Bosworth. It also offers special events with a medieval theme on summer Sundays, and there is an annual re-enactment of the battle. The Battlefield Line runs steam and diesel trains from Shenton Station, an easy walk from the Visitor Centre, to Shackerstone, where there is a railway museum, via Market Bosworth.

The Alternative Battlefield

The alternative battlefield lies south of Ambion Hill, with the Ashby-de-la-Zouch Canal and a disused railway line curling across it. It is easily viewed by leaving the Battle Trail and walking south along the old railway line, crossing the canal and then walking about 200 yards (180 m) east along the tow-path. A natural bowl lies south of the canal, and looking across it the churches of Dadlington (to the left) and Stoke Golding (to the right) appear on the high ground on its far side. The fields are lush, with a stream, edged by willows, running through them. The Roman road from Stoke Golding to Fenny Drayton (still called Fenn Lanes) is built up to cross this depression.

My interpretation would place the marsh in this area. Oxford's division would have swung north to avoid it, and the fight between Oxford and Norfolk would have taken place just to the south-west edge of Ambion Wood, perhaps where the old railway now crosses the canal.

Contemporary accounts say that Richard was killed at Sandeford. The suffix 'ford' on a place-name need not refer only to river or stream crossing. It could also indicate a causeway, and it may well be that the Roman road crossed the wetlands in this area on a causeway: even now it is taken over several streams on substantial culverts. There was a Sand Pit Close just south of Fenn Lanes, where the Roman road swings north-eastwards near Greenhill Farm, in 1849. My best guess, and it can be no more than that, places the last mêlée somewhere near the irregular quadrant between the Roman road, the minor road to Dadlington, the canal, and the footpath connecting Fenn Lanes to the towpath. This interpretation would leave the victorious Henry in a good position to retire to Crown Hill, to the south, and would account for the presence of bodies in Dadlington Church.

The happy combination of footpaths and minor roads enables the visitor first to view the area from the towpath south of Ambion Wood, and then drive along Fenn Lanes to Dadlington. The churchyard offers a good view of Ambion Hill, and the pub opposite provides wholesome and copious bar food. A footpath connects the north-west edge of Dadlington with Fenns Lanes, enabling the zealous vistor to walk off lunch and continue the process of battlefield speculation.

Richard's Well, on Ambion Hill, marks the spring where Richard is believed to have drunk before the battle: the Richard III society holds a service there on 22 August each year. By tradition Richard heard mass in the church of St James, Sutton Cheney, on the morning of the battle, and a memorial there urges us to:

Remember Before God
RICHARD III
King of England
and those who fell
at Bosworth Field
Having Kept Faith
22 August 1485
Loyaulté me lie

CHAPTER 4

Naseby
1645

Background

Whatever his failings, Charles I was no coward. On the morning of his execution in January 1649, a month so cold that the River Thames froze, he wore two shirts, lest any shivering be misunderstood. But on 14 June 1645, he was preparing to charge at the head of his cavalry reserve when:

the earl of Carnwath, who rode next to him…on a sudden laid his hand on the bridle of the King's horse, and swearing two or three full mouthed Scots' oaths (for of that nation he was) said, 'Will you go upon your death in an instant?' and, before His Majesty understood what he would have, turned his horse around… Upon this they all turned their horses round and rode upon the spur, as if they were every man to shift for himself.

It is likely that the battle was already lost. Yet perhaps Charles could, even then, have tilted the balance of the day by throwing himself into the scales: had he failed, he might have met a more fitting end on Naseby field than on a scaffold in Whitehall.

The Tudors
It was less than a century and a half since Richard III had died at Bosworth, but in that time England had been transformed. John Guy suggests that the nation 'was economically healthier, more expansive and more optimistic under the Tudors than at any time since the Roman occupation of Britain.' Its population grew from 2.26 million in 1525 to 4.1 million in 1601; agriculture flourished and prices rose. Yet it was not a comfortable era to

This plate from a pre-Civil War drillbook shows a musketeer, match glowing, blowing loose powder from his priming pan. Charges hang from his bandoleer. By 1645 dress was less elaborate and musketeers had discarded the forked musket-rest. The matchlock musket *(left)* was the most common firearm of the period. Although cumbersome and inaccurate it was robust and simple to maintain.

live through, as dispossessed countrymen flocked to the towns or strove to survive as vagabonds.

Henry VII (Henry Tudor) inaugurated the political stability which made this economic success possible. Although he began with important advantages, his reign was not secure at its outset. Richard III had removed most contenders for the throne, and the Earl of Warwick, a possible claimant, was in Henry's custody. Henry's judicious marriage to Edward IV's daughter Elizabeth of York helped mollify many Yorkists. However, in 1487 Viscount Lovell, the Earl of Lincoln and disaffected Yorkists invaded from Ireland, using a boy called Lambert Simnel to masquerade as the Earl of Warwick. They were defeated at Stoke, where Lincoln was killed. Lambert Simnel was more fortunate: he was taken into royal service as a kitchen-boy.

It was typical of Henry's wily nature that he dated his reign from the day before Bosworth, making traitors of those who fought against him. Yet he was relatively merciful, and Sir William Catesby was one of the few executed after the battle. There was heavier retribution after Stoke, but discontent continued to bubble up. Northumberland was murdered on a tax-collecting expedition in 1489, allegedly because of 'his disappointing of King Richard at Bosworth', and Sir William Stanley, whose defection had done much to win the battle, was executed for treason six years later. Another impostor, Perkin Warbeck, who claimed to be Richard of York, one of the princes who died in the Tower of London, was seized and later executed, and the real Earl of Warwick was beheaded to deter future imitators.

Historians once wrote of a 'Tudor revolution in government' instituted by Henry VII, but most would now recognize that Henry adapted existing mechanisms and enforced old obligations rather than developing new ones. He made ruthless use of royal patronage, awarding titles, lands, offices and pensions, in order to control the political nation. Command of castles and garrisons was concentrated in reliable hands, and noblemen who kept liveried retainers were heavily fined. Henry watched royal finances like a hawk, and some of his methods of raising money from his subjects scarcely fell short of extortion.

It is small wonder that Henry's death in 1509 was greeted with universal rejoicing. His son Henry VIII, who succeeded him, made what might have seemed a good start by marrying his late brother's widow, Catherine of Aragon; and by executing his father's two most unpopular ministers. For the first years of his reign, when Cardinal Wolsey was his chief minister, the King spent much of his time hunting, dancing or playing the lute, though his appetite for glory led him into costly wars against France.

His attempt to divorce Catherine, who had failed to produce a living male heir, in order to marry Anne Boleyn, precipitated the real crisis of Henry's reign. Henry's failure to persuade the Pope to agree to a divorce encouraged him to claim supremacy over the English Church, and in the early 1530s the Church's connection with Rome was legally severed and Henry was established as its head. Shortly afterwards the monasteries were dissolved, and though the Crown obtained their lands, most were sold to cover Henry's profligate expenditure.

The break with Rome sealed Wolsey's fate, and Thomas Cromwell, who master-minded the dissolution, was soon jettisoned. The King's headstrong character and poor judgement was reflected in a succession of royal marriages, and Henry wooed the British Isles no less roughly. A northern rising, the Pilgrimage of Grace, was brutally suppressed. Wales was effectively annexed, and in 1542 Henry assumed the title of King of Ireland, though he still tried to govern through the chiefs who controlled the country beyond Dublin. The Scots were beaten at Flodden in 1513 and Solway Moss in 1542, but their nationalism could not be expunged and their 'auld alliance' with France repeatedly threatened to open up war on two fronts.

The reign of Henry's devoutly Protestant son Edward VI was dominated by two protectors. The first, Edward Seymour, Earl of Hertford and then Duke of Somerset, pursued expensive wars with France and Scotland and provoked rebellion at home. In 1549 he was overthrown by the Earl of Warwick, who elevated himself to Duke of Northumberland. Northumberland made peace with France and Scotland, and might be more favourably remembered but for an attempt to win the throne for his daughter-in-law Lady Jane Grey, daughter of the Marquess of Dorset and next in succession after Henry VIII's daughters Mary and Elizabeth. Although the dying Edward disinherited his sisters, Jane ruled for only nine days before Mary entered London: Northumberland and his chief adherents were executed.

Henry VIII's quarrel with Rome had been principally political, but there were other pressures on the Church. Resentment of its privilege and wealth was an undercurrent throughout the age, and there were demands for religion to be more accessible and to reflect the mood of reform and humanism that was sweeping the Continent. Henry's ecclesiastical revolution had not been accompanied by doctrinal change, but under Edward Protestant theologians flocked into England and reformers dominated the Church.

Mary, a devoted Catholic, brought the kingdom back into obedience to Rome and burnt several leaders of Edwardian Protestantism. Many opponents escaped abroad, from whence they poured a stream of propaganda against the Queen and her advisers. Mary married Philip, son of the Holy Roman Emperor Charles V, and when Philip became King of Spain in 1556 England was dragged into war with France. In 1558 the French took Calais, the last relic of English victories in the Hundred Years War: its loss was bitterly resented.

Mary died childless in November 1558, and was succeeded by her sister Elizabeth, fruit of Henry VIII's liaison with Anne Boleyn. She was to rule for 44 years, in a reign replete with military and political triumphs. The Anglican church was firmly established, and in 1588 England survived its sternest test when the Spanish Armada, intended to seize control of the English Channel and convoy the Duke of Parma's army from Holland, was defeated. Plots and risings were suppressed, and local government, run by the gentry, was conducted with exemplary efficiency.

Yet all this success rested on weak foundations. Despite the Queen's parsimony, royal income, aided by parliamentary subsidies, could not keep pace with growing costs. The religious settlement was popular neither with extreme Protestants nor with Roman Catholics. A long war in Ireland ended in English victory, but did not create the conditions needed for lasting peace. Too many workers chased too few jobs, and the population grew faster than food resources.

The Stuarts

It would have been astonishing had these pressures not come to a head under that unlucky dynasty, the Stuarts. James I, son of Mary, Queen of Scots, was already unpopular in Scotland, where he had reigned since 1567, because of his favouritism. He was an intelligent man who hoped for a genuine union between England and Scotland and a wide measure of religious toleration. He made little progress in religious or constitutional matters, partly because of an unwise affair with George Villiers, Duke of Buckingham, but handed over a stable kingdom to his son Charles I in 1625.

The chaste and chilly Charles was a stark contrast to his scruffy father. He cleaned up a sleazy court, sharpened royal administration and ensured that the Crown could 'live of its own' in peacetime, albeit by exploiting some obsolete feudal practices. After clashing with Parliament he ruled without it, and the mid-1630s saw him apparently triumphant. However, religious conflict helped tarnish this image. William Laud, Archbishop of Canterbury, did not merely offend Puritans by attempting to make them conform with the 1559 Prayer Book, but alienated many others by striving to increase the Church's wealth and jurisdiction.

Attempts to extend Laud's religious reforms into Scotland provoked resistance which flared into outright war, and it was the two Bishops' Wars (1639–40) that highlighted the weakness of Charles's position. He could not fight without parliamentary subsidies, and summoning Parliament unleashed demands for the redress of financial and religious grievances and the punishment of the King's 'evil counsellors'. A rising in Ireland, where rebels massacred several thousand Protestants, added to the mood of crisis.

Long-term economic, religious and social pressures contributed to the breakdown. Yet Charles might still have averted it, had he shown better judgement or behaved with greater determination. He acquiesced in the execution of the Earl of Strafford, who was accused of planning to use an Irish army against Parliament, the imprisonment of Laud (who was later executed), and gave in to most of Parliament's demands. Yet when the Grand Remonstrance, a condemnation of Charles's rule, was passed by a narrow majority in the Commons, Charles tried to arrest five leading members of the Opposition. It was a humiliating fiasco, and on 10 January 1642 he left London to the mercy of a hostile mob and his enemies in Parliament. He was never to return as a free man.

The Civil War Begins

The process of taking sides in the Civil War was infinitely more complex than the simple terms Royalist or Parliamentarian imply. If men at the political or religious extremes found it easy to decide where their loyalties lay, it was harder for most of the political nation. Sir Edmund Verney, for example, was a Puritan and hoped that the King would yield to Parliament's demands, but declared: 'I have eaten his bread and served him near thirty years, and will not do so base a thing as to forsake him; and choose rather to lose my life (which I am sure to do) to preserve and defend these things which are against my conscience to preserve and defend.' He was killed at Edgehill, the first battle of the war: his eldest son fought for Parliament and two others for the King.

Economic interests, religious sensibilities, political, personal, family and local loyalties all played their parts, and many strove to remain neutral until they were drawn into the conflict. Lines of cleavage could be wafer-thin. Sir William Waller and Sir Ralph Hopton were close friends, had served together in the Thirty Years War (1618–1648), and were members of the Parliamentary opposition. Yet Hopton felt that ultimate sovereignty resided in the monarch, and Waller did not. They commanded rival armies in the South-West, personal friendship rising above what Waller called 'this war without an enemy'.

Charles I and his younger son James, Duke of York, the future King James II. Like most portraits of Charles, this painting by Sir Peter Lely catches his regal chilliness. Behind this austere exterior lay a man who found it hard to adopt a settled course of action and was often powerfully influenced by unreliable advisors.

On 20 August 1642 Charles raised his royal standard at Nottingham, an act which symbolized the outbreak of war. Both sides had been raising troops for months, but hoped that outright war could be averted. On 23 October there was an inconclusive battle at Edgehill between the King's main army and Parliament's principal force under the Earl of Essex. The King pushed on to take Brentford, only to find his route to the capital blocked at Turnham Green. He established his capital at Oxford instead, and both sides spent the winter in fruitless negotiation and preparing for a renewal of the fighting.

The war's inherent localism was evident in 1643, when the Royalists secured the South-West, taking Bristol, the country's second port, on 26 July. They were unsuccessful at Gloucester, and fought a drawn battle at

Newbury against the Parliamentarian army that had marched out from London to relieve Gloucester. In the North the Royalist grandee the Duke of Newcastle strengthened his grip on much of Yorkshire, despite spirited opposition from Lord Fairfax and his son Sir Thomas. In East Anglia the Parliamentarian Eastern Association gained the upper hand, with Oliver Cromwell, a Huntingdonshire squire and MP, establishing a growing military reputation. The year's most important event was political: in September the Solemn League and Covenant, an alliance between Parliament and the Scots, was signed, and the Scots began to raise troops. They could not afford to be single-minded in their commitment to their allies, however, because the Marquis of Montrose, Charles's captain-general in Scotland, won a string of remarkable victories over the Covenantors.

The year 1644 was also indecisive. Although Charles fought a successful campaign in the West Country, totally defeating Essex's army, on 2 July his nephew Rupert was beaten by the allies at Marston Moor, the war's largest battle, and York fell shortly afterwards. On 27 November a promising Parliamentarian plan misfired at the second Battle of Newbury. The acrimonious debate which followed it highlighted the lack of resolve in the Parliamentarian command.

'Gentlemen,' pleaded the Earl of Manchester, 'I beseech you let's consider what we do. The King need not care how oft he fights... If we fight 100 times and beat him 99 he will be King still, but if he beats us but once, or the last time, we shall be hanged, we shall lose our estates, and our posterities be undone.'

'My Lord,' replied Cromwell, 'if this be so, why did we take up arms at first? This is against fighting ever hereafter. If this be so, let us make peace, be it never so base.'

Changes in Military Organization and Weaponry

Parliament's alliance with the Scots, its possession of most major ports, and its control of the fleet and the wealth and manpower of London, and a central tract of territory meant that it was likely to win a war of attrition. It could not do so, however, without an army capable of closing the deal. The inquiry into failure at Newbury soon deepened into an examination of the conduct of the war in general, and on 23 November the Committee of Both Kingdoms, with both English and Scots members, directed the Commons 'to consider a frame or model for the whole militia'. The Self-Denying Ordinance, which excluded members of both Houses of Parliament from military command, passed the Commons on 9 December. The Lords initially threw it out, but the Committee of Both Kingdoms had already sketched out a force under central command with a strength of some 22,000 men. This was to become the New Model Army, instrument of Parliament's victory.

There had been no standing army under the early Stuarts. In Elizabeth's reign the general obligation of Englishmen to serve in time of need was reflected in the organization of county militias, known as trained bands. These were sometimes efficient, especially in counties liable to invasion, with their training administered by professional soldiers, but there is little doubt that if Parma had landed in the Armada in 1588 his tough veterans would have made short work of them. Troops were specially raised for overseas expeditions: in 1585, for instance, the Earl of Leicester led 6000 men to help the Dutch against the Spanish.

Britain exported military talent. Well-born young men served abroad as gentlemen volunteers, and scions of impecunious gentry went off to make their fortunes in the wars. Irishmen fought for France or other Catholic powers, and there were Scots and Englishmen on both sides during the Thirty Years War. When the Civil War broke out hundreds of these men returned to provide a leaven of military experience on both sides. With them came foreigners, like the King's nephews Rupert and Maurice, sons of the Elector Palatine and Charles's sister Elizabeth of Bohemia. Some professionals imported the culture which had helped make the Thirty Years War so bitter and destructive. 'I care not for your cause,' said one. 'I come to fight for your half-crown and your handsome women.'

Historians debate whether the term 'military revolution' accurately describes the changes in organization and weaponry which took place at this time. If they were spread over too long a period (and embodied too much of what had gone before) to constitute a real revolution, they were nonetheless profound. Armies became bigger, coming more firmly under the control of states in whose formation they played a crucial part. The proliferation of gunpowder weapons was accompanied by the need for drill. Military organization took on characteristics which are with us still: the titles of many modern military ranks and bodies date from this period.

Infantry formed the bulk of armies. About two-thirds of foot-soldiers carried the matchlock musket, loaded by tipping black powder down its barrel, following this with a ball, and tamping the charge down with wadding – tow, paper or even grass. It was fired when the match, a length of smouldering cord held in the jaws of the cock, was dropped into the priming pan, thus igniting the weapon's charge. Misfires or accidents were common, and rainy or windy weather might render the musket useless.

The musket fired a bullet weighing 12 to the pound, lethal at up to 400 yards (365 m) but really effective at much less, perhaps 150 yards (137 m). A musketeer had once fired his weapon from a forked rest, though this was obsolete by 1645, and carried spare charges in tubular containers hung from his bandoleer. He wore a sword, though for close combat he generally took to 'clubbing them down', swinging his musket by the barrel.

The musketeer relied for close protection upon the pikeman. The pike was a long spear with a regulation length of 18 feet (5.5 m), although there were complaints that men cut their pikes down to make them less cumbersome. In Elizabeth's time pikemen had worn a gorget at the throat, a cuirass (breast- and back-plate), a steel helmet and tassets covering the thighs, but gorgets and tassets were abandoned at the start of the Civil War and it is possible that the New Model Army's pikemen were not issued with any armour. The crux of infantry battle came when the foot came to 'push of pike'. Musketeers would try to get off a volley just before impact, 'doubling their ranks' so that two or three ranks fired at once.

At the start of the war, in 1642, some cavalry had worn armour, but by 1645 most troopers on both sides wore a cuirass and a lobstertail helmet: the latter was certainly not confined to Parliamentarian cavalry. Some preferred a broad-brimmed felt hat with a metal 'spider' beneath it to protect the skull. A stout leather buff-coat was worn under or instead of the cuirass. Cavalrymen carried a long, straight sword and a pair of wheel-lock pistols, fired when a toothed wheel revolved against a piece of iron pyrites held in the jaws of the cock. Some had carbines, short muskets.

Cavalry tactics had been warmly debated. Disciples of the Dutch school maintained that each rank of horsemen should trot up to pistol range of their enemy, fire, and wheel about to reload. At the other extreme, followers of the Swedish school argued that cavalry achieved the best results by shock action: pistols ought not to be used until horsemen had charged home. By the time of Naseby the Swedish school was in the ascendant, although commanders might provide cavalry with firepower by attaching groups of 'commanded musketeers' to them.

The dragoon was a hybrid. Although he was mounted, his horse was primarily a means of transport rather than a fighting platform, and was much cheaper than the cavalryman's steed. He had no armour, wore a cloth rather than a buff-coat, and carried both sword and musket. In the advance dragoons moved with the vanguard to hold key features or defiles until the infantry came up; and in retreat they often formed part of the rearguard. Dragoons, and the infantry who guarded the train of artillery, were usually equipped with the more modern snaphance musket, forerunner of the flintlock which was later to become the standard infantry weapon.

Artillery was still comparatively poorly developed. Cannon graduated from the tiny robinet, with its ¾ lb (0.3 kg) ball, through falconet, falcon, minon, saker, demi-culverin, culverin, demi-cannon and cannon, to the

Far left: This Victorian painting of the execution of Charles I outside the Banqueting House in Whitehall (Horse Guards now stands almost directly opposite) catches the mood of that freezing day well. Musketeers and pikemen surround the temporary scaffold. Although pikemen traditionally wore armour, there is no evidence that the New Model's pikemen had it at Naseby. The horsemen are members of a cavalry regiment. *Left:* Many cavalrymen on both sides wore a stout leather buff-coat, thick enough to turn a sword-cut, with breast- and back-plate over it. The lobstertail helmet drew its name from the articulated plates covering the neck. By the time of Naseby cavalrymen were trained to charge home with their swords, using point and edge in hand-to-hand combat.

cannon royal which fired a 63 lb (27 kg) ball. The 5-pounder (2.3 kg) sakers and 9-pounder (4 kg) demi-culverins were the most commonly used field guns. They were usually positioned in groups, and were unlikely to move during the course of an action. Smaller, more mobile pieces, would deploy in the intervals between bodies of infantry.

Stubby, high-trajectory mortars, with their exploding bombs, were useful in siege warfare, but field-guns fired solid roundshot which trundled through the enemy's ranks, killing and wounding as they went. At close range, gunners used caseshot, a canister of small balls which spread in a wide arc on leaving the muzzle. Each gun was manned by the gunner, his mate, and a number of labourers or matrosses.

The New Model Army
The regiment, named after its colonel, was the standard unit of horse and foot. The New Model Army's infantry regiments had an establishment strength of 1200 men divided into ten companies. The colonel's company, commanded by his captain-lieutenant, was 200 men strong, the lieutenant-colonel's 160 and the major's 140: other companies were commanded by captains and numbered 100 men apiece. Each company had its own colour, carried by the ensign, the most junior of its three commissioned officers. Cavalry troops, the equivalent of companies, had a standard each, and dragoon companies a guidon. Regiments of horse or foot were often brigaded together under a general or senior colonel.

A captain-general or lord-general commanded an army, with a lieutenant-general as his second-in-command, and each of the major arms – horse, foot and guns – might have a general and lieutenant-general, though not all posts were usually filled. The foot also had a sergeant-major-general (soon abbreviated to major-general) and the horse a commissary-general.

Convention decreed that armies formed up with their foot in the centre, with its most senior regiment on the right, the next most senior to the left, and so on. Cavalry stood to the flanks, with the senior cavalry general on the right flank and his junior on the left. Amongst the staff were the scoutmaster-general (responsible for the collection and processing of intelligence) and the carriage-master-general, who supervised the baggage train.

Civil War armies were poorly administered, with the arrival of pay and rations far from certain. Soldiers were entitled to a daily ration or cash instead. Sir James Turner tells how:

they allow so much bread, flesh, wine or beer to every trooper and foot soldier, which is ordinarily alike to both, then they allow to the officers, according to their dignities and charges, double, triple and quadruple portions... The ordinary allowance for a soldier in the field is daily, two pound of bread, one pound of flesh, or in lieu of it, one pound of cheese, one pottle of wine, or in lieu of it, two pottles of beer.

The soldier who received this was fortunate. All too often he was reduced to living at 'free quarter', billeted on civilians who fed and sheltered him (paid either in cash or with debentures which could in theory be cashed in but were often worthless). Horses too had to be fed: the New Model's baggage-train contained over a thousand horses, not to mention the mounts for senior officers and the cavalry, all munching their way through fodder.

When the New Model was raised its officers and men were promised 'constant pay', and this was to be furnished by a monthly assessment on property levied in 17 counties. Officers were to receive 'respited pay' – payment only partly in cash, with the remainder secured by a debenture until the end of the war. Initial delays in collection meant that pay was in arrears: nevertheless, the New Model was better-paid than its Royalist opponents.

Sir Thomas Fairfax who became the New Model's commander-in-chief, was a 33-year-old Yorkshireman whose dark hair and swarthy features earned him the nickname 'Black Tom'. He had served in Holland and as a colonel of foot in the first Bishop's War before commanding the horse under his father Lord Fairfax in Yorkshire in 1642–3. At Marston Moor he had led the right wing, which was roughly handled by the Royalist cavalry. Fairfax was a dashing and enterprising commander with abundant common sense. When the lord-general's regiment claimed that its status exempted it from rearguard duties, Fairfax is reported to have simply dismounted and led it to the rear of the army.

Sir Thomas Fairfax, Lord-General of the New Model Army. Fairfax was a tough fighting Yorkshireman whose personal contribution to victory at Naseby was considerable. He had little taste for politics, and did not sign Charles's death-warrant.

Oliver Cromwell was the New Model's lieutenant-general, commanding its cavalry, at Naseby. He succeeded Fairfax as lord-general and later became Lord Protector and head of state. This portrait of him by Robert Walker shows him in armour, probably rather more than he would have worn at Naseby. He holds the baton which marks him out as a senior officer. A page is tying his sash. Officers on both sides wore silk sashes, sometimes so wide that they could make improvised stretchers. Royalist sashes were red, Parliamentarian sashes orange-tawny. Cromwell was not a vain man and, when painted by Lely, urged the artist to show him 'warts and all'.

Oliver Cromwell, Fairfax's lieutenant-general, had also been lieutenant-general to the Earl of Manchester in the Eastern Association. He was 12 years older than Fairfax, and had no pre-war service but had risen from captain of horse by sheer merit. Part of his skill lay in personnel selection. 'I had rather have a plain russet-coated captain that knows what he fights for and loves what he knows,' he affirmed, 'than that which you call a gentleman and is nothing else.' Although he was an MP he was to be exempted from the Self-Denying Ordinance (which excluded Members of both Houses of Parliament from military command) to become lieutenant-general shortly before Naseby. His commissary-general, appointed on the eve of the battle, was his close associate Henry Ireton, who became his son-in-law the following year. Philip Skippon, a veteran of the Dutch service who had commanded the London Trained Bands and then served as major-general to the Earl of Essex, was responsible for the New Model's infantry.

The New Model was to comprise 12 regiments of foot with a strength of 1200 men apiece; 11 regiments of horse, each 600 strong; and 1000 dragoons in ten companies. The artillery train, under Lieutenant-General Thomas Hammond, included at least three demi-culverins, a mortar, nine sakers and three smaller guns. Three regiments each of horse and foot came from Essex's army, two of foot from Waller's and nine of horse and four of foot from the Eastern Association's. Other regiments were disbanded to bring the New Model up to strength, and some men were drafted in from civilian life. Fairfax and Skippon spent much of April 1645 in the far from painless business of 'New Modelling', and it is thanks to their practical common sense that the process went as well as it did.

The New Model has been the subject of such varied judgements that it is difficult to assess it objectively. It has been hailed, on the one hand, as a force with a strong political and religious identity, and on the other as just another seventeenth-century army, irregularly paid and indifferently fed: the truth embodies elements of both extremes. In 1645 it was not, as its critics opined, 'an army of sectaries', officered by low-born men of extreme Independent rather than moderate Presbyterian views. Denzil Holles, a leading member of the pre-war Opposition, concluded that the army was more of a danger than the King, and complained:

All of them, from the general (except what he may have in expectation of his father's death) to the meanest sentinel, are not able to make a thousand pounds a year [from the rent of their] lands; most of the colonels are tradesmen, brewers, tailors, goldsmiths, shoemakers and the like. These to rebel against their masters!

There was only a measure of truth in Holles's complaint. Parliament had to approve Fairfax's list of officers, and the Lords objected to two colonels – the 'dangerous' Independents Edward Montague and John Pickering, as well as 40 captains. The list eventually scraped by with a majority of just one. Some officers were not gentlemen: Lieutenant-Colonel Thomas Pride of Harley's Regiment had been a drayman before the war and Lieutenant-Colonel John Hewson of Pickering's a cobbler.

Remodelling gave Fairfax and his generals complete control over the appointment of officers, subject to parliamentary approval, and the quality of its officers was one of the New Model's greatest strengths. John Rushworth, writing after Naseby, declared that:

from the beginning I was confident, a blessing from heaven did attend this army, there were in it so many pious men, men of integrity, hating vice, fighting not out of ambitiousness or ends, but aiming at God's glory and the preservations of liberty and religion, and the destruction of the enemy.

Nonetheless, there were complaints that competent officers had been 'put out' because of their religious or political views, and Joshua Sprigge, an army chaplain, agreed that some 'were better Christians than soldiers and wiser in faith than in fighting'.

The rank and file was more uneven in quality. At one extreme the horse, particularly the old Eastern Association regiments, was very good. At the other, the infantry was patchy. About half the foot-soldiers had been conscripted, and they deserted in large numbers. Thus, while the New Model, in its newly issued red coats, struck Sir Samuel Luke as 'the bravest that I ever saw for bodies of men, both in numbers, arms or other accoutrements', its commander was warned by an unnamed great person that 'he was sorry that I was going with the army, for he did believe we should be beaten'.

The Royalists
Many Royalists cracked jokes about the 'New Noddle', though these could scarcely conceal the fact that their own army had been harrowed by three years of war and now lacked a large enough territorial base to make good its losses. Nevertheless, the King's cause seemed far from hopeless at the outset. Detachments of sturdy foot still trudged in from Wales, nursery of the Royalist infantry; a cessation of hostilities in Ireland enabled the King to use 'Irish' troops in England, though at terrible risk, for Parliament had decreed that they were to be killed if captured; and in Scotland the Marquis of Montrose was tying down a growing proportion of the Scots army.

The key strategic question of early 1645 was the use to which the King's main army should be put, and there was no unanimity amongst the men who debated it. Charles was captain-general but, though he had performed well in the West Country in 1644, he was ill-suited to command in the field. He was weak and indecisive, often influenced by the last person to advise him, yet could turn stubborn over what he regarded as issues of principle. He was a poor judge of men, and in 1645, when there were good arguments for concentrating to meet the New Model, he gave an independent command in the South-West to that engaging drunkard and womanizer, George, Lord Goring.

Charles's lieutenant-general and nephew, Prince Rupert, had begun his military service at the age of 14. He had a considerable reputation before the war, and his many achievements during it had earned him the respect of his own men and the hatred of his enemies. Unfortunately not all the latter were in Parliament's ranks. Rupert had allies, notably his brother Maurice, commanding in Wales and the Marches, and Colonel Will Legge, Governor of Oxford. Amongst his opponents was George, Lord Digby, one of the King's secretaries of state, who exercised great influence over Charles. The King had decided to establish his son Charles, Prince of Wales, at Bristol with his own council, and many of his more level-headed advisers had been sent off with the prince, strengthening the malign influence of Digby.

In March 1645 Charles wrote to his wife Queen Henrietta Maria that there was 'a great division... amongst his own friends upon the conditions of peace out of the universal weariness of the war'. Rupert and his supporters favoured streamlining the Royalist chain of command in much the same way as Parliament had with the New Model, and fighting for a compromise peace. Digby, in contrast, encouraged Charles to believe that the war could be won. He was not alone, for in January, Montrose, with another stunning victory behind him, had told the King:

Forgive me, sacred Sovereign, to tell your Majesty that, in my opinion, it is unworthy of a King to treat with rebel subjects... Through God's blessing I am in the fairest hopes of reducing this kingdom to your majesty's obedience, and... I doubt not before the end of this summer I shall be able to come to your Majesty's assistance with a brave army.

Campaign and Battle

Rupert's plan of campaign for 1645 was robust. Garrisons around Oxford would be pared down to strengthen the field army, while artillery and engineer stores would be concentrated in the city. The army would then concentrate on Worcester and move north to relieve besieged Chester, drawing recruits from Wales as it went. It could raise more men in Lancashire and in Yorkshire, and then perhaps even join Montrose in Scotland. Speed was of the essence, for there was everything to be gained by moving before the New Model was ready.

Royalist preparations so alarmed the Parliamentarians that Cromwell, who arrived at Windsor ready to relinquish his commission under the terms of the Self-Denying Ordinance, was immediately given a brigade of cavalry and sent off to disrupt them. On 24 April he beat the Earl of Northampton's cavalry brigade at Islip Bridge, and went on to summon the garrison of Bletchington House to surrender. The governor, Colonel Francis Windebank, was unnerved by the presence of his young wife and some of her friends, and immediately gave up to save his guests from the horrors of an assault which Cromwell, with no infantry at his disposal, was in a poor position to deliver.

Two days later, Cromwell's horse, swinging north and west of Oxford, dealt with some Royalist cavalry and then overwhelmed 350 foot-soldiers at

Bampton-in-the-Bush. He summoned Faringdon Castle to surrender, but its governor replied 'You are not now at Bletchingdon.' Although Cromwell brought up infantry from the Parliamentarian garrison of Abingdon, when he attempted to storm Faringdon he was beaten off. News that Goring was on his way from the South-West persuaded Cromwell to fall back, but in the space of a few days he had unsettled the Royalists and, no less importantly, swept up many heavy draught horses which were to have been used for moving the train of artillery but had not yet been taken into Oxford.

The Siege of Oxford

If the King's Council was unsure of how to prosecute the war, Parliament's Committee of Both Kingdoms scarcely had any better idea. The Scots, in the North, demanded help against Langdale's marauding cavalry, and there were urgent requests that besieged Taunton should be relieved. On 28 April the Committee ordered Fairfax to march to the relief of Taunton, and he set off two days later. He was at Blandford in Dorset on 8 May, with Cromwell well off to his right flank in case the Oxford army moved south. He now received new orders. The King's army was moving north, and he was to detach a brigade to relieve Taunton and take the remainder of the New Model towards Oxford. Fairfax obediently sent Colonel Weldon with four regiments of foot and one of horse to Taunton and set off northwards.

Rupert and Maurice had reached Oxford on 4 May, and Goring rode in the following day. The King left Oxford on 7 May with his lifeguard, the Oxford infantry and the artillery, and the next day Sir Marmaduke Langdale brought his Northern Horse down to a general rendezvous on Bradford Down. A council of war was held in Stow-on-the-Wold that evening.

Rupert reiterated the case for marching on Chester: if it fell, then it would be impossible to bring any more troops over from Ireland. The weakened and disillusioned Scots could be dealt with, and only then should the Royalists risk fighting the New Model. Langdale supported him: his own men were happier closer to home. Digby and Goring favoured tackling the New Model head on. Rupert seems to have suggested a compromise: Goring would return to the West to hold up the New Model while the rest of the army marched north. The Earl of Clarendon claims that Rupert hoped to be rid of Goring because 'he was like to have most credit with the king in all debates' and got on well with Digby. Goring was happy with the scheme, which would give him an independent command, and even if Rupert was less devious than Clarendon suggests the arrangement suited him too, for Goring's fondness for the bottle had made him increasingly unreliable. It was a disastrous decision, for whatever Goring's failings he was a superb cavalry leader, and his horse would have made a real difference at Naseby.

The Royalists marched north, joined by reinforcements as they went. The most substantial contingent, 3300 infantry, appeared at Evesham on 9 May. With it came Lord Astley, major-general of the foot, 'as fit for the office he exercised,' records Clarendon, 'as Christendom yielded and was so generally esteemed.' He was a short, white-haired man – Elizabeth of Bohemia had called him 'my little monkey' – 66 years old but in sprightly good health. Jacob Astley's enormous experience in the Dutch service, personal courage and forthright honesty earned him wide respect. He deserves remembering for the brief prayer he uttered before leading the Royalist foot forward at Edgehill: 'O Lord! Thou knowest how busy I must be this day. If I forget thee, do not thou forget me – march on boys!'

Cromwell, still without a commission in the New Model, shadowed the Royalists, at first hoping that Fairfax would join him, but soon hearing that the New Model had been ordered to besiege Oxford. He was told to send Colonel Vermuyden with a brigade of horse to support the Scots contingent in Derbyshire, and then fell back to join Fairfax.

On 20 May the King was at Market Drayton, where he heard that the Parliamentarians had raised the siege of Chester. Thus far the campaign was going his way. Parliament had hoped that the Scots and local forces would prevent the King from moving north, but the Scots, concerned for their lines of communication and well aware that Montrose was on the rampage in their homeland, withdrew from Derbyshire into Westmorland. The Midlands and the North were dangerously exposed, and Charles's arrival transformed the local balance of power.

After hearing the good news from Chester, Charles decided to march eastwards, hoping to draw cavalry out of the Royalist enclave of Newark to strengthen his own horse and then to move on to raise the sieges of Pontefract and Scarborough. The Scots were very relieved at his change of direction: 'I was much afraid,' wrote one, 'that the north of England should have joined with him, and fallen first on our army, and then on Scotland.'

Fairfax, meanwhile, was stuck fast before Oxford, able to cut off the city but too short of heavy guns to begin a formal siege. He asked why 'we should spend our time unprofitably before a town while the King hath time to strengthen himself and by terror to enforce obedience of all places where he come.' Although the city was well defended and provisioned, Sir John Culpepper, who had been left there, warned Digby that 'the temper of those within the town, the disaffection of the townsmen…and the vast importance of the place and persons within the town' made it imperative for Oxford to be relieved.

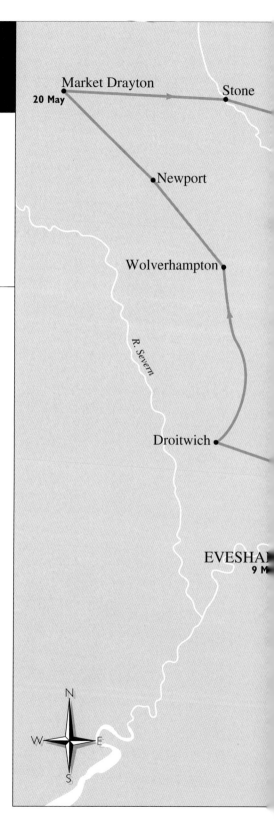

THE NASEBY CAMPAIGN
1645: Main Armies Only

→ Royalist
troop movements

→ New Model
troop movements

0 ——————— 10 Miles

0   10   20 Kms

Market Drayton

20 May

Stone

Newport

Wolverhampton

R. Severn

Droitwich

EVESHA[M]
9 M

N
W   E
S

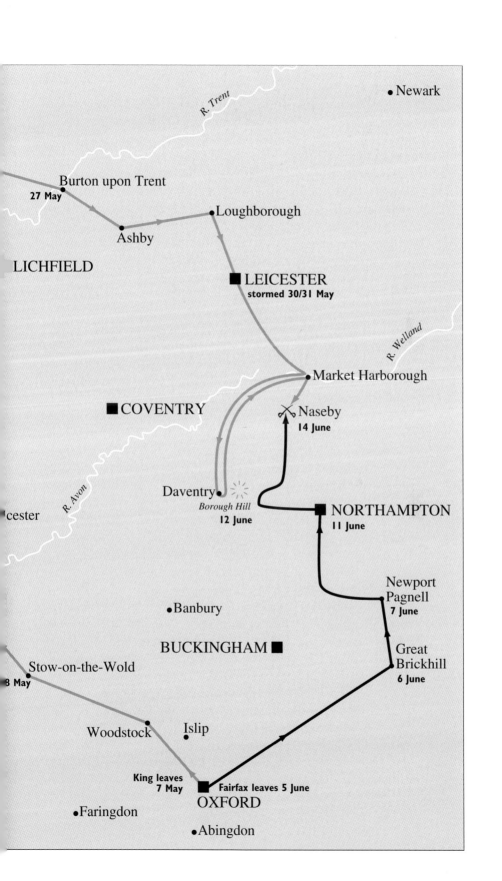

• Newark

R. Trent

Burton upon Trent
27 May

Loughborough

Ashby

LICHFIELD

■ LEICESTER
stormed 30/31 May

R. Welland

Market Harborough

■ COVENTRY

⚔ Naseby
14 June

R. Avon

Daventry •
Borough Hill
12 June

■ NORTHAMPTON
11 June

cester

Newport
Pagnell
7 June

• Banbury

BUCKINGHAM ■

Stow-on-the-Wold
8 May

Great
Brickhill
6 June

Woodstock

Islip

King leaves
7 May

Fairfax leaves 5 June

OXFORD

• Faringdon

• Abingdon

A council of war, held at Burton upon Trent on 27 May determined that the best way to raise the siege of Oxford would be 'to fall upon some place possessed by the Parliament'. This would draw Fairfax away from Oxford and would bring about battle on the most favourable terms. Sir Charles Gerard was told to bring his horse across from Newark, and Rupert ordered Goring to make for Market Harborough with his horse and any spare foot, pausing at Oxford to collect the remainder of the artillery. Knowing that Goring might not obey an order from Rupert, Digby reinforced the summons with one of his own. 'For God's sake use diligence and come as strong as you can,' he urged. 'In my conscience it will be the last blow in the business.' He did not know how right he was.

The Siege of Leicester
Leicester, with a population of about 4000, was prosperous but weak, and would have preferred to continue 'uneasy neutrality' than stand a siege. Its castle had been re-fortified, and the adjacent Newarke suburb was surrounded by medieval walls. The town itself had lost its walls, though their gates remained, and earth and timber defences had been thrown up in their place. Some prominent buildings outside the defences which might offer cover to a besieger had been demolished, but many had survived, doubtless because of the influence of their owners.

There were about 600 foot and 420 horse in the garrison, with some 900 well-disposed townsmen ready to assist them. Although the County Committee had reported that Leicester was short of cannon, no more had been sent by the time the Royalists arrived, and the defenders had only nine. The garrison was fortunate that two experienced officers from the New Model, Colonel Sir Robert Pye and Major James Innes, were fortuitously caught up in the siege and were able to advise the governor, the inexperienced Colonel Grey.

Leicester was cut off by Langdale's horse and then, on 29 May, surrounded by the Royalist foot. Rupert threw up a six-gun battery on Raw Dykes, south of the town, facing the walls of the Newarke. The next day he sent a trumpeter to demand the town's surrender, and when the governor asked for more time 'the battery began to play...and made such a breach, that it was thought counsellable, the same night to make a general assault with the whole army, in several places, but principally at the breach...'

The defenders, working frantically, built a retrenchment behind the breach, and when the assault came they fought like tigers, repulsing three Royalist attacks. The attackers did better elsewhere, using primitive hand-grenades to drive back the defenders, and scaled the defences in three separate places. Pye led a cavalry counter-attack, and garrison and townsmen fought with extraordinary determination. A Royalist officer wrote of how:

they fired upon our men out of their windows, from the tops of the houses, and threw tiles upon their heads...finding one house better manned than ordinary, and many shots fired at us out of the windows, I caused my men to attack it, and resolved to make them an example for the rest; which they did; and breaking open the doors, they killed all they found there without distinction.

The attackers, their blood up, drew no easy distinction between soldiers and non-combatants. The Parliamentarian press reported that all Scots in the garrison were killed out of hand and many women murdered or ravished. Even if the butchery was on a lesser scale than hostile reports suggested, there is no doubt that the organized pillage which followed the storm was extreme by the standards of the Civil War. It was claimed that 140 cartloads of goods were sent off to Newark, and when the Mayor turned out to greet the King on 1 June his silver mace was snatched as he awaited the monarch's arrival.

The fall of Leicester and its horrific aftermath sent shock-waves through Parliamentarian garrisons in the Midlands and greatly encouraged the Royalists. Even before the fall of Leicester Cromwell had been sent up to the Isle of Ely to put its defences in order in case the Royalists struck deep into East Anglia, and on 2 June Fairfax was at last ordered to raise the siege of Oxford and march towards the Eastern Association.

A Royalist council of war at Leicester reiterated the usual arguments. Rupert was for marching north, and perhaps coming to terms with the Scots who were increasingly disillusioned with Parliament's shift away from Presbyterians towards the Independents. The courtiers argued in favour of returning to Oxford – they did not yet know that the siege had been lifted – and fighting the New Model if they met it. Charles decided to go back to Oxford, and dawdled south-west to Daventry, a change of direction which produced a temporary mutiny amongst the Northern Horse. There he heard that Fairfax had left Oxford, and told the Queen: 'I may without being too much sanguine affirm that since this rebellion my affairs were never in so hopeful a way.'

Rupert was less cheerful. Goring had still not appeared. Leicester had cost the army perhaps 700 killed and wounded, a garrison had been left to hold it, and some men had disappeared with their loot. Although he could not have known it, Parliament had at last given Fairfax a free hand, and on 8 June his council of war had decided to make the King's army their fixed object. Fairfax was marching north, bent on battle.

The Armies Converge

The Royalists remained around Daventry throughout the second week in June, awaiting the return of a cavalry escort (which had taken a provision convoy into Oxford and would return with ammunition to replenish that expended at Leicester) and plundering villages for miles around. Rupert had secured the huge Iron Age hillfort on Borough Hill, which dominated western Northamptonshire, but his army was widely spread.

Fairfax reached Newport Pagnell on 7 June, and then moved more cautiously. Sir Samuel Luke, the town's governor, received regular reports from surrounding garrisons and was well aware of the Royalist progress, and Fairfax's scoutmaster-general, Major Leonard Watson, sent his own mounted scouts well ahead of the New Model. Fairfax still had important changes to make to his command structure. He was able to persuade Parliament to grant Cromwell a lieutenant-general's commission regardless of the Self-Denying Ordinance. Vermuyden's brigade, which had been sent on a fruitless mission to join the Scots, rejoined the army in Newport Pagnell, and its commander announced that he wished to go abroad: this left the way clear for Ireton's appointment as commissary-general, Cromwell's second-in-command.

The New Model reached Northampton on 11 June, and that day Fairfax ordered Skippon to frame a 'form of battle' in brigades of horse and foot which would be its standard disposition for battle. On 12 June he was at Kislingbury, about 7 miles (11 km) as the crow flies from Borough Hill. That evening the King was hunting in the deer park at Fawsley, 3 miles (5 km) south of Daventry, when he heard that Parliamentarian horse had surprised Colonel Carey's cavalry regiment at Flore, only 5 miles (8 km) to the east. Rupert drew the army together in a general rendezvous on Borough Hill at midnight and kept it stood to arms all night, but Fairfax had no intention of attacking such an advantageous position.

The Oxford convoy rejoined the Royalists that night, and not long after first light they were on the move, marching through Daventry in a column perhaps 6 miles (10 km) long. They were heading for Market Harborough and Melton Mowbray, whence they would make for Newark to obtain reinforcements before heading north. This is an index of just how badly the Royalists had misjudged the tactical situation: with the New Model so close there was no real prospect of escaping without a battle. They probably swung north-eastwards up the Avon valley, through the Kilworths and Husbands Bosworth, to reach Market Harborough after a march of some 23 miles (37 km). The King spent the night in the Old Hall at Lubenham, and Rupert was in Market Harborough itself. The army was in the town and surrounding villages, with a cavalry outpost in Naseby, to the south-south-west.

The New Model spent the night in and around Guilsborough, and a cavalry patrol drove the Royalists out of Naseby: one source says that troopers of Rupert's Lifeguard were surprised playing quoits, while another has them caught at dinner in Shuckburgh House, opposite the church. News of this clash brought the King to a council of war at Rupert's headquarters, traditionally the King's Head Inn. We should not be surprised that there was a difference of opinion. Although there are contradictory accounts, it seems certain that Rupert and his supporters favoured marching north (though with the New Model so close it is hard to see how guns and baggage could have been transported safely), while Digby and the courtiers wanted to offer battle. The King backed Digby, and if Rupert had advocated caution he subsequently gave little sign of it, and the next few hours saw him galvanized with all his old enthusiasm.

The Royalists were numerically weaker than the New Model. Glenn Foard, whose *Naseby: The Decisive Campaign* is unlikely to be bettered as a scholarly assessment, reckons that there were between 9500 and 12,500 Royalists and 15,200 to 17,000 Parliamentarians, depending on the method of calculation. As to quality, the Royalists had more experienced officers, though the composite character of their army meant that it contained more smaller units than the New Model. If few of the New Model's officers had served on the Continent, most had been in arms during the war. Both armies contained some recently drafted, part-trained men. There were more of these in the New Model than the King's army, and Fairfax used some local forces to compensate for the brigade sent to Taunton. Within each army there were sharp differences in quality, and the best, like Rupert's Bluecoats or Cromwell's own regiment of horse, were amongst the finest of the age.

The battle was to be fought north of Naseby, largely on unenclosed open fields. There was pasture near the villages, but for the most part the fields were composed of unhedged cultivated strips of brown loam with patches of gorse at their fringes. A walled rabbit warren, with a warrener's cottage, stood a little over a mile (1.6 km) due north of Naseby, and the battlefield's left flank was defined by robust hedges on the edge of the enclosed pasture fields of Sulby. The Naseby–Sibbertoft road (then as now) divides the battlefield. The ground rises north of Naseby to cross the long ridge of Mill Hill–Fenny Hill. North of this lies the long valley of Broad Moor, with Dust Hill, connected to the Sibbertoft plateau by a narrow neck of land, behind it.

The Royalists were on the move well before first light, and drew up on 'rising ground of very great advantage', the ridge south of East Farndon crossed by the Naseby road. There was no sign of the enemy, and Francis

Ruce, the scoutmaster-general, was sent forward but failed to find any trace of them. It is probable that another report then arrived saying that the New Model was retreating. Rupert at once set off southwards with a party of horse supported by musketeers, whether to check on the reports or, as his enemies were to maintain, because his natural impetuosity impelled him to risk a battle whatever the terms, we cannot be sure. As he passed through Clipston he saw the New Model forming up to the south-west, blocking the road in the area of New House Farm.

Both armies then edged westwards, probably with the New Model beginning the process first and making for Mill Hill. Rupert summoned his own army, possibly because he thought that, as the Parliamentarians were pulling back off the ridge, Fairfax was trying to get away. The Royalists came forward, as Colonel John Okey of the New Model's dragoons put it, 'in a very stately way in a whole body towards us...' By mid-morning the rival armies were arrayed on the low ridges on either side of Broad Moor, their western flanks resting on the Sulby hedges and their eastern flanks bordering the thicker furze where the ground begins its long ripple down towards the Naseby–Clipston road.

The Battle is Joined
There are two good contemporary plans of the battle, one published by Streeter in *Anglia Rediviva*, an account by the Parliamentarian chaplain Joshua Sprigge, and the other a manuscript sketch by the Royalist engineer Sir Bernard de Gomme. Glenn Foard's analysis now enables us to place the armies with some confidence. The Parliamentarians were in two main lines, Cromwell's horse on the right and Ireton's on the left, with Skippon's foot in the centre. A 'forlorn hope' (in this context a forward screen) of musketeers stood to Skippon's left front, and Lieutenant-Colonel Pride commanded a rearguard behind his centre. Cromwell's strong right wing formed three lines rather than two because the ground was too broken up with furze and rabbit holes to enable it to extend further to the east. The baggage train, escorted by its snaphance-armed guard (matchlocks and powder barrels were an unwise combination) was probably on the north-west edge of Naseby. The New Model's field-word, to aid identification in battle, was 'God is our Strength', and some Parliamentarians wore a piece of white linen or white paper in their hats.

The Royalist deployment was more complex. Rupert drew his army up in three lines, with musketeers between the cavalry, and a regiment's worth of cavalry interleaved between the infantry brigades. The former was a continental practice designed to give firepower to cavalry, and the latter was intended to shore up the outnumbered infantry. Rupert

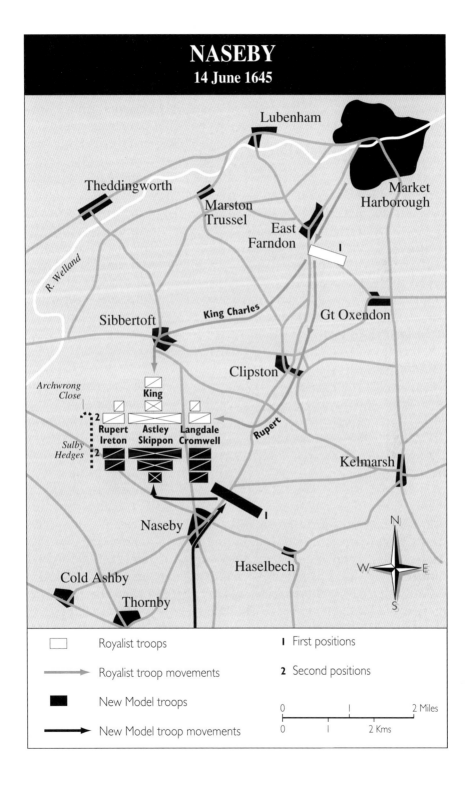

NASEBY
14 June 1645

Lubenham

Market
Harborough

Theddingworth

Marston
Trussel

East
Farndon

R. Welland

Sibbertoft

King Charles

Gt Oxendon

Clipston

Archwrong
Close

King

2

Rupert   Astley   Langdale
Ireton   Skippon   Cromwell

Sulby
Hedges   2

Rupert

Kelmarsh

Naseby

N

Haselbech

W   E

Cold Ashby

S

Thornby

☐ Royalist troops   I First positions

→ Royalist troop movements   2 Second positions

■ New Model troops

0   I   2 Miles
0   I   2 Kms

→ New Model troop movements

commanded five regiments of horse on the right, and Langdale his under-strength Northern Horse on the left. Jacob Astley's foot formed three tertias or brigades commanded by Sir Bernard Astley, Sir Henry Bard and Sir George Lisle. The King, well back on the slopes of Dust Hill, was surrounded by a mixture of horse and foot including his own Lifeguard and Prince Rupert's Bluecoats. The baggage train was well back, and recent finds of coinage suggest that it might have been east of Sibbertoft, near the Sibbertoft–Clipston road. 'Queen Mary' was the Royalist field word, and many Royalists had put beanstalks in their hats, taken from the bean fields they had crossed during their advance.

The New Model formed up just south of the crest-line so that it was not visible to the Royalists, although the 'forlorn hope' on the forward slope and senior officers on the crest-line must have made the general outline of deployment clear enough. Cromwell, struck by the importance of the Sulby hedges, found Colonel John Okey of the dragoons issuing ammunition to his men behind the Parliamentarian lines, and ordered him to secure the hedged close on the army's left. Recent evidence of musket-balls and pewter tops from the charge-boxes on bandoleers suggests that the close in question was Archwrong Close, well forward of the Parliamentarian left, not simply a hedge-line at right angles to the main line of deployment as was once believed. Okey moved fast, and on arrival one man in ten held the horses while the other nine prepared to defend the hedges with their muskets. Rupert reacted immediately with infantry and cavalry, but Okey reported that: 'it pleased God that we beat off both the horse and foot on the left, and the right wing, and cleared the field, and kept our ground.'

It may be that the dragoon battle goaded the Royalists into attacking, or that Rupert hoped to catch the Parliamentarians before they were fully formed up. In any event, between 10 and 11 a.m. both armies advanced, drums beating and colours flying. Fairfax halted his men on the crest, but the Royalists came on, receiving a spattering of shot from the 'forlorn hope' of musketeers, which fell back up the hill. Both armies had cannon drawn up between their front-rank infantry regiments. The Royalists fired at most a round or two apiece, and although the Parliamentarian guns fired more, their effect was no more than irritating.

It was axiomatic that horse under attack should not receive the charge standing still, but advance to meet it, and when Rupert led his wing forward Ireton's men moved down the slope. This advance, the boggy ground around a stream in the valley bottom, or perhaps a parish boundary hedge, caused Rupert to pause before he thundered up the slope 'at full career', taking the fire of Okey's men in his right flank as he did so.

Although this attack was launched by the best of the Royalist horse the result was no foregone conclusion, for the Parliamentarians did not break at first impact but fought back hard. In fact Ireton's right-hand units had the better of the encounter, enabling Ireton to lead them in against the Royalist foot. However, his horse was killed, and he was run through the thigh with a pike, gashed in the face by a halberd, and taken prisoner. Rupert charged again, this time breaking both Ireton's lines, driving many – but by no means all – of his troopers in disorderly flight to the south and pounding after them.

Astley's foot came on no less gallantly than Rupert's horse. The Parliamentarians advanced to the crest-line to meet them – Clarendon says that 'the Foot on either side scarcely saw each other till they were within carbine-shot' – and fired a volley, which seems to have done little damage. The Parliamentarians held the first attack, but the second, supported by the cavalry attached to the infantry for just this purpose, proved more serious, and Sir Edward Walker saw how the Royalist foot 'falling in with sword and butt end of musket did notable execution; so much as I saw their colours fall and their foot in great disorder.' Pickering's and Montague's regiments broke and ran, opening a gap in the centre. Though Skippon's, on the left, was terribly hard hit, assailed in front by the King's foot and in its left flank by some of Rupert's horse, it fought on.

The Royalists flooded through the gap ripped in the Parliamentarian centre, over-running six guns. They now had only the second line to beat, and as Skippon led it forward he was hit under the ribs by a musket ball which pierced his armour. However, as Fairfax wrote: 'he continued in the field with great resolution: and when I desired him to go off the field he answered, he would not go as long as a man could stand...' His personal example helped avert disaster, for the second line held. Archaeological evidence suggests that most of the firing took place at this stage in the battle, with the foot on both sides firing steadily. The wind was blowing from the north-west, a disadvantage for the Parliamentarians as the powder-smoke blew back in their faces.

It was only on the eastern flank that the Parliamentarians gained an early decisive advantage. Although Langdale's horse was much-criticized for its failure, it is clear that the northerners fought hard against the first wave of Cromwell's attack: Whalley's regiment suffered more casualties

Overleaf: Streeter's 1647 engraving of the battle in *Anglia Rediviva*, written by the Parliamentarian chaplain Joshua Sprigge, is an important source. Although not wholly accurate, it helps us relate the armies to the ground and helps us understand their layout. The obelisk north-east of Naseby stands on the site of the windmill.

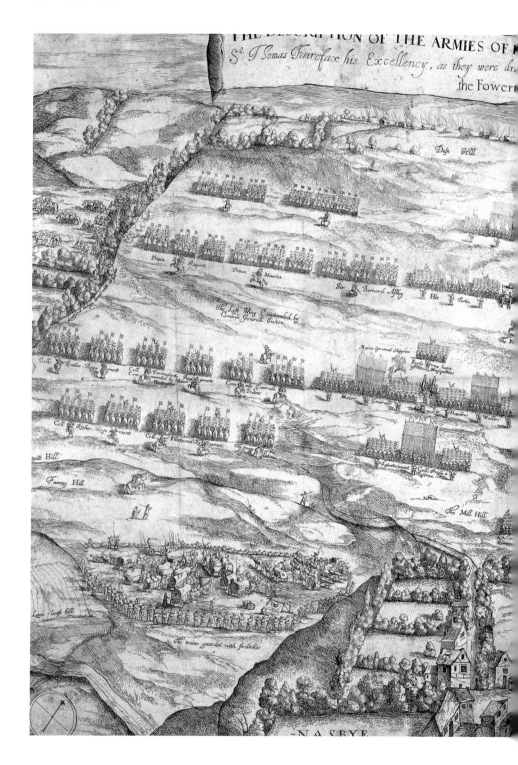

ND FOOT OF HIS MAJESTIES
ll bodyes, at the Battayle at NASBYE
of June 1645

than any other Parliamentarian cavalry regiment, and its commander 'had his coat cut in many pieces'. But Langdale faced impossible odds: he was outnumbered at least two to one by the New Model's best cavalry, charging with the advantage of the slope. Cromwell sent part of his force after Langdale, to prevent him from rallying, and had the bulk of it available to throw against the Royalist infantry.

Once battle was joined all along the line, Fairfax rode from place to place giving orders, and was personally involved in the cavalry attack on the unbroken third line of foot, which included Rupert's Bluecoats who 'stood to it very stoutly' and received the charge 'like a wall of brass'. Fairfax had already had his helmet knocked off. He met his Lifeguard, commanded by Captain Charles D'Oyley, wheeling away from a body of foot, probably the Bluecoats, which they could not break. Fairfax took some troopers and charged from the rear while D'Oyley attacked from the front. The infantry broke at last, and Fairfax cut down an ensign, whose colour was picked up by a trooper who boasted about his valour. D'Oyley reprimanded the man, but Fairfax replied: 'I have honour enough, let him take that to himself.'

Many historians – myself included – have written of the rapid collapse of the Royalist foot once the horse from Cromwell's victorious right wing surged in against it. However, musket-ball scatters, discovered by metal-detectors, suggest that parties of Royalists, horse and foot alike, fought on across Broad Moor and Dust Hill although the day was clearly lost. Some may have been Irish who 'chose rather to die in the field than be hanged' but the overall picture can only pay tribute to the King's foot, who, as a Parliamentarian admitted, 'did as gallantly as ever men on earth could do'.

It was now that the King was dissuaded by Lord Carnwath from charging with his remaining horse, and as he wheeled from the battlefield there was a temporary panic. It seems likely that the shaken horse soon rallied and charged, but the odds were hopeless and they fell back once more.

Rupert now returned to the field. He had chased the broken portion of Ireton's wing for some miles, and, in the process, encountered the Parliamentarian baggage train. The guard commander mistook Rupert for Fairfax, doffed his hat and asked how the day was going, and only realized his mistake when Rupert asked him if he would surrender. Although John Rushworth says that the guard 'gave fire and instantly beat them off', several members of the train were killed and wounded, suggesting that Rupert may have made a more determined attack. Rupert did manage to rally most of his men before he returned to the battlefield, but when he arrived he found that all was already lost. He could do nothing for the infantry, and he joined the King's party only to find that they were faced by a reconstituted Parliamentarian army. Sir Walter Slingsby admits that: 'they being horse and foot in good order, and we but a few horse only, and those mightily discouraged, that so we were immediately made to run...' The Royalists fled with Fairfax's horse in hot pursuit: 'happy was he that was best mounted'. A substantial musket-ball scatter on high ground north of the Sibbertoft–Clipston road suggests that some of the infantry made a last stand, but it was a hopeless venture.

The Aftermath of the Battle
Near Clipston the pursuing Parliamentarians caught several hundred women from the baggage train: some were killed and the others marked as whores by having their faces slashed or noses slit. Although they were described as 'Irish women, of cruel countenance', armed with long knives, it is likely that they were Welsh and that the knives were for no more sinister purpose than to prepare food for the infantrymen they followed. Of more political significance was the capture, in the King's coach, of the royal correspondence, which was later published as *The King's Cabinet Opened* and contained damaging admissions about Charles's dealings with the French and Irish.

The pursuit went on to the gates of Leicester, and only about 4000 Royalists escaped. Fairfax marched on to Market Harborough, regrouped his army and told Parliament of its staggering victory. He was soon complaining that the sheer quantity of booty taken at Naseby had induced many of his men to desert, and his infantry were only at half their establishment strength. The New Model had lost perhaps 300 men killed in action and another 44 who died of wounds. Royalist losses were much heavier: perhaps 1000 killed; as many seriously wounded; and 5000 captured. What made Naseby decisive was the destruction of the King's 'old infantry'. Charles was never to have an army approaching such quality again.

Although Charles got clear of the battlefield, halted briefly at Leicester, and then set off for Hereford where he began to raise fresh infantry, his cause was lost. Fairfax marched into the West Country, beat Goring at Langport on 10 July and then attacked Bristol, held by Prince Rupert. With his defences pierced, Rupert surrendered on favourable terms, but found himself exiled by his infuriated uncle. The King's last armies were snuffed out, and on 20 March 1646 Lord Astley, on his way to Oxford with 3000 foot, was caught by superior forces at Stow-on-the-Wold. The brave old gentleman surrendered at last. As he sat on a drum he told his captors: 'You have done your work, boys, and may now go play, unless you will fall out amongst yourselves.'

They were prophetic words. A second Civil War, with the captive Charles supported by the Scots, ended with Cromwell's victory at Preston in August 1648. Cromwell was fast becoming the most powerful figure on the Parliamentarian side, and his conviction that Charles was inherently untrustworthy encouraged him to press for the King's execution in January 1649. A third Civil War saw Charles II's Scots supporters defeated at Dunbar in 1650 and Worcester a year later. Cromwell strove without success to find a lasting constitutional settlement, and eventually became Lord Protector in 1657. When he died the following year there was nobody of his status who could hold the reins of power, and the monarchy was restored in May 1660.

A View of the Field

Time and the antics of town planners have not dealt kindly with Leicester, but the Castle Park area, south-west of the city centre, has retained several areas of interest. The original gateway into the Newarke was built during the fourteenth century, used for the storage of arms during the Civil War and subsequently known as the Magazine. It stands in a sprawl of main roads on the south-eastern edge of Castle Park, and now houses the museum of the Royal Leicestershire Regiment.

The Newarke
About 200 yards (180 m) to the west is the Newarke Houses Museum, maintained by Leicester City Museums. It is devoted to the social history of Leicester during the last 500 years. The room on the right of the entrance was panelled in the seventeenth century, possibly to repair damage suffered during the siege. It contains contemporary furniture and artefacts, amongst them a cuirass (breast- and back-plate) and lobstertail helmet of the Naseby period. Upstairs is the militia gallery, which contains the town's armour and some Civil War pottery hand-grenades –'grenadoes' to the men who used them. Leave the museum, turn right and right again to gain access to the gardens. The wall behind them is part of the original defences of the Newarke, and its soft stone is still pierced by the loopholes cut in 1645 to enable Parliamentarian musketeers to fire on the Royalists.

Naseby Field
The field of Naseby was remarkably unspoilt until the recent construction of the A14 across its southern edge. Despite this piece of insensitivity the

battlefield remains easy to interpret, although one must always remember that there were almost no hedges in 1645. Many fields still show signs of the distinctive ridge and furrow field system which characterized pre-enclosure agriculture. There are good examples, for instance, where the little road to Marston Trussel heads north from the Sibbertoft–Clipston road.

An obelisk about 1 mile (1.6 km) north-east of Naseby, on the Market Harborough road, bears a plaque whose inscription warns of the importance of kings not exceeding their just prerogatives. The A14, which clips along noisily just to its north, is on the approximate site of the New Model's first position. The Royalist first position was probably along the road between East Farndon and Great Oxenden – line up the two church towers and you have it – with Market Harborough lying in the valley behind it: it remains 'rising ground of great advantage'.

The little road which heads due north from Naseby goes squarely across the battlefield. Just off its western verge, 1½ miles (2.4 km) from the village, is a memorial which pays tribute to Cromwell but actually stands just forward of the New Model's infantry line. A panel helps the visitor interpret the ground. Broad Moor, a natural amphitheatre, though a tiny stage for such an important play, falls away to the north, and Dust Hill rises on its far side. The woods, Naseby Covert due east and Long Hold Spinney to the north-east, post-date the battle. Both, however, are helpful guides to its dimensions: Cromwell's horse formed up where Naseby Covert now stands, and Langdale's Northern Horse on the ground now covered by Long Hold Spinney. There is no public access to Archwrong Close, seized by Okey's dragoons at the start of the battle, but a bridleway running south-west from the southern edge of Sibbertoft passes just north of it and gives a good feel for the western edge of the battlefield.

Naseby Village

Naseby Battle and Farm Museum, in Purlieu Farm just south of the village, is open on Sunday and Bank Holiday afternoons between Easter and the end of September. It contains some relics and a model of the battle; and a sword, probably dating from 1645, hangs in Naseby church. Naseby Hall, where some of Rupert's troopers were surprised the night before the battle, was demolished to make way for a newer building, but its dining table – 'Cromwell's table' – is also in the church. It looks modest enough, but run a hand over its gnarled surface, close your eyes, and you can almost catch the whiff of sweat and tobacco, and hear those sunburnt troopers, in their buff-coats and top-boots, toasting 'Charles, King of England, and Rupert of the Rhine'.

CHAPTER 5

The Boyne
1690

Background

The Boyne was not a big battle. It was not even the bloodiest battle of the Williamite War in Ireland – that honour goes to 'Aughrim of the slaughter', fought a year later. Yet it struck a particular chord. It was the only battle where the contenders for the British throne, James II and William III, met in person, and they did so on the banks of a river which courses through Irish history. Its images are compelling: William's Dutch Guards marching to the river to the accompaniment of the popular tune 'Lilliburlero'; asthmatic little William crossing the water on horseback under fire; and the Duke of Berwick, James's illegitimate son, leading charge after charge.

But the Boyne has cut a deeper groove in history than its military importance might suggest. To the Protestants of the North it became symbolic of the defeat of Catholicism. Although the battle itself was fought on 1 July, calendar changes adopted in the eighteenth century pushed anniversary celebrations on to 12 July. The Boyne anniversary is the highlight of the 'marching season', when flute bands in their distinctive liveries parade through the streets of Northern Ireland. The Loyal Orange Institution, whose members originally swore to 'support and defend the king and his heirs as long as he or they support the Protestant ascendancy' makes much of the Boyne and its victor, and William, splendidly mounted on a white charger, is an enduring piece of Orange ideography. The battle lives on in songs, one of which concludes:

Orangemen remember King William
And your fathers who with him did join
And fought for our glorious deliverance
On the green grassy slopes of the Boyne.

Above: James II had fought bravely on land and sea in his youth, but the Boyne campaign found him past his best, probably because his expulsion from England in 1688 had done serious damage to his self-confidence.
Left: He is said to have worn this armour at the Boyne: the sliding grille protecting his face is pierced with the royal arms. He holds a commander's baton, and would have carried a pair of holster pistols, one visible here, as well as a sword.

The English Conquest of Ireland

The fate of Ireland was bound up in all the battles described thus far. After the Norman conquest of England, Norman lords sailed to Ireland and established themselves there: the great keep of Carrickfergus Castle, overlooking Belfast Lough, is one of their enduring monuments. But Norman rule was never comprehensive. Gaelic chieftains remained powerful, and over the next three centuries increased their influence through intermarriage with Norman families and military victory. By 1435 the Irish Council reported to Henry VI that his writ ran only in a small area around Dublin: the Pale, a fortified barrier, was built to defend it.

English kings styled themselves lords of Ireland, and it was only Henry VIII who assumed the title of king. He declared that English laws automatically applied in Ireland, and that the Irish Parliament could legislate only with his consent. In practice he exercised little real power beyond the Pale, and relied heavily on the support of the Gaelic chiefs.

In Elizabeth's reign periodic rebellions by the Gaelic chiefs, together with the risk that Ireland, scarcely touched by the Reformation, might provide a springboard for a Spanish attack on England, persuaded the Queen to embark on full-scale conquest. It was a bitter war, with its share of English reverses. In 1598 Sir Henry Bagenal was defeated by Hugh O'Neill, Earl of Tyrone, at Yellow Ford on the River Blackwater, a rout 'so disastrous to the English and successful in action to the Irish as they shaked the English government in this kingdom till it tottered, and wanted little of fatal ruin.'

O'Neill was a charismatic commander, and the Irish Council believed that, under his leadership, the Irish sought 'to recover their ancient land and territories out of the Englishmen's hands, and [strive] for the restoring of the Romish religion, and to cast off English laws and government…' Although O'Neill developed his force from guerrilla bands into something approaching a regular army, he was ground down by the weight of numbers deployed by Elizabeth's Lord Deputy, Lord Mountjoy. In September 1601 3500 Spaniards landed at Kinsale, just south of Cork, and on Christmas Eve the allied Spanish and Irish advanced to attack Mountjoy's camp. It was badly beaten in what emerged as the war's decisive battle, and by 1603 the English conquest of Ireland was complete.

Under James I 'plantations' of Protestant Scots and English migrants were established in the North. 'Make speed, get thee to Ulster, serve God and be sober,' urged one Norfolk gentleman who took possession of a grant of land in Fermanagh. James gave great tracts of land to the City of London, whose livery companies built a walled city at the old settlement of Derry, renamed, like the county around it, Londonderry.

The English Civil War and the Restoration
In October 1641 the Irish of Ulster rose against English rule, and stories
of the atrocities committed by the rebels made a powerful contribution to
the air of crisis on the eve of the English Civil War. During that struggle
Charles I concluded a truce or 'cessation' with the rebels in order to
employ Irish troops in England. Parliament riposted by ordering any Irish
taken in arms to be executed without further ado.

Parliament's victory in England left Ireland in the hands of unrepen-
tant Royalists, and in 1649, Cromwell, who had succeeded Fairfax as
Lord-General, departed to bring them to heel. In the process he added a
new layer to the dreadful strata of atrocity and counter-atrocity which
were coming to characterize Irish history. The garrisons of Drogheda and
Wexford were amongst those that resisted him, and both were massacred
when the towns were taken.

Although it can be argued that Cromwell was not departing from the
strict rules of war at the time – defenders put their lives at risk if they
continued to fight once their walls were breached and assault was imminent – the assaults on Drogheda and Wexford were brutal, even by the
standards of the age. At Drogheda some of the defenders took refuge in a
church, which was fired. Cromwell wrote that one of them yelled from
the midst of the flames 'God damn me, God confound me; I burn, I burn',
while another, who jumped from the tower, was spared 'for the extraordi-
nariness of the thing'. The governor, a testy veteran called Sir Arthur
Aston, was beaten to death with his wooden leg; and captured priests, as
Cromwell admitted, 'were knocked on the head promiscuously'.

Cromwell ruthlessly suppressed the Roman Catholic Church in
Ireland, destroying its buildings and transporting its priests to Barbados.
The lands of most 'Irish papists' east of the Shannon were confiscated,
and their former owners sent 'to Hell or Connaught' on its far side. With
the restoration of Charles II in 1660 the Irish Catholics, many of whom
had bravely supported the King and his father, Charles I, hoped to have
their lands returned and their Church revived.

Neither proved easy. It was impossible to restore land to the Catholics
without alienating the new owners, whose support underpinned the
Restoration settlement. The eventual compromise, which gave back about
a third of the confiscated land, pleased nobody, and left much of the
Catholic nobility and gentry potentially disaffected. The plight of the
Catholic Church was no more encouraging. The established church, the
Church of Ireland, catered for perhaps 100,000 of Ireland's 300,000
Protestants – most of the rest were Scots Presbyterians, mainly living in
the North. The land's 800,000 Catholics were severely handicapped by

being unable to take the oath of supremacy required of holders of public office, civil and military, for it acknowledged the king's supreme authority in all matters spiritual and temporal. Catholic clergy were poor and sometimes persecuted, notably during the 'popish plot hysteria' towards the end of Charles II's reign.

James II Comes to the Throne

The accession of Charles's Catholic brother, James II, in 1685, offered hope to the Catholics. Despite James's initial desire not to alienate Irish Protestants, it soon became clear that changes were under way, and in January 1687 Richard Talbot, Earl of Tyrconnell, a Catholic landowner who, as a young officer, had managed to escape the carnage of Drogheda, arrived as Lord Deputy (in effect, Viceroy). His appointment elated Catholics and depressed Protestants, and the delight of the former is mocked in the doggerel set to Purcell's tune 'Lilliburlero' by Thomas, Lord Wharton:

> Ho, Brother Teague, dost hear the decree?
> Dat we shall have a new deputy.
> Ho, by my shoul, it is de Talbot,
> And he will cut de Englishmen's throat.

If Tyrconnell's aims were in fact less sanguinary than Wharton suggested, he certainly lost no time in restoring Catholics to political and military dominance. The Irish army was purged of its Protestant officers, enabling both native Irish and 'old English' to return to a profession which was regarded as natural for a gentleman. The removal of Protestants from the civil administation was less rapid and less thorough, and nothing was done about the vexed question of land settlement.

In England, James II sought to repeal anti-Catholic legislation, and, recognizing that the weight of the political nation was firmly against him, tried to gain approval of both Catholics and Protestant dissenters, granting freedom of worship to the latter and reorganizing local government so as to give them greatly increased power. In 1685 a rising by James's nephew, the Duke of Monmouth, attracted considerable support in the West Country, but was put down at Sedgemoor.

More generally, opposition was muted both by the memory of recent civil war and by the belief that James's unpopular policies would be short-lived. The King was 50 years old. His second wife, Mary of Modena, had no surviving child and had not given birth for several years. It was assumed that when he died his Protestant daughter Mary, married to the Dutch ruler William of Orange (himself son of James II's sister Mary), would succeed him.

William Lands in England

The birth of a son and heir, James Edward, in June 1688, changed the prospect at a stroke. The opposition leaders invited William to come to England, and William was prepared to take the risk of doing so because victory would enable him to mobilize Britain's financial, naval and military resources against his long-standing enemy, Louis XIV of France. William landed at Torbay on 5 November. James advanced to Salisbury to meet him, but was held up by a series of nosebleeds and displayed alarming behaviour which encouraged many senior officers, like John Churchill (the future Duke of Marlborough and the real architect of victory at Sedgemoor), to desert him.

James might yet have won. As a young man he had fought bravely on land and sea, but now his nerve deserted him and he fled to London. He was soon captured, allowed to escape, inconveniently recaptured and permitted to escape once more: the crown was then offered jointly to William and Mary. Most modern historians take a cautious view of the 'Glorious Revolution' of 1688, which was in many respects what Paul Langford terms 'a palace coup than a genuine shift of social or political power'. But the settlement, based as it was on the legitimization of an evidently illegitimate act, did embody the crucial notion of contract between rulers and ruled. William and Mary reigned not because of Divine Right, but because of the will of the people as expressed by Parliament.

If the revolution was largely bloodless in England, it was less so in Scotland, where James's supporters – the Jacobites – had to be defeated by force of arms. In Ireland its consequences were even more bloody, although the slide into conflict was slow. News of James's fall aroused fears in Catholics and Protestants alike, but Tyrconnell did his best to preserve calm, and it briefly seemed that he might negotiate with William.

William sent out Richard Hamilton, a scion of the Irish noble house of Ormonde, major-general in James's army and a close personal friend of Tyrconnell's, in an effort to persuade the Earl to surrender. Hamilton, however, seems to have urged him to hold out, and Tyrconnell raised fresh troops, asking James (exiled in France) to send both money and arms.

By April 1689 Tyrconnell controlled all Ireland with the exception of parts of Ulster. Derry had declined to accept a Jacobite garrison; in Enniskillen the local Protestants formed their own garrison under Gustavus Hamilton; and the Earl of Mountalexander headed a 'Supreme Council' based in Hillsborough in County Down. Richard Hamilton was sent north to subdue Ulster, dispersed Mountalexander's troops with little difficulty, and snapped up the smaller garrisons, leaving only Londonderry and Enniskillen in Protestant hands.

James II Lands in Ireland

James landed in Ireland on 12 March 1689, the first English king to visit for more than 300 years. Although Louis XIV's advisers were divided as to the wisdom of the expedition, Louis eventually decided that it was very much in his interest to support the Irish Jacobites. They would be a thorn in William's flesh, and would prevent him from concentrating British resources against France. Ireland might be a springboard from which James could invade Scotland, where he still enjoyed substantial support, or even England itself. News of James's arrival alarmed William's English supporters. 'If Ireland be lost,' warned one MP, 'England will follow.'

James arrived at Kinsale in a fleet of 22 ships. With him came numerous Irish, Scots and English supporters, his two illegitimate sons (the Duke of Berwick and the Grand Prior of France), a substantial contingent of French troops under General Conrad von Rosen, and the Comte d'Avaux (an experienced diplomat who was to give James political guidance and to report back to Louis). James went straight to Cork, where he rewarded Tyrconnell by making him a duke. He was greeted on his journey from Cork to Dublin 'as if he had been an angel from heaven', and entered Dublin Castle beneath a banner which read:

Now or never
Now and forever.

As soon as he arrived in Dublin, James summoned a parliament which was to meet on 7 May. All but six members of the House of Commons were Catholics, and most of them looked forward to repealing the anti-Catholic laws, reforming the land settlement, strengthening the economy and generally making Ireland less dependent on England.

James and his English advisers were less enthusiastic, because such changes would make it harder for James, once fully restored to his throne, to control Ireland. Measures which gratified Irish Catholics would be almost guaranteed to offend many of James's potential supporters in England. James saw Ireland, just as Louis hoped, as a stepping-stone to his restoration in England. His Irish supporters hoped for much more than he would willingly grant.

The land settlement was duly overturned, offering the prospect of the recovery of land confiscated by Cromwell and not restored under Charles II, although military events moved too quickly for a large-scale redistribution to take place. An act of attainder condemned James's opponents as traitors, subject to the death penalty and the confiscation of their property. Parliament agreed to grant James a subsidy to prosecute the war, although it proved difficult to collect. A shortage of precious metal compelled

James to mint coins from brass and copper, and Tyrconnell later complained to Mary of Modena that even base metal was so scarce that 'we are forced to coin our brass guns for want of it'.

Not only did James and his Irish supporters have different ambitions, but political squabblings distracted them from conducting what was by now a war. In late April a French fleet disembarked Irish regiments raised in France in Bantry Bay, and had rather the better of a battle with an English squadron. It was typical of James that he did not know quite what to make of the encounter. While a French victory was in his interests, he could not bear to think of his old fleet being defeated, and when told that the English had been beaten he snapped, 'It is the first time, then.'

Changes in Military Organization
Each of Charles II's three kingdoms had its own army, and it was the Irish army, Protestant under Charles but transformed into a Catholic force by Tyrconnell, that formed the basis of James's army. Its establishment varied little throughout the war, and in 1689 comprised a Lifeguard, seven regiments of cavalry, eight of dragoons and 45 of foot.

There was initially much variation in the establishments of individual units, with some infantry regiments having up to 45 companies, but soon most foot regiments comprised 13 companies, each with a theoretical strength of 62 private soldiers, five non-commissioned officers (or NCOs) and three officers – captain, lieutenant and ensign. The regiment's three field officers, its colonel, lieutenant-colonel and major, were also company commanders. Its wartime strength was 43 officers, 65 NCOs and 650 privates, but detachments, casualties and desertion would reduce this. The cavalry regiment, whose six troops corresponded to infantry companies, was supposed to number 527 officers and men, but was only likely to produce 3–400 on the battlefield. Dragoon regiments had 10 or 12 companies, and in the Jacobite army they had retained their old role of acting essentially as mounted infantry, using their horses for transport to the battlefield, where they generally fought on foot.

In the armies of the age, colonels were more than mere regimental commanders. Their regiments usually took their colonel's name, and the regiment's colours – once a colour for each company, but now generally a colour for each field officer – might bear devices from the colonel's coat of arms or be the hue of his livery. Colonels were responsible for raising and equipping their regiments and had much influence, sometimes amounting to effective control, over the appointment of their officers. Often they held other senior military or political appointments which kept them away from their regiments, so that the real work was done by the lieutenant-colonel. If all went well there was money to be made from a colonelcy, for even if pay was in arrears, an astute colonel might pocket the difference between the money granted for clothing and equipment and the real cost of items purchased.

Because most Catholics had been excluded from British military service for a generation, James's experienced colonels were officers who had served in other European armies. Perhaps the best-known is Patrick Sarsfield. The first Sarsfield to arrive in Ireland had done so in the retinue of Henry II in 1172, but since then the family had intermarried with the native Gaels: Sarsfield's father married Anne O'Moore, daughter of Rory O'Moore, one of the leaders of the 1641 rebellion. Sarsfield was typical of the 'old English', deprived of their lands in the Pale by Cromwell and packed off to Connaught, resentful over the land settlement and religious discrimination, and with a cultural identity blurred by five centuries in Ireland .

In the 1660s and 1670s a series of legal actions failed to give the Sarsfields possession of their old estate, and Patrick decided to become a soldier. As a Catholic he could not hold a commission in the British Isles, so he became an officer in an English regiment raised to fight for Louis XIV as part of a secret agreement concluded between Charles II and Louis in 1670. Still unable to hold a commission in England, he fought bravely at Sedgemoor as a gentleman volunteer, was rewarded with a captaincy and was specifically exempted from taking the oath of allegiance and supremacy. He was a lieutenant-colonel in 1688, and showed characteristic flair in a patrol action near Wincanton.

As he approached, an enemy officer shouted: 'Stand! For who are ye?'

'I am for King James,' replied Sarsfield, 'Who are you for?'

'I am for the Prince of Orange.'

'God damn you!' came the reply, 'I'll *prince* you!'

Sarsfield had the better of the skirmish, which hardly guaranteed him a future in William's army, and he joined James in France.

Not all the Jacobite colonels were men of Sarsfield's experience, but were given regiments because of their political clout or personal wealth. Lord Bellew had a 6000 (2400 hectare) acre estate but no prior military service, while his neighbour Lord Louth had 4000 acres (1600 hectares) and had joined the army as a captain only in 1686. Usually inexperienced colonels were given veteran lieutenant-colonels – Lord Galway, for instance, had Laurence Dempsey, who had served in Portugal and France. Over 200 Frenchmen served as officers in the Jacobite army, one (the Marquis de Boisseleau) commanding a foot regiment.

As Diarmuid and Harman Murtagh have observed, 'a regiment resembled a business, managed by the colonel, with the other officers as junior partners. They tended to be drawn from the colonel's relatives, neighbours, "conections", and, very probably, those who were prepared to invest in the enterprise.' There were 10 other Plunketts besides the colonel in Lord Louth's regiment, and Colonel Art MacMahon's regiment was officered by MacMahons and O'Reillys, with a leavening of Bradys and Duffys.

Changes in Weaponry

In the 45 years separating Naseby from the Boyne the art of war had moved on apace. The matchlock musket was being superseded by the flintlock, whose charge was ignited by the sparks from a flint which struck a steel frizzen when the trigger was pressed. Flintlocks were more reliable than matchlocks, but more expensive to manufacture and maintain, and the Jacobite army was always short of them. The proportion of pikemen to musketeers was declining. Sir Edward Dering's regiment, in William's service, had two-thirds musketeers to one-third pikemen in 1689, but by 1691 the English regiments which left Ireland for Flanders had only 14 pikemen per company (less than a quarter of their strength).

The development of the bayonet contributed to the pikeman's demise. The first bayonets were fitted with tapered hilts which simply plugged into the musket's muzzle, and it was not until the early eighteenth century that the socket bayonet, which fitted over the muzzle, became generally available. The musket could not be fired when its plug bayonet was fixed, a fact which contributed to the defeat of a Williamite force by the Scots Jacobite John Graham of Claverhouse, Viscount Dundee, at Killiecrankie in July 1689. Government muskets were – not for the last time – no match for the broadswords of charging Highlanders, but Dundee himself was shot dead in the moment of victory and the rising soon collapsed without him.

The Jacobite army was constantly under-equipped. Not only were most of its muskets matchlocks, but there were never enough even of them, and

Most of William's musketeers carried the new flintlock musket, known as a 'dog-lock' because of the catch (dog) that holds it safely at half-cock. The hilt of the plug bayonet was simply inserted into the musket's muzzle when required.

in 1689 there were reports that whole regiments were equipped with sharpened sticks, clubs or even scythes. In March 1690 Tyrconnell complained that he was short of 20,000 muskets and had so little gunpowder that two-thirds of his men had never fired a shot. Eight major arms convoys arrived from France, but Louvois, the Minister of War, had never been in favour of the enterprise, and even Louis regarded it as simply a means of diverting William from the Continent. There were never enough French arms, and those that appeared were usually old or in poor repair. Private purchase was sometimes more successful: flintlocks and cannon were bought in Portugal, and Mary of Modena pawned her jewellery to buy 2000 muskets.

The Jacobite foot-soldier looked very similar to his opponent. He wore a full-skirted coat, long waistcoat, shirt, cravat, loose-fitting breeches, woollen stockings, brogues, and a broad-brimmed hat. One company in each regiment contained grenadiers, who needed to sling their muskets over their shoulders in order to throw their hand grenades (cast-iron globes filled with gunpowder and ignited by a burning fuse), and so wore low caps instead of hats. Most Jacobite regiments, in common with their English opponents, wore red coats, although white, grey and perhaps blue were also used. There was much variety in the colour of the coat's lining and the wide, turned-back cuffs. The Jacobite cavalry impressed friend and foe alike. At the start of the war it was well-mounted and had the best of the officers. Cavalrymen wore long coats, breeches and high jackboots, and carried a sword, a pair of flintlock pistols and a flintlock carbine. Dragoons carried sword and musket, and wore short boots and a cap similar to that worn by grenadiers in the infantry.

James was poorly provided with artillery. Shortage of guns was one reasons for his failure to take Londonderry, and at the Boyne he had perhaps 16 field-guns. He was scarcely better off for engineers or doctors, and Ireland's notoriously poor roads caused constant difficulties for his transport train which comprised 170 wagons and 400 carts in 1691.

The Jacobite army was of uneven quality. It lacked experienced officers, was wretchedly paid, and shortage of modern weapons told against its infantry. Yet it often fought remarkably well. John Stevens, an Englishman who served as an officer in the Grand Prior's Regiment, commended the army's 'courage and resolution', adding, 'Let not any mistake and think I either speak out of affection or deliver what I know not; for the first I am no Irishman to be anyway biased, and for the other part I received not what I write by hearsay, but was an eyewitness.' 'Never was an attack made with more bravery and courage, and never was it known that the Irish fought with more resolution' was a Williamite's verdict on Jacobite performance at Aughrim.

The Sieges of Derry and Enniskillen

By the time James arrived Tyrconnell had done his work well and all the country, except Enniskillen and Derry, was in Jacobite hands. In April he approached Derry, hoping that his presence would persuade the citizens to open their gates, but was disappointed: on 18 April he was fired upon and some of his entourage were killed. After a council of war it was decided that James would return to Dublin while the French Lieutenant-General Maumont besieged Derry, with Richard Hamilton as his second-in-command.

The siege of Derry was the first major act of the Williamite war. The city's governor, Lieutenant-Colonel Robert Lundy, fled in suspicious circumstances – his effigy is burned annually – and Henry Baker and the Reverend George Walker were appointed joint governors. The able-bodied male citizens, some 7500 men, were formed into eight regiments, each assigned to a sector of the walls. Cannon were positioned along the walls, covering the gates, and on the tower of St Columb's Cathedral.

The besiegers, numbering perhaps 20,000 men, had too few cannon to breach Derry's walls, but fired mortar bombs into the city – George Walker thought that at least 600 people were killed by them – and tried to starve out the defenders. On 21 April the defenders mounted a sortie against Pennyburn, a mile (1.6 km) north of the city, killing Maumont in the process. Early the following month a small fort built round a windmill on the southern edge of the city was captured by the Jacobites and then recaptured by the garrison.

Rosen arrived with reinforcements in June, and the besiegers tightened their grip, blocking the River Foyle with a wooden boom to prevent relief by water. Bad weather and shortage of food added to the discomfort of besiegers and besieged alike. Walker admitted that one extremely fat man feared that he would fall victim to cannibalism, and from the other side of the lines a French officer wrote that 'the troops are tired and many of them are ill…' On the evening of Sunday 28 July the boom was broken and two merchant ships full of provisions reached Derry. With no prospect of starving the city into submission, the Jacobites abandoned the siege.

Enniskillen, the other centre of Protestant resistance, was also be-sieged. Although it lacked Derry's stout walls, its position, on an island where Upper and Lower Lough Erne join, gave it great natural strength. Its defenders were never as closely besieged as the garrison of Derry, and were able to make damaging raids against Jacobite lines of commu-nication. In July Viscount Mountcashel and Major-General Anthony Hamilton (Richard's brother) launched a deliberate attack on Enniskillen, trying first to take Crom Castle on Upper Loch Erne. They were badly beaten there, and the victors capitalized on their success by attacking Mountcashel at Newtownbutler.

The Enniskilleners were tough adversaries – 'I have seen them, like mastiff dogs, run against the bullets,' said one amazed Englishman – and the force of their assault was too much for Mountcashel's men. Mountcashel himself was dangerously wounded and then captured: perhaps 2000 of his men were killed and another 500 taken. The defence of Derry and Enniskillen, and the battle of Newtownbutler, raised Protestant morale, and hard on their heels came more good news: William was sending an expedition to Ireland.

Schomberg Arrives in Ireland

William had originally hoped to persuade Tyrconnell to capitulate; he then offered the Jacobites religious toleration and security of property, but confiscation of their land if they did not submit. This had no effect, and it became clear that he would have to recapture Ireland by force of arms. William was not confident enough of the English regular army's loyalty to use it in such an attempt. Instead, he brought over Dutch troops, supplemented by English regiments specially raised for the expedition, and officered by Irish Protestants in exile in England. Other regiments were recruited from French Huguenots, who had been forced to emigrate when Louis XIV had revoked the Edict of Nantes (which had given them religious freedom) in 1685. In command was the 74-year-old veteran Frederick Hermann, Duke of Schomberg. He had served in the Portuguese, Brandenburg and French armies, becoming a marshal of France in 1675 but, a Protestant, leaving France in 1685. He had been William's military commander in 1688: active, experienced and methodical, he was a natural choice for command in Ireland.

Schomberg landed in Bangor Bay in mid-August, and at once laid siege to Carrickfergus Castle, which surrendered on terms after a stout defence. Word of Schomberg's arrival, coming hard on the heels of bad news from Derry and Enniskillen, provoked something approaching a panic in Dublin. James considered returning to France, but soon decided to go forward to Drogheda, ordering Tyrconnell to follow with the army, while Berwick delayed Schomberg's advance around Newry by breaking up the roads and laying waste the countryside.

In early September Schomberg ground to a halt at Dundalk, and the adversaries remained facing one another, in growing discomfort from sickness and bad weather, till early October when James withdrew to Ardee, and thence to Dublin, and Schomberg fell back to winter quarters of his own in Lisburn. The campaign had proved utterly inconclusive, and William was not pleased. He concluded that 'nothing worth while would be done' unless he went to Ireland himself, though he was reluctant to do so because it would keep him from the Continent during the 1690 campaigning season.

Campaign and Battle

Both sides built up their forces for the coming campaign. In 1689 William had begun negotiating the hire of troops from the King of Denmark, and in March 1690 1000 Danish cavalry and 6000 infantry, commanded by the Duke of Wurttemberg-Neustadt, arrived in Ireland. More English, German and Dutch troops arrived over the next two months, and steps were taken to improve the regularity of the army's pay and supply of rations.

William was assisted by the fact that his navy was able to control the Irish Sea so that convoys could cross without interference. Sir Cloudesley Shovell, the enterprising commander of the squadron of warships protecting communications with Ireland, was delighted that the French made no serious attempt to interfere. He made several raids on Jacobite bases, and even managed to cut out a 20-gun frigate from Dublin Harbour.

The Jacobites, meanwhile, exchanged a brigade of Irish infantry under Lord Mountcashel (who had succeeded in escaping from Enniskillen) for a brigade of French under the Comte de Lauzun. Mountcashel's men formed the nucleus of the many 'Wild Geese' who were to serve France, especially after the final collapse of the Jacobite cause in Ireland in 1691.

Louis XIV got the best of the deal. Lauzun was ambitious, inexperienced and on bad terms with Louvois, the Minister of War, whose support was essential. D'Avaux was recalled to France at the same time, and was not sorry to go, as he expected to fall out with Lauzun, and he may well have been right, for it was soon reported that the Count had boxed the ears of the Governor of Dublin. Three of Lauzun's five regiments were French, one was Walloon (from what is now Belgium) and the remaining one, Zurlauben's, was German. Some were Protestants, who deserted to William after the Boyne, and they were far less well-equipped than the reinforcements William was sending to Ireland. Nor was this all. Lauzun had been told to remain on the defensive and play for time, for Louis now saw little hope of James re-establishing himself in England.

William Arrives in Ireland

William sailed from Hoylake in Lancashire on 11 June and, escorted by Shovell's squadron, reached Carrickfergus three days later. With him came another 14,000 men, a train of artillery from Holland, a full war-chest and a veritable galaxy of notables. William was 39 years old, the son of William II, Prince of Orange and Stadholder of the United Provinces of the Netherlands, and his wife Mary, eldest daughter of Charles I of England. William's father had died shortly before his birth, and the House of Orange had lost its power to an oligarchy of wealthy citizens which failed to make preparations to meet the rising power of Louis XIV. When the French attacked in 1672 'the United Provinces collapsed like a bad soufflé', and three provinces were actually over-run. William inspired the defence, and the following year he began the counter-offensive by taking the town of Naarden.

William's recovery of the lost provinces made him a national hero. 'The hereditary establishment of his offices made him, in all but name, a constitutional monarch,' wrote his biographer Stephen Baxter, and 'the Prince had become a professional soldier and a very hard man.' In 1672 he married Mary, daughter of James Duke of York, the future James II. Although the marriage developed into a love match, the princess was shocked by the first sight of her future husband. He was half a head shorter than she was, hunchbacked, pockmarked and asthmatic: his only remarkable feature was a pair of brilliant eyes.

It may have been William's unprepossessing appearance as much as their own unfamiliarity with monarchy that gave the people of Belfast pause for thought when William entered the city. One eyewitness said that

Above: **The Norman castle at Carrickfergus had been taken by Schomberg in August 1689: William arrived with substantial reinforcements on 14 June 1690.** *Above right:* **Sir Godfrey Kneller's formal portrait of William sets out the sharp lines of his features, but does not reveal that he was short, stooped and pockmarked. William was a brave man and a seasoned soldier: on campaign he lived with his troops in a portable 'cabin' designed by Sir Christopher Wren.**

they 'did nothing but stare, never having seen a king before in that part of the world; but after a while some of them beginning to huzza the rest all took it (as hounds do a scent).' William declared that he had not come to let the grass grow under his feet, and he made plans to move his 36,000 men south as quickly as he could. He himself made for Dundalk by way of Newry and the Moyry pass, sending part of his army via Armagh and Newtownhamilton.

The Jacobite Advance

James had set off for Dundalk with the main body of his army, some 26,000 strong, on 16 June. His men were optimistic: 'Some were so open as to tell their Protestant friends very lately that they would be glad to go to mass within this twelve months.' They believed that the French fleet would sever William's communications with England, or that their would be a Jacobite rising there. Lauzun was more hard-headed. James was short of supplies and his men were poorly armed: if he went forward to Dundalk he risked being cut off from Dublin. Although a Jacobite screening force fought a brief delaying action in the Moyry pass, James wisely decided not to hold it in strength because he risked being outflanked by the advance from Armagh.

In truth James had few options. The ground between Dundalk and Dublin is generally low and easily crossed. All its rivers flow eastwards to the sea and must therefore be crossed by an invader moving southwards, but neither the Fane, Glyde and Dee in County Louth, nor the Nanny in County Meath are serious obstacles. If James moved westwards he would simply uncover Dublin, for William could advance directly on it, keeping himself supplied by sea.

James knew that he was outnumbered, and, misled by information from a prisoner taken in the Moyry pass, may well have believed William to be stronger than he actually was. But as he was to maintain:

What induced the king to hazard a battle on this inequality was that if he did not there he must lose all without a stroke, and be obliged to quit Dublin and all Munster, and so be reduced to the province of Connaught, where having no magazines he could not subsist very long, it being the worst corn country in Ireland. Besides his men seemed desirous to fight, and being new raised would have been disheartened still to retire before an enemy and see all their country taken from them without one blow for it, and by consequence be apt to disperse and give all for lost.

James's only chance was to face William behind the best obstacle he could find: the Boyne water.

Yet even the Boyne was far from perfect. James acknowledged that the position he chose was 'an indifferent good one (and indeed the country afforded no better)'. It had two chief disadvantages. The first was that the Boyne swings north near Rossnaree to loop round Oldbridge before resuming its journey eastwards to the sea through Drogheda. Classical military theory warns against defending the curve of a river which faces the enemy, for an opponent who attacks where the river bends is effectively behind the defenders of the loop, who risk being cut off if the attack succeeds. In James's case this warning was particularly appropriate, for the small town of Duleek, where the road to Dublin from Oldbridge crosses the River Nanny, actually lay closer to attackers across the Boyne at Rossnaree than to the defenders at Oldbridge.

Worse still, the Boyne was fordable in many places, although the practicability of these fords remains a matter of debate. Lauzun observed that when the Jacobites crossed the river at low tide on 29 June their drummers continued beating, without having to lift their drums to protect them from the water. He then rode along the course of the river to Slane, finding it fordable everywhere. However, given Lauzun's instructions only to risk a battle on favourable terms, and the part he was to play in persuading James to flee, he is scarcely an impartial witness. Two of his French subordinates found the river a much more formidable obstacle, and the commissary Coubertin thought that only the ford at Rossnaree offered a realistic prospect of crossing upstream of Oldbridge.

The Williamites were certainly impressed by the Jacobite position. William's confidant the Earl of Portland believed that the King found the fords 'not only difficult, but almost impracticable', and Captain Robert Parker of Lord Meath's Regiment thought that 'it would be a difficult matter to force them from their ground, unless some measures were taken before the battle which might oblige them to break up the order they were drawn up in'.

The Deployment of the Armies
The most recent terrain analysis of the battlefield of the Boyne, conducted by Donal O'Carroll in 1990, concludes that the position did indeed have considerable natural advantages, but that these were not properly appreciated by James. The Oldbridge area and the lofty Donore Hill to its south were its vital ground, and the only realistic prospect of outflanking this came from the Slane/Rossnaree area. Even if an attacker did cross the river at Rossnaree, it would be no easy matter for him to reach Duleek because of the very boggy ground. The battlefield, O'Carroll sensibly maintains, 'had a potential for defence that would have belied later events'.

William's army reached the Boyne early on 30 June and encamped near Tullyallen, facing James's main body on Donore Hill. 'His troops had marched out properly,' wrote a Danish officer, 'and were divided by brigades very advantageously on the other side of the river. The crossing a little way off [Oldbridge] was strongly held by the enemy.' William's Dutch guards, in their distinctive blue coats, were engaged by Jacobite cannon covering the crossing. When William's guns arrived in the afternoon they were brought onto action on 'a furry bank over against the pass', probably the rising ground just north of Oldbridge, and took on the

IRELAND
The Williamite War

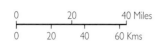 Provinces of Ireland

0		20		40 Miles
0	20	40		60 Kms

MUNSTE

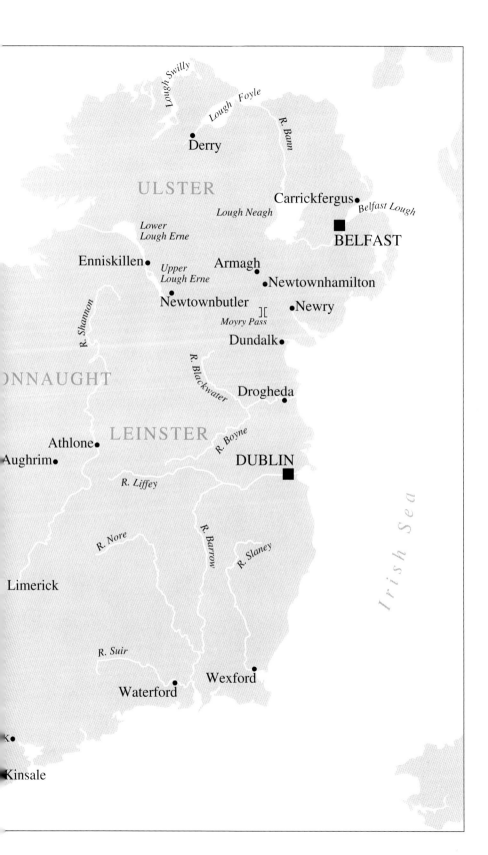

Jacobite guns, apparently persuading James to move his headquarters back to the ruined church atop Donore hill.

William himself went down to the river shortly afterwards, looked at Oldbridge ford and then rode upstream. He dismounted to relax, and no sooner was he back in the saddle than a cannon ball, possibly fired from one of a pair of field-pieces brought forward with a party of cavalry and concealed behind a hedge, 'grazed upon the bank of the river, and in the rising slanted upon the King's right shoulder, tore out a piece of his coat, and tore the skin and flesh, and afterwards broke the head of a gentleman's pistol.' William made light of it, quipping that it could have come nearer, but spent the evening riding about his camp to show his men that he was not badly hurt.

William held a council of war that night. It was clear to all present that their choices were limited to an attack at Oldbridge, an outflanking move by way of Slane/Rossnaree, or a combination of the two. There was a bridge at Slane, but the Jacobites had in fact broken it down; though the bridges at Drogheda were intact, the town was strongly held. Schomberg favoured making a feint at Oldbridge and sending the bulk of the army upstream to find a crossing. Count Solms, commander of the Dutch contingent, disagreed, and recommended throwing the whole army across the river at Oldbridge.

William hit upon a judicious compromise. A strong detachment of cavalry, infantry and dragoons, some 10,000 men in all, probably under the overall command of Lieutenant-General James Douglas, would march upstream towards Slane/Rossnaree. Douglas expected to make for Slane bridge, but was to be redirected to Rossnaree. Schomberg's son, Count Meinhard Schomberg, moved first with part of the force, making for the ford at Rossnaree. The remainder of the army was to cross at Oldbridge. This plan would give William the flexibility of exploiting success at either crossing, and he might have hoped that news of young Schomberg's approach would persuade James to weaken his strong position around Donore: this is precisely what happened.

Schomberg's party moved off at about 5 a.m. on the morning of 1 July, and reached the river at Rossnaree perhaps an hour later. They found the ford defended by Colonel Neil O'Neill's dragoon regiment. As commissary Coubertin pointed out, the ford was so important that it merited a strong garrison, and O'Neill, under orders to 'defend that pass as long as he could, without exposing his men to be cut to pieces', had no realistic prospect of stopping Schomberg.

Schomberg sent 100 elite mounted grenadiers down to the ford to draw the defenders' fire, and followed up with his Dutch dragoons, driving O'Neill's men back. O'Neill himself, who proudly celebrated his ancestry by dressing like an Irish chief rather than a colonel of dragoons, was mortally wounded. With Schomberg's cavalry across, his infantry followed, and an officer was sent back to tell William the good news. William then ordered Douglas to support Schomberg with the remainder of the flanking force.

The threat to his left induced James to shift troops across to strengthen it. He sent off two regiments of cavalry, one of them Sarsfield's, together with Lauzun and his French infantry, followed by some of the Irish infantry until about half the Jacobite army was on its way towards Rossnaree. James expected that the whole Williamite army would follow young Schomberg, but when he rode forwards he found Tyrconnell with the right wing of cavalry and two brigades of infantry facing William's men at Oldbridge.

James then rode westwards and joined Lauzun's force near Corballis. It was drawn up perhaps 500 yards (460 m) from the Williamites, with boggy ground and two deep, high-banked ditches between the armies. The Williamite Lord Meath complained that 'a damned deep bog lay between us; we could not pass it', and Colonel Richard Brewer 'thought the Devil himself could not have got through'. James had now checked the flanking attack, but at the price of weakening his centre, and while he was talking to Lauzun a messenger arrived with the worst possible news: the Williamites had crossed the Boyne at Oldbridge.

The Battle Begins
The first crossing began just after 10 a.m., when William's Dutch guards, nearly 2000 strong, advanced to the strains of 'Lilliburlero'. The Reverend George Story tells how 'the Dutch beat a march till they got to the river's side, and then, the drums ceasing, they went in some eight or ten abreast'. When they were about halfway across the defences of Oldbridge blazed into life, and 'a whole peal of shot came from the hedges, breastworks and houses'. The fire was not notably effective, but when the Dutch reached the shore the Royal Regiment of Foot took them on hand to hand, Major Arthur Ashton rushing forward to pike a Dutch officer as he scrambled from the water, only to be shot a moment later. 'The fighting was so hot,' recorded Story, 'that many old soldiers said they never saw brisker work.'

The Dutch guards pushed the Jacobites out of Oldbridge and then formed up on its far side. While they were doing so, other Williamite troops prepared to cross downstream; as they marched to their crossing-points Tyrconnell launched his cavalry against the Dutch while he prepared to meet the fresh attacks. The charge was led by James's natural son the Duke of Berwick, whose horsemen 'rushed sword in hand' upon the guards. William, watching through a telescope from the other side of the river, was, according to his Secretary at War, George Clarke, 'in a good deal of apprehension for them, there not being any hedge or ditch before them nor any of our horse to support them, and I was so near His Majesty as to hear him say softly to himself "my poor guards, my poor guards, my poor guards".' The Dutch formed square and stood their ground with musket and bayonet, bringing down horse and rider. William was mightily relieved, and 'breathed out as people used to after holding their breath upon a fright or suspense, and said that he had seen his Guards do that which he had never seen foot do in his life.'

The two Huguenot regiments of Cambon and Caillemotte, together with William's northern Irish foot (notably Gustavus Hamilton's Enniskilleners), Nassau's Dutch regiment and two English regiments crossed a little downstream from the guards. Lieutenant-General Richard Hamilton led some Jacobite foot against them, only to see his inexperienced men break and run as the Williamites crossed. He galloped across to some nearby cavalry and led them in a series of charges which not only checked the Williamite advance but forced some of the infantry back into the river, and came close to breaking Caillemotte's regiment. Colonel de la Caillemotte, mortally wounded, was carried back across the river, shouting: '*À la gloire, mes enfants, à la gloire*'.

His men were at their last gasp when the Duke of Schomberg rode up, drew his sword, pointed at the Jacobites and reminded the Huguenots of the miseries inflicted on them by Catholics. '*Allons, messieurs,*' he cried, '*voila vos persecuteurs*' – 'Come, gentlemen, there are your persecutors.' The appeal worked and Caillemotte's men rallied.

The Duke of Wurttemberg-Neustadt led his Danish troops across the river at Yellow Island, almost a mile (1.6 km) downstream from Oldbridge, carried on the shoulders of his grenadiers. 'Where your Majesty's Guards crossed,' he later reported to the Danish King Christian V, 'the water was so deep it came up to their armpits. We marched across by division. The bottom was very boggy.' No sooner did the Danish guards reach the southern bank than they were bravely attacked by Jacobite horse – 'the Irish cavalry behaved very well,' wrote Wurttemberg-Neustadt, 'but the foot behaved very badly.' The guards beat off the charge and formed a bridgehead where they were joined by the Danish cavalry, de la Mellonière's Huguenot regiment and Cutts' English regiment in Dutch pay.

William's men were now across the river in such strength that Tyrconnell's plight was hopeless. Nevertheless, he sent all his cavalry

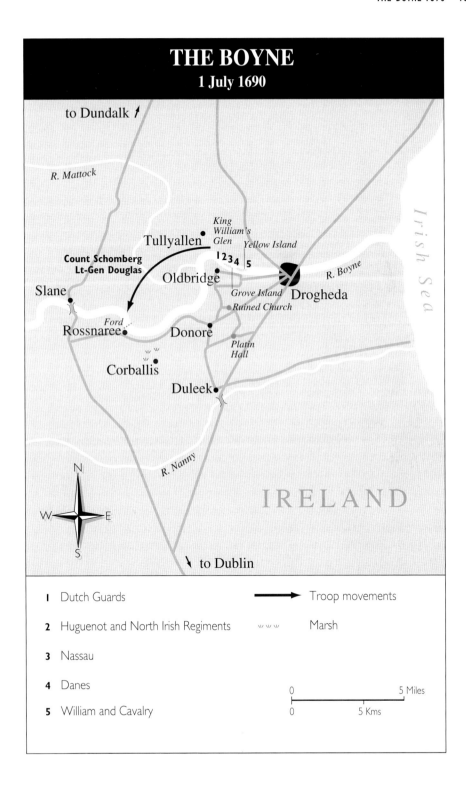

THE BOYNE
1 July 1690

to Dundalk

R. Mattock

Tullyallen

King William's Glen

Yellow Island

Count Schomberg Lt-Gen Douglas

Oldbridge

1 2 3 4 5

Grove Island

R. Boyne

Drogheda

Ruined Church

Slane

Ford

Rossnaree

Donore

Platin Hall

Corballis

Duleek

R. Nanny

IRELAND

Irish Sea

N
W   E
S

to Dublin

1	Dutch Guards		Troop movements
2	Huguenot and North Irish Regiments		Marsh
3	Nassau		
4	Danes		0 ——————— 5 Miles
5	William and Cavalry		0 ——————— 5 Kms

William's cannon, north of the Boyne, support the crossing at Oldbridge. Many Jacobite regiments and the French brigade had been shifted from the high ground opposite to deal with the crossing at Rossnaree, well to the right of this picture.

forward in a desperate attempt to thrown the Williamites back into the river in a charge which excited the admiration even of its intended victims. 'The enemy's horse fought wonderfully bravely as ever men could do,' acknowledged James Douglas, while Sir Thomas Bellingham wrote that: 'The enemy's horse of Tyrconnell's regiment behaved themselves well but our Dutch like angels.'

Berwick's horse was killed under him, but the Duke was helped to safety by a trooper. Old Schomberg was less fortunate. He was with the Huguenots and Enniskilleners when a bullet hit him in the neck. The Danish ambassador thought that it was fired 'by our men, who were crossing the river and discharging their pieces as they advanced', though the Jacobites were to claim that the fatal shot was fired deliberately by Sir Cathal O'Toole. Schomberg fell from his horse and 'died immediately without uttering a word'. Another distinguished casualty was George Walker, once Governor of Londonderry and now Bishop-Elect of Derry, serving as chaplain with the Enniskilleners. William had no time for warrior-priests and, when told that Walker had been killed, asked sarcastically: 'What took him there?'

Although William had not been pleased with Schomberg's performance the previous year, he realised that news of the Duke's death might have a detrimental effect on his men's morale, and determined to cross the river himself. He had already ordered Godart de Ginkel to find a ford below Yellow Island and cross there with his cavalry regiment and two regiments of dragoons.

William reached the river while the crossing was still in progress and, seeing Lord Walter Dongan's Jacobite dragoons riding down to intercept Ginkel, organized covering fire from two field-guns and some Danish infantry. Dongan was killed and his men were driven off. William then crossed the river. He could not wear a cuirass because of the wound he had received the previous day, carried his sword in his left hand because his right arm was so sore, and was a prominent sight in the sash and star of the Order of the Garter. The Danish ambassador admitted that at this stage in the battle he and a colleague fell back behind the King, 'not deeming it our duty to expose ourselves to musket shots and sabre cuts'.

The crossing was so boggy that William had to dismount, and the stress of tramping through the mud brought on an asthma attack. Yet he was soon back in the saddle, leading his cavalry in an effort to cut off the Jacobite infantry around Oldbridge. Once again the Jacobite cavalry bore the brunt of the battle, checking the pursuit and falling back onto the slopes of Donore. Even Tyrconnell now realized that the game was up, and decided to withdraw to Duleek, ordering Richard Hamilton to keep the Williamites back as best he could.

William, anxious to press the Jacobites, approached the Enniskillen cavalry regiment, commanded by an Englishman, Colonel William Wolseley. The troopers did not recognize him in the dust and smoke until Wolseley saw the star and sash and shouted: 'It's the King!' William stood up in his stirrups and cried: 'Gentlemen, you shall be my guards today. I have heard much of you. Let me see something of you!' Then he led them up Donore hill towards Hamilton's rearguard.

There was a desperate fight around Donore Church. 'The place was unfortunately full of holes and dung pits and the passages narrow,' recalled Sir Robert Southwell:

but above all the dust and smoke quite blinded them. His Majesty was here in the crowd of all, drawing his sword and animating all that fled to follow him... Nay one of the Inniskilleners came with a pistol cocked to His Majesty till he called out 'what, are you angry with your friends?' The truth is the clothes of friends and foe are so alike that His Majesty had the goodness to excuse all that passed.

188 OF THE BOYNE 1690

Richard Hamilton was wounded and captured, and William rode over to
see him, asking him if he thought the Jacobites would charge again.

'Yes, upon my honour, I believe they will,' replied Hamilton, 'for they
have a good body of horse still.'

'*Your* honour?' riposted William, mindful of the fact that he had sent
Hamilton to Ireland in 1689 to persuade Tyrconnell to surrender.

James heard of the defeat of his right wing at about 2 p.m., and whis-
pered to Lauzun that their only hope was to charge the younger Schomberg's
detachment before their soldiers found out what had happened and became
disheartened. Lauzun and his cavalry commander, the Marquis Lery de
Girardin, agreed that the ground made this quite impossible. However, his
second-in-command, the Marquis de la Hoguette, was soon to write that the
bog and ditches could have been crossed. It is, however, likely that he wrote
with a view to discrediting Lauzun, for even the fiery Patrick Sarsfield
believed that 'it was impossible for the horse to charge the enemy.'

The Jacobite Retreat

At this moment the Williamite dragoons mounted, and Schomberg's force
turned right and began to march southwards as if to gain the Dublin road.
This manoeuvre threatened to outflank the whole Jacobite army, and Lauzun
at once ordered de la Hoguette to march off by the left flank and make for
Dublin. James claimed that Lauzun pressed him to take his own regiment of
horse, which was then at the head of the column, and some dragoons, head
straight for Dublin, and then 'to go with all expedition to France to prevent
his falling into the enemy's hands…' Lauzun pressed the cavalry to go faster,
and when de la Hoguette remonstrated that this would imperil the infantry,
Lauzun retorted that all that now mattered was saving the King.

The retreat speedily got out of hand. Lieutenant Stevens describes how
the Grand Prior's Regiment of Foot had begun to withdraw, in good order,
down a sunken road leading towards Duleek, when a fleeing cavalry
regiment burst upon them:

so unexpected and with such speed, some firing their pistols, that we had no time
to receive or shun them, but all supposing them to be the enemy (as indeed, they
were no better to us) took to their heels, no officer ever being able to stop the
men after they were broken…some throwing away their arms, others even their
coats and shoes to run lighter.

There was a dreadful scramble when the two retreating wings collided at
Duleek, where a single bridge crossed the narrow River Nanny. De la
Hoguette later told Louvois that: 'The Irish troops were not only beaten;

A later print showing the flight of James II from the Boyne. Most senior officers wore broad-brimmed hats rather than helmets (see page 163). James was hustled from the field by Lauzun, commanding the French contingent, who was anxious to prevent him from being killed or captured.

they were driven before the enemy like sheep.' Colonel Conrad von Zurlaben reported that his French comrades-in-arms behaved little better, and it was his own bluecoats, mainly German and Swiss, who helped the Jacobite cavalry cover the retreat.

William did not press his beaten enemies. The Jacobite Colonel O'Kelly claims that it was because James's men fell back in such good order. This may have been true of Zurlaben's regiment, the cavalry, and some gunners, probably French, who checked the pursuit for an hour and a half near Duleek, but it scarcely applies to the rest of the army. Bishop Burnet suggests, more plausibly, that William believed that James's army would disintegrate and there was little to be gained from a vigorous pursuit with the attendant loss of life. Jacobites found on the field were certainly shown little mercy: 'they shot them like hares amongst the corn and in the hedges as they found them in their march,' admitted George Story. The Danish envoy noted that Count Schomberg had received no orders to cut off the Jacobite retreat, and that William himself may have wished 'to put into practice Caesar's maxim and leave his enemies a golden bridge' over which to retire.

The first fugitives from the Boyne reached Dublin at about 5 p.m. that afternoon, and the trickle soon became a flood. James himself arrived at 10 p.m., accompanied by 200 of Sarsfield's horse. It was said that the Duchess of Tyrconnell offered him food, but he replied that after such a breakfast he had little stomach for supper. He consulted such Privy Councillors as could be found and asked them whether he should return to France (he later made much of the fact that amongst his letters from Mary of Modena was one advising exactly that). Tyrconnell soon arrived and recommended withdrawal to France, and Lauzun sent a note with the same suggestion.

Early the next day James told some of his leading supporters that the Irish had played him false. 'When it came to a trial,' he bleated, 'they basely fled the field and left the spoil to the enemy...henceforth I never determined to head an Irish army, and do now resolve to shift for myself, and so, gentlemen, must you.' He rode south at once, and a St Malo privateer took him from Duncannon to Kinsale, where he had landed a year before. He paused long enough to write orders for Tyrconnell, telling him that he was now Viceroy, and then, on 4 July, left Ireland for ever.

William's army had spent the night of 1 July on the battlefield. The most senior officers slept in their coaches, but most officers and men bivouacked, as best they could, in the field. Some made bonfires of discarded pikes and muskets to keep themselves warm, and others poked about in the Jacobite camp, finding gold watches and silver dinner-services. Surprisingly few soldiers had been killed: most estimates suggest that about 1000 Jacobites and 500 Williamites perished.

The Decline of the Jacobites

The Boyne did not end the war, which dragged on for another year. William was repulsed from Limerick in August, after a spectacular raid by Sarsfield crippled his siege train, and returned to England almost immediately, leaving the conduct of the war in the hands of Godart de Ginkel, whom he created Earl of Athlone. Tyrconnell and Lauzun left for France, and in May 1691 the former returned with a new French commander, the experienced Marquis de St Ruth.

It was like 'pouring brandy down the throat of a dying man', and the Jacobite cause enjoyed a last revival. On 12 July St Ruth was engaged in a desperate battle at Aughrim when a cannon ball killed him. His army, fighting remarkably well until then, panicked, and may have lost as many as 7000 men killed, including 400 officers. After Aughrim the decline was rapid. The Jacobites fell back on Limerick, where Tyrconnell died of a stroke, and his successors squabbled hopelessly. Ginkel laid siege to the city, and on 3 October the adversaries signed a draft treaty.

The Treaty of Limerick allowed the French to return home and guaranteed safe conduct to Jacobites who wished to do the same or to serve abroad. Jacobite estates would not be confiscated, and Catholics would receive 'not less toleration' than they had enjoyed under Charles II. The treaty was not ratified. A million and a half acres (600,000 hectares) were confiscated, and penal laws bore down on Catholics and dissenting Protestants alike.

It is small wonder that when the Irish brigade spearheaded the successful French attack at Fontenoy in 1745 that its soldiers shouted: 'remember Limerick and English treachery!' Sarsfield was long dead, mortally wounded at Neerwinden in Holland in 1693. His last words were 'If only it was for Ireland.' The Irish did not find it easy to forgive James for using them as a mere tool in his own political ambitions. He became *Seamus an Chaca*, 'James the shithead', and after the Boyne Irishmen fought to drive out the English, not in support of a King who had betrayed them.

Indeed, James must bear a great share of the blame for what happened that day, and many Irish officers could not but compare the soldierly William with the irresolute James. Let us leave the last word to the gallant Sarsfield. 'As low as we now are,' he declared, 'change but kings with us and we will fight it over again with you.'

A View of the Field

Drogheda
The pleasant little town of Drogheda is a good starting-point for a visit to the battlefield of the Boyne. It was held by the Jacobites during the battle, and its defenders surrendered on terms on 3 July 1690. Officers were allowed to keep their swords and the garrison was given safe conduct to Athlone.

The prominent Millmount Fort, on Duleek Street, south of the Boyne, is known locally as the cup and saucer. The hillock was fortified by the Normans in the twelfth century, and was Sir Arthur Aston's headquarters when Cromwell stormed the town in 1649, though the present pill-box tower dates from 1808 and was damaged in 1922. The tower offers an excellent view across Drogheda; and the Millmount Museum, in a converted barracks at the foot of the mound, has a small collection of material relating to the Battle of the Boyne.

Parts of Drogheda's medieval walls and gates survive. St Laurence Gate stands at the head of St Laurence Street at the eastern edge of the town, with a pub named after Patrick Sarsfield just outside it. Dr Oliver Plunkett, Roman Catholic Archbishop of Armagh, was implicated in the popish plot in Charles II's reign, and convicted of treason on the false witness of Titus Oates and others. He was hanged, drawn and quartered in 1681, and canonized in the 1980s. His head is now kept in an imposing shrine in St Peter's Church. Some may find this a macabre relic, but it is a striking symbol of the immediacy of Irish history.

Oldbridge

The N51 runs from Drogheda to Slane by way of Oldbridge. North of Oldbridge a narrow wooded valley, still known as King William's Glen, runs up towards Tullyallen: it provided the Williamites with an admirable covered approach to the ford. William's guns were probably deployed on the rising ground just east of the glen.

The Boyne is now crossed by an iron girder bridge and the village of Oldbridge, once on its southern side, has disappeared altogether: not even ruins remain. The river is deeper now than it was in 1690, but still looks eminently fordable just upsteam of the bridge, where a pleasant meadow is today the haunt of anglers rather than Dutch guardsmen and Jacobite foot.

A large overgrown plinth on the northern bank marks the site of a pillar dedicated to the Duke of Schomberg. For many years it was believed that this had been blown up by the IRA in 1922, but recent evidence suggests that post-prandial high spirits on the part of officers from the Free State Army's garrison in Drogheda were responsible.

The canal which parallels the Boyne at Oldbridge postdates the battle by almost two centuries. South of it a minor road runs parallel with the river, giving a good view of the Williamite crossings. The fierce cavalry charges came down from the high ground to the south, and the Dutch guards beat them off in the open ground just above Oldbridge Hall.

Donore and the Boyne

The ruins of the old church at Donore have all but disappeared, but the cemetery which surrounds them remains. It is reached down a long straight track which strikes northwards, through a farmyard, on a sharp bend where the road from Sheephouse, south of Oldbridge, nears Newtown Platin. It offers a superb view over the whole of the central part

William, crossing the Boyne on a white charger, is a popular image in some Protestant areas of Northern Ireland.

of the battlefield, and Drogheda itself is clearly visible to the north-east.

From the village of Donore, confusingly well to the west of the old church, a road follows the course of the Boyne: across the river is the grave at Newgrange, now recognized as dating from around 3200 BC and predating not only Stonehenge but also the pyramids. The Boyne Valley Visitors Centre (under construction when this book went to press) will include a full-scale replica of the tomb. The site of the ford at Rossnaree, bravely defended by Sir Neil O'Neill's dragoons, lies just east of Rossnaree House, and a well-used parking spot gives a good view of the river there. The road joins the main N1 at McGruder's Cross-Roads, and leads on to Slane, with its splendid bridge, damaged by the Jacobites in 1690. The gates of Slane Castle, famous for its rock concerts, can be seen from the bridge.

The difficulties facing the retreating Jacobites can easily be grasped by visiting Duleek, south of Donore and just off the road connecting Drogheda with the N2. The Nanny is much smaller than the Boyne, but a long causeway crosses meadows which remain liable to flooding. A stone memorial, its lettering worn with age, on the causeway's south-western end commemorates something older than the Battle of the Boyne: beaten Jacobites and victorious Williamites alike would have passed it on their way south.

CHAPTER 6

Waterloo
1815

Background

The Waterloo campaign is a bloody addendum to the Napoleonic Wars. Napoleon's star began to fall with his invasion of Russia in 1812. In 1813 he was beaten at Leipzig, and although he showed flashes of his old fire the following year he could not deflect the armies that converged on Paris. The Allies were not vindictive and Napoleon was sent to rule the Mediterranean island of Elba, whence he kept a close watch on France, now governed by Louis XVIII. The trappings of the old regime were resented by men who had fought under the eagles, *émigrés* were employed while veterans were retired, and peasants feared that land confiscated after the Revolution would be redistributed. There had been widespread war-weariness during the last years of the Empire, but Napoleon's absence made French hearts grow fonder. In March 1815 he re-established himself as emperor and, against all the odds, in 100 hectic days fought a campaign which he came within an inch of winning.

The Evolution of Weaponry
It is ironic that most men who fought at Waterloo carried weapons which, in range, accuracy and rate of fire, were inferior to the longbow. There were many reasons for the bow's decline. England ran short of archers, partly because of the decline in practice, signalled by warnings that 'now the art is become totally neglected'. Complaints like this were made during as well as after the great age of archery, so we cannot assume that the rise of the 'dishonest games' signalled its end. The Wars of the Roses (1455–85) were at least as important in creating a shortage of archers. Contemporary opinions of the carnage of Towton

The Duke of Wellington was at the height of his powers in 1815. He did not spend long in bed – 'when it is time to turn over, it is time to turn out' – but his camp bed and other possessions are preserved in the regimental museum of The Duke of Wellington's Regiment in Halifax. Most of the Duke's infantry carried the flintlock musket, pictured here, known as 'Brown Bess'. Colonel George Hanger wrote: 'I do maintain and will prove ... that no man was ever killed at 200 yards, by a common musket, by the man who aimed at him.'

(1461), the bloodiest battle fought on English soil, must be treated with caution. Even so, there may have been 16 000 casualties, most of them archers or spearmen. Other factors were at work. Firearms were so noisy that they terrified men and horses. They represented fashionable modernity which made them attractive to monarchs forging nation states. It was easy to teach men to use them, and also to make them, as the hard-won skills of bowyer and fletcher were blotted out by the smoke of the Industrial Revolution.

When Michael Roberts produced his thesis on the 'military revolution' of the seventeenth century he laid emphasis on the rise in firepower produced through reforms instigated by Maurice of Nassau (1567–1625). These led to the standardization of drill and weaponry and the creation of a disciplined army, with the Swedish army of the Thirty Years War (1618–48) as its paradigm. The thesis linked changes in military organization with the shift of power within the state. New tactics demanded larger, more professional armies, which in turn aided the rise of absolutist states by taking power from subjects and concentrating it in the hands of monarchs.

Historians who develop innovative theories stride into shafts of criticism. Michael Roberts was no exception, and the military revolution thesis must now be substantially qualified. However, we must recognize that even if changes bridging the gap between Agincourt and Waterloo do not pivot on a single revolution, more a succession of key developments, with as much migration of ideas as genuine innovation, their effects on the way men fought were nothing less than revolutionary.

Armies grew bigger and were maintained in peace as well as war. In 1786, the year Frederick the Great died, Prussia had 190 000 men under arms. Although Frederick tried to reduce demands on national manpower by recruiting foreigners, a system of registration permitted swift conversion of young men into recruits. Where Prussia led others followed. First with the standing armies of the eighteenth century and then, in more dramatic guise, with the French *levée en masse* of 1793, we see the strengthening of that link between citizenship and military service which looms large in the remainder of this book. Britain was different because its navy rather than its army was the bulwark of defence. Young Britons were not conscripted into a regular army which was much smaller than those of Continental powers, but the press gang showed that Britain could be as remorseless as her neighbours when it came to securing manpower for vital functions.

Military service was not always willingly embraced, and tens of thousands of conscripts deserted. As Christopher Duffy affirms, 'desertion was the bane of the Prussian army', and during the Seven Years War (1756–63) one of its regiments lost the equivalent of its full complement through desertion. It took a unique mixture of patriotic fervour and robust discipline to bring desertion in the French army down to only 4 per cent of its strength by 1793: the number had doubled two years later.

There were sharp constraints on war-making. Successful French intervention in the American War of Independence imposed a financial burden on the country which was not least amongst the title-deeds of revolution. Even when armies took the field they were hard to feed without cumbersome baggage-trains and provision magazines located in fortresses whose attack and defence became a quintessential feature of war. Cannon brought the high stone walls of medieval castles crashing down. In their place came artillery fortification: low, geometrical works in whose development the French military engineer Sébastien le Prestre de Vauban (1633–1707) played such an important part.

In the age of the French Revolution and Napoleon, war broke free of many old bonds. Napoleon's techniques were as much a reflection of their eighteenth-century background as sparks flying from an outstanding military intellect. Napoleonic warfare rolled across Europe with unprecedented scale and rapidity. In August 1805 Napoleon led an army of over 200 000 men from Boulogne on the French coast to what is now the Czech Republic. In October, operating on a front 150 miles (240 km) wide, his army engulfed an Austrian force at Ulm, and on 5 December it trounced a superior Austro-Russian army at Austerlitz. Napoleon's ability to manoeuvre hinged on his development of *corps d'armée*, all-arms formations which marched on separate routes, making best use of roads and locally obtained provisions, but which fought united.

Napoleon sought to fight decisive battles and to win them by offensive action. At his best he moved fast so as to surprise, confuse and unbalance before striking. At his worst he relied on the power of his artillery and the morale of his soldiers to break an enemy by brute force. Napoleon recognized that much of war depended on the imponderables of the human spirit and took infinite pains, from an imperial word of approval here to an award of the Légion d'honneur there, to foster morale. Yet he had a hard edge of cynicism which saw men as a resource like any other. 'You cannot stop me,' he warned the Austrian statesman Metternich, 'I can spend thirty thousand men a month.'

Battles were linear. Formations of close-packed infantry engaged one another with the flintlock musket, whose slow rate of fire (about three rounds a minute), close range (an enemy line would receive little damage at 200 yards [180 metres]) and inherent unreliability (one shot in five

The eagles of the French 45th and 105th Regiments were captured when Ponsonby's Union Brigade charged. Sergeant Charles Ewart of the Royal Scots Greys took the former, after a desperate hand-to-hand struggle: '... the bearer thrust at my groin. I parried it off and cut him down through the head. A lancer came at me – I threw the lance off by my right side and cut him from the chin upwards, which cut went through his teeth. Next I was attacked by a foot soldier who, after firing at me, charged me with his bayonet ... I parried it, and cut him down through the head; so that finished my contest for the Eagle.'

normally misfired, and in rainy conditions it was hard to fire at all) reduced the soldier to a tiny cog in a ponderous machine. There were important exceptions. Light infantry, who fought outside the line and sometimes carried more accurate rifled weapons, were useful, especially when straight lines and massed volleys were inappropriate. The Revolutionary armies used swarms of *tirailleurs* (light infantry) who buzzed ahead of the main body, galling the enemy's line before it was ever seriously attacked.

For years writers contrasted French preference for the column with British predilection for the line. The truth is more mundane. Columns were useful for road or cross-country movement and essential for keeping men together in an assault. In about 1700 the plug bayonet, jammed inconveniently into the musket's muzzle, was replaced by the socket bayonet, which fitted round the barrel. Infantrymen were trained to push home their attack with the bayonet, but in practice large-scale clashes between bayonet-wielding infantry were rare. The steady advance of a column, well prepared by *tirailleurs* and artillery, and accompanied by whoops, patriotic songs and martial music, often proved too much for its intended recipients, who departed before the cold steel arrived.

If fire was required, then deployment in line enabled the maximum number of muskets to bear. During the Peninsular War in Spain and Portugal (1808–14), the Duke of Wellington made skilful use of the ground so that startled French columns, configured for movement, often collided with the British, deployed to fire. A variety of compromises was possible, based on versions of 'mixed order', where columns, closed up for movement or attack, were preceded by lines. If attacked by cavalry, infantry battalions formed hollow squares, with officers and colours inside and rows of uninviting bayonets outside.

As the close-range firepower of infantry grew it became harder for cavalry to break infantry by the physical impact of man and horse, even aided by the psychological blow of the charging mass. There were times when cavalry used surprise, smoke, broken ground or the fire of other arms to ride down infantry, but these were few and far between. Yet cavalry was essential for screening (preventing enemy patrols from penetrating its own outposts), reconnaissance (getting inside the enemy's cavalry screen to glean information) and pursuit (pressing a beaten foe to turn retreat into rout).

Artillery had grown markedly in power. Guns threw heavier projectiles and were increasingly grouped in massed batteries to produce concentrated fire. Field artillery enjoyed mobility that would have stunned Henry V's gunners, and horse artillery, with all its gunners mounted, could keep pace with cavalry. Field guns provided direct fire, engaging targets visible to their detachments, their usual missile an iron ball whose weight defined the piece's calibre. The 12-pdr, Napoleon's favourite, fired its ball to a maximum range of 1200 yards (1100 metres) but was really effective at perhaps half this distance.

At close range the most deadly projectile was case shot, a container filled with musket balls which split open at the muzzle to turn the piece into a gigantic shotgun. Explosive shells were fired from howitzers. Common shell was an iron sphere packed with gunpowder, and spherical case shot, sometimes called after its inventor, Henry Shrapnel of the Royal Artillery, had musket balls mixed with a bursting charge and was designed to explode in the air above its target. Inconsistencies in fuses, gunpowder and metallurgy limited the effectiveness of this sort of ammunition. Nor did they do much for the primitive rockets used by the British. When Wellington ordered a rocket battery to be equipped with more conventional weapons he was told that this would break its com- mander's heart. 'Damn his heart: let my orders be obeyed' was the duke's blunt response.

Campaign and Battle

On 1 March 1815 Napoleon landed at Fréjus and set off for Grenoble. Troops defected to him on the way and Grenoble opened its gates, giving him a rapturous welcome. Marshal Ney had left Paris promising to bring him back 'in an iron cage', but when they met at Auxerre on 14 March the marshal's men defected and Ney followed suit. Five days later Louis XVIII left Paris for Belgium. There could be no question of Napoleon's reassumption of power being accepted by the Allies, whose representatives were at Vienna discussing the post-war settlement. They immediately buried their differences and set about planning the invasion of France.

This was to take the form of a concentric attack involving up to one million men. The Austrians would concentrate in northern Italy and the lower Rhine; the Prussians would send an army to eastern Belgium; an Anglo-Dutch force would concentrate in western Belgium; and a Russian army would advance through Poland. Organizing operations on this scale was not the work of a moment: the Austrians would not be ready until July, and the Russians might take even longer.

Napoleon quickly set about raising troops. After only eight weeks he had nearly 300 000 men under arms, and another 150 000 would be added once the conscripts of the class of 1815 were available. He could

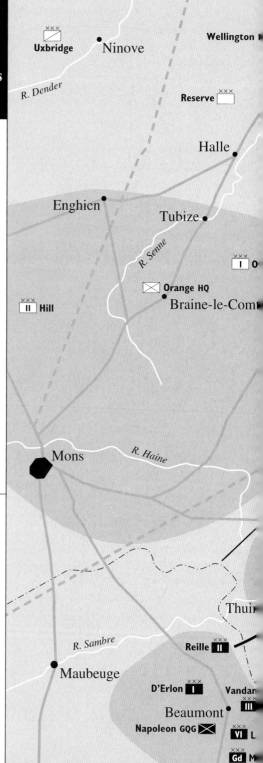

THE WATERLOO CAMPAIGN

Position of French and Allied Armies, and French Lines of Advance at Dawn on 15 June

▭	Allied troops (British/Dutch-Belgian/Prussian)
◼	French troops
→	French troop movements
▨	Army areas
– ×××× –	Army boundary
–·–·–·	Frontier, 1815
▬▬	Roads with metalled surface, 1815
– – –	Roman roads

```
0        2        4        6 Miles
├───┬───┬───┬───┬───┤
0    2    4    6    8    10 Kms
```

Louvain

Brussels

Forest of Soignies

BELGIUM

N
W E
S

R. Lasne

lsemberg

La Hulpe

R. Dyle

Waterloo

Bierges

Wavre

Ohain

nt-St

Chapelle-St Lambert

Jean

Lasne

Ottignies

Mont-St Guibert

Sart-lez-Walhain

Genappe

R. Orne

elles

uatre-Bras

Tilly

Gembloux

Pirch I ××× II

Marbais

Frasnes

Sombreffe

Ligny

Fleurus

Blücher HQ

Gosselies

Namur

en HQ

Charleroi

Marchienne

Châtelet

Ciney

I ××× Ziethen

Thielmann ××× III

R. Meuse

××× ×××

Gérard ××× IV

Boussu

FRANCE

play for time, raising more troops and opposing each Allied thrust, or might repeat the pattern of 1814 and stab at invading armies in turn. He realized that his only hope lay in defeating his opponents in detail, and determined to move north as soon as possible.

Wellington's 'Infamous Army'
There were some 79 000 infantry, 14 000 cavalry and 196 guns in Wellington's Anglo-Dutch field army in Belgium. He had not used permanent corps in Spain but introduced them for the Waterloo campaign, although they had little effect on the battle when the duke commanded his army as he pleased. The Prince of Orange, twenty-three-year-old heir to the throne of the Netherlands, commanded 1st Corps (two British and two Dutch-Belgian divisions) from Braine-le-Comte. Lieutenant-General Lord Hill's 2nd Corps (two British divisions, a Dutch-Belgian division and a Dutch-Belgian brigade) was around Ath, and the Reserve Corps (two British divisions, a corps of Brunswickers under their duke, and a Nassau detachment) was under Wellington's hand around Brussels. The eleven brigades of British, Hanoverian and Dutch-Belgian cavalry were commanded by Lord Uxbridge.

The components of Wellington's force were of markedly different quality. Only six of his twenty-five British battalions had served in Spain. Others had been involved in Sir Thomas Graham's unsuccessful attack on Bergen-op-Zoom in 1814, and many had not recovered from the experience. The King's German Legion (KGL), recruited in George III's German possessions, was first-rate, encouraging Wellington to reduce its eight battalions from ten to eight companies apiece and use the spare officers and NCOs to stiffen less reliable Hanoverian units. Dutch-Belgian units were of similarly varied calibre, and Wellington observed that many of their officers 'had risen under Bonaparte and are admirers of his system and government'.

Wellington, at forty-six the same age as his opponent, had earned his first laurels in India in 1803. He defeated the French at Vimeiro in Portugal in 1808, and from 1809 he campaigned in Spain and Portugal, crossing the Pyrenees into France in 1814. Wellington had never met Napoleon in battle but had dealt with a succession of his marshals. He was more than just a canny defensive practitioner. On 22 July 1812 he caught Marshal Marmont off-balance at Salamanca with a meticulously timed attack which, it was said with little exaggeration, routed 40 000 men in 40 minutes.

Wellington's talents were not confined to the battlefield. He was a careful administrator and knew that there was an intimate connection between the maintenance of discipline and the regular arrival of rations. The duke was not helped by the fact that the commissariat, which provided the army with supplies, was administered by the Treasury and employed civilian officials who were not under military command. Soldiers were entitled to a daily ration of $1\frac{1}{2}$ lb (0.7 kg) bread or 1 lb (0.5 kg) biscuit, 1 lb (0.5 kg) beef or mutton, $\frac{1}{2}$ pint (0.5 litres) wine or $\frac{1}{3}$ pint (0.3 litres) rum, although they often found themselves on half-rations or no rations at all.

The drink ration was insufficient for many. Wellington believed that: 'Some of our men enlist from having got bastard children – some for minor offences – many more for drink; but you can hardly conceive such a set brought together, and it really is wonderful that we should have made them the fine fellows they are.' Even so, the lure of drink regularly proved too much for them. There were outbursts of collective disorder, and at the individual level many good soldiers were ruined by drink. Discipline was harsh, with flogging for minor offences. Rifleman Harris of the 95th thought it a necessary evil. 'I detest the sight of the lash,' he wrote, 'but I am convinced that the British army cannot go on without it.'

British soldiers had volunteered for service. A few joined to escape justice, and Philip Haythornthwaite is right to suggest that these formed the basis for the 50–100 incorrigibles in every regiment. Others were attracted by the enlistment bounty; found the delights of the open-air life extolled by recruiting sergeants more appealing than the drudgery of the counting house or weaving shed; were led from the militia by officers eager for the regular commission granted them for presenting forty volunteers; or simply got drunk and woke up a soldier.

Many were labourers, a description as often based on hope as on experience, and depressions in the textile trade generated waves of unemployed weavers. Recruits from the teeming industrial cities were smaller than countrymen, and most were shorter and narrower in the chest than modern recruits: in 1812 the 10th Hussars demonstrated that it was a regiment of rare distinction by announcing that it would accept no men below 5 ft 7 in (1.7 metres). Scotland and Ireland were fecund recruiting grounds, and the Irish were everywhere, manning Irish units like the inimitable 88th Connaught Rangers and leavening many an ostensibly English regiment.

The origins of officers were scarcely less diverse. Michael Glover and others have demolished the myth that the army withered 'under the cold shade of the aristocracy'. Abuses like the commissioning of children had been ended, although a young man could still buy a commission by furnishing the money for his rank. An ensigncy, the junior commissioned

The artist Denis Dighton made drawings at Waterloo after the battle. Here he shows Light Companies of the Coldstream Guards during the early stages of the fight for Hougoumont. The massive south gate can be seen centre left, and to its right some guardsmen are firing over the garden wall.

rank in the infantry, cost £400, and appointments in the Guards or cavalry were more expensive. Promotion could be purchased if an officer had sufficient service to be eligible for the next rank and could find the extra money. Many promotions went by regimental seniority: several distinguished officers, such as Harry Smith and George de Lacy Evans, rose without buying a single step. Officers of the Royal Artillery and Royal Engineers purchased neither first commissions nor subsequent promotion and, unlike their brothers of horse and foot, had to receive training at the Royal Military Academy at Woolwich before being commissioned.

This 'infamous army' had extraordinary qualities. Its soldiers were inured to hardship and had their own rough pride. In a crowded field-hospital Sergeant Michael Connolly of the 95th reprimanded a man for groaning in the presence of French wounded. 'Hold your tongue, ye blathering devil,' he barked, 'and don't be after disgracing your country in the teeth of these 'ere furriners by dying hard … For God's sake die like a man before these 'ere Frenchers.' Ensign Leeke of the 52nd heard only one man cry out in pain at Waterloo, 'and when an officer said: "Oh man, don't make a noise," he instantly recollected himself and was quiet.' Officers tried to show gentlemanly 'bottom' at all times, and most saw death as preferable to loss of status, however recently acquired.

Wellington was chatting to the diarist Thomas Creevey in the park at Brussels when he saw a private of the line wandering about gaping at the statues. 'There,' said the duke, jabbing with a long finger. 'It all depends on that article whether we do the business or not. Give me enough of it and I am sure.' This confidence was reciprocated. Lieutenant John Kincaid of the 95th recalled that: 'We would rather see his long nose than a reinforcement of 10 000 men any day.' Private Horesfield of the 7th Fusiliers put it in blunter vernacular: 'Whore's ar Arthur? Aw wish he wor here.'

Blücher's Men

Wellington's Prussian ally, Field-Marshal Gebhard Leberecht von Blücher, had spent most of his seventy-two years fighting. His men called him 'Old Forwards', and neither considerable eccentricities nor devotion to a pungent mixture of gin, rhubarb and garlic shook their regard. Blücher lacked Wellington's grasp of detail, but his chief of staff, August Wilhelm von Gneisenau, plied pen to balance his master's sword. Blücher's 121 000 men and 300 guns formed four corps: Ziethen's I Corps around Fleurus and Charleroi; Pirch's II at Namur; Thielmann's III at Ciney; and Bülow's IV near Liège.

Blücher's lines of communication ran through Liège into Germany, while Wellington's went from Brussels to Alost and the Channel. There was a risk that, under pressure, each commander would fall back on his own lines, and when the two met on 3 May 1815 they agreed that the Anglo-Dutch would concentrate on Nivelles and the Prussians on Sombreffe if the French attacked. Liaison officers were exchanged, Colonel Hardinge joining Blücher's headquarters and Baron Müffling reporting to Wellington's.

Napoleon's Campaign

Napoleon was not at his best. David Chandler tells us that 'his mind was as alert as ever but physically he was out of condition'. Marshal Berthier, his former chief of staff, had declined to serve, and in his place Napoleon had appointed Marshal Soult, an experienced commander but not a natural staff officer. The Armée du Nord, 124 000 men and 366 guns, formed two wings and a reserve. Emmanuel de Grouchy, newly promoted marshal and a stranger to high command, led the right wing (Vandamme's III and Gérard's IV Corps with five smaller cavalry corps) south of Charleroi. Marshal Michel Ney's left wing (Drouet d'Erlon's I Corps and Reille's II) was around Maubeuge. The red-headed Ney deserved his sobriquet 'the bravest of the brave', but he had never been the same since 1812, when he was the last Frenchman out of Russia, a musket in his hand. Close to his headquarters at Beaumont Napoleon held his reserve, Marshal Mortier's Imperial Guard and Lobau's VI Corps. The army was riddled with faction, old Bonapartists mistrusting converted royalists, and not without reason, for the defection of a divisional commander was an early feature of the campaign. The French historian Henri Hossaye affirmed that: 'Napoleon had never before handled an instrument of war that was so formidable and so fragile.'

Early on 15 June the French headed for the frontier. Although bad staff work caused traffic jams, they crossed the Sambre at Charleroi despite resistance from Ziethen's Prussian I Corps. Napoleon told Ney to advance up the Brussels road while Grouchy took the Fleurus road towards Sombreffe. As for the Allies, Gneisenau ordered a concentration on Sombreffe while Wellington, who did not receive details of the attack until mid-afternoon, wrongly scented danger from the direction of Mons and decided to concentrate on Nivelles. By nightfall Napoleon had won the first round, for while Blücher was obligingly moving into his grasp, Wellington was swinging away from his ally.

Wellington attended the Duchess of Richmond's ball in Brussels that night. Absence would have heartened Napoleon's Belgian supporters, and it was useful to have senior officers to hand at the gathering. He

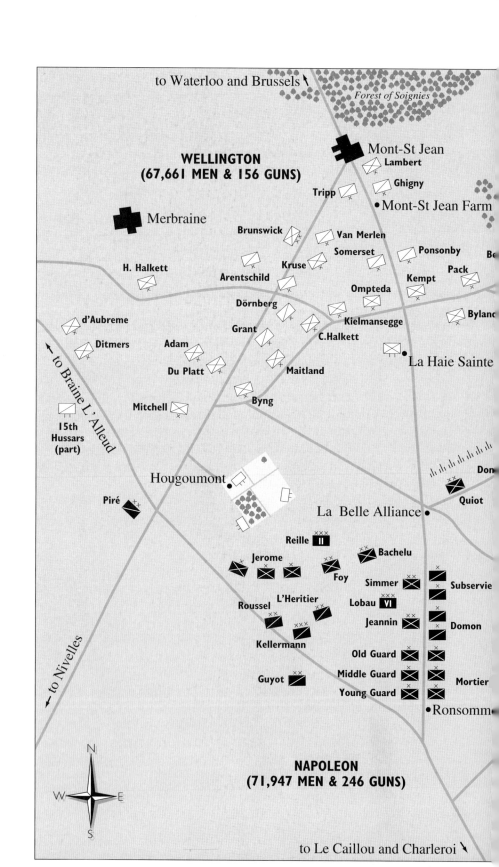

to Waterloo and Brussels ↘

Forest of Soignies

WELLINGTON
(67,661 MEN & 156 GUNS)

Mont-St Jean

Lambert

Ghigny

Tripp

● Mont-St Jean Farm

Merbraine

Brunswick

Van Merlen

Somerset

Ponsonby

Be

H. Halkett

Kruse

Pack

Arentschild

Kempt

d'Aubreme

Dörnberg

Ompteda

Ditmers

Grant

Kielmansegge

Bylanc

Adam

C.Halkett

La Haie Sainte

Du Platt

Maitland

Mitchell

Byng

15th
Hussars
(part)

to Braine L' Alleud →

Hougoumont

Don

Piré

Quiot

La Belle Alliance ●

Reille **II**

Bachelu

Jerome

Foy

Simmer

Subservie

Roussel

L'Heritier

Lobau **VI**

Jeannin

Domon

Kellermann

Old Guard

Guyot

Middle Guard

Mortier

Young Guard

● Ronsomm

to Nivelles →

N
W E
S

NAPOLEON
(71,947 MEN & 246 GUNS)

to Le Caillou and Charleroi ↘

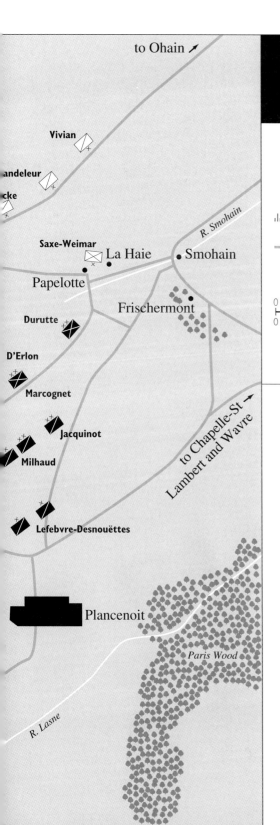

to Ohain ⤢

Vivian

andeleur

cke

Saxe-Weimar

La Haie

Smohain

R. Smohain

Papelotte

Frischermont

Durutte

D'Erlon

Marcognet

Jacquinot

Milhaud

to Chapelle-St
Lambert and Wavre ⤢

Lefebvre-Desnouëttes

Plancenoit

Paris Wood

R. Lasne

WATERLOO
18 June 1815:
Situation at 11.30 a.m.

☐   Allied troops (British/
      Dutch-Belgian/Prussian)

■   French troops

╷╷ ╷╷ ╷╷   Napoleon's Great Battery

━━━   Roads with metalled
       surface, 1815

```
0    200   400   600   800 Yds
0    200   400   600   800 Metres
```

heard of the Prussian move to Sombreffe before leaving for the ball, and was later told that Ney had pushed Prince Bernhardt of Saxe-Weimar's brigade of Perponcher's Dutch-Belgian division out of Frasnes on the Brussels road, but that the French had been held south of Quatre-Bras, the next major junction to the north. Wellington asked the Duke of Richmond if he had a good map, retired into the dressing room, and told his host: 'Napoleon has humbugged me, by God! He has gained twenty-four hours' march on me.' Richmond asked him what he intended to do. Wellington replied that he would concentrate at Quatre-Bras, 'but we shall not stop him there, and if so I must fight him' – his thumbnail described a line across Mont-St Jean, a little to the north – '*here.*'

Wellington rode out of Brussels at seven on the morning of 16 June. The leading division of his reserve, under Sir Thomas Picton, had already left for Quatre-Bras. The junction was only held thanks to the 'intelligent disobedience' of the Prince of Orange's chief of staff, Constant de Rebecq, who encouraged Prince Bernhardt to stand his ground and supported him with Major-General Count Bylandt's brigade of Perponcher's division.

De Rebecq's bluff worked because of misunderstandings between Napoleon and Ney. Napoleon expected the Prussians to retire out of reach and proposed to deal with Wellington first. Ney thought that because his wing was entrusted with the day's main effort he should not attack until the reserve arrived. Reille, his leading corps commander, had fought in Spain and was nervous of long crest-lines which might have nasty surprises behind them. It was not until 1 p.m. that Ney was urged to attack without delay, but by this time Napoleon had changed his plan. Blücher had not withdrawn and so while Grouchy launched a frontal assault on him, Ney was to take Quatre-Bras and move along the Nivelles–Namur road against his flank.

A Day of Battles
There were two battles on 16 June. At Ligny, on Napoleon's right, the Prussians were attacked by Vandamme and Gerard, with the Guard putting in the final assault. By nightfall the Prussians were in full retreat, having lost over 16 000 men and 21 guns and inflicted 11 500 French casualties. Blücher, leading his cavalry forward at the very end of the day, was unhorsed and ridden over before being rescued and bundled back with the fugitives.

On Napoleon's left, Ney spent the afternoon hammering the Allies at Quatre-Bras. Wellington commanded in person, his conduct of battle dictated by a bare trickle of reinforcements. Reille's French corps was checked with difficulty in the cornfields south of the junction. Sir Thomas Picton arrived in time to take the weight off Perponcher, but there was heavy fighting in which the Duke of Brunswick was killed and, by 4 p.m., with d'Erlon's corps about to engage, Wellington's plight seemed hopeless. At this juncture a staff officer from Napoleon ordered d'Erlon eastwards to take on the Prussians. He had almost reached Ligny, where the appearance of his unidentified troops stalled the French attack, when Ney, furious at his own lack of progress, ordered him back. He arrived too late to help, and in his absence the balance tilted in Wellington's favour.

Quatre-Bras was no easy battle. Very late in the afternoon French cuirassiers commanded by Kellermann, coming on very fast, caught Colin Halkett's newly arrived brigade of Alten's division in line, a formation decreed by the Prince of Orange, and cut it about badly. Ney had insufficient infantry on hand to secure the results of the charge, and the arrival of Cooke's Guards division gave Wellington the reinforcements he needed to re-establish control over the battlefield.

Blücher and Wellington had met at Bussy mill near Brye that morning, and the duke agreed to support the Prussians 'provided I am not attacked'. Gneisenau was no anglophile, and as he briefed senior officers that night he was inclined to fall back on the Prussian lines at Liège. The best route, the Nivelles–Namur road, was already lost, and it was agreed that the army would regroup at Wavre and then make for Liège. When Blücher reappeared he would not hear of it: common sense and military honour demanded that he should support Wellington.

The Eve of Waterloo
On 17 June Wellington slipped away from Quatre-Bras, his retirement covered by a spectacular rainstorm. He was too fast for Napoleon who, by nightfall, was in the farmhouse of Le Caillou, beside the Brussels road, with Wellington's army on the ridge just to his north. Napoleon received a message from Grouchy which suggested that the Prussians were falling back on Wavre, but it was not until 10 a.m. the next day that he sent Grouchy an order, and then only an imprecise one. Napoleon intended Grouchy to keep the Prussians away from Wellington, but he did not say so in as many words. When Soult suggested that the army should fight united, Napoleon turned on him: 'Because you have been beaten by Wellington you consider him a good general but I tell you that Wellington is a bad general and the English are breakfast.'

Wellington had first seen the ridge with the village of Mont-St Jean in its centre on his way to Paris in 1814. It was not an ideal position, but its slopes offered good fields of fire to their front and shelter behind. There were three robust farms on the forward slope: Hougoumont to the west, La Haie Sainte in the centre, and the Papelotte/La Haie/Smohain complex to the east. The valleys of the Dyle and Lasne rivers and Paris Wood gave some protection to the eastern flank. The western flank was open, which encouraged Wellington to post 15 500 men at Halle and Tubize, 8 miles (13 km) away.

The remainder of the duke's army, 67 661 men and 156 guns, took post along the ridge, its line running from Braine L'Alleud to Papelotte/La Haie/Smohain. Cavalry watched both flanks, but most of Wellington's horsemen were drawn up behind his centre. Almost all the cavalry and much of the infantry were behind the crest-line, and shoulder-high corn helped to screen the position. Bylandt's brigade, just east of the main road, was less lucky because a gash in the ridge meant that there was nothing Wellington could do to protect it.

The farms were held by picked troops. Battalions contained a grenadier company of tall and stalwart soldiers and a light company of lithe and nimble men, in addition to their eight 'battalion companies'. The Guards light companies garrisoned the farm of Hougoumont, with a Nassau battalion and two companies of Hanoverian riflemen supporting them. The remainder of the Guards division was not far behind, south of the crest but partly screened by the trees around Hougoumont and able to reach the farm down a sunken lane. Major Baring's 2nd Light Battalion KGL held La Haie Sainte, and the 95th a sandpit on the other side of the road. Both units carried the Baker rifle, a more accurate weapon than the Long Land Pattern musket, popularly known as Brown Bess, carried by line regiments. Saxe-Weimar's brigade of Perponcher's division garrisoned the buildings around Papelotte on the left.

The weather was worse than the night before Agincourt. Private William Wheeler of the 51st was pleased to discover that there was a good deal of drink about, so he and his comrades were 'wet and comfortable'. Comfort was strictly relative:

It would be impossible for any one to form an opinion of what we endured that night. Being close to the enemy we could not use our blankets, the ground was too wet to lie down, we sat on our knapsacks until daylight without fires, there was no shelter against the weather: the water ran in streams from the cuffs of our jackets, in short we were as wet as if we had been plunged over head in a river. We had one consolation, we knew the enemy were in the same plight.

Some officers and men huddled under the 'pitching blankets' that made improvised tents. Ensign Short of the Coldstream Guards admitted: 'I with another officer had a blanket, and with a little more gin we kept up very well.'

The Battle for Hougoumont

Soldiers set about cleaning their muskets as soon as it was light, and started by firing the charge already in the weapon. Private Matthew Clay of the 3rd Guards aimed his 'at an object, which the ball embedded in the bank where I had purposely placed it as a target.' He commented that 'the flint musket then in use was a sad bore on that occasion, from the effects of the wet, the springs of the lock became wood-bound and would not act correctly, and when in action the clumsy flints also became useless.'

The weather did little for Napoleon, who decided to delay the opening of the battle to allow the ground to dry out so that guns could move more easily. Late that morning his infantry drew up astride the Brussels road, with d'Erlon to the east, Reille to the west and most of the cavalry behind them. Lobau's corps, with the Guard to its rear, waited parallel with the road, between an inn called La Belle Alliance and the hamlet of Ronsomme. A battery of eighty-four 12-pdrs stood on a low rise just east of the Brussels road and hinted at the emperor's intention, made clear when he issued his orders at 11 a.m., to launch Ney straight against Wellington's centre. He had 72 000 men and 246 guns, and proposed to hit the Anglo-Dutch army as hard as possible in the hope of breaking it.

Reille's French corps started the battle at about 11.50 a.m. with an attack on the Hougoumont farm, intended to draw troops from Welling-ton's centre. His leading division was commanded by Prince Jerome, Napoleon's youngest brother, who sent four regiments into the wood south of the farm. Its Nassau and Hanoverian defenders fought well and fell back only slowly. When the attackers burst through a hedge at the northern end of the wood it was to find themselves facing the farm's south gate and long garden wall, pierced with loopholes by the defending guardsmen. The French did their best to break into the enclosure, grab-bing muskets protruding from loopholes and even exchanging bayonet thrusts across the top of the wall, but could make no progress and fell back into the wood.

The battle for Hougoumont was still isolated, allowing Wellington to devote his attention to it. He sent Lieutenant-Colonel Lord Saltoun with the light companies of Maitland's brigade to relieve the Nassauers, in dif-ficulties in the orchard; posted Bull's howitzer battery behind the farm with orders to shell the wood; and brought du Plat's KGL brigade of Clinton's division down to join Byng's Guards brigade just behind

Hougoumont. Scarcely less important was the contribution made by Joseph Brewster of the Royal Wagon Train, who took a tumbril of ammunition down into Hougoumont, under fire the whole way. Part of the wood was reoccupied, but when Jerome's French troops renewed their efforts about half an hour later, assisted by elements of Foy's division, they quickly regained lost ground and surged right round the buildings to attack the north gate.

Second Lieutenant Legros of the 1st Light Infantry, a giant of a man nicknamed 'the smasher', weakened the gate with an axe and led a rush which burst it open. The defenders fought back with bayonet and butt, aided by musket fire from the surrounding buildings until eventually Legros and all but one attacker were killed. The fight was still raging when a fresh wave of attackers appeared at the gate, and Lieutenant-Colonel Macdonnell, commanding the light companies of Byng's Guards brigade, collected a party of officers and men who closed the gates and jammed them shut.

Further attacks fared no better, and reinforcements were constantly slipped down the covered way. Some set about raiding the cherry trees in the orchard, oblivious of the heavy fire and the fury of Macdonnell, who roared out: 'You scoundrels! If I survive this day, I will punish you all.' At 2 p.m. the French belatedly brought up a howitzer, and followed it with others. Their shells set fire to the buildings but could not shake the defence. Matthew Clay recalled that his officer placed himself across the door of an upstairs room and would not allow the defenders to leave until just before the floor gave way, and some guardsmen perished when floors collapsed beneath them. The wounded had been carried into the great barn, and when it began to burn there were agonized cries but no one could be spared to rescue them. Corporal James Graham, one of the party which had closed the gates, asked Macdonnell for permission to save his wounded brother Joseph, then dragged him from the burning barn and returned to the fight.

The struggle at Hougoumont raged on without reference to the rest of the battle, and Ensign Wedgwood of the 3rd Guards acknowledged that he had no idea what was happening outside his own field of interest. 'I remember that I was myself completely ignorant of what was going on or what the result of the action was likely to be,' he wrote, 'until we saw parties of the French passing us in full retreat with the Brunswickers in pursuit ...'

About 10 000 men fell in and around Hougoumont. The overwhelming majority were French, for Wellington used only about 3500 men in all to hold the farm. The action exhausted the French divisions under

Although, at 46, Napoleon was the same age as Wellington in 1815, he was out of condition, and looked less trim than he did when this painting by Robert Lefevre was completed three years before. Napoleon had replaced the fleur de lys of the Old Regime with the imperial eagle, which adorned French uniforms, accoutrements and regimental colours. A gilt eagle topped the staff which bore a regiment's colours and these were defended not only by the officer who carried them but also by an escort of veteran NCOs.

Jerome and Foy and made inroads into Bachelu's men but did not succeed in inducing Wellington to weaken his centre. The duke had no doubt that Hougoumont was the pin on which the battle turned, and affirmed afterwards that victory had depended on closing its gates.

The battery opposite Wellington's centre thudded into action at about 1 p.m. Gunners tried to hit the ground just in front of the enemy so that cannon balls would ricochet through an entire formation. Not only did the French have few infantry to aim at, but the soggy ground absorbed many projectiles which might have bounced over the crest to plough into troops on the far side. Bylandt's brigade was more visible than most and suffered accordingly, but overall the bombardment was disappointing for the French.

So too was the news that troops seen on the French right, at first believed to be Grouchy's, and therefore French, were in fact Prussian. Napoleon sent two cavalry divisions and part of Lobau's corps to keep them off, and remarked that although the odds had shifted they were still in his favour. Then, at about 1.30 p.m., he ordered Ney to unleash d'Erlon's infantry. The centre pair of d'Erlon's four divisions, under Donzelot and Marcognet, advanced in thick columns. Only two cavalry brigades went forward with the corps, one on its extreme left and the other down the line of the Brussels road. The lack of a cavalry threat enabled Wellington's infantry to await the attack in line, and his gunners did frightful damage to the French columns as they moved up. The garrison of La Haie Sainte and the 95th on the other side of the road raked Quiot's division with rifle fire, although when the Prince of Orange sent a battalion down the slope to reinforce the riflemen it was destroyed by French cavalry hovering on the left flank of the attack.

Despite the ghastly effect of artillery fire – muskets, packs and limbs were thrown into the air by its impact – the French columns reached the hedge beside the Ohain road. Their evident bravery, the moral effect of their advance, the growling of their drums and yells of '*Vive l'Empereur!*' all contributed to shake the defence. Bylandt's men, sorely tried by the artillery fire, slipped back, and Sir Thomas Picton, whose division awaited the assault on the far side of the road, was shot through the head.

Lord Uxbridge chose this moment to launch two brigades of heavy cavalry, husbanded on the reverse slope for just such an eventuality. Somerset's Household Brigade charged west of the road, driving off French cavalry and cutting down many of Quiot's men. Corporal Shaw of the Life Guards may have killed as many as nine Frenchmen before he died: he had been at the gin that morning and was fighting drunk. East of the road the Union Brigade – English, Scots and Irish regiments –

smashed squarely into Donzelot and Marcognet, as Major George de Lacy Evans testified. 'By the sudden appearance and closing of our cavalry upon them (added to their previous suffering from musketry and grape),' he wrote, 'they became quite paralysed and incapable of resistance, except occasionally, individually, a little.'

The British charge broke both divisions and took two eagles, and had the horsemen rallied at once all would have been well. But although the brigade commander, Sir William Ponsonby, and most of his officers knew what would happen if the charge carried on there was no way of stopping the men. As Evans lamely explained: 'Finding that we were not successful in stopping the troops we were forced to continue on with them in order to continue our exclamations to halt.' The cavalry hurrooshed on into the great French battery, cutting down gunners and artillery drivers: an officer recalled that the latter were 'mere boys', sabred as they sat on their horses and weeping helplessly. The inevitable counter-attack by French lancers and cuirassiers herded the survivors back up the slope: of the 2500 British horsemen who had charged at least 1000 were killed or taken.

D'Erlon's counter-attack was not a total failure because his right-hand division, Durutte's, took the farm of Papelotte. The British cavalry brigades of Vivian and Vandeleur helped to extract the survivors of the charge and prevented Durutte from exploiting his success. Wellington, meanwhile, made some adjustments to his centre. He was only just in time, because Ney sent some of d'Erlon's surviving battalions against La Haie Sainte – the attack was beaten off, but the defenders' rifle ammunition was running very low – and then followed them with Milhaud's cuirassiers who spurred up the slope at about 4 p.m. in the first of the series of cavalry charges which characterized this phase of the battle.

Allied Tactics

Infantry was trained to receive cavalry in a square whose formation was a matter of a commander's judgement and his soldiers' skill. By forming too early, a battalion presented artillery with an attractive target, for a cunning cavalry leader would alternate charges with the fire of horse artillery. By forming too late it invited a mêlée in which an empty musket was rarely a match for a sabre. There were many ways of forming squares; oblongs, whose extended sides gave a better volume of fire, were widely used.

The principles were always the same. Fire was carefully controlled, with half-company volleys crashing out at targets within 50 yards (46 metres). Major Eeles of the 95th saw the effect of volleys from his company

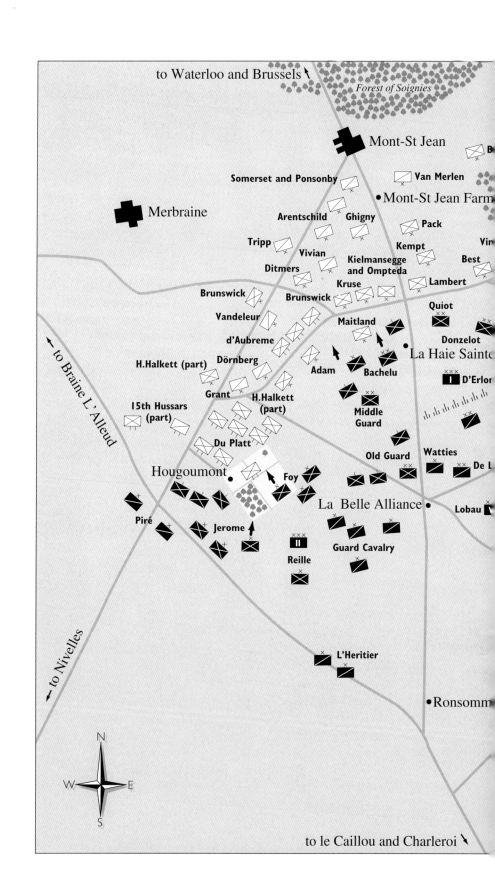

to Waterloo and Brussels ↖

Forest of Soignies

Mont-St Jean

B

Van Merlen

• Mont-St Jean Farm

Somerset and Ponsonby

Merbraine

Arentschild   Ghigny   Pack

Tripp   Kempt   Vin

Vivian   Kielmansegge   Best

Ditmers   and Ompteda

Kruse   Lambert

Brunswick   Brunswick

Quiot

Vandeleur   Maitland   Donzelot

d'Aubreme   La Haie Sainte

H.Halkett (part)   Dörnberg   Adam   Bachelu   D'Erlon

Grant   H.Halkett   Middle   Guard

15th Hussars   (part)   Guard

(part)

Du Platt   Old Guard   Watties   De L

Hougoumont   Foy   La Belle Alliance   Lobau

Piré   Jerome   Guard Cavalry

Reille

L'Heritier

• Ronsomm

to Braine L'Alleud ↑

to Nivelles ↙

N
W   E
S

to le Caillou and Charleroi ↘

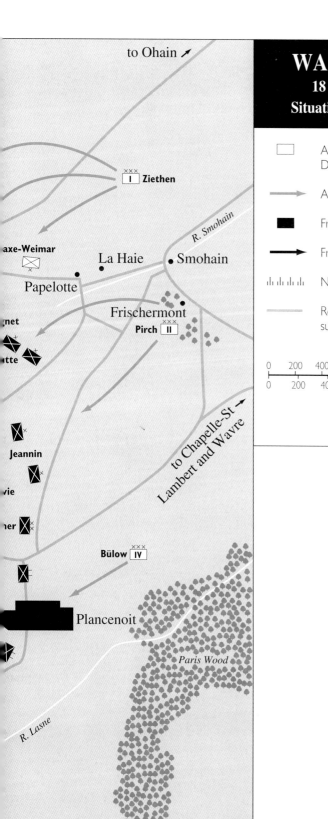

to Ohain

WATERLOO
18 June 1815:
Situation at 7.30 p.m.

Allied troops (British/
Dutch-Belgian/Prussian)

Allied troops movements

French troops

French troop movements

Napoleon's Great Battery

Roads with metalled
surface, 1815

0   200   400   600   800 Yds
0   200   400   600   800 Metres

I Ziethen

axe-Weimar

La Haie

Smohain

R. Smohain

Papelotte

Frischermont

net

Pirch II

tte

to Chapelle-St
Lambert and Wavre

Jeannin

vie

ner

Bülow IV

Plancenoit

Paris Wood

R. Lasne

and a square of the 71st on a body of French cuirassiers. 'I certainly believe that half the enemy were at the instant on the ground,' he remembered, 'some few men and horses were killed, more wounded, but by far the greater part were thrown down over the dying and wounded.' Private Wheeler thought that his comrades did rather better: they fired a volley at nearly a hundred cuirassiers and when the smoke cleared they could see only one, making off on foot.

At all costs men had to face outwards, front rank kneeling with muskets braced against the ground. Avoiding incoming roundshot, which bounded along with deceptive slowness, was discouraged. Wellington's battalions were fortunate that Ney did not combine cavalry and artillery more carefully, but standing firm in square was one of their greatest trials that day. If a square was under fire with its men already shaken, as many were, officers and sergeants had to strain every nerve to keep it together. Captain Cavalié Mercer of the Royal Horse Artillery watched the Brunswick squares near his own battery. 'The Brunswickers were falling fast,' he recorded in his journal, 'the shot every moment making great gaps in their squares, which the officers and sergeants were actively employed in filling up by pushing men together and sometimes thumping men ere they could make them move.'

When ammunition ran short, individual horsemen might approach unscathed, and many combatants remembered a very personal battle. Moustachioed cuirassiers, grimacing in impotent fury, induced one officer to get his men to scowl back. 'Now, men,' he ordered, 'make faces!' Mercer was narrowly missed by a *tirailleur* 'so I shook my finger at him, and called him *coquin* etc. The rogue grinned as he reloaded, and again took aim.' The shot missed Mercer but killed one of his drivers. It was hard not to admire French bravery. 'By God,' muttered an officer, 'those fellows deserve Bonaparte: they fight so nobly for him.' The defenders of Hougoumont respected their assailants' bravery but gave them no quarter: the only survivor of Legros' assault group was a drummer boy.

Roundshot, grape and musketry caused a variety of wounds. One of Wheeler's comrades was 'knocked to atoms' by a roundshot, and Driver Crammond of Mercer's troop lost 'the whole head except barely the visage, which still remained attached to the torn and bloody neck'. Limbs were shot off or left dangling by a thread, abdominal wounds grew progressively more painful, and head shots produced a variety of effects from sudden death through snuffling mimicry of sleep to shot-rabbit jerks. Some wounded were carried back to reeking field-hospitals behind the crest, but many had to remain in the squares: Ensign Gronow of the 1st Guards thought that the inside of his square, with its piles of

wounded, was 'a perfect hospital, being full of dead, dying and mutilated soldiers'.

There was gallows humour at death's door. An ensign, bearing his
colour inside a square, was splashed by the brains of a soldier and
drawled 'how extremely disgusting' in his best Pall Mall voice. A doctor
carrying an umbrella to ward off a sudden shower 'lounged up' to
Mercer's guns during a lull in firing, and when 'the heavy answers' began
to arrive made off at once. One shot passed just over his head, so he
dropped to his hands and knees and, umbrella still erect, 'away he scrambled like a great baboon … whilst our fellows made the field resound
with shouts and laughter.'

The attack and defence of colours had a logic of its own. Some bore
scars of previous campaigns and others, like that carried by Lieutenant
Robert Belcher of the 32nd, were brand new. In either case they were natural targets. When d'Erlon's men attacked Picton's division, a French
officer, who had just extricated himself from beneath his dead horse,
grabbed the staff of Belcher's colour. Belcher retained the colour itself,
and 'the Covering Colour Sergeant, named Switzer, thrust his pike into
his breast, and right rank and file of the division, named Lacy, fired into
him.' Colours were passed amongst the subalterns as their bearers were
hit, sergeants carried them if all junior officers were down, and no one
flinched from the deadly honour of bearing them. Lieutenant Edward
Macready's 30th Regiment was so weakened that it could no longer guarantee to protect its colours, which were marched off the field. 'I know I
never in my life felt such joy,' he wrote, 'or looked on danger with so
light a heart, as when I saw our dear old rags in safety.'

The French Response

Ney's horsemen were still eddying around the squares when the Prussians took Plancenoit. It was retaken, lost, and retaken again as first
Lobau and then the Imperial Guard tried to bolster up the sagging flank.
Napoleon eventually had the situation well enough under control to pull
the Guard back into reserve, but he was still dealing only with Bülow's
corps. Of the other Prussian troops, Pirch was close behind, Ziethen was
marching on Mont-St Jean by the Ohain road, and Thielmann was holding off Grouchy. Gneisenau knew that the fate of the Allied campaign
hung in the balance, and turned down an appeal for help from Thielmann. 'It doesn't matter if he is crushed,' he snapped, 'providing that we
gain the victory here.'

The Allies came close to losing when Ney threw everything into a last
attack at 6 p.m. It was far better co-ordinated than his previous efforts.

La Haie Sainte was taken after its defenders ran out of ammunition: Baring and forty-two of his men escaped. The Prince of Orange ordered Baron Ompteda to counter-attack with his KGL brigade. Ompteda knew the task was impossible, but the prince pressed the point and the baron had to obey. Both Ompteda's nephews were serving with him: he asked a brother officer to try to save them, and then went for the enemy with such courage that French officers vainly tried to prevent their men from killing him. He was shot dead at close range and his brigade was cut to pieces. A French battery unlimbered nearby and subjected Major-General Sir John Lambert's brigade of the British 6th Division, east of the Brussels road, to a fire which left the 27th 'lying dead in square'. Colin Halkett warned Wellington that two-thirds of his men were down and begged for his brigade to be relieved. The duke's reply caught the dour mood of the moment: 'What he asks is impossible: he and I, and every Englishman on the field, must die on the spot which we now occupy.'

The duke knew that this was the crisis of the day. Napoleon, unable to feel the battle's pulse, did not. When Ney asked for more troops the emperor snapped: 'Some more troops! Where do you expect me to get them from? Do you want me to make them?' Ney might have pointed out that part of the Guard was still fresh, and David Chandler has argued that if they had been committed at this moment 'the battle would almost certainly have been won'.

Wellington's line held by the thinnest of margins. The Prince of Orange, his personal courage of higher order than his tactical judgement, was wounded on the spot where the Lion Monument now stands, and Sir Hussey Vivian, bringing his cavalry brigade across from the eastern flank, crossed 'ground that was actually covered with dead and dying, cannon shots and shells flying thicker than I ever heard musketry before, and our troops – some of them – giving way.' Somehow the tired Allied battalions stood their ground and as the attackers slid back gunners emerged from squares in which they had taken refuge to pound them. Müffling led up the first units of Ziethen's Prussian corps, and the worst was over.

The End of the Battle

Napoleon played his last card too late. At about 7 p.m. he led part of his Guard forward in person before handing it over to Ney. As the Guard, probably eleven battalions strong, began its advance there was an attempt to raise morale in the rest of the army by spreading the word that the troops coming up on the right were French rather than Prussian. We cannot be sure of the details of the Guard's attack, but it seems likely that the column began its advance west of the road in a single mass perhaps 60 yards (55 metres) broad and 500 yards (457 metres) deep, grim-faced veterans stepping out under colours whose battle honours embodied a decade of imperial glory. The column detached two battalions to face Hougoumont and then inclined westwards, away from the road and up the trampled slope, splitting into three smaller columns, two of grenadiers and one of *chasseurs*, as it did so.

Two grenadier battalions, with some support from d'Erlon's men, reached Wellington's line close to the Brussels road, forcing back Halkett's exhausted brigade before being repulsed by Chassé's Dutch-Belgians. The main body of grenadiers, marching into a gale of shot, approached the Ohain road where the guardsmen of Maitland's brigade were sheltering behind the high banks. The duke was right behind them and called out 'Now, Maitland! Now is your time,' before ordering: 'Up Guards! Make ready! Fire!' Maitland's line overlapped the head of the column, and the French grenadiers could make no response to the half-company volleys that crashed out at point-blank range. It was an unequal contest, and the grenadiers were driven back down the slope. The *chasseurs* hit Adam's brigade, partly concealed by corn. Colonel John Colborne swung the 52nd, an experienced Peninsular War battalion, out at right angles to the line and fired into the *chasseurs*' left flank while the remainder of the brigade took on the head of the column. The result was the same, and the *chasseurs* too fell back.

This shocking repulse snapped French morale. There were cries of '*Trahison*' and '*Sauve qui peut*', and most of the army dissolved into rout. Several Guards battalions retained cohesion, checking the pursuit and enabling Napoleon to leave the field. Wellington doffed his hat and motioned his whole army forward, anxious that the French should not be given a chance to rally. He met Blücher at La Belle Alliance at about 9.30 p.m. They embraced on horseback and the old Prussian, who had been treating himself with gin and rhubarb, apologized: 'I stink a bit.' When he tried to describe the day, somehow only French would do: '*Quelle affaire.*'

Waterloo might not have been decisive in itself. On the French side, Napoleon lost 25 000 men in the battle and another 8000 afterwards, while Grouchy lost 2600 at Wavre. The Allies were scarcely better off: Wellington suffered 15 000 casualties and Blücher 7000 at Waterloo, and another 2500 Prussians were killed or wounded at Wavre. The Allies, with fresh armies on their way, could sustain these losses while the French could not, and defeat had broken Napoleon's spell. An armistice was signed on 3 July and the Allies entered Paris four days later. This time the quality of their mercy was decidedly strained. Napoleon was packed off to the rocky island of St Helena in the South Atlantic, and stayed there until he died six years later.

A View of the Field

The field of Waterloo remains evocative although it is often extremely crowded, and has been affected by 'commemoration' and other works. The Lion Monument, erected in 1823–6 on the spot where the Prince of Orange was wounded, consumed 42 000 cubic yards (32 000 cubic metres) of earth and altered the topography of the centre of the battle-field. An autoroute, mercifully in a cutting, separates Braine L'Alleud from the rest of the field, and the old Brussels road is so busy as to make walking along it scarcely less hazardous today than on 18 June 1815. The proprietors of cafés and souvenir shops have not missed a trick, and a visitor might be forgiven, looking at their wares, for imagining that Napoleon had been victorious.

Quatre-Bras
It is best to approach the battlefield as Napoleon did, from the south along the Brussels road, and the visitor who can afford the time should start at Quatre-Bras, now just on the Belgian side of the Franco-Belgian border. A large monument on the road's eastern edge south of the junc-tion marks the spot where the Duke of Brunswick was killed. The French attacked from the south and took Gemioncourt Farm, a block of build-ings on the modern border, early in the battle and then advanced up the slope. Their approach was obstructed by Bossu Wood, which stood well to the west of the road but has now disappeared, and by Materne Lake, east of the road, which is now somewhat larger than in 1815.

Looking east from the Brunswick monument the visitor gains a good impression of the ground held by Picton's men on the afternoon of 16 June 1815, although we must remember that there was standing corn which offered cover until it was trampled down. Halkett's brigade went into action on the other side of the road, and was mauled by Keller-mann's cuirassiers charging straight up its axis. The 69th Regiment was caught in line and broken perhaps 150 yards (137 metres) north-west of the monument.

Genappe
The Brussels road, now the N5, bypasses Genappe but in 1815 it ran right through the little town. Napoleon, hotly pursued after Waterloo,

abandoned his coach in the Place de l'Empereur. The old inn, Au Roi d'Espagne, is now a house bearing the number 58. On 16 June Wellington lunched there, probably lightly because he was an abstemious man. The French commanders Reille and Jerome dined at the inn the following day, and late on the 18th it became Blücher's headquarters. General Duhesme, mortally wounded while commanding the Young Guard at Waterloo, died there and is buried in the nearby churchyard of St Martin des Ways.

Museums and Monuments
The farmhouse of Le Caillou, where Napoleon spent the night before the battle, is further towards Brussels. It is now a museum of Napoleonic memorabilia, and a museum of the Dutch-Belgian contribution to the battle stands nearby. Still further north is the Wounded Eagle monument, which marks the spot where the last squares of the Old Guard held the Allies so the emperor could get away. On the other side of the road, a column commemorates the French writer, Victor Hugo. Hugo grew up when France was trying to put the Napoleonic experience into context, and described the emperor as the 'mighty somnambulist of a vanished dream'. Although Hugo did not always write accurately of Waterloo, his own thoughts, and those of so many Frenchmen of his generation, were haunted by the place.

Plancenoit, Papelotte and La Haie Sainte
La Belle Alliance, where Wellington and Blücher met after the battle, is now a restaurant. A short way down the Plancenoit road, which breaks eastwards off the N5, is a spot marked as L'Observatoire de Napoleon. The emperor and his staff used this as a forward command post at various stages of the battle and it still offers an admirable view of Wellington's left centre and left. The Lion Monument is clearly visible and to its right, by a cluster of trees, the Ohain road crosses the Brussels road. The Ohain road runs along the ridge in the middle distance – traffic usually obligingly materializes to mark its route. Well over to the right is the big farm of Papelotte which was taken by the French under Durutte. La Haie is on its right and Smohain even further to the right.

  Plancenoit is a short walk away. It was viciously disputed between French and Prussians and badly damaged in the process. A Gothic monument in the village marks the spot where a battery of Bülow's corps fought, and commemorates the Prussian dead. The Prussians called the battle La Belle Alliance, which is scarcely surprising as they went nowhere near Waterloo itself, which is well behind the battlefield. Mont-St

Jean might have been a better name for the battle, but perhaps Wellington feared that his countrymen would never get their tongues round it, and so Waterloo it was.

The farm of La Haie Sainte, which was held by Major Baring's 2nd Light Battalion KGL until the French took it, stands beside the Brussels road just short of the Ohain crossroads. Visitors must bear in mind that it is a working farm and also beware of the juggernauts barrelling along to Brussels. It is not now entered by the gates on the main road, but by a track leading down the hill from opposite the 1815 Hotel, west of the crossroads. It is easy to see why the spot was so important, standing in front of Wellington's main line like a ravelin on a Vauban fortress. Turning along the Ohain road towards the Lion Monument we pass across the front held by Ompteda's and Kielmansegge's brigades of Charles Alten's 3rd British Division. The road was sunken in 1815 and is scarcely so today (the Lion Monument has seen to that) but we should be cautious in believing Victor Hugo's description of a chasm which swallowed up charging French cuirassiers: Maitland's men, a little ahead of us, were able to use the banks as cover.

The Visitor's Centre below the mound has excellent electronic maps and a film show, although I find the older-style Waterloo Panorama, with its circular painting of the battle at the time of the French cavalry charges, almost as telling. Directly opposite, on the ground floor of the Hôtel du Musée, built by Sergeant-Major Edward Cotton in 1818, is the Waxworks Museum, with life-sized models of the leading participants in the battle.

Studying the Field

Much as I abuse the Lion, his mound, ascended by 226 steps, offers an unrivalled view of the field. Looking east, the Ohain road runs off to Papelotte. Due south the straight line of the Brussels road disappears behind the roofs of La Haie Sainte and goes on to La Belle Alliance over a gentle swell which marks the site of the grand battery. With the ground so wet, gunners would not have wished to haul 12-pdrs or ammunition wagons far from a cobbled surface, and we would have expected to see some guns on both sides of the main road.

Opposite the Waxworks Museum a tiny road leads to the area where Maitland's guardsmen repulsed the French grenadiers and Mercer's troop of horse artillery took on the French cavalry. Mercer did not fire until the head of the column, led on at a steady and deliberate trot by a heavily decorated officer, was 50–60 yards (46–55 metres) away, and his guns were loaded with both roundshot and case. When they fired: 'The effect was terrible. Nearly the whole leading rank fell at once, and the round-shot, penetrating the column, carried confusion throughout its extent.' There is a monument to Mercer himself and another to Lieutenant Augustin Demulder of the 5th Cuirassiers, perhaps one of the victims of that dreadful fire. By turning eastwards just beyond the Mercer monument, the visitor can take a track which runs all the way to La Belle Alliance and the Brussels road.

The Farm of Hougoumont
Hougoumont, now known as Goumont, is best approached along the Ohain and Brussels–Nivelles road. A long metalled track leads to the farm, which is a working concern like La Haie Sainte. It was badly damaged in the fighting and has been altered since, but it is hard to grasp its importance without a visit. In 1815 its buildings formed a rectangular enclosure pierced by several entrances, with a great barn on the western side, other domestic and farm buildings and a chapel. A formal walled garden stood at its eastern end, with an orchard beyond that. A track bordered by a stout hedge ran parallel with the southern edge of the garden wall, and a substantial wood stretched off to the south.

The northern section of Hougoumont has been substantially altered, but the southern gate and the garden wall defended by the Guards light companies look the same today as in contemporary illustrations, and many loopholes are intact. The Guards had improvised a firestep which enabled them to fire over the top of the wall as well as through it, and we can sense the fury of Jerome's men when faced with what was, to unsupported infantry, an impenetrable obstacle. The tiny chapel can usually be visited, and there are several memorials on and around it. The graves of Captain John Lucie Blackman of the Coldstream, killed in battle, and Sergeant-Major Edward Cotton, who wrote *A Voice from Waterloo*, made a good living as a guide to the battlefield, and died in 1849, are on the southern edge of the old orchard.

Wellington's Positions
To reach Wellington's left centre we retrace our steps, taking the Ohain road to its junction with the Brussels road where there are monuments to the young Colonel Sir Alexander Gordon of Wellington's staff and the Dutch-Belgian dead. Wellington spent much of the battle here, near an elm tree on the south-western edge of the junction. The original tree has long since disappeared but it has a more recent replacement. A tramway built along the eastern edge of the main road altered the area's complexion and filled the sandpit held by the 95th: the base of

Gordon's monument shows where the ground level used to be.

Bylandt's brigade stood immediately east of the crossroads within view of the grand battery, and Lambert's men, slightly further back, were hard hit once Ney had remembered to bring guns up. The Ohain road was sunken here as it was on the other side of the junction, and was bordered by hedges so stout that British gunners had hacked holes in them. The gallant Sir Thomas Picton had warned the duke that his nerves were not up to the strain of another campaign. 'I must give up,' he begged. 'I am grown so nervous that when there is any service to be done it works upon my mind so that it is impossible for me to sleep at nights.' But he turned

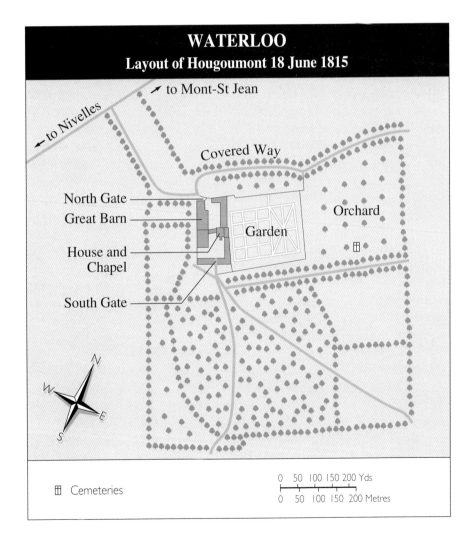

WATERLOO
Layout of Hougoumont 18 June 1815

to Mont-St Jean

to Nivelles

Covered Way

North Gate
Great Barn
House and Chapel
South Gate

Orchard

Garden

⊞ Cemeteries

0 50 100 150 200 Yds

0 50 100 150 200 Metres

out to command his division as ordered, and a memorial marks the spot where he fell, in civilian frock coat and top hat. Another monument stands where the dead of the 27th marked the position of its square.

The Town of Waterloo

Waterloo itself is well off the battlefield, further along the N5. The former Hôtel Boderglieu, just across the main road from St Joseph's church, is now the Wellington Museum, containing helpful maps of the battle and an interesting assortment of memorabilia including the wooden leg worn by the Marquess of Anglesey, as Lord Uxbridge became. Wellington ate supper at the hotel after the battle, looking sadly at the door to see if any of his young sparks would come in to fill those empty places at the table. Some historians suggest that Colonel Gordon died in the duke's bed while Wellington slept on a pallet on the floor, although the museum has beds for both officers. When woken and told that Gordon had died, this iron man wept, tears furrowing the grime on his cheeks. 'Well, thank God, I don't know what it is to lose a battle,' he said in a broken voice, 'but certainly nothing can be more painful than to win one with the loss of so many of one's friends.'

CHAPTER 7

Mons and Le Cateau
1914

Background

On 23 August 1914 fighting spread westwards along the Mons–Condé Canal like flame through brushwood. German columns, flowing down through Belgium towards France in a grey torrent, found the British Expeditionary Force directly in their path. The battle of Mons, the first major engagement of the First World War, was a day of shock and confusion, characterized by the unequal contest between Germans and British, the former advancing in formations which might not have astonished Wellington, the latter delivering firepower which the deftest archer would have envied. Corporal John Lucy of the Royal Irish Rifles told how, when the Germans appeared:

A great roar of musketry rent the air … The satisfactory sharp blasts of the directing whistles showed that our machinery of defence was working like the drill-book, and that the recent shelling had caused no disorganization … For us the battle took the form of well-ordered rapid rifle-fire at close range as the field-grey human targets appeared, or were struck down … after the first shock of seeing men slowly and helplessly falling down as they were hit [it] gave us a great sense of power and pleasure. It was all so easy.

Waterloo ushered in a long peace in Europe. In France, neither the Bourbons nor the July monarchy which replaced them in 1830 could compete with Bonapartist mythology or do much for the thousands who flooded into the towns from

Harry Easton joined the 21st Lancers
in 1906, but transferred to the 9th to
go to South Africa, where this picture
was taken, the following year. He went
onto the reserve after spending seven
years with the colours, and was a
Berkshire policeman when mobilized
in August 1914. Captured during the
charge near Audregnies on 24 August,
Easton (seated) spent part of his cap-
tivity working on a farm in Germany.
British cavalry carried the same rifle
as the infantry, this Short Magazine
Lee Enfield. Adopted in 1902, it
weighed just over 8lb (18kg) and one
expert called it 'one of the most efficient rifles ever to be put into the
hands of a fighting soldier.'

a saturated countryside, providing Victor Hugo with raw material for *Les Misérables*. After a foray into republicanism, France found herself an empire once more with Napoleon III, the great man's nephew, on her throne. Although he claimed that 'the empire is peace', Napoleon pursued foreign policy intended to give his countrymen a taste of the glory that had faded with their defeat at Waterloo. The French army played a major role in the Crimean War in 1854–6, invaded Austrian-occupied northern Italy in 1859, and even sent an expedition to Mexico in 1862–6. Those who knew it well realized that its victories owed much to a tactical style which would have suited an old bruiser like Marshal Ney, and that the reform needed to fit it for European war would take more courage than the government possessed.

The Franco-Prussian War
At the beginning of the nineteenth century, Germany was divided into a score of states linked largely by language. Even those who sought a united Germany were divided between the big solution, with Austria in, or the small, with Austria out. Otto von Bismarck, Minister-President of Prussia, the dominant north German state, had to cope with Liberal opposition in parliament and, at the same time, advance towards his goal of German unification. He grabbed Schleswig and Holstein from the Danes in 1864–5, isolated Austria, enabling the reformed Prussian army to show its mettle and eliminating Austria from German affairs (1866), and then deluded the government of Napoleon III into declaring war in the summer of 1870.

The Franco-Prussian conflict of 1870–1 is the military watershed between 1815 and 1914. It was the first war in which the infantry on both sides carried breech-loading rifles, their deadliness awesomely demonstrated when the Prussian Guard lost over 8000 men while attacking St-Privat on 18 August 1870. Gunners still used direct fire, but shells had replaced roundshot and the Germans had excellent breech-loading Krupp guns. The French even had a machine-gun, the Mitrailleuse, but this had been kept a secret from friends as well as enemies and was largely ineffective. Cavalry had a dangerous and disappointing time. For every successful charge like von Bredow's death-ride (16 August 1870), there were a dozen others which ended in heaps of dead men and kicking horses.

Some of the most important developments were less spectacular. The telegraph enabled Helmuth von Moltke, the German commander-in-chief, to maintain contact with his armies as they sprawled across France. Contemporaries focused on the first phase of the war, marked by the destruction of the imperial armies in August–October 1870, to produce the paradigm of lightning war. Yet it was not lightning war at all. With her regulars dead or captured and her capital besieged, France fought on, conjuring up the Armies of National Defence to wage a war marked by deepening bitterness.

The war laid the foundations of future conflict. For France, the loss of the provinces of Alsace and Lorraine was a profound national humiliation, while Germany found in victory and the proclamation of William I of Prussia as German emperor the impulsion towards militarism. For the next forty years European diplomacy was played out with an arms race as its backcloth. The great powers fine-tuned arrangements for mobilization, bought modern arms and equipment and encouraged young men to anticipate a struggle of national survival from which only the worthless would hang back.

French Planning

The first French plans were defensive, and fortifications marked the new Franco-German border. Although the alliance between army and nation which had followed the Franco-Prussian War faltered with the Dreyfus affair, planners grew confident enough to adopt bolder schemes. In 1913 Plan XVII decreed: 'Whatever the circumstances, it is the Commander-in-Chief's intention to advance with all forces united to attack the German armies.' The edge of the sword was tempered by doctrine which knew no law save that of the offensive, and was applied by determined soldiers in long blue overcoats and red trousers. Fire support came from the legendary *soixante-quinze*, the 75mm quick-firing gun which was 'Father, Son and Holy Ghost' to French tacticians. One realist remarked that it would have been nice to have seen it surrounded by a few saints of heavier metal.

The Schlieffen Plan

The Germans could not afford to be so single-minded, for they had dangerous neighbours to east and west. In 1894 France and Russia concluded an entente, convincing Count Alfred von Schlieffen, German chief of the general staff from 1891–1906, that Germany would fight her next war on two fronts. He believed that he could win only 'ordinary victories' over the Russians, who would retreat into the fastnesses of their empire, and that the highest expression of military art was a battle of encirclement, like that won by Hannibal against the Romans at Cannae in 216 BC. Logic urged him to deal with France first, but he could not do so by direct attack because of those fortresses along the frontier.

Schlieffen's solution was the plan which bears his name, although its final version owed much to his successor, the younger Moltke, nephew of the architect of victory in 1870–1. Three armies, 1st, 2nd and 3rd, would sweep into northern France, passing through Belgian territory to do so. The 4th Army would turn in north of Sedan, while the 5th, 6th and 7th would defend Alsace-Lorraine. Schlieffen emphasized that the 1st Army must swing wide, passing west of Paris before jabbing in to fight a battle of encirclement in Champagne. Schlieffen always had reservations about the scheme, doubting whether even the German armies were strong enough for it. Moltke had abandoned Schlieffen's notion of violating Dutch as well as Belgian neutrality, so the armies of his right wing would have to pass through the corridor between the 'Maastricht appendix' of Dutch territory and the hilly Ardennes, dealing with the mighty fortress of Liège.

Britain's Position
Britain, concerned with the preservation of her empire and the maintenance of maritime power, was a latecomer to the Continental ball. In 1870 her sympathies had largely been with the Prussians, but as the war went on they swung towards the French. Nevertheless, old habits and colonial rivalries contributed to Anglo-French coolness, while there were sympathetic ties with Germany. William II was Queen Victoria's grandson and a field marshal in the British army, and many British regiments had fraternal relations with their German counterparts.

These British regiments had been having a frustrating time. In the South African War of 1899–1902 they had found it hard to defeat the tiny armies of the Boer republics and the mobile commandos which waged a long guerrilla struggle. The war showed that military reform was indispensable, and the most important work was carried out under the aegis of R.B. Haldane, secretary of state for war in the Liberal government which took office in late 1905. It was becoming clear that Britain's main rival was not France but Germany, and that Britain was more likely to become involved in a European war than to fight Russia on the north-west frontier of India. In 1904 Britain and France concluded the Entente Cordiale and in 1906 Haldane authorized the newly created general staff to open 'conversations' with the French on the understanding that they were not politically binding.

If the army was to operate on the Continent alongside a major ally it would be more than 'a bullet fired by the navy' and in so doing would alter the balance of British defence policy. Major-General Henry Wilson, who became director of military operations in 1910, was an ardent francophile, committed to the recovery of France's lost provinces. When discussing the size of the British contingent he asked General Ferdinand Foch what the smallest useful force would be. 'One single private soldier,' replied Foch, 'and we would take good care that he was killed.'

Haldane's reforms produced a regular expeditionary force of one cavalry and six infantry divisions, brought up to strength on mobilization by ex-regulars and members of the part-time Special Reserve. Most non-regular forces were combined into the Territorial Force of fourteen infantry divisions and fourteen brigades of yeomanry cavalry. It was intended to defend Britain while the expeditionary force departed overseas, but on outbreak of war many Territorials volunteered for foreign service and the first Territorial battalion was in action in October 1914.

Some saw the Territorial Force as little more than a device for avoiding conscription. The National Service League argued that Britain could not fight a great power while retaining a system of recruitment which Wellington would have recognized. The army's structure had certainly changed. The Cardwell reforms of the early 1880s had combined pairs of numbered regiments into the 'linked battalion' system of county regiments. John Colborne's 52nd, for instance, joined the 43rd, its Peninsular War comrade-in-arms, to form the Oxfordshire and Buckinghamshire Light Infantry. By 1914 this had two regular battalions, a Special Reserve Battalion and two Territorial battalions. In the pages that follow I adopt the practice of the British official history of the First World War by styling 1st Battalion The Oxfordshire and Buckinghamshire Light Infantry as 1/Oxfordshire and Buckinghamshire, and do the same for other regiments.

Most recruits were unemployed, and only half even claimed to have a trade. There were more 'town casuals' than countrymen, and areas such as Ireland, Scotland, London and Birmingham supplied soldiers to many regiments which claimed English county connections. One man spoke for many when he said that 'unemployment and the need for food' had driven him to enlist. There were scores of other reasons. Fred Milton left his farm to see the bright lights of Newton Abbot and finished up in the Devons. William Nicholson was attracted by family tradition – a grandfather had charged at Balaclava – and the glamour of full dress. R.G. Garrod, a young clerk, saw 'a gorgeous figure in blue with yellow braid and clinking spurs and said to myself "That's for me" ...' John Lucy and his brother went 'a bit wild' when their mother died. Bored with small-town life they joined the Royal Irish Rifles.

Although officers no longer bought commissions, it was hard to survive without a private income. Most went from public school to Sandhurst for the infantry and cavalry, or to Woolwich for gunners and

Ca'

Boulogne •

R. S

Main British port of entry

Le Havre

Rouen **By rai**

R. Seine

FRANCE

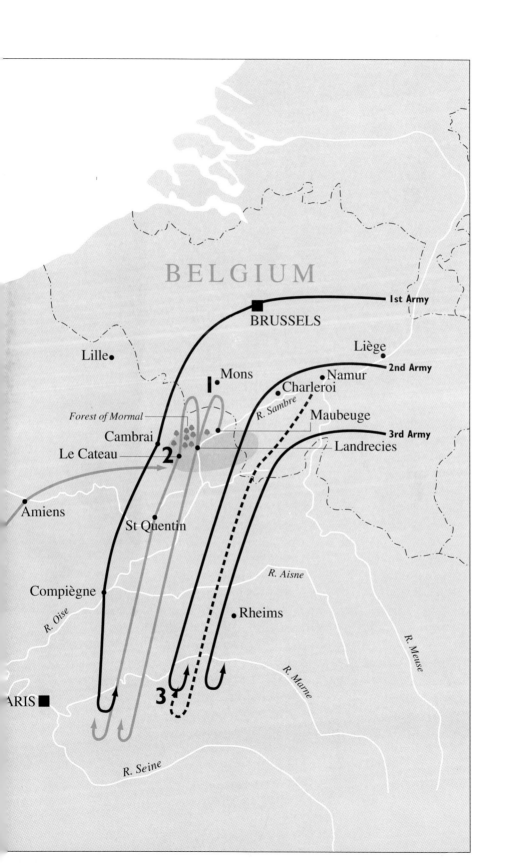

BELGIUM

1st Army

BRUSSELS

Liège

Lille

Mons

Namur

2nd Army

Charleroi

Forest of Mormal

R. Sambre

Maubeuge

Cambrai

Le Cateau

3rd Army

Landrecies

Amiens

St Quentin

Compiègne

R. Aisne

Rheims

R. Oise

R. Meuse

R. Marne

PARIS

R. Seine

Field Marshal Sir John French, seen disembarking from HMS Sentinel at Boulogne on 14 August 1914 *(above)* had a history of poor relations with General Sir Horace Smith-Dorrien *(right)*. Smith-Dorrien's decision to fight at Le Cateau on 26 August proved crucial.

sappers. Promotion was slow, and although efforts to improve training lengthened the working day there was plenty of time for sport. Relations between officers and men were formal and sometimes remote, but there were often bonds of mutual regard linking them. Company Sergeant-Major Ernest Shephard described his company commander as 'a real sample of the Regular "Officer and Gentleman" ... Absolutely fearless and first and last thought for his men.'

It was the assassination in Sarajevo, on 28 June 1914, of the Arch-duke Franz Ferdinand, heir to the throne of Austria-Hungary, that struck the spark which blew the old world apart. The Austrians blamed the Serbs for the outrage and demanded humiliating concessions. The Serbs appealed to their Slav brothers in Russia, and on 1 August Russian mobilization provoked a German declaration of war. France would not guarantee to remain neutral, and reports of fictitious French border violations were used to justify the German declaration of war on France on 3 August. Britain might have held aloof, but on 4 August the Cabinet was told that the Germans had violated the Belgian neutrality guaranteed by Britain, and duly declared war on Germany.

Campaign and Battles

A Council of War met at 10 Downing Street on 5 August and agreed to implement the existing plan for concentration around Le Cateau and

Maubeuge on the left of the French 5th Army. Only the cavalry division and four infantry divisions would be sent out at first, under the command of Field Marshal Sir John French, a cavalry officer who had made his reputation in South Africa. They would form two corps: 1 Corps (1st and 2nd Divisions) under Sir Douglas Haig, a quiet Lowland Scot who had once served as French's brigade-major; and 2 Corps (3rd and 5th Divisions) under Sir James Grierson, a more affable character who quipped that the medals on his well-filled chest commemorated many a battle with knife and fork.

French was given his orders by the newly-appointed secretary of state for war, Field Marshal Lord Kitchener. They did not get on: French was a mercurial man with an eye for the ladies, while Kitchener was dour and monkish. French was told to 'coincide most sympathetically with the plans and wishes of our ally' but was warned not to expose his force unduly and reminded that 'you will in no sense come under the orders of any Allied general'. Sir John visited Paris on 15 August and went on to see the French commander-in-chief, General Joseph Joffre, the following day. Joffre assured him that all was going well, and that the British Expeditionary Force (BEF) would at the worst be facing two German corps and a cavalry division.

The Arrival of the BEF
Most of the BEF landed at Le Havre, Rouen and Boulogne between 12 and 17 August and went on to its concentration area by train. British soldiers were surprised by the warmth of the French welcome. A guardsman did his best for Anglo-French relations by yelling '*Vive l'Empereur*', and Sergeant William Edgington of the Royal Horse Artillery (RHA) recorded 'enthusiastic reception by French population who shower us with flowers (and kisses) …' Private Frank Richards of the Royal Welch Fusiliers, like many of his comrades a recalled reservist, was pleased to discover that many girls proved themselves 'true daughters of France'. His mates left cap-badges as souvenirs, along with other mementoes which would not make their presence felt for a few months. One soldier, wandering around Amiens cathedral, told Richards that it would be a fine place to loot.

Sir James Grierson got no further than Amiens. He died of a heart attack on the train and was replaced by Sir Horace Smith-Dorrien, an experienced but irascible infantry officer who had been one of the few survivors of the Zulu victory at Isandalwana. Smith-Dorrien was not French's first choice, and their relationship was not improved when Sir Horace announced that King George V had asked him to keep him informed of the doings of 2 Corps. By this time French's confidence had been jolted by a frosty interview with General Lanrezac, commander of the 5th Army, and by 'silly reports of French reverses'.

On 19 August the Royal Flying Corps mounted its first-ever operational sortie. It saw no Germans, but the next day sighted a huge column moving through Louvain. Liège had held up the Germans, but its forts were smashed by heavy howitzers and the Belgian field army fell back on Antwerp, enabling the Germans to occupy Brussels on 20 August. Even Joffre could not ignore this news. He shifted the weight of his attack to the north and sent one of his cavalry corps on a circuitous march behind the BEF to come up on its left flank.

By the time the BEF set out towards the Belgian mining town of Mons on 21 August the Allied plan had gone badly wrong: the French attack, pressed home with all the dash demanded by theorists, ran bloodily into German machine-guns and howitzers. British soldiers on the long and baking road had no inkling that their allies were being so roughly handled in the opening of what became known as 'the Battle of the Frontiers'. Lieutenant James Pennycuik of the Royal Engineers, riding up from Landrecies, remembered: 'I got quite good at cracking an egg on my saddle and swallowing it raw,' although his fellow sapper, Second Lieutenant Kenneth Godsell, witnessed an unforeseen result of gifts of fruit and wine when 'falling out among the troops became very frequent and men were seen rolling in agony by the roadside'.

Not all the agony was gastronomic. Cobbled roads made for difficult marching, especially for reservists with new boots. Each man's kit, consisting of a loaded pack, webbing equipment, an entrenching tool, ammunition, rifle and bayonet, weighed about 80 lb (36 kg) and bore down on his back. Private Harry Beaumont of the Royal West Kent wrote: 'We all began to feel the effects of the intense heat. Some were more or less in a state of collapse, and had to be supported by their comrades, while others carried their rifles.'

The Battle of Mons
The first British shot of the war was fired on the morning of 22 August when C Squadron 4th Dragoon Guards clashed with German cavalry at Casteau, on the Mons–Brussels road. That day saw the BEF move up with 1 Corps, on its right, north-east of Maubeuge, and 2 Corps, on its left, reaching the line of the Mons–Condé Canal. Sir John French still believed that he was participating in a general advance, but Lieutenant Edward Spears, liaison officer with the 5th Army, knew that Lanrezac's men had been fought to a standstill around Charleroi, and on the night of

the 22nd he visited French at Le Cateau and warned him that Lanrezac was not attacking. When, shortly afterwards, French was asked to fall on the right flank of Germans facing Lanrezac he declined to do so but agreed to hold his ground for twenty-four hours. The scene was set for the battle of Mons.

Sir John French saw his corps commanders early on 23 August at Smith-Dorrien's headquarters at Sars la Bruyère. It seems likely that the commander-in-chief passed on some of his doubts and warned corps commanders to be prepared to advance or retreat. Smith-Dorrien was worried that his corps, 3rd Division to the right and 5th to the left, was stretched across 20 miles (32 km) of difficult country. He was already preparing the canal bridges for demolition and reconnoitring a line south of Mons on to which he could withdraw his right-hand formation, 8th Infantry Brigade, exposed in the Nimy–Obourg bend of the canal. French's main headquarters was in Le Cateau with an advanced element at Bavay, but he planned to be up and about. He had been told that 4th Division was being sent to join him, and converted the infantry assigned to the lines of communication into 19th Infantry Brigade, which he was to visit that day.

The 'close, blind country' around Mons was a mining area, with pit-heads, slag-heaps, rows of miners' cottages fronting on to narrow cobbled streets, and 'mineral railways' taking coal to the main line. Corporal W.H.L. Watson, an Oxford undergraduate who had volunteered to serve as a motor-cycle dispatch rider, had a frustrating time. 'The roads wandered round great slag-heaps,' he wrote, 'lost themselves in little valleys, ran into pits and groups of buildings … Without a map to get from Elouges to Frameries was like asking an American to make his way from Richmond Park to Denmark Hill.'

The canal had been dug when Napoleon was emperor. It was an average of 64 feet (19 metres) wide and 7 feet (2 metres) deep, and was crossed by eighteen road and railway bridges in addition to lock gates which infantry could use. Smith-Dorrien had too few engineers, too little explosive and too little time to destroy them all, but his sappers did what they could, and Kenneth Godsell received an insouciant wave from the driver of a shunting engine which puffed across the bridge at St Ghislain as his men were laying demolition charges.

The troops holding the canal had arrived on the 22nd, too late to do more than scratch 'lying trenches' on and around the towpath, and use furniture to barricade the village streets behind. There was a cement factory at Obourg, and the soldiers of 4/Middlesex, holding the station, improvised defences from sacks of cement. The British had fought in

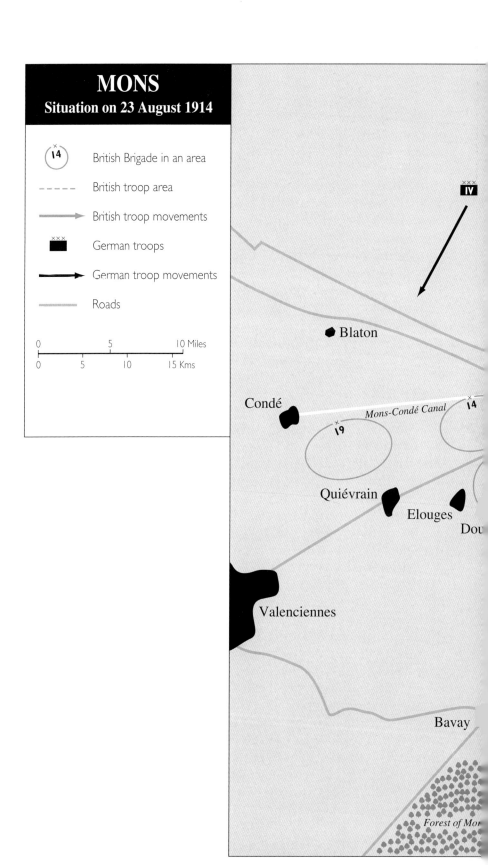

MONS
Situation on 23 August 1914

(14)	British Brigade in an area
- - - - -	British troop area
→	British troop movements
■	German troops
→	German troop movements
━━	Roads

```
0          5          10 Miles
|----------|----------|
0     5        10    15 Kms
```

IV

● Blaton

Condé

Mons-Condé Canal

14

19

Quiévrain

Elouges

Dou

Valenciennes

Bavay

Forest of Mor

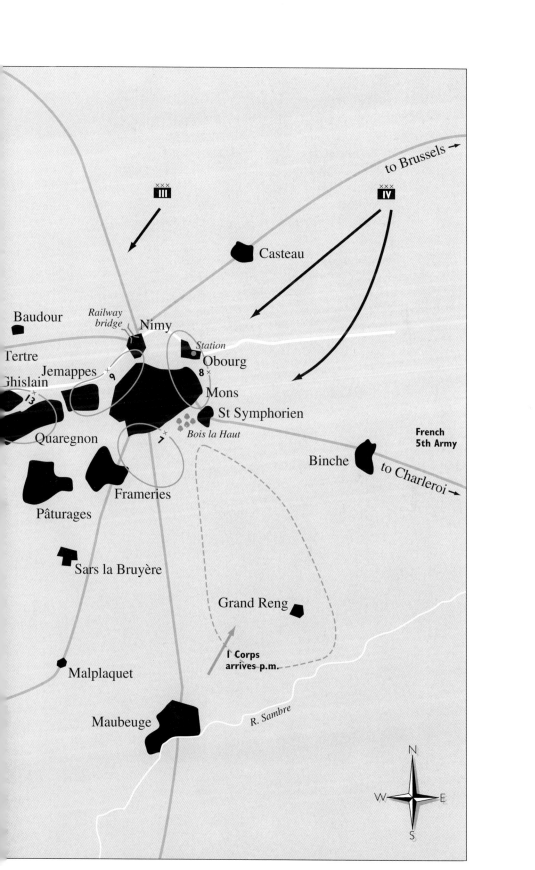

to Brussels →

×××
III

×××
IV

Casteau

Baudour

Railway bridge Nimy

Tertre

Jemappes + 9

Ghislain

+ 13

Quaregnon

Station

Obourg

8 ×

Mons

St Symphorien

Bois la Haut

+ 1

Frameries

Pâturages

French 5th Army

Binche

to Charleroi →

Sars la Bruyère

Grand Reng

I Corps arrives p.m.

Malplaquet

Maubeuge

R. Sambre

N
W   E
S

khaki since the 1880s, and the South African War had reminded them of the importance of fieldcraft and marksmanship. The .303 Lee-Enfield rifle carried by infantry and cavalry alike was sighted up to 2000 yards (1830 metres) and men shot regularly at targets 600 yards (550 metres) away. They were expected to put fifteen shots a minute into the 2-foot (60-cm) circle of a target 300 yards (225 metres) away, and many could do better. Marksmen received proficiency pay which added to the pleasures a man might find foaming in the wet canteen or loitering outside the barrack gate.

Like his Continental counterpart, the British soldier was taught that wars were not won by defence, and Infantry Regulations enjoined him to use his skill in musketry to get to close quarters and take the bayonet to the king's enemies. At the moment of the assault 'the men will cheer, bugles will be sounded and pipes played'. Belief in the offensive had a rationale of its own. Nobody could ignore the advances in killing-power that had come with smokeless powder, the magazine rifle and the machine-gun: there were two belt-fed Vickers-Maxim machine guns in every British battalion. But without 'unconquerable and determined offensive spirit' men would go to ground and firepower would impose a paralysis that would lead to long and exhausting wars.

There was offensive spirit aplenty that Sunday morning of the 23rd. The German soldiers of Colonel-General Alexander von Kluck's 1st Army, marching south-west, had no idea of what lay before them. Kluck

Field-grey replaced the blue uniforms of German infantry for manoeuvres and war, and their spiked helmets had a cloth cover with the regiment's number stencilled on it.

knew that the British were in France, because one of their aircraft had been brought down by ground-fire and news of the cavalry action at Casteau had reached him. However, he thought that the BEF had landed at Ostend, Boulogne and Calais, had detrained at Lille and so were probably at Tournai. Mist kept his aircraft on the ground until midday, and the action at Casteau helped to give British cavalry an edge over his own. At the back of Kluck's mind was the principle which had stood the Germans in good stead in 1870–1. Attacking infantry did well if they pinned an enemy to his position and prevented him from manoeuvring. While they fixed, others could strike, seeking flanks and rear so that the defender's success in holding ground, and thus making it easier for his attacker to get in behind him, only made his eventual destruction more certain.

At 6 a.m. German horsemen approached the canal. They had been on the move since crossing the frontier over two weeks before, and their first contact with British infantry was a shock. The Middlesex at Obourg shot the first horsemen who appeared, and when a patrol galloped down the road towards the swing bridge at Nimy, 4/Royal Fusiliers killed four men and wounded the officer, Lieutenant von Arnim, whose father was commanding the German IV Corps a few miles away. The infantry came later, trudging down the road in column. 'They were only about 1000 yards [900 metres] distant,' records the Fusiliers' regimental history, 'and the rapid fire, aided by the machine-guns, in a few minutes destroyed the leading section of fours.' The Middlesex also had the best of the early

Men of 4/Royal Fusiliers in the square at Mons on 22 August 1914. This battalion, consisting largely of reservists, held the Nimy sector of the Mons–Condé canal the next day.

action: a battery unlimbered in the open 1500 yards (1370 metres) from the canal and was driven off by their machine-guns.

Then the tone of battle changed. German guns deluged the canal line with a fire to which the British made no response. This was because the bulk of 2 Corps' artillery, of limited use around Mons, was away to the west, with most of the cavalry, helping to cover the open flank. Guns could now engage a target invisible from the gun-line, but communication between observer and battery was by semaphore or telephone. The Germans moved with artillery well up the line of march and soon had telephone lines laid and guns in action.

After the shelling came German infantry, advancing shoulder to shoulder in the face of fire which cut them down like corn before the scythe. The Middlesex regimental history acknowledges that 'they were brave fellows, those Germans ...' On the north-eastern edge of the Nimy–Obourg salient, Germans began to cross the canal to the east, using unguarded bridges, and to work their way through the broken ground behind the station. As the battle gained momentum 2/Royal Irish, in reserve on the edge of Mons, was ordered forward to support the Middlesex, but by early afternoon it was clear that both battalions would have to fall back.

The Royal Fusiliers at Nimy were also under pressure. Shelling caused casualties amongst soldiers on the canal bank, and the machine-gun section, under Lieutenant Maurice Dease, was cruelly exposed up on the abutment of the railway bridge. Dease was hit twice and then mortally wounded as he went back and forth keeping his guns in action. Eventually, with the gunners all dead or wounded, Private Sid Godley climbed up on to the bridge, hauled the bodies out from behind a gun, and kept firing until he ran out of ammunition. He beat the gun against a bridge stanchion and staggered off into Nimy, where he collapsed from loss of blood. Lieutenant Dease and Private Godley were both awarded the Victoria Cross, the first of the war. By this time the Fusiliers had been ordered to withdraw to the new line south of Mons. One brave German, Private Niemayer of the 84th Regiment, swam the canal and clambered up to operate the bridge mechanism and swing the bridge back across the canal. He was killed, but as the Fusiliers withdrew through Nimy the Germans were close behind them, with local inhabitants – fugitives or hostages – between the combatants.

Things were more difficult for the Middlesex and Royal Irish. Smith-Dorrien's right flank, running back from Obourg on to the wooded eminence of Bois la Haut, was vulnerable because 1 Corps did not arrive to extend the line to the south-east until early afternoon. There were also problems of co-ordination which left the Bascule crossroads, directly behind the Middlesex, unguarded. Regimental Quartermaster Sergeant Fitzpatrick of the Royal Irish was in the Segard Brewery, where the road from Bascule enters Mons, sending beer forward to the firing-line. He looked up towards the junction, saw soldiers of his battalion falling back across the road, and at once collected about forty cooks, grooms and storemen and took them to the crossroads.

Fitzpatrick was just in time to take on the leading elements of the German 35th and 85th Infantry Regiments, moving straight up the road. An officer of the Gordon Highlanders, the next battalion to the south-east, arrived but was hit almost immediately, and more volunteers came up with a machine-gun. The little band held on until well past midnight, when the Royal Irish and Middlesex had been gone for hours, and withdrew after burying their fifteen dead and smashing the machine-gun. Fitzpatrick was awarded the Distinguished Conduct Medal and a commission for the day's work: he was a Lieutenant-Colonel by the end of the war.

Fighting spread along the canal, and the action at St Ghislain is typical of a dozen other clashes. A Company 1/Royal West Kent was north of the canal, between Tertre and Baudour, covering 5th Division's cavalry squadron, which was to retire as the Germans approached. The battalion's other three companies were on the south bank, and to the left 2/King's Own Scottish Borderers covered the St Ghislain bridge: four field guns had been manhandled on to the towpath.

Captain Walter Bloem, a forty-six-year-old German reserve officer snatched from a comfortable literary existence to command a company of 12th Brandenburg Grenadiers, approached Tertre after a sweaty morning's march. His men had been joking about the British in their funny scarlet tunics, and Hussar patrols announced that the country was clear for 50 miles (80 km) ahead. The mobile cookers had just been brought up with lunch when two wounded Hussars galloped up with the news that the British were on the canal. A third limped past carrying his bloodstained saddle: they were in Tertre too.

The Brandenburgers went forward at once. A battalion attacked Tertre, and Bloem's men made for the wood south-west of the village. As he passed farm buildings Bloem saw a group of horses, and a British cavalryman was shot dead as he ran for cover. There was no sign of the British on the water meadows, but fire from invisible marksmen left German dead and wounded to mark the ground gained. Cows in fields ahead bellowed and collapsed, and men followed suit. Bloem described the scene:

'I'm hit, sir! O God! Oh, mother! I'm done for!'

'I'm dying, sir!' said another one near me. 'I can't help you, my young man – come, give me your hand.' …

Behind us the whole meadow was dotted with little grey heaps. The hundred and sixty men that had left the wood with me had shrunk to less than a hundred.

About 500 yards (460 metres) from the canal Bloem stopped to let his men catch their breath. The fire ceased when they lay down, because the embankment on the German side created a wafer of dead ground invisible to the defenders. A raffish corporal produced a bottle of champagne. Bloem shared it with Lieutenant Gräser, the corporal and an orderly, and ordered his men on again.

The enemy must have been waiting for this moment to get us all together at close range, for immediately the line rose it was as if the hounds of hell had been loosed at us, yelling, barking, hammering as a mass of lead swept in amongst us … 'Gräser!' I called out. 'Where is Lieutenant Gräser?' And then from the cries and groans all around came a low-voiced reply: 'Lieutenant Gräser is dead, sir, just this moment. Shot through the head and heart as he fell. He's here.'

They were little further forward by nightfall, and when Bloem met his battalion commander he found that he was the only captain left. 'Our grand regiment, with all its pride and splendid discipline, its attack full of dash and courage, and now only a few fragments left,' mused Bloem. It had lost 25 officers and more than 500 men. The survivors would not have enjoyed hearing Harry Beaumont of the Royal West Kent call them 'easy targets'.

Smith-Dorrien pulled back that night, sappers blowing up as many bridges as they could: Captain Theodore Wright and Lance-Corporal Charles Jarvis were both awarded the VC for their part in the work. The British had lost 1642 men, most of them from the Royal Fusiliers, Middlesex and Royal Irish. German losses cannot have been less than 5000 and may easily have been much more.

The Retreat from Mons
The British corps chiefs of staff were given orders for withdrawal to a line running east-west though Bavay at 1 a.m. on 24 August, and told to agree details between themselves. It was fairly easy for 1 Corps to break clear but 2 Corps had a testing time. Smith-Dorrien decided to get 3rd Division away first. By mid-morning 5th Division's commander, Major-General Sir Charles Fergusson, learned that the cavalry had already gone, exposing his left flank, and a German corps was making for it. He sent Lieutenant-Colonel Ballard with 1/Norfolk, 1/Cheshire and 119th

Battery Royal Field Artillery (RFA) to attack the Germans, but this order was soon modified. Ballard was to hold the ridge between Audregnies and Elouges and buy time, and Fergusson asked Major-General Edmund Allenby of the cavalry division to support him.

Ballard's detachment formed a line on the ridge. The Cheshires, on the left, had a company in Audregnies itself, and the Norfolks, on the right, continued the line north-east towards Elouges, with 119th Battery towards the middle. L Battery Royal Horse Artillery joined in from the high ground on the eastern edge of Audregnies. Two German divisions, each of four three-battalion infantry regiments, swept down towards Ballard's force, supported by nine batteries firing from the Quiévrain–Mons road.

Captain Wilfrid Dugmore of the Cheshires lay in the open while shrapnel hit the ground around him. 'The situation seemed pretty miserable,' he told his wife, 'the fire was so heavy as to defy description … I was dead-beat not having touched a mouthful of food for over twenty-four hours, nor had a drink, less than two hours sleep, we had been marching in a sort of trance, receiving orders which were promptly counter-ordered … I think I would have welcomed a bullet through a vital spot.'

His opponents were also taking punishment. Major Tom Bridges of the 4th Dragoon Guards saw the gunners of L Battery at their work 'as steadily as if they had been on the ranges at Okehampton,' and Major 'Sally' Home of Allenby's staff watched the German infantry debouch from Quiévrain into their fire: 'Every shell burst low over them: they stood it for five minutes and then bolted.'

Dismounted cavalry had already joined the firefight when Allenby rode up and ordered Brigadier-General de Lisle of 2nd Cavalry Brigade to charge the guns. De Lisle shouted to Lieutenant-Colonel David Campbell of the 9th Lancers: 'I'm going to charge the enemy. The 4th Dragoon Guards will attack on your left. As soon as you see them deploy, attack on their right with at least two squadrons.' Corporal Harry Easton was doing so well against easy targets that he missed the order to cease fire, and got back to his troop just in time to hear Captain Francis Grenfell say: 'Get mounted, lads, we're going to charge the guns.' Private Wells scrawled snatches of those last few seconds: 'Move off at trot and ride knee to knee. "Carry Lances." See figures running about in distance. "Lance Engage." Gallop …'

In a flash of clarity, Easton looked to his left and saw his boyhood friend Jackie Patterson riding with the Dragoon Guards. Then it was chaos, as Second Lieutenant Roger Chance of the Dragoon Guards recalled:

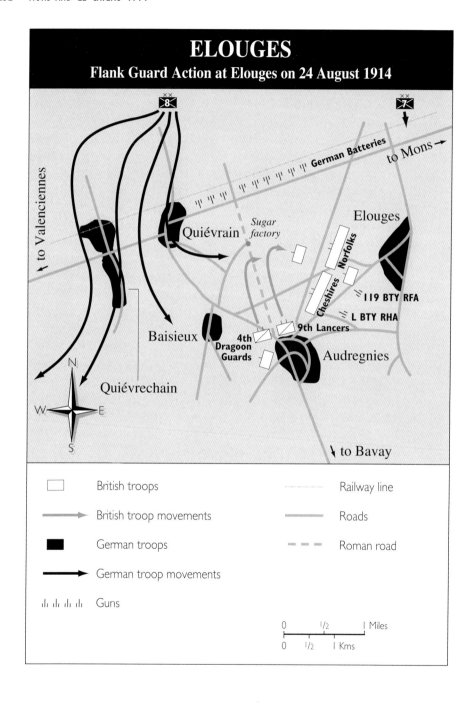

ELOUGES

Flank Guard Action at Elouges on 24 August 1914

British troops

British troop movements

German troops

German troop movements

Guns

Railway line

Roads

Roman road

0   1/2   1 Miles

0   1/2   1 Kms

A cloud of dust has risen ahead, pierced with the flash of shell bursts. If there is a hail of bullets I am not aware of it, as with [Sergeant] Talbot glimpsed alongside, the men thundering after us, I endeavour one-handed to control my almost run-away steed … He has gone – Talbot has gone down in a crashing somersault, to be ridden over dead or alive, and no sooner is he lost to us than I am among the ranks of those who, halted by wire, were right in disorder like a flock of sheep.

The wire fence ran in front of a sugar-beet factory on a Roman road leading from Audregnies towards the guns. Easton came down just short of it, and staggered to his feet, lance gone, rifle still with his horse and the Cheshires' fire cracking overhead: he was captured moments later. Tom Bridges, unhorsed and stunned, was helped on to a loose horse and galloped back up the Roman road. He lost that horse too, and was wafted off to safety by the brigade signals officer in a blue and silver Rolls-Royce. Despite Ballard's best efforts, the Cheshires never received the order to withdraw and fought on until the survivors surrendered at 6.30 p.m. The battalion had gone into action nearly one thousand strong: two officers and two hundred men answered their names at roll-call that evening.

The first day of the retreat, 24 August, cost the BEF almost 2600 men. The next was quieter, although the forest of Mormal which lay behind the BEF split its retreat as the cutwater of a bridge divides the torrent; 1 Corps marched to its east and 2 Corps to its west, competing for road space with refugees whose plight many soldiers found more depressing than their own. Men were already very tired: John Lucy thought that he

British horsemen during the retreat from Mons. They carried a sword, hung from the saddle on the horse's left, and a rifle, in a leather bucket on its right.

had covered '75 miles [120 km] in five days and a battle into the bargain'. Refugees, hovering German cavalry, heat and lack of food bore
down on the retreating columns, and on the evening of the 24th a spectacular summer thunderstorm left them soaked as well.

The Battle of Le Cateau

GHQ moved back from Le Cateau to St Quentin on the 24th and ordered
both corps to spend the night on a line running east-west through Le
Cateau, and to move off again the following morning. It was a bad night.
The Germans clashed with 1 Corps at Landrecies, and the normally
stolid Haig, tired and inconvenienced by a radical cure for constipation,
sent worrying messages back to GHQ. Smith-Dorrien, in the village of
Bertry, south-west of Le Cateau, learned at midnight that the cavalry had
relinquished the ridge covering his bivouacs and that his rearguards were
still coming in, dead-beat. Unless he was clear by first light the Germans
would be on him. He decided to fight in the hope of striking 'a stopping
blow'. Both Allenby and Major-General Snow of the newly arrived but
incomplete 4th Division agreed to fight under his orders. GHQ was less
than convinced, and eventually approved his decision in a telegram
replete with double negatives: 'Although you are given a free hand as to
method this telegram is not intended to convey the impression that I am
not anxious for you to carry out the retirement and you must make every
endeavour to do so.'

2 Corps fought on the ground it occupied. There were a few troops in
Le Cateau itself: most got clear before the Germans entered at 6.30 a.m.
on the 26th, the day of the battle. Smith-Dorrien's own divisions, 5th on
the right and 3rd on the left, took up post south of the ruler-straight road
from Le Cateau to Caudry, whence 4th Division took the line on towards
Esnes to the south-west. As the day wore on Sordet's cavalry corps at last
reached the British left, and the rapid fire of its 75mm guns helped to
hearten the defence.

On the British right, the artillery commanders of 3rd and 5th Divisions agreed to push batteries forward to hearten the infantry, and some
were tucked into folds of ground between the main road and a sunken
track which runs parallel to it to the south. A prominent knoll on 5th
Division's right, held by 2/Suffolk, had three batteries, eighteen guns in
all, right up on it. There would be occasions in future when British gunners would engage targets with direct fire, but Le Cateau was the last
battle when it would be done deliberately on this scale. As the attack
gained momentum, with columns rolling down from the north, gunners
fought like their ancestors at Waterloo. Officers took over as men fell.

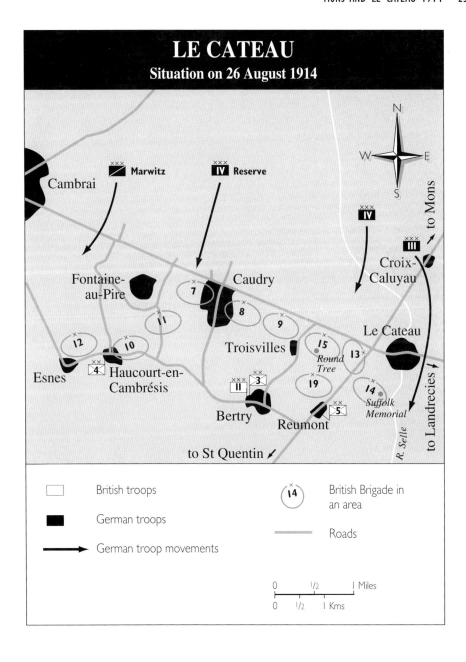

LE CATEAU
Situation on 26 August 1914

Cambrai

Marwitz

IV Reserve

IV

III

Croix-Caluyau

Fontaine-au-Pire

Caudry

7

8

9

11

12

10

Troisvilles

15

13

Le Cateau

Esnes

4

Haucourt-en-Cambrésis

3

II

19

Round Tree

14

Suffolk Memorial

Bertry

5

Reumont

to St Quentin

R. Selle

to Mons

to Landrecies

☐ British troops

■ German troops

➡ German troop movements

(14) British Brigade in an area

━━ Roads

0   ½   1 Miles

0   ½   1 Kms

Lieutenant Tom Butt of the King's Own Yorkshire Light Infantry, in the angle between the main road and the Bavay–St Quentin road, saw the gun behind him manned by the battery commander and his sergeant-major, and Lieutenant Rory Macleod, up with the Suffolks, remembered the rattle of rifle-fire against the shield of the gun he served.

Not all the gunnery was old-fashioned. In addition to its fifty-four 18-pdr guns and eighteen 4.5-inch howitzers, each division had a four-gun battery of 60-pdr heavy guns manned by the Royal Garrison Artillery. The RGA was heir to a more scientific tradition than its more swash-buckling brothers of the RFA and RHA. The heavy battery of 5th Division, tucked into a re-entrant north-east of Reumont, spotted flashes from German guns around Croix-Caluyau on the Bavay road and brought a destructive fire to bear on them. Later, when the Suffolks had been engulfed, the battery burst shells right on the knoll. The big 60-pdrs and their sturdy Clydesdales became something of a totem, and exhausted infantrymen patted the guns as they staggered past.

The Germans made little progress against the front of Smith-Dorrien's position but pushed back his left flank and, more threateningly, lapped entirely right round his right. Although the Suffolks were supported by elements of 2/Manchester and 2/Argyll and Sutherland Highlanders,

An 18-pounder near Ypres in October 1914. At Le Cateau there was no time to construct positions like this: guns were fought in the open, using whatever natural cover was available.

their position was untenable. The Germans dragged machine-guns up from the main road to rake the knoll, two field howitzers shelled it over open sights and infantry lurked in gullies behind. The Suffolks' commanding officer was killed early on, and the second-in-command was wounded taking ammunition to the machine-guns. By midday Fergusson, who could see the battle from a rooftop in Reumont, knew that his right was near collapse, asked Smith-Dorrien for permission to withdraw, and decided to get his guns away.

Field guns and howitzers were attached to a limber drawn by six horses. After the guns had been brought into action the teams were led off, to be brought back when the guns were to be moved. Rory Macleod was serving one of his battery's two surviving guns when he looked back to see the teams hurtling up. 'Shells were bursting all round them,' he recalled. 'It was a magnificent sight. Now and then a man or a horse or a whole team would go down. It was like Balaclava all over again!' Three VCs were won for saving one of 37th (Howitzer) Battery's pieces, and so stirring was the sight of teams at the gallop that the Royal West Kent rose and cheered as they tore through its line south of the sunken road.

On the edge of the sunken road, 122nd Battery RFA had been hard hit by the time its teams arrived. Second Lieutenant 'Clarrie' Hodgson watched the Germans redouble their fire as they reached the position: 'Men and horses were just blown to pieces.' The gun-line was a shambles, and he was relieved when a shout went up: 'Every man for himself. Destroy the guns.' Lieutenant Lionel Lutyens saw one of his two guns away safely, but as the other team reached the sunken road the horses jibbed, and fire felled horses and drivers. Lutyens looked behind and saw that his groom was still there with his charger, Bronco. He found it hard to mount, but eventually got up. He:

… let him go down the road as fast as he could gallop … it was an extraordinary sight, a wild scene of galloping horses, and then everyone gone, dead horses and dead men everywhere, four guns left solitary on the position, a few wagon limbers lying about and one standing on the skyline with its pole straight up in the air. *Voilà tout*.

At 1.40 p.m., Fergusson was given permission to withdraw. Once 5th Division was on the move, 3rd would follow suit, with 4th Division moving last of all. The retirement went better than might have been expected, and Smith-Dorrien thought the retreating men resembled a crowd coming away from a race meeting. The Suffolks were swamped at about 2.45 p.m., and 1/Gordon Highlanders, over at Audencourt, never received an order to withdraw, remained on the position until nightfall, and were forced to surrender as they stumbled into superior German forces in the dark. Although 2 Corps lost 7812 men and 38 guns, Smith-Dorrien had succeeded in his aim: the pursuit was never as pressing again. French paid him a handsome tribute in his dispatch, but he was never comfortable with the decision to stand and fight, and Smith-Dorrien's dismissal in 1915 has an echo of Le Cateau to it.

The Continuing Retreat

The retreat from Mons went on until 5 September, taking the BEF beyond the River Marne, where it contributed to the counter-attack which halted the German advance and then turned it into a retreat. As they reached the River Aisne the Germans dug in, and the war of movement began to freeze into immobility. Sir John French had had a trying campaign, and his suggestion that the BEF should withdraw from the line to refit had earned him a difficult interview with Lord Kitchener. But he caught the new tone of the war very quickly, telling the king: 'I think the battle of the Aisne is very typical of what battles in the future are most likely to resemble. Siege operations will enter largely into the tactical problems – the *spade* will be as great a necessity as the rifle, and the heaviest calibres of artillery will be brought up in support on either side.' It is as well that soldiers cannot see too far into the future. On their retreat, some of Smith-Dorrien's men crossed a little river at Voyennes, which Henry V's men had passed on their way to Agincourt. It was, of course, the Somme.

A View of the Field

The town of Mons was fought over in August 1914, and again when the Canadians liberated it in November 1918, but it sustained little damage. Its ring road and one-way system are unforgiving, but the town centre is unquestionably worth a visit. The Grande Place, at its centre, is largely unspoilt, and there is a museum in the Jardin du Mayeur behind the town hall, reached through an archway off the square. Its ground floor is devoted to the First World War and contains a good selection of Allied and German uniforms, weapons and equipment. The machine-gun in the entrance hall was used by the Cheshires at Audregnies and buried to avoid capture, and there is a photograph of Regimental Quartermaster Sergeant Fitzpatrick nearby. One of the upstairs floors contains a collection of ceramics, and the other is a sombre record of Mons under occupation.

Casteau

The British army's first and last shots of the war were fired on opposite sides of the N6 Brussels road in Casteau, across the canal from Mons. Just beyond Supreme Headquarters Allied Powers Europe, a monument north of the road commemorates the action of the 4th Dragoon Guards on 22 August 1914. Tom Bridges, the squadron leader, had prepared an ambush on the road with a mounted troop under Captain Charles Hornby ready to exploit it. An oncoming German cavalry patrol smelt a rat and fled, but Hornby pursued and there was a brief mounted clash before the Germans met the rest of their leading troop east of Casteau. Both sides dismounted, and Corporal Edward Thomas fired the first shot at a German officer who fell to the ground. The 4th Dragoon Guards then galloped on to Soignies where there was a more serious mounted action in the village street. 'Captain Hornby ran his sword through one Jerry,' remembered Private Ted Worrell, 'and Sergeant-Major Sharpe got another. I got a poke at a man but I don't know what happened to him.' Further down the road more German cavalry and lorried *jäger* appeared and the pursuit was called off. Across the road from the 1914 memorial, a plaque on a wall recalls the fact that Canadian infantry fired the last shots of the war nearby on 11 November 1918.

Nimy and Obourg

In the inter-war years the Mons–Condé Canal was re-routed to become part of the Canal du Centre, and now runs north-westwards towards Blaton from a new large pool at Nimy. A sadly diminished version of the old canal follows more or less its original path in a grubby concrete channel, but the old bridges have disappeared. Between Nimy and Obourg the canal follows its old route and, although wider and deeper, looks much the same as it did in 1914. Both Nimy Bridge and Obourg station are worth a visit. The former can be approached by parking in the little square at Nimy, just south of the modern span which replaces the old swing bridge, or driving on to the towpath. The current railway bridge is a girder construction much like its predecessor. Dease's guns were up on the abutments, and it is easy to see why the Fusiliers manning them fell like flies. A plaque beneath the bridge pays tribute to Dease, an Irishman from Meath, and Godley, a solidly built Londoner who sported the bushy moustache so characteristic of the Old Bills of 1914.

Obourg station is also on the south bank of the canal, east of the belching chimneys of Obourg cement works, the major local employer now that the mines have closed. When the old station building was demolished, a small section of wall was left to commemorate the stand made by 4/Middlesex and, in particular, one unknown hero. As the company at the station withdrew a soldier climbed on to the roof to cover his comrades' retreat, and continued to fire until the burning roof fell in. The nearby Middlesex Farm, defended by A Company 4/Middlesex, was, and still is, owned by the Abell family. A was Able Company in the phonetic alphabet of the day, and its commander, killed in action, was coincidentally called Major Abell.

The Bascule crossroads, where the N90 to Binche and Charleroi meets the N40 to Beaumont, is very busy, but there is a lay-by on the N90 and parking near an electrical showroom with the inspired name of So Watt. The Obourg chimneys help to establish the position of the canal, and the Middlesex and Royal Irish had a difficult time pulling back south-westwards, from right to left as we face the chimneys, through the tangle of houses, gardens and little woods, not to mention convent and town cemetery, between the canal and Mons itself.

The Château Gendebien lies amongst trees where the Bois la Haut begins to rise west of the crossroads. It was used as a field hospital in 1914 and was badly damaged by fire started by shells aimed at Fitzpatrick's men. It now houses NATO's Supreme Allied Commander Europe and is not open to the public. On one side of the Binche road a large monument, once in the centre of Mons, marks the town's significance for the British army of the First World War. On the other stands a Celtic cross, unveiled by Sir John French, a memorial to the Royal Irish Regiment whose forebears had fought for Marlborough nearby at Malplaquet.

War Graves

It was not until the First World War that British soldiers killed in action received individual burial as a matter of course. Most dead of battles such as Waterloo were stripped of anything of value by comrades, enemies or the looters who flocked to battlefields like vultures round a carcass, and were then tumbled, half-naked, into communal grave-pits. Officers might be interred in individual graves or repatriated in one grisly guise or another. In 1914 it soon became clear to Fabian Ware, then a Red Cross volunteer, that the nation would demand some account of its dead, and he was appointed to head the Graves Registration Commission which grew in 1917 into the Imperial (now Commonwealth) War Graves Commission.

Trips around battlefields often degenerate into cemetery crawls. It is easy to see why, for there is something unutterably poignant about these silent cities. They offer so much. Family inscriptions on headstones range from heart-rending through mawkish to triumphal. There are stark reminders of the age of the dead, from fourteen (Private John Condon of

British officers at the memorial commemorating the battle of Malplaquet (1709). The cobbled road is now busy tarmac: Mons lies a few miles beyond the crest.

the Royal Irish, killed in May 1915) to sixty-eight (Lieutenant Henry Webber of the South Lancashires, died of wounds in July 1916). Then there is military demography by microcosm, with old reservists with Boer War medals, youthful colonels with Distinguished Service Orders and Military Crosses and, most tragically, boys consumed by an omnivorous army as Britain ran out of men. 'School, War, Death' reads a family's bitter inscription on a headstone near Cambrai. Finally, there is pure military history, with those cap-badges of yesteryear, shining pride turned to stone.

If you only visit one war cemetery then St Symphorien, on a gently wooded hillock just down the Binche road, should be it. It was started by the Germans for their own and the British dead of Mons, although many others lie elsewhere. Heavy German headstones of regimental pattern bear a man's name, rank, unit and home town, and officers are buried separately. The first British were interred on the same basis, and there is a short 'officers' row' at the back of the cemetery. Many of the defenders of Obourg were buried in a mass grave, above which the Germans raised a column to the *Royal* Middlesex Regiment, taking the view that a unit which fought so hard must have been royal. A circle of British headstones around it names the men who are known to rest beneath.

Lieutenant Dease lies in the first group of British graves across from the left-hand entrance gate, with Private Price, the last Canadian killed, behind him. Where the path begins to wind around towards the rear of the cemetery lies Private Parr of the Middlesex, killed on reconnaissance, as the amended date on his headstone tells us, on 21 August 1914. On the other side of the path is Private Ellison of the 5th Lancers (private soldiers in line cavalry regiments were not called troopers until 1922) killed on 11 November 1918 and the last British fatality of the war. Futility, courage and irony are all there, and in the War Graves Commission's tending of this peaceful spot we are reminded that even in war, when human life may count for little, the human spirit is all.

Elouges

The scene of the flank-guard action near Elouges can be reached via the N30, which grinds its way out of Mons through forlorn suburbs. It is easier to take the autoroute, turning off at the Ville Pommeroeul exit and then heading south. The Roman road, down whose axis the 4th Dragoon Guards and 9th Lancers charged, runs from the northern end of Audregnies, past the sugar factory, to the N30, then the German gun-line. Tom Bridges and Roger Chance were on the road itself, and David Campbell's lancers charged through the field to their east. The road is barely passable to cars, but there is a good walk from Audregnies towards the sugar factory, and by turning right in a sharp cutting and then right again at l'Avaleresse (a colliery works in 1914) one can follow a narrow metalled road back to Audregnies on precisely the line held by the Norfolks and the Cheshires.

The Forest of Mormal

The direct route to the forest of Mormal crosses the border into France just south of Audregnies. A diversion takes the visitor through Hergies, Hon-Hergies and Taisnières-sur-Hon to the sprawling village of Malplaquet. Beyond its northern edge, close to the border, is an obelisk in the centre of the position defended, on 11 September 1709, by a French army under Marshal Villars. Although the Allies emerged as masters of the field it cost them 25 000 men and was Marlborough's bloodiest victory.

The forest of Mormal still divides major roads, but there are pleasant drives through it and a number of sylvan *auberges* at their quiet junctions. It was not impassable in August 1914, although poor maps and fear of ambush deterred most British units from using it.

Le Cateau

Le Cateau lies south of the forest in the valley of the little River Selle. It was the birthplace of Napoleon's Marshal Mortier, whose statue presides over the long and narrow square. In 1914 GHQ was in the attractive neo-classical school at the lower end of the square. The building now houses the Matisse Museum, for the painter is another of Le Cateau's sons.

The sunken road runs south of the N43 Le Cateau–Cambrai road. It is crueller to cars than the Roman road at Audregnies, but a walk down it from Troisvilles towards Le Cateau puts Smith-Dorrien's right flank into perspective. Half-way along stands a prominent tree – l'Arbre Rond on the IGN map. This replaces a tree which stood there in 1914, on part of the road held by Ballard's Norfolks. The battalion stood in the second line that day with 1/Bedford towards the main road on its left front and 2/King's Own Scottish Borderers to its right. The tree was an obvious aiming mark for German gunners, and Ballard ordered his pioneers to fell it. The tree was almost down when the wind changed and threatened to blow it into the lane, blocking this valuable covered route. It had to be guyed up with ropes and was eventually pulled down into the field behind.

On the track's northern edge, just before its junction with the D932 St Quentin road, was 122nd Battery RFA. Lionel Lutyens and his fellow section commanders stood on the track, their six guns – a pair for each of the battery's three subalterns – in the field, sheltered from frontal fire by a smudge of rising ground. The gun-line soon became very unsafe, and we can see why. The spire of St Martin's church in Le Cateau, into which the Germans had inserted machine-guns, peeps up over the crest-line, and there were more machine-guns on the near lip of the cutting carrying the Cambrai road through a spur: a water tower stands helpfully above it.

To the right of the church, as Lutyens would have seen it, a handsome cenotaph in a square of trees shows where the Suffolks stood. The tracks on the far side of the St Quentin road are not helpful to the walker, and the Suffolk memorial is best reached by driving into Le Cateau, swinging south at the first set of lights and parking near the Collège J. Rostand before walking up on to the knoll. It is easy to see why the Suffolks and their supporting gunners were so vulnerable to fire from front and right flank and to attack by infantry seeping up the re-entrant behind the cenotaph. Reumont, whence Sir Charles Fergusson commanded his division, is visible on a rise on the D932. There was once a plaque on the house itself, the second on the left when entering the village: its screw-holes still remain. A water tower in the centre of the western horizon marks the position of Bertry, Smith-Dorrien's headquarters, central in his corps' position. It is a tiny battlefield, and Wellington would have understood so much about it. Lines of infantry, kept steady by discipline, the bonds of mateship, a touch of sheer nastiness – Frank Richards hoped for 'a bang at the bastards' – brave leaders and the remembrance of things past. Gunners who would abandon neither the pieces they served nor the infantry they supported. Le Cateau was the last battle of the old war.

CHAPTER 8

The Somme
1916

Background

At 7.30 a.m. on 1 July 1916, 60 000 British soldiers scrambled out of their trenches on the uplands north of the Somme to begin the 'Big Push'. By noon almost 100 000 had been committed to battle, and by nightfall 57 470 were dead, wounded or missing. The British army lost more soldiers than it had fielded at Waterloo, Mons or Le Cateau, and probably more than fought on either side at Agincourt. It was the first day of a battle that ground on until November, and by its close there were 418 000 British casualties. These were the best of the nation's volunteer manhood, and the merest glance at its casualty roll shows what the Somme did to the old world of brass bands and cricket fields, pit-head cottages and broad acres.

It levelled the exalted. The prime minister's son, Lieutenant Herbert Asquith, and Lieutenant the Hon. Edward Tennant were part of that fusion of Leicestershire hunting world and London society known as the Souls: they lie in the same cemetery at Guillemont. Nearby, Second Lieutenant George Marsden-Smedley, not long out of Harrow, where he had captained both the cricket and football teams, died in his first action. It mauled the artistic. H.H. Munro, who wrote short stories as Saki, was killed while serving as a Lance-Sergeant in the Royal Fusiliers. Lieutenant William Noel Hodgson MC, poet and Cambridge contemporary of Rupert Brooke, had begged for strength to face the death he found on 1 July.

> By all the delights that I shall miss,
> Help me to die, O Lord.

George Butterworth, the composer, whose music for *A Shropshire Lad* breathes the scent of peacetime's last summers, died as a captain in the

With Loving Greetings

To My Truest of Pals.
"MY MOTHER."

May the LORD watch for ever between me and thee
When we are absent one from the other :
Are the words that I send with heart full of love,
To the best of dear pals MOTHER.

For King, Queen and Country we're fighting,
" Honour and Right " is our watchword true ;
Tho' " Might " at first seemed to hold the sway,
Naught shall conquer the Red, White and Blue.

Twas some time since that I left my loved home,
To answer old England's cry ;
The parting was hard, and tho' she tried to be brave,
There was a tear in my dear mother's eye.

" God bless you " said she, " God bless her," say I,
For of mothers' no man had a better ;
And while I'm at FOVANT or when I go to the Front
She knows I shall never forget her.

So, cheer up, Dear Mother, my Truest of Pals,
Tho' at parting your heart may feel sore,
We will all look forward with hearts full of hope
To true happiness when peace comes once more.

From

"FIT AND READY."

The first day of the Somme saw terrible losses amongst the Pals' battalions of wartime volunteers. H.D. Riley *(above, centre)* founded the Burnley Lads' Club in 1905, and in 1914 commanded the Burnley company of the Accrington Pals *(below)*. He died, with many of his men, on 1 July 1916. The words of this postcard reflect the fact that many of the Pals were very young.

Durham Light Infantry, and like so many of his comrades has no known grave.

It blighted families. Sergeant George Lee and his son Corporal Robert Frederick Lee died on 5 September. Lieutenant Arthur Tregaskis lies beside his brother Leonard in Flat Iron Copse Cemetery with two other pairs of brothers, Corporal T. and Lance-Corporal H. Hardwidge, and Privates Ernest and Herbert Philby. It decimated communities. Three battalions of Lancashire Fusiliers, recruited from 'the docklands, engineering workshops, mines and mills of Salford', lost 41 officers and 942 men on 1 July.

It savaged the new world as it rallied to the old. The Newfoundland Battalion lost 715 officers and men on 1 July, the heaviest casualty rate of any battalion that day. Later, the South Africans suffered in Delville Wood and the Canadians at Courcelette. The Australians lost an appalling 23 000 men at Pozières. It is difficult to be objective about the Australian experience, shot through with myth and counter-myth. Even at the baldest level there was something remarkable about those rangy characters in slouch hats, summoned to a distant fight that brought disillusionment or death. Lieutenant Bert Crowe scribbled his last lines home:

The pain is getting worse and worse. I am very sorry dear, but still you will be well provided for and I am easy on that score. So cheer up dear I could write on a lot but am nearly unconscious. Give my love to Dear Bill and yourself, do take care of yourself and him. Your loving husband Bert.

They expected no privileges: W.J. Johnson, a member of the Australian parliament, fell as a private in the infantry. And above all they tried to die game. Lieutenant Archie Dean appeared at a dressing station with a verse from a popular song – 'Here we are! Here we are! Here we are again!' – and the top blown off his skull. 'He was as game as any man could be,' wrote his platoon sergeant, 'and refused attendance until the wounds of the others were dressed.' He died nearly five months later.

The Progress of the War

The Somme was the misshapen child of 1915. By Christmas 1914 the British Expeditionary Force (BEF) had lost 90 000 men: in those thousand-strong battalions which had marched up to Mons in August there remained on average one officer and thirty men. France's losses were even more catastrophic, approaching a million men and nearly half her regular officers. The Western Front was locked in stalemate, and in 1915 the Allies hoped to break the deadlock either, as the 'Westerners' argued, by beating the Germans in France or, as the 'Easterners' hoped, by find-ing another, more promising, theatre.

They failed. Attempts to break the German line by assault – the British attacked at Neuve Chapelle, Festubert and Aubers Ridge in the spring and at Loos in September 1915 – made little progress. Sir John French blamed early defeats on lack of ammunition, and the ensuing 'shells scandal' helped to replace the Liberal government with a coali-tion. Although the one major German offensive in the west, at Ypres in May, was repulsed, it claimed many men and much ground. A bid to knock Germany's ally Turkey out of the war failed when an Anglo-French force was unable to secure the Gallipoli peninsula.

In December 1915 Allied representatives met at Chantilly to deter-mine strategy for the coming year. They concluded that a decision could only be achieved on those fronts where the enemy was massed: France, Italy and Russia. Offensives were to be co-ordinated so that German reserves could not be moved from one front to another. Local attacks to wear out the Germans could be launched 'by those powers which still have abundant reserves of men'. With ninety-five divisions on the West-ern Front, France was beginning to reach the end of her available man-power. Britain had thirty-eight divisions in France and fifty-one in training or in other theatres, and her human resources had never been better. It was evident that whatever form the war took in 1916, Britain's share of the burden could only increase.

Sir John French was one of the casualties of Loos: on 18 December 1915 he was replaced by Sir Douglas Haig, who had commanded 1 Corps at Mons. Scarcely had Haig assumed command than the French announced that they were only strong enough for one major attack that year, which they proposed to co-ordinate with a Russian effort in July. They hoped that the British would undertake 'wearing-out fights' to whit-tle down German resources. Haig argued that these would 'entail consid-erable loss on us with little to show for it'. On 14 February 1916 he persuaded the French commander-in-chief, General Joseph Joffre, to abandon them, and in return agreed that 'the main French and British attacks are to be "jointives", that is, side by side' where the Allied armies met on the Somme. In fact, Haig was not convinced. There were com-pelling arguments for an offensive at Ypres, where a short advance might put the key rail junction at Roulers within reach. Nor were his political masters any clearer, and it was not until April that they formally agreed to support a joint offensive in the west.

By this time circumstances had changed. General Erich von Falken-hayn had replaced the worn-out Moltke as *de facto* commander-in-chief of the German army in autumn 1914. In December 1915 he concluded that Germany's most obdurate foe was England, and that his best chance of victory was to knock 'England's best sword', the French army, from her hand. This could be achieved by attacking an objective 'for the retention of which the French General Staff will be compelled to throw in every man they have. If they do so the forces of France will bleed to death …' The chosen target was Verdun, and the attack began in February 1916, supported by the heaviest artillery concentration the world had seen. It soon bogged down, and if the French were being bled white the Germans were also haemorrhaging. Verdun not only demanded a speedy opening of the Allied offensive but also reduced the number of French troops available for it.

We cannot be sure of Haig's real hopes for the Somme. The evidence suggests that he hoped to break through the German lines although he was unwilling to tell the cautious government so. The British military theorist Basil Liddell Hart maintained it was only when it was evident that there would be no quick victory that 'the story was spread by officially inspired apologists that Haig was throughout aiming at a campaign of attrition and had not dreamt of a "breakthrough".' General Sir Henry Rawlinson, whose 4th Army was to launch the attack, thought that the commander-in-chief hoped for a breakthrough. He himself had more restrained expectations, and favoured 'bite and hold' operations, with artillery rendering the German front line untenable so that it could be occupied with little cost. Haig felt that Rawlinson's proposals did not go far enough, and urged him to consider 'the possibility of pushing our first advance further than is contemplated in your plan'. Rawlinson did so, although he confided to his diary: 'I feel pretty confident of success, though only after heavy fighting. That the Boche will break and a debacle will supervene I do not believe.'

As the British army expanded it took over the front from the French, and by July 1916 its line ran from Ypres to Maricourt, above the Somme. The Ypres area was held by 2nd Army, 1st Army covered the low-lying ground around Loos and La Bassée, 3rd Army was responsible for Vimy Ridge and Arras, handing over to Rawlinson's 4th Army south of Gommecourt. A new Reserve Army, intended to capitalize on 4th Army's breakthrough, had just been formed under Lieutenant-General Sir Hubert Gough, and during the Somme fighting it became 5th Army.

Kitchener's 'New Armies'
This astonishing growth in the size of the British army owed much to Lord Kitchener. Whatever his failings, the secretary of state for war was

amongst the minority who believed that the war would not be over by Christmas 1914. No sooner was he in office than he took steps to increase the army and called for 100 000 volunteers. He had a mistakenly low regard for the Territorial Force and, instead of recruiting through its County Associations, he raised the 'New Armies' through the Adjutant-General's Department at the War Office. Further appeals produced sufficient volunteers to send thirty New Army divisions abroad by 1 July 1916. Such was the scale of this achievement that, as Peter Simkins points out, 'more men joined the Army voluntarily between August 1914 and December 1915 than were conscripted in 1916 and 1917 combined.'

Patriotism, duty, boredom, pressure from friends or employers, the lure of adventure or momentary whim all encouraged men to enlist. Mining and industrial areas were well represented: Lancashire, Yorkshire and Scotland between them provided more than one-third of the overall total of 250 New Army battalions. Many of 'Kitchener's men' came from backgrounds which had not usually furnished soldiers. Lieutenant-Colonel C.H. Cobb, commanding 5/Oxfordshire and Buckinghamshire Light Infantry, recalled:

There were a great many from the most respectable homes and businesses. Some gentlemen, many indoor servants, grooms, gardeners, gamekeepers, well-to-do tradesmen, hotel-keepers, clerks, etc., etc., to say nothing of the engineers, fitters and hands from the great works in Birmingham and Coventry. All these men had left good, comfortable homes, with good wages, and had come voluntarily out of a sheer sense of duty.

Lieutenant Charles Douie of 7/Dorsets agreed. His comrades 'took soldiering seriously, as a means to an end, in their hope of a rapid end. The war was not a crusade in their eyes; it was a disagreeable job which had to be seen through, however long it took and whatever sacrifice it entailed …'

Most volunteers joined 'Service' battalions of county regiments, numbered consecutively after Regular, Special Reserve and Territorial battalions. Many were raised locally, with eager support from civic authorities, and rejoiced in names which never appeared on the Army List but summed up identity better than a formal title ever could. Glasgow's three new units were battalions of the Highland Light Infantry. The 15th, recruited from employees of the City Tramways, was the Tramways Battalion; old members of the Boys' Brigade joined the 16th, the Boys' Brigade Battalion; while the 17th, raised by the Chamber of Commerce, answered to the name of the Glasgow Commercials.

Let one of these Pals' battalions speak for so many others. Councillor

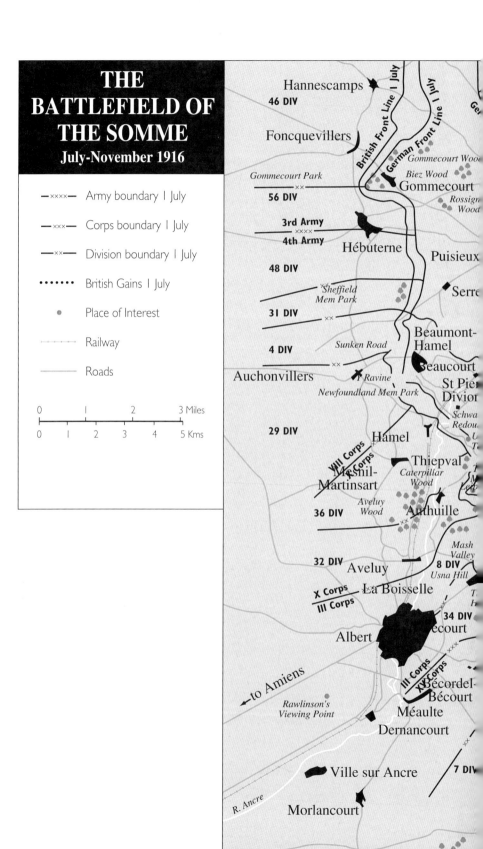

THE BATTLEFIELD OF THE SOMME
July-November 1916

—×××× — Army boundary 1 July

—××× — Corps boundary 1 July

—×× — Division boundary 1 July

••••••• British Gains 1 July

• Place of Interest

+·+·+·+ Railway

——— Roads

0	1	2		3 Miles
0	1	2	3	4	5 Kms

Hannescamps

46 DIV

Foncquevillers

British Front Line 1 July

German Front Line 1 July

Ger

Gommecourt Wood

Gommecourt Park

Biez Wood

Gommecourt

56 DIV

Rossign
Wood

3rd Army
————
4th Army

Hébuterne

Puisieux

48 DIV

Sheffield
Mem Park

Serre

31 DIV

Beaumont-
Hamel

4 DIV

Sunken Road

Beaucourt

Auchonvillers

Ravine

St Pier
Divion

Newfoundland Mem Park

Schwa
Redou

29 DIV

Hamel

Caterpillar
Wood

Thiepval

VIII Corps

X Corps

Mesnil-
Martinsart

Aveluy
Wood

36 DIV

Authuille

Mash
Valley

32 DIV

Aveluy

8 DIV
Usna Hill

La Boissele

X Corps
III Corps

34 DIV
court

Albert

III Corps
XV Corps

Bécordel-
Bécourt

to Amiens

Rawlinson's
Viewing Point

Méaulte

Dernancourt

Ville sur Ancre

7 DIV

R. Ancre

Morlancourt

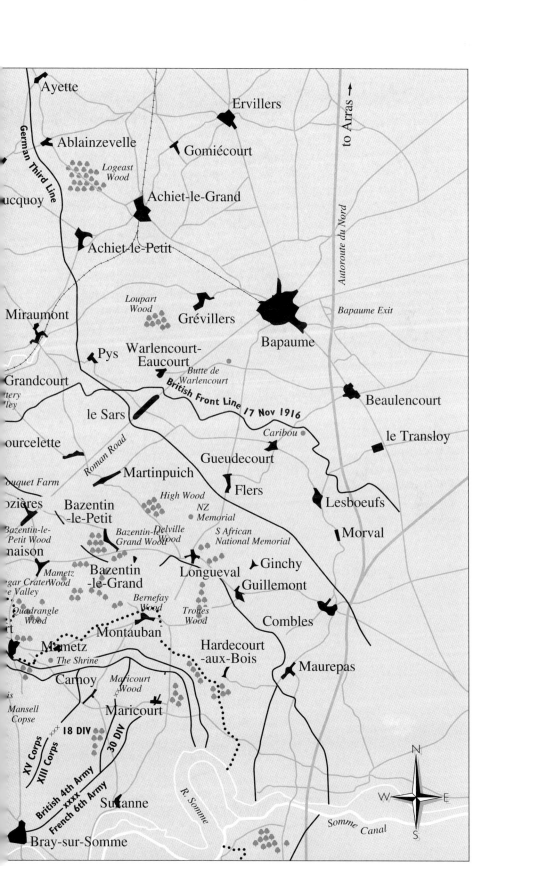

Ayette

Ervillers

Ablainzevelle

Gomiécourt

to Arras →

German Third Line

Logeast
Wood

ucquoy

Achiet-le-Grand

Autoroute du Nord

Achiet-le-Petit

Miraumont

Loupart
Wood

Grévillers

Bapaume Exit

Pys

Warlencourt-
Eaucourt

Bapaume

Butte de
Warlencourt

Grandcourt

British Front Line 17 Nov 1916

Beaulencourt

tery
ley

le Sars

Caribou

le Transloy

ourcelette

Roman Road

Gueudecourt

uquet Farm

Martinpuich

Flers

ozières

High Wood

NZ
Memorial

Lesboeufs

Bazentin
-le-Petit

Bazentin- Delville
Grand Wood Wood

S African
National Memorial

Morval

Bazentin-le-
Petit Wood

naison

gar Crater Wood
e Valley

Mametz

Bazentin
-le-Grand

Longueval

Ginchy

Guillemont

Quadrangle
Wood

Bernefay
Wood

Trônes
Wood

Combles

rt

Mametz

Montauban

Hardecourt
-aux-Bois

Maurepas

The Shrine

Carnoy

Maricourt
Wood

Mansell
Copse

is

Maricourt

18 DIV

30 DIV

XV Corps

XIII Corps

British 4th Army

xxxx

French 6th Army

Suzanne

R. Somme

Somme Canal

N
W E
S

Bray-sur-Somme

John Harwood JP, Lord Mayor of Accrington, offered to raise a battalion. The War Office accepted his proposal, and he began recruiting in and around Accrington on 7 September 1914. In 10 days 36 officers and 1076 men joined what was officially the 11th (Service) Battalion The East Lancashire Regiment, but which has left its mark on history as the Accrington Pals. Loyalties within the battalion mirrored peacetime associations. H.D. Riley, prominent local employer and Justice of the Peace, was a leading supporter of the Burnley Lads' Club. In September 1914 Riley volunteered for D (Burnley) Company of the Pals, and seventy Lads' Club members enlisted with him. Councillor Harwood selected his own officers, and it was natural that Riley should command D Company.

The case of the Accringtons highlights the problem of providing officers and NCOs. Martin Middlebrook, whose book *The First Day of the Somme* broke new ground in the historiography of the war, examined the 21st Division and found that every battalion commander had been a retired officer on the outbreak of war. Of the other officers, only fourteen had any military experience. The remainder, over 400, were newly commissioned. Some had been on a War Office list of 2000 'young gentlemen' who had just left public school or university, and others were professional men. Yet not all professional men wanted to be officers. The 1st Sportsmen's Battalion (23/Royal Fusiliers) included in its ranks two England cricketers, the country's lightweight boxing champion and the former lord mayor of Exeter. 8/East Surreys found itself with one sergeant-major as its only NCO. A dozen old reservists were made lance-corporals, 'much to their horror and indignation,' and anybody 'who had been in charge of anyone else or who wanted to be' also found himself a lance-corporal. The adjutant acknowledged that it was 'a rough and ready system, but it worked out well and nearly all of them made good'.

It was less easy to improvise weapons and equipment, and some battalions spent their first weeks in tented camps with no uniforms. Blue serge uniforms, unpopular because they resembled those worn by postmen, were eventually replaced by khaki. Rifles were slow in coming: the 12/York and Lancaster, the Sheffield City Battalion, received its full complement in November 1915. Machine-guns were as hard to acquire, and much early training was carried out to the accompaniment of policemen's rattles. Gunners were even worse off: 34th Division's artillery had only three days' practice on real weapons before embarkation.

Lack of experienced officers and NCOs combined with the shortage of modern weapons to restrict training, and not all divisional commanders were as imaginative as Major-General Maxse of 18th Division, who placed special emphasis on the thorough training of platoons by the young officers in command of them. In any event it was not clear what training should consist of. As Paddy Griffith has demonstrated in *Battle Tactics of the Western Front*, the British army had begun to develop doctrine for trench warfare. Nevertheless, it was poor at distillation of best practice, and Griffith is right to maintain that in July 1916 the 'machine looked magnificent on the drawing board, but … in reality was unready in almost all of its parts'. The Somme turned a largely inexperienced mass army into a largely experienced one. But the men who were to attack on 1 July had not come to the Somme to learn: they had come to win the war.

The Battle

There was no particular merit to attacking on the Somme: it was simply where the Allied armies met. The Roman road from Albert to Bapaume slashes the battlefield. When Henry V passed on his way to Agincourt, Albert was known as Ancre from the river of that name which winds southwards to join the Somme at Corbie. It had been a pilgrimage centre, although the number of pilgrims had never come up to expectations and the basilica of Notre-Dame-des-Brebières, topped by a gilded statue of the Virgin, seemed large for a town of 9000 souls. It is a big, confident landscape, downland sprinkled with woods, large hedgeless fields growing wheat and sugar-beet, farms four-square like fortresses, and villages of close-ranked redbrick houses.

The sector had been quiet since the front solidified in 1914, and German positions took advantage of the fields of fire offered by open countryside and the protection afforded by villages. As it ran down from the north, the German front line looped in front of Gommecourt Wood and crossed the fields between Hébuterne and Serre, the latter, like other front-line villages, a self-contained strongpoint. After dipping across the Serre–Mailly-Maillet road the line clung to the crest of what the British called Redan Ridge, then slid into a re-entrant on the western edge of Beaumont-Hamel to ascend Hawthorn Ridge, where a redoubt dominated the approaches from Auchonvillers.

Just beyond Hawthorn Ridge Redoubt the line jinked south-eastwards through the gash of Y Ravine and then fell gently into the marshy valley of the Ancre, rising again to curl with the contours in front of Thiepval and Ovillers. It followed the Roman road on the northern edge of La Boiselle, crossing south-west of the village to stretch out over the ridge to the western edge of Fricourt. From Fricourt the line turned to run almost due west to the Maricourt–Longueval road, where British and French forces met. Although the Germans looked down from the long ridge from Mametz to Montauban, the ground favoured them less in this sector than on those spurs further north, each dominated by its fellows to left and right so that local successes would be cancelled out by flanking failures.

In the Trenches
The trenches of 1916 bore as much relation to the scratchings of British defenders of Mons as a jumbo jet does to a paper dart. The Germans had originally believed in having 'one good line and that a strong one', but experience of 1915, where the British had broken through the front line to be stopped further back, had shown the value of depth, and by 1916 the Germans thought in terms of forward, reserve and support positions. Each position comprised several parallel trenches, connected to one another and to positions further back by communication trenches. Second and third positions on the Somme were incomplete, but the ridges lent themselves to defence in depth and the Germans had done much work on a second position running across the crest behind Pozières and had begun a third through Le Sars.

The construction of front-line trenches varied, but most were about 8 feet (2.5 metres) deep, with a parapet of earth and sandbags facing the enemy and a lower parados at the rear. Sides were revetted with planks, wattle or corrugated iron, and a firestep enabled occupants to step up from the comparative safety of the duckboards to peer out across the parapet. Narrow trenches known as saps, with listening posts at their ends, poked out towards the enemy. Trenches followed the crenellated line of a Greek frieze so that the effect of shellbursts would be minimized and enemy intrusions contained. A belt of barbed wire, often 20–30 yards (18–27 metres) deep, ran on the enemy side of the trench. There was a strip of no man's land, whose width varied from a few yards to several hundred, then the enemy's wire and finally his own trench systems.

Although most infantrymen carried a rifle, this was of limited use in trench warfare. When field guns were not busy on other tasks they were laid on what the British termed 'SOS lines' in front of trenches, their fire called down by field telephone or signalling pistol. Trench-mortars lobbed 'toffee apples' or 'flying pigs' to blow in sections of trench; snipers picked off individuals; and machine-guns, sited to fire obliquely along the wire, dealt with larger targets. Both armies still manned medium machine-guns on tripods or sledges, but had developed lighter versions, the Lewis for the British and the 08/15 Spandau for the Germans.

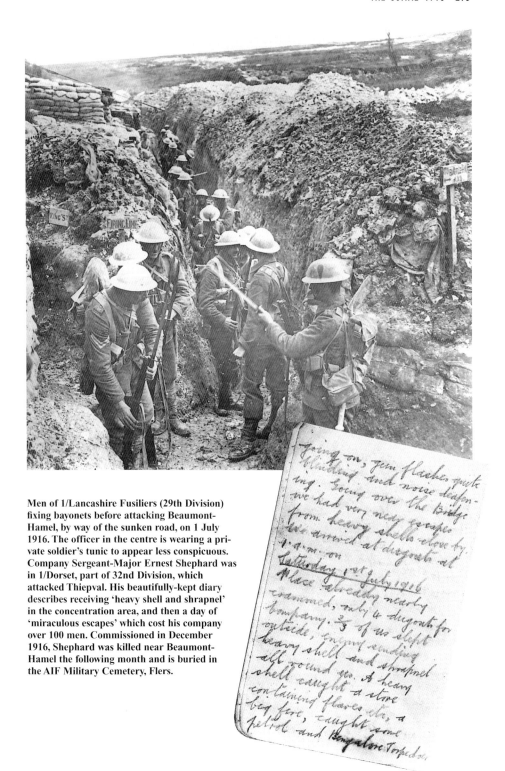

Men of 1/Lancashire Fusiliers (29th Division) fixing bayonets before attacking Beaumont-Hamel, by way of the sunken road, on 1 July 1916. The officer in the centre is wearing a private soldier's tunic to appear less conspicuous. Company Sergeant-Major Ernest Shephard was in 1/Dorset, part of 32nd Division, which attacked Thiepval. His beautifully-kept diary describes receiving 'heavy shell and shrapnel' in the concentration area, and then a day of 'miraculous escapes' which cost his company over 100 men. Commissioned in December 1916, Shephard was killed near Beaumont-Hamel the following month and is buried in the AIF Military Cemetery, Flers.

Once attackers entered a trench they relied heavily on hand grenades, the British Mills bomb and the German stick grenade, and would try to bomb their way from traverse to traverse, bayonet men dashing in as grenades exploded.

Units rotated between tours of duty in front-line trenches, support systems and rest or training: a German battalion might spend four days in the front line, two in support and four at rest. Soldiers lived in dug-outs, entered by steps leading down from the trenches. Somme chalk lent itself to dug-out construction and the Germans, with no advance in mind, had built some splendid specimens, 30–40 feet (9–12 metres) deep, many with electric light and wood-panelled walls. These were impenetrable by all but the heaviest guns, although a direct hit could blow in a dugout's entrance and entomb the occupants.

The Plan of Campaign

We have seen that Haig and Rawlinson had different expectations. Haig directed Rawlinson to advance 1½ miles (2.4 km) on a front of 14 miles (23 km) on the first day of the Somme, enabling Gough's Reserve Army to push through the gap and seize Bapaume before swinging north towards Arras. Although Rawlinson doubted if things would be this simple, he was confident that the German first position would be taken, and the process could be repeated as 4th Army chewed its way to Bapaume bite by bite. Brigadier-General Gordon of 8th Infantry Brigade was expounding orthodoxy when he told men that they could 'slope arms, light up your pipes and cigarettes, and march all the way to Pozières before meeting any live Germans'.

This assurance stemmed from the fact that 1 500 000 shells were to be fired in the week before the attack, 18-pdrs working on wire and trenches, and heavier pieces concentrating on strongpoints and batteries. Once the battle began, a 'creeping barrage', a novelty for its day, would move ahead of the infantry. The artillery preparation proved inadequate and, on 1 July, men discovered to their cost that many Germans had survived in their dug-outs. There were proportionately fewer guns than had been available at Neuve Chapelle: the French to the south had twice as many heavy guns per yard of front line. A combination of faulty fuses and shot-out barrels meant that as many as one in three shells failed to explode. It was difficult to cut wire with shrapnel, and a high-explosive round with a 'graze' fuse was not readily available. There was no universal answer to the problem of dug-outs. However, the most menacing German positions would be dealt with by eight large and eleven small mines. Tunnels were dug forward from the

British lines to create explosive-packed chambers beneath features like the Hawthorn Ridge Redoubt. Most of these were to be blown at 7.28 a.m., two minutes before the assault began.

The bombardment began on 24 June. 'My Lord the gun has come into his own,' wrote one artillery officer, 'and his kingdom today is large: it is the world.' Another, standing on a gun-pit in the dark, felt 'the thousands of tons of metal rushing away from one'. A major in the Grimsby Chums reflected on the beauty of the German trenches under fire, 'our shells bursting over them in yellow, black or white puffs, many of the trenches covered by a bright yellow weed; while between the heavy white lines of chalk marking the principal trenches, there are frequently large fields of brilliant scarlet poppies.'

Above the battlefield, reconnaissance aircraft took photographs and spotted for the guns. Lieutenant C.S. Lewis found it hard to hold his plane steady in the torrent of shells. 'At two thousand feet [610 metres] we were in the path of the gun trajectories,' he wrote, 'and as the shells passed, above or below us, the wind eddies made by their motion flung the machine up and down as if in a gale. Each bump meant that a passing shell had missed the machine by four or five feet [1.2–1.5 metres] …' The attack had been intended to start on 29 June, but heavy summer storms restricted visibility, vital for accurate observation of artillery fire, and persuaded Rawlinson to delay it until 1 July.

Postponement tweaked pre-battle nerves. Patrols brought in news that the wire was uncut, and a gunner officer in 29th Division told his headquarters that the barrage would move faster than the infantry could follow. The plan was too complex to be altered by mere fact. Rawlinson had long since closed the debate, warning that 'All criticism by subordinates … of orders received from superior authority will, in the end, recoil on the critics.'

As battalions packed the crowded trenches on the night of 30 June, men asked themselves how they would cope with the challenge that approached with every tick of the watch. Many realized that they had no time to say all they needed to, and did their best in last letters. Second Lieutenant J.S. Engell told his parents:

The day has almost dawned when I shall really do my little bit in the cause of civilization … Should it be God's holy will to call me away, I am quite prepared to go … I could not wish for a finer death, and you, dear Mother and Dad, will know that I died doing my duty to my God, my country and my King.

Another officer gazed at the stars, and mused: 'What an insignificant thing the loss of say 40 years of life is to them …Well, Goodbye, you darlings.'

The Start of the Battle

At 7.20 a.m. on 1 July, as the bombardment reached its crescendo, the Hawthorn Ridge mine was blown, and the others exploded eight minutes later in what was then the loudest ever man-made sound. At 7.30 a.m. officers blew whistles and led their men across the parapet, through pre-cut gaps in the British wire and out into no man's land to form up for the assault. Most battalions were expecting to move forward at a walk, occupying defences levelled by artillery, not conducting a fighting advance against determined opposition, and men were heavily laden. General Sir Anthony Farrar-Hockley declared that 'no man carried less than 65 lb [29 kg]. Often additional grenades, bombs, small arms ammunition or perhaps a prepared charge against obstacles increased the load to 85 or 90 lb [38 or 41 kg].'

The difficulties of forming up a battalion of 600–800 men on ground hacked by shell-holes and trenches and strewn with wire merit consideration. What were to look like lines of advancing infantry were a series of columns moving side by side, with battalions moving on a front of one or two companies, and most covering perhaps 400 yards (365 metres) of frontage and a depth of 900 yards (823 metres). Control was by voice and whistle, although some officers tied pennons or handkerchiefs to walking sticks to help men to find them, and at least one wore his sword. Coloured triangles fixed to packs distinguished officers and NCOs, and tin reflectors worn on the back helped low-flying 'contact patrols' of the Royal Flying Corps to identify British troops.

What happened after 7.30 a.m. followed no consistent pattern, although there were grim similarities. In the north, at Gommecourt, two Territorial Divisions of 3rd Army mounted a two-pronged attack designed to draw in German reserves. The elaborate digging of trenches for waiting troops had left the Germans in no doubt of what was to come, and attackers in the northern division, 46th North Midland, were hewn down by machine-gun fire as they bunched in front of the few gaps in the German wire. The southern division, 56th London, fought its way into Gommecourt Wood. Some brave souls almost reached the point at which they were to have met the Midlanders, but were swamped by the inevitable counter-attack. One defender felt 'it wasn't fair to send these young soldiers against us. Some of them were only students and we felt very sorry for them.'

The story was the same opposite Serre, where the 31st Division left its strength on the German wire. Across the Serre road, elements of 4th Division took the Heidenkopf strongpoint on Redan Ridge and briefly got some little way beyond it. Further south, opposite Beaumont-Hamel, the attackers came from the last of the old regular divisions, a veteran of Gallipoli. It is no reflection on the quality or courage of what was widely known as the 'incomparable' 29th Division that it made no progress whatsoever.

Things were different south of the Ancre. The Schwaben Redoubt, dominating the high ground between the river and Thiepval, was attacked by the 36th Ulster Division. This had largely been recruited from members of the pre-war Ulster Volunteer Force, sworn to resist the imposition of Home Rule. It is as difficult to be objective about the Ulster Division as it is about the Australians. In fact, it contained soldiers from both sides of Ireland's cultural divide, although the majority were indeed Protestant. Some wore their Orangemen's sashes over their equipment, and there was a mood of exultation that would not brook waiting about in no man's land.

The Ulstermen were fortunate in that their assembly area in Thiepval Wood was close to the German front line and in dead ground, and at 7.30 a.m. they were into the German position before survivors had a chance to emerge from their dug-outs. The official history speaks of 'a steady pace with the precision of a parade movement', but one of the reasons for the division's success was its dash and momentum. The Schwaben was captured after the sort of hand-to-hand fighting that a veteran of Agincourt might have identified with. Men killed one another with bayonet and butt, shovel and explosive. Attackers dropped bags of grenades and trench-mortar bombs into dug-outs: one remembered that 'the yells and screams of those boys down there were wicked'.

A follow-up brigade tried to push through into the German second position, but machine-guns in Thiepval laced the flanks of the advance and artillery drew a curtain of fire across no man's land. When his West Belfast Company wavered, Major George Gaffikin took off his orange sash and waved it, bellowing 'Come on, boys! No surrender.' A few of the Ulstermen got into the second line but, unsupported, could not remain there. Nevertheless, although the Germans regained the Schwaben late in the afternoon, when 36th Division was relieved that night it handed over 800 yards (730 metres) of German front-line trench.

The Thiepval spur was the key to the whole front between the River Ancre and the Roman road. Thiepval's houses had been demolished by shellfire, but their debris covered deep cellars and defenders had tunnelled between them to create a position of enormous strength. On the

Overleaf: Artist André Devambez has caught French troops at the moment of assault on the Somme. Belts of French and German wire are clearly visible. Attacking troops are climbing ladders out of the front-line trench, into no-man's land, while others pack the communication trenches behind them.

southern face of the spur, grinning out south and west, stood the Leipzig Redoubt. When 32nd Division attacked Thiepval its only success came at the Leipzig. Brigadier-General Jardine had been attached to the Japanese army during the Russo-Japanese War (1904–5), and had noticed that successful Japanese infantry assaults went in over very short distances. Accordingly, at 7.23 p.m. the leading companies of Glasgow Commercials crept close to the German line and rushed it when the barrage lifted. They were in the Leipzig before its defenders surfaced.

Between Thiepval and the Roman road, 8th Division attacked Ovillers, its right flank pushing up Mash Valley, a long re-entrant with the La Boisselle spur to its south. The feature was twinned with Sausage Valley, named after the German observation balloons which had flown above it, on the other side of the spur. That day it was mash valley indeed, and 2/Middlesex, whose commanding officer had been concerned about the problem of flanking fire, lost 623 of its soldiers.

The fate of 34th Division, on the other side of the spur, was even crueller. Only two of its brigades could start from the British front line at the foot of the slope, and the third, 103rd (Tyneside Irish) Brigade, had to begin its advance from the far side of a low ridge, its twin peaks known as Tara and Usna hills, moving almost 1 mile (1.6 km) across open country to the front line. The explosion of the huge Lochnagar mine and a cluster of smaller mines further north enabled assaulting battalions to penetrate the German front line, and isolated parties got as far as Contalmaison, deep in the second position. But the flanks of the penetration were not secured, and as Tyneside Irish marched forward, keeping step to the beat of a single bass drum in the centre of the brigade, they were subjected to unceasing and accurate machine-gun fire. The division lost 6380 men that day, including a brigadier and seven out of twelve battalion commanders.

At Fricourt, further south, 21st Division made poor progress, but on its right 7th Division took and held Mametz. Major-General Maxse's 18th Division pushed on to seize Montauban Alley, the trench system on the far side of the Mametz–Montauban road. As for 30th Division, it did even better. It profited from the fact that the French, on its immediate right, were well provided with heavy guns and the bombardment was unusually effective. However, a single German machine-gun, firing with cool deliberation from 18th Division's sector into the flank of the advance, hit every company commander in the leading waves and remained in action until knocked out by a Lewis gun team of 2/Manchester Pals.

The performance of German machine-gunners attracted the admiration of many British soldiers. One officer called them: 'Topping fellows.

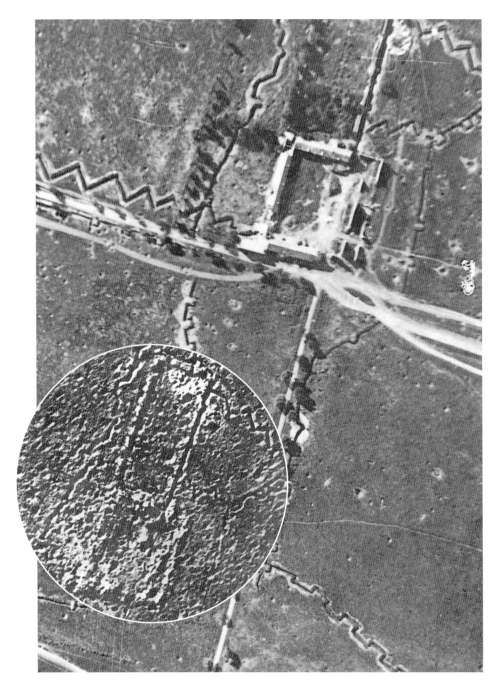

This aerial view of Mouquet Farm, strongpoint in the German second position, was taken in July and shows the outline of trenches and the fact that little damage had been done to defences this far back. The inset was taken in September, revealing how incessant bombardment transformed the area.

Fight until they are killed. They gave us hell.' Another saw a grey-haired German machine-gunner slumped behind his gun surrounded by a pile of empty cases almost as high as the gun. When an advancing section passed a dead machine-gunner, one of its members heard 'a murmur of approbation' from his mates.

Despite the efforts of the unknown machine-gunner, 30th Division took Montauban and the nearby brickworks. North of the Somme, General Balfourier's 'Iron' Corps had made good progress, while south of the river, where the French achieved surprise by attacking at 9.30 a.m., results were even more impressive. They had heavier guns than the British: eighty-five heavy batteries had engaged 7983 yards (7300 metres) of trench for nearly eight days. Their tactics were more flexible, attackers shoving on in small groups, ducking and weaving their way forward and supporting one another by fire.

This had little to do with abstract thought and much to do with experience. The first day of the Somme was the 132nd day of Verdun, and the French had been learning. The British, too, were to learn fast, although we must doubt whether 57 470 men were a fair price for the teaching. The Germans, for their part, lost 2200 prisoners, and casualties for the bombardment and the first day of the battle may have totalled 8000.

The Battle Goes On

Over the next few days Haig shifted his balance, giving Gough command north of the Roman road, where the German first position was largely intact, while south of the road Rawlinson took on the second position. This ran along Longueval Ridge, with two prominent woods, Delville Wood and High Wood (Bois des Fourcaux) astride it. Its fall would expose Pozières and in turn isolate Thiepval, undermining the German position south of the Ancre. Before Rawlinson's men could get to grips with the position they had to deal with Mametz Wood, 'that menacing wall of gloom', which stood like a bastion in front of it. Most of its trees – oak, beech and birch – were still standing, and those that had been blown down by shellfire thickened the tangled undergrowth. Second Lieutenant Siegfried Sassoon's 2/Royal Welch Fusiliers had approached it on 3 July, passing British dead 'their fingers mingled in bloodstained bunches, as though they were acknowledging the companionship of death,' to discover that even if the wood had been empty two days before it was now 'full of Germans'.

On 7 July, Mametz Wood was attacked by the New Army's 38th (Welsh) Division, whose composition owed much to the political influence of David Lloyd George. It had not fought a major action before, and

Sassoon found his trench filled by 'a jostling company of exclamatory Welshmen ... I understood the doomed condition of these half trained civilians who had been sent up to attack the Wood.' An initial attack failed, and on 10 July the division mounted a more forceful effort under a new commander, crashing into the wood from the south.

The attackers tried to clear the wood in sections, ride by ride, but it was impossible to keep direction in the tangle. Shelling only worsened matters. Lieutenant Wyn Griffith saw 'limbs and mutilated trunks, here and there a detached head, forming splashes of red against the green leaves ... one tree held in its branches a leg, with its torn flesh hanging down over a spray of leaf.' Captain Robert Graves crept into the wood at night in search of German overcoats to use as blankets, and found it 'full of dead Prussian Guards Reserve, big men, and dead Royal Welch and South Wales Borderers of the New Army battalions, little men.' By the time it was relieved by 7th and 21st Divisions on 12 July, when the wood was at last cleared, 38th Division had lost 4000 men, including seven battalion commanders.

The attack on Longueval Ridge was altogether more successful. On the night of 13/14 July Rawlinson launched 22 000 men against it after only a short bombardment. By mid-morning the second position was breached all along the ridge, and for a few heady moments there was a possibility of exploitation as cavalry moved up to High Wood. But the opportunity slipped away, and for most of that unseasonably wet summer 4th Army was stalled in front of High Wood and Delville Wood. Shelling reduced both to what Lieutenant Max Plowman called 'a collection of stakes stuck upright in the ground like the broken teeth of some vicious beast.' The Germans were able to relieve their garrisons by trickling troops up from the dead ground behind the woods while attackers had to cross the shell-scoured slopes to their front.

There had been gradual progress on the Roman road. La Boisselle fell on 7 July and Ovillers on the 16th but Pozières remained obdurate. In pitch darkness on 23 July the Australians were launched against the village, keeping close to the barrage to take their first objective in the almost unrecognizable heap of ruins. The Germans always riposted sharply – Falkenhayn ordained that 'the first principle of position warfare must be to yield not one foot of ground; if it be lost, to retake it immediately by counter-attack ...' – and an immediate counter-attack was driven off with heavy loss. As John Terraine has observed, the texture of the Somme was 'attack, counter-attack; attack again; counter-attack again' and when attackers knew their business these counter-attacks were very roughly handled.

On 7 August, after bludgeoning through Pozières yard by filthy yard, the Australians shrugged off the last counter-attack to remain masters of the village. They then edged north to attack Mouquet ('Mucky') Farm whose capture was expected to unlock Thiepval, still standing secure on its bluff. On 5 September they were relieved by the Canadians and left the sector with deepening contempt for 'the British Staff, British methods and British bungling'. As Peter Charlton tells us in his fine book *Australians on the Somme: Pozières 1916*: 'If Australians wish to trace their modern suspicion and resentment of Britain to a date and a place, then July–August 1916 and the ruined village of Pozières are useful points of departure. Australia was never the same again.'

The First Tanks in Action

Even before Pozières fell, Haig was warned by Robertson that there was widespread disquiet over huge losses for small gains. Haig replied that he proposed to maintain steady pressure to wear down the Germans and would snatch any chance of a break-out. Another major effort would be made in mid-September, and as part of it he intended to use what he termed 'a rather desperate innovation'. There was nothing new in the notion of what H.G. Wells had called 'The Land Ironclads', but stalemate had encouraged the British to experiment with an armoured, trench-crossing machine whose box-like structure inspired the dissembling name of tank. The crews, provided by the Heavy Section Machine-Gun Corps, were subjected to deafening noise from the engine and guns, thrown about by the monster's lumbering gait and nauseated by its exhaust fumes. The tanks arrived at Abbeville in early September, were moved up to a railhead at Bray-sur-Somme, and thirty-two of them were available on 15 September when the battle of Flers-Courcelette, the last major offensive on the Somme, began.

The distinction of being the first tank in action went to 'D1', which cleared an isolated pocket of resistance on the eastern edge of Delville Wood shortly before the main attack began at 6.20 a.m. on the 15th. In the north, Gough allocated all his tanks to 2nd Canadian Division, which intended to use them in its drive on the sugar factory at Courcelette. This was taken without the aid of the tanks, which broke down or failed to keep up with the infantry. On the Canadian right, 15th Scottish Division took Martinpuich with the help of four tanks. Another four were assigned to assist 47th London Division in its attack on High Wood – 'Ghastly by day, ghostly by night, the rottenest place on the Somme.' Tank officers had warned that their machines were likely to belly on tree-stumps. Three eventually ditched, and the fourth reached the

German support line where it was destroyed by a shell. The Londoners took the wood after a trench-mortar battery put 750 bombs into it in seven minutes, at last knocking the fight out of the Bavarian defenders.

It is an indication of the massive concentrations now applied to small objectives that XV Corps had three divisions available for its attack on Flers across the strip of blighted landscape between High Wood and Delville Wood. Fourteen of the eighteen tanks allocated had reached their points of departure, and when the battle opened they jarred and rumbled their way forward. There was little the German infantry could do: it took a direct hit from a field gun or, more commonly, an obstacle or a mechanical breakdown, to stop them. 'The monsters approached slowly,' wrote one German, 'hobbling, rolling and rocking but they approached. Nothing impeded them: a supernatural force seemed to impel them on. Someone in the trenches said, "The Devil is coming" …' A British pilot reported 'A tank is walking up the High Street of Flers with the British Army cheering behind it,' but the truth was more familiar: the gap was sealed before advantage could be taken of it.

The End of the Battle

Although there were further successes – Morval and Lesboeufs fell on 25 September and Thiepval, at long last, on the 26th – the fighting petered out in a sea of mud on what was barely recognizable as the German third position. Lieutenant E.G. Bates of the Northumberland Fusiliers described: 'Ponds of standing water; what looks like a fairly safe crossing, in reality a 10-foot [3-metre] shell-hole; trenches falling in and impossible to repair; men done up before they ever get under fire.' Max Plowman saw how: 'Corpses lie along the parados, rotting in the wet; every now and then a booted foot appears jutting over the trench. The mud makes it all but impassable.' The battle struck its dying fall with the capture of Beaumont-Hamel – a 1 July objective – on 13 November.

Even now we cannot be certain how many men died or were wounded on the Somme. Allied casualties totalled about 600 000, two-thirds of them British. Differences in casualty reporting procedure mean that the official German figures are certainly too low, although many have accused Brigadier-General Sir James Edmonds, the British official historian, of over-optimism in inflating them to 660–680 000. It is safer to suggest that the Germans lost 600 000 men, many in counter-attacks and more to artillery. Erich von Ludendorff, deputy to Field-Marshal von Hindenburg, who had replaced the discredited Falkenhayn in August 1916, admitted that the Germans were 'completely exhausted', and a survivor wrote:

'The Somme was the muddy grave of the German field army.'

That the Somme had worn down the German army and contributed to the tactical skill of the British cannot be denied. But much else had been worn down, and the New Armies had lost their innocence. On 1 July a soldier of 12/London Regiment emerged from Gommecourt Wood with a smashed arm and a gashed head, asking where the dressing station was. A signaller told him to wait while he found a stretcher-bearer. 'I don't want him for *me*,' said the young man tersely, wiping blood out of his eyes. 'I want someone to come back with me to get my mate. *He's hurt!*'

A View of the Field

If any battlefield can be described as a congenial spot for a long walk then the Somme is it. We might do best to drive on to it, passing through Querrieu on the Amiens–Albert road, which Sassoon remembered as 'a big village cosily over-populated by 4th Army Staff'. Rawlinson's head-quarters were in the château where the road from Amiens swings right on entering the village. Its owners, the Count and Countess d'Alcantara, are generally prepared to receive visitors who phone in advance – the number is (22) 4011409 – and have converted their stables into pleasant bed and breakfast apartments which can be booked on the same number.

Rawlinson did not spend all his time at Querrieu. Sassoon got 'a glimpse of his geniality' as he 'squelched among the brown tents in his boots and spurs'. He observed the opening of the battle from 'the Grand-stand' near Dernancourt, and the military historian Martin Middlebrook, whose knowledge of the battle is encyclopaedic, has found it. A minor road connects the Amiens–Albert highway with Dernancourt, in the Ancre valley south of Albert. A metalled farm track strikes off north-eastwards 150 yards (137 metres) north of a copse equidistant between Dernancourt and the main road, and from the end of the track the entire southern portion of the battlefield can be seen. Ulster Tower, close to the site of the Schwaben Redoubt, cuts the skyline to the north-north-east, with the Thiepval Memorial to its right. Further right, past Ovillers and Pozières, both Mametz Wood and Delville Wood are smudges on the horizon.

Albert
Albert is a bustling town, overlooked by the rebuilt basilica and its golden Virgin. The tower was hit by shellfire in January 1915 and the statue began to list dangerously, but French engineers secured it with steel cable and it remained 'the hanging Virgin' for most of the war.

Some said that the war would end when the statue fell, and others unkindly maintained that it was the only virgin to be found in Albert. The town was taken by the Germans in their spring offensive in 1918, and on 16 April British guns levelled the tower to prevent artillery observers from using it. After the First World War the presence of an aircraft factory south of the town led the citizens to fear air raids in future conflicts, and shelters in the square beneath the basilica now house a rather jumbled war museum.

Following the Front Line
The 1 July front line can be followed for almost all its length. Gommecourt Wood New Cemetery, on the D6 linking Gommecourt to Foncquevillers, provides a clear view of the ground over which 46th Division attacked. Looking north, a small copse in the valley bottom marks a bulge in the German line called Schwalben Nest by the men who held it and The Z by the British. The German front trench ran along the edge of Sartel Wood, on the right, and there were further trenches in the wood behind it. A battalion of 91st Reserve Regiment held the sector attacked by the twelve battalions of 46th Division, a similar ratio of defence to attack on many other parts of the front that day.

The two forward brigades of 46th Division – 137th on the right and 139th on the left – formed up in no man's land east of Foncquevillers, but when they advanced most were stopped by wire, machine-gun and artillery fire although a few got into the wood. The follow-up brigade, 138th, with four battalions of Sherwood Foresters, did somewhat better, and a few attackers crossed the first German trench. Five battalion commanders were killed and one, Lieutenant-Colonel C.E. Boote of 1/6th North Staffordshire, a Boer War veteran, is buried in the cemetery.

Captain J.L. Green, medical officer of 1/6th Sherwood Foresters, was hit while treating the wounded in no man's land, and was eventually killed as he dragged a wounded officer back towards British lines. He won one of the nine VCs awarded that day, and lies in Foncquevillers Military Cemetery. Captain Green's death points up one of the sad truths of the first day. The proportion of killed to wounded (21 000 to 36 000) was unusually high because many who could have recovered with prompt attention perished as they lay in no man's land. Initially the Germans took few chances, and men who moved between the lines were sniped or machine-gunned. Later, especially in areas where the attack had palpably failed, they sometimes allowed the wounded to be recovered. Often men took huge risks to drag in survivors or search for friends, and many remembered the

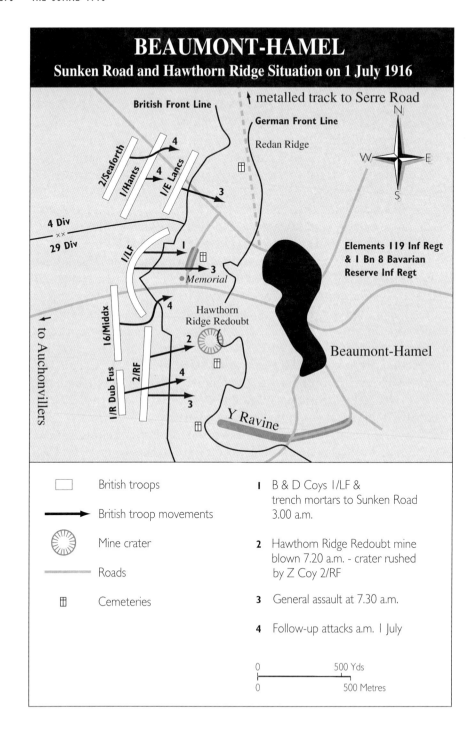

BEAUMONT-HAMEL
Sunken Road and Hawthorn Ridge Situation on 1 July 1916

British Front Line

metalled track to Serre Road

N

German Front Line

Redan Ridge

2/Seaforth

1/Hants

1/E Lancs

4

4

3

W—E

S

4 Div
××
29 Div

1/LF

1

3

Elements 119 Inf Regt
& 1 Bn 8 Bavarian
Reserve Inf Regt

Memorial

Hawthorn
Ridge Redoubt

16/Middx

4

2

4

Beaumont-Hamel

to Auchonvillers

1/R Dub Fus

2/RF

3

Y Ravine

British troops

British troop movements

Mine crater

Roads

Cemeteries

1 B & D Coys 1/LF &
trench mortars to Sunken Road
3.00 a.m.

2 Hawthorn Ridge Redoubt mine
blown 7.20 a.m. - crater rushed
by Z Coy 2/RF

3 General assault at 7.30 a.m.

4 Follow-up attacks a.m. 1 July

0   500 Yds

0   500 Metres

cries of the wounded, sounding like fingernails being dragged down glass, as the most distressing aspect of the day.

Bravery at Serre

To trace 31st Division's attack on Serre, park in front of Serre Road Cemetery No. 1, where the Serre–Mailly-Maillet road (D919) dips south of Serre. Then walk up a long track north of the farm, following the Commonwealth War Graves Commission (CWGC) signs to Luke Copse British Cemetery, as far as the wood now known as Sheffield Park. In 1916 there were four copses here – Matthew, Mark, Luke and John. The British front line ran along the edge of the wood, and can still be seen as an unmistakable ditch. The 94th Brigade attacked Serre, just over the crest-line to the east, from this line, with two of its battalions in the first wave. The Accrington Pals were on its right, where the gates lead down to Railway Hollow Cemetery, and on its left, where the copse peters out, stood the Sheffield City Battalion.

Both battalions began to form up in no man's land at 7.20 a.m. on 1 July 1916. They were immediately machine-gunned from the German front line, about 100 yards (90 metres) beyond the small cemeteries east of Sheffield Park, and field guns bombarded the British front line. Neither counter-battery fire nor a hurricane bombardment from Stokes mortars which preceded the assault made any difference, and at 7.30 a.m. Germans could be seen running out to man their fire positions.

The Accringtons and the City Battalion attacked regardless. 'The extended lines started in excellent order but gradually melted away,' recorded Sir James Edmonds.

There was no wavering or attempting to come back. The men fell in their ranks, mostly before the first hundred yards of No Man's Land had been crossed. The magnificent gallantry, discipline and determination shown by all ranks of this North Country division were of no avail against the concentrated fire-effect of the enemy's unshaken infantry and artillery, whose barrage has been described as so consistent and severe that the cones of the explosions gave the impression of a thick belt of poplar trees.

Captain Riley led his Burnley lads into the maelstrom and was shot through the head: his commanding officer, Lieutenant-Colonel Rickman, survived the battle, although the official history reported him killed, only to be electrocuted at home in 1925.

A few men from each battalion managed to enter Serre. A gunner officer saw some of the right-hand Accrington Company disappear into the village, and when it was briefly entered in November the bodies of some Sheffield men were found in its north-west corner. The Accringtons lost 585 officers and men and the Sheffield City Battalion 512. Many are buried in the cemeteries around Sheffield Park, amongst them Private Alf Goodlad, who lies in Railway Hollow Cemetery, and whose proud parents inscribed a sentence from one of his letters on his tombstone. France was, he told them, a grand country, well worth fighting for.

A metalled track, which leaves the Serre road almost opposite the track to Sheffield Park, leads across Redan Ridge to Beaumont-Hamel. On entering the village turn right towards Auchonvillers and walk as far as a track leading north to a memorial to 8/Argyll and Sutherland Highlanders. The mound it stands on gives a good view of the defences of Beaumont-Hamel, with the German front line running along the wood edge to the east and the position of Hawthorn Ridge Redoubt marked by trees and bushes across the road to one's right front.

Don't be Alarmed, the Accrington Pals are on guard at Carnarvon.

The Accringtons left Lancashire for Carnarvon in early 1915, and this postcard dates from their time there. The reality of the Somme had little to do with this image: most men were tired after a long march to the front the night before the battle. Yet the attack aroused great admiration. The commander of 94th Infantry Brigade wrote: 'I have been through many battles in this war and nothing more magnificent has come to my notice. The waves went forward as if on a drill parade and I saw no man turn back or falter.'

Memorials and Cemeteries

The sunken road, a continuation of the track, was occupied on the night of 30 June 1916 by B and D companies of 1/Lancashire Fusiliers and eight Stokes mortars which were to fire a hurricane bombardment to cover the assault. The Germans dropped shells into the road at 7 a.m., and the explosion of the Hawthorn Ridge Redoubt mine drew heavier fire. The two leading companies were, in the words of Lieutenant-Colonel Martin Magniac, 'mown down' as they left the road, and the other two companies suffered heavily just to reach the road. Corporal George Ashurst jumped breathlessly into it: 'My God, what a sight! The whole of the road was strewn with dead and dying men. Some were talking deliriously, others calling for help and asking for water.' The second wave attacked with no better success. Some Lancashire Fusiliers lie in the cemetery which marks the front edge of the German wire, but most have no known graves. Although 2/Royal Fusiliers, across the road to the right, sent men racing for the mine-crater they were unable to secure it, and once the Germans had re-established themselves, further efforts were hopeless.

It is possible to walk up to Newfoundland Park, a large area of preserved battlefield south-west of Beaumont-Hamel or to drive there by way of Auchonvillers. A bronze caribou, bellowing out across the battlefield, commemorates the Newfoundlanders, whose front and support trenches are marked. A short walk out across no man's land, past the 'Tree of Death' which marks the limit of the Newfoundland advance, takes the visitor to Y Ravine Cemetery and, further on, to the German front line, which still gives a good impression of its former strength. The statue of a kilted soldier celebrates the capture of Beaumont-Hamel by 51st Highland Division in November 1916.

The 36th Division is commemorated by Ulster Tower, on the far side of the Ancre. It is a replica of Helen's Tower, in the Marquess of Dufferin and Ava's park at Clandeboye, near Belfast, where the division had trained, and there is a good little museum, with a knowledgeable curator, just behind it. To reach the site of the Schwaben Redoubt we must walk past Mill Road Cemetery, whose gravestones are laid flat because the ground is so unstable. There is usually a practicable route along a field edge east of the cemetery, and about 300 yards (275 metres) further on tussocks interlaced with occasional broken bottles mark the site of the Schwaben.

Thiepval is crowned by Sir Edwin Lutyens' Memorial to the Missing which bears the names of 73 412 British and South African officers and men missing on the Somme in 1916–17. Names are arranged in panels

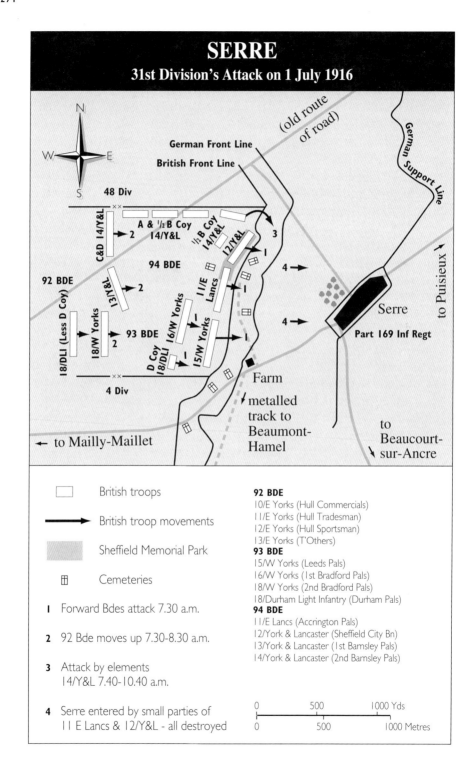

by regimental seniority, beginning with cavalry and gunners up to the left as one approaches. It includes neither British soldiers missing in the fighting of 1918 nor Empire or Dominion missing who are commemorated elsewhere. The Anglo-French cemetery in front of the memorial contains 300 dead from each nation and symbolizes the joint effort of the Allies. It stands on the front line vainly attacked on 1 July by 16/Northumberland Fusiliers, the Newcastle Commercials.

The road south winds past the Leipzig salient and, with a left turn short of Aveluy, goes on to meet the Roman road at La Boisselle. Snaking through the village and following signs for La Grande Mine takes the visitor past craters called 'The Glory Hole', where the track for Lochnagar crater leaves the village: broken ground caused by mining can be seen on the right. Although some of the mines that exploded beneath Messines Ridge in 1917 contained more explosive, Lochnagar is the largest surviving crater. It was created by 60 000 lb (27 215 kg) of ammonal exploded beneath the German front line and was taken by the Tyneside Scottish, some of whom were hit by lumps of chalk flung into the air by the blast. An Englishman, Richard Dunning, bought the crater in 1970, having seen how farming was gradually changing the battlefield.

It makes a profound impression, and the pockmarked ground around it offers a good view of the Tara–Usna line from which the Tyneside Irish began their doomed advance.

No book of this length can hope to do justice to the whole of the 1 July front, but one remaining spot is more than worth a visit. Due south of Mametz, 8/ and 9/Devons of 7th Division attacked from Mansell Copse, on the lip of the valley south of the Fricourt–Maricourt road. The civilian cemetery of Mametz stands on the other side of the road. Captain D.L. Martin, one of 9/Devons' company commanders, had made a Plasticine model of the area and predicted that the machine-gun dug in below the base of The Shrine (the crucifix in the cemetery, replaced but easily visible) would catch his battalion as it breasted the rise and made for the German front line to its north, obliquely to the gun. He was right, and he lies with 123 other Devons, including Noel Hodgson the poet, in Devonshire Cemetery. This was a trench burial, with the dead interred *en masse* in the old front-line trench. A wooden sign, now replaced by stone, proudly proclaimed:

> The Devonshires held this trench
> The Devonshires hold it still

Mametz Wood is in private hands, but the track leaving Mametz village for Bazentin curls along its eastern edge, passing the new dragon memorial

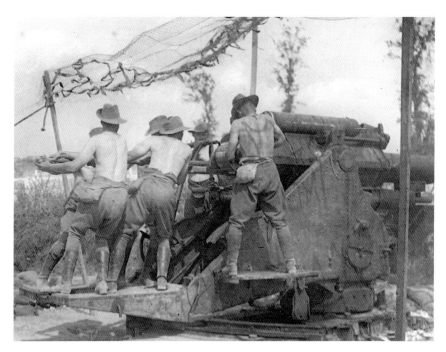

Australian artillerymen serving a 9.2-inch heavy gun during the battle for Pozières in August. They are shirtless in the heat, but have retained their khaki fur-felt hats, the symbol of the 'digger.'

to 38th Division and then running past Flat Iron Copse Cemetery, which began as a dressing station set up shortly after 7th Division took Bazentin on 14 July. The track emerges on the Contalmaison–Longueval road, and it is possible to walk to High Wood along a track which heads off almost opposite the turning down to Bazentin-le-Grand, or to go straight on into Longueval.

Delville Wood lies east of Longueval, and amongst the divisions which fought for 'Devil's Wood' was 9th Scottish, which included a South African brigade. The South African National Memorial within the wood was built in 1987 around the original Voortrekker's Cross which commemorated the 10 000 South African dead of the First World War. The rides in the wood have stone markers recording street names given to them by 9th Scottish Division. A convenient café stands near the entrance to the wood. On the open ground between Delville Wood and High Wood is the New Zealand Division Memorial: the New Zealanders crossed this ridge on 15 September 1916, making good progress once the fall of High Wood had cleared their left flank. High Wood itself cannot be entered, but a walk around its edge shows what a commanding view its garrison enjoyed.

Pozières and Mild Trench

Two remaining spots help us to understand the Somme. Pozières, with its Australian memorials and idiosyncratic Burma Star Café, dominates the surrounding countryside, and it is easy to see why the village was important. On the northern side of the Roman road is the site of Pozières Mill, the highest spot on the entire battlefield. Just across the road the Tank Memorial, which bears Second World War damage, marks the spot from which tanks of C Company, Heavy Section Machine-Gun Corps, set off to accompany 2nd Canadian Division on 16 September.

Having seen one caribou in Newfoundland Park, we can find another north-east of Gueudecourt. He stands on a pocket-handkerchief of ground slashed by a trench. This is purportedly Hilt Trench, taken by the Newfoundlanders on 12 October, but is actually Mild Trench, captured by 2/East Lancashires two weeks later. It stands at the furthest point of the British advance. On a good day the Thiepval Memorial, almost due west, is visible with the naked eye, and to the north Bapaume, an early objective for Gough's cavalry, stands on the horizon. On a bad day the wind keens across the ridge, reminding us that by November 1916 there was sheer desolation to the west, with no metalled track or light railway until the other side of the Longueval Ridge. By the time the battle finished, soldiers up here were dying of exhaustion and exposure. Whatever historians now say about the Somme, when soldiers of a later generation sought a telling comparison it always came to mind. 'This,' they would say, 'is the biggest balls-up since the Somme.'

CHAPTER 9

Arras
1940

Background

In May 1940 the Germans rolled across the battlefields of 1914–18 with a speed which amazed them. 'It was hardly conceivable,' wrote Major-General Erwin Rommel. 'Twenty-two years before we had stood for four-and-a-half years before this self-same enemy and had won victory after victory and finally lost the war.' 'What was up with the famous French army, which in the First World War had fought against us so bravely and on equal terms?' asked Captain Hans von Luck. 'Le Cateau, then Cambrai, Arras, always far in front of everybody else,' exulted Rommel. The word *blitzkrieg*, meaning 'lightning war', summed it up perfectly.

The Aftermath of the First World War
In 1919 the Treaty of Versailles had confirmed Allied victory. Germany had already lost her imperial crown, for the Kaiser fled in November 1918, and Versailles went on to strip her of territory, returning Alsace and Lorraine to France. The German army was restricted to 100 000 men, without tanks, heavy guns or aircraft, and the general staff was abolished. Germany accepted guilt for causing and prosecuting the war, and was to pay huge reparations. France was to administer the coal mines in the Saar for fifteen years to compensate for damage to her own mining heartland. The peacemakers redrew the map of Eastern Europe, creating the new states of Czecho-slovakia and Yugoslavia, and re-establishing Poland, leaving East Prussia isolated from the remainder of Germany.

Some felt that this settlement was too harsh: others thought that it was not punitive enough. Marshal Foch, Allied generalissimo in 1918,

Men of 4/Royal Tank Regiment, in their distinctive black berets, at work on Infantry Tanks Mk I. This tank was nicknamed Matilda because of its comic duck appearance, but the nickname was soon applied to the more powerful Mk II. Tank crews carried .38 Enfield revolvers, introduced into service in 1932: this version has no hammer spur, making it less likely to catch on clothing or equipment in a tank. Most British soldiers who fought in the 1940 campaign were entitled to the 1939-45 Star, generally awarded for six months' service in an operational command – though a single day at Dunkirk qualified a soldier for the medal.

believed that it was merely a twenty-year armistice. The great powers stalked away from the peace table in a sour mood. President Wilson, who had done much to shape the settlement, could not sell it to his own countrymen. Britain speedily dismantled a war-winning instrument. In November 1918 she had 3½ million men under arms: two years later there were 370 000. The army reverted to its traditional role of imperial policing. Public disillusionment with war combined with official attempts to reduce the burden imposed by defence. The Ten Year Rule, formulated in 1919 but slipped forward year by year until 1932, decreed that planning was to proceed on the basis that there would be no major war for ten years. As late as May 1938 a senior RAF officer declared: 'Never again shall we even contemplate a force for a foreign country. Our contribution is to be the Navy and the RAF.'

The mood in France was no more buoyant. First World War casualties had been proportionately heavier than in Britain or Germany: one-third of young Frenchmen had been killed or crippled. War memorials embodied the moral credit which France believed herself to have earned, but the sacrifice they represented counted for little. Inflation hit bourgeois and peasant alike, and former allies seemed reluctant to force Germany to pay reparations. When she defaulted in 1923 the French and Belgians occupied the Ruhr, increasing German bitterness and worsening her economic state. The Wall Street crash of 1929 plunged the Western world into crisis, and in Germany it fuelled hyper-inflation which encouraged extremist politics and permitted the rise of Hitler, who exploited resentment against Versailles and found scapegoats, internal and external, to blame for the country's plight.

France had a seat on the Council of the League of Nations and tried, through alliances with Czechoslovakia and Poland, to maintain international support. Her quest for security solidified along the Franco-German border in a barrier which took its name from André Maginot, the Verdun veteran who steered its credits through parliament. There was some logic behind the Maginot Line. Commissions had noted the relatively small amount of internal damage suffered by the Verdun forts. Tens of thousands of Frenchmen had fallen trying to expel the Germans from France. The line would prevent rapid invasion and give time for the mobilization of a mass army.

This logic collapsed under the pressure of events. In 1936 Belgium became neutral. Although money was found for some fortifications on the Franco-Belgian border, these were not on the same scale as the line proper. It was impossible to link defensive strategy with alliances in Eastern Europe. Colonel Charles de Gaulle, one of the army's most radical thinkers, warned that if war came all the French would be able to do was watch, from behind their barricades, the enslavement of Europe. The cost of the line meant that there was little left over for modern weapons and equipment. When the Popular Front came to power in 1936 and attempted to improve military preparedness, it found that French arms production failed to match that of Germany. Lastly, the line contributed to a defensive mentality and discouraged progressive military thought.

In fact, there were innovators in all the contending nations. The manoeuvres of the British Experimental Mechanized Force in the late 1920s broke new ground and Provisional Regulations of 1927 were a powerful influence on Heinz Guderian, who helped to inspire the development of German armoured troops. The apostles of mobility – men like Guderian in Germany, de Gaulle in France and Basil Liddell Hart and Major-General J.F.C. Fuller (the Tank Corps' chief of staff in the First World War and a prolific military writer) in Britain – disagreed on points of detail, but all rejected systematic attrition and envisaged a war characterized by manoeuvre. Building on infiltration tactics developed during the First World War, they emphasized the importance of achieving surprise, attacking an enemy's points of weakness, and tapping out a tempo which left him paralysed.

Many, even in Germany, regarded them as heretics. General Hans von Seekt, commander of the 100 000-man *Reichswehr*, who used a variety of measures to circumvent the Treaty of Versailles, favoured infiltration tactics; he had no particular regard for tanks, and many of his fellow officers were deeply conservative. Guderian and the 'Young Turks' made slow progress and needed high-level political support. In early 1934, a year after Hitler had become chancellor, Guderian showed him a primitive, mechanized combined-arms force at Kummersdorf. 'That's what I need,' said Hitler. 'That's what I want to have.' Yet he was no easy convert to armoured warfare. He thought that the tank would earn him prestige, and it was probably not until 1939 that he glimpsed the weapon's real potential.

Other reformers fared less well. De Gaulle was struck off the 1936 promotion list for writing a controversial book. Fuller retired as a major-general after being offered an appointment he regarded as insulting. Liddell Hart, who had left the army after the First World War, enjoyed considerable influence as adviser to the secretary of state for war in 1935–7 but was bitterly resented by the military establishment.

Germany Develops Armoured Warfare
The expanding German army gained three panzer divisions in 1933, but

the first General der Panzertruppen, Otto Lutz, was opposed by officers
who hoped to use the tank to support infantry and feared these divisions
would consume resources best spread across the whole army. However,
experience gained in the Spanish Civil War and in the invasion of
Poland in September 1939 helped the Germans to develop armoured
warfare. Surprise, speed and concentration were its essence, encapsu-
lated in Guderian's slogan '*Klotzen, nicht Kleckern*' – 'Smash, don't
tap.' Their new air force, the *Luftwaffe*, not only prevented enemy aircraft from interfering in the ground battle but became 'flying artillery'
for the panzer divisions.

These were not simply tank formations, but included mechanized
infantry (called rifle regiments in 1940); reconnaissance; field, anti-tank
and anti-aircraft artillery; and engineers. Of all their weapons, the radio
was the most potent. Communications had been the single greatest con-
straint on First World War tactics: how different the first day on the
Somme might have been in 1916 had the attackers been able to identify
and reinforce their success faster than the defender could rectify his failure. General Ludwig Beck had asked Guderian how he proposed to lead
a panzer division. 'From the front – by wireless' replied 'Hurrying
Heinz'. 'Nonsense!' retorted Beck. 'A divisional commander sits back
with maps and a telephone.' He could not do so in 1940 and hope to win.

Campaign and Battle

When Britain and France declared war in September 1939 in response to
the German invasion of Poland, there was little they could do for the
Poles. The French mounted an irresolute offensive into the Saar, settled
down in the Maginot Line and began preparing for a long war. It was the
coldest winter for years, and morale plummeted. Major-General Edward
Spears had been a liaison officer in the First World War, knew the French
army well, and found its condition 'horribly depressing'.

Allied Plans
The French commander-in-chief, General Maurice Gamelin, was based
in the Château de Vincennes, on the eastern outskirts of Paris, within
sight of the donjon in which Henry V had died. He issued orders to the
North-East Front through its commander, General Georges, at La Ferté-
sous-Jouarre. Georges disposed of three army groups, with General
Gaston Billotte's No. 1 Army Group responsible for the Franco-Belgian
border. It comprised four French armies – Blanchard's 1st, Huntziger's
2nd, Giraud's 7th and Corap's 9th – as well as Lord Gort's British Expe-

ditionary Force (BEF). In practice, Gort, a grenadier with a formidable fighting reputation from the First World War, received his orders from Gamelin via Georges. He also enjoyed right of appeal to the British government should he receive orders which appeared to imperil his force. Spears described him as 'a simple, straightforward but not very clever man ... who felt above all else that orders must be obeyed.' There were to be times in the coming campaign when Gort's moral courage would stand him in good stead.

In February 1940 air zones were created to correspond with these army groups: General d'Astier de la Vigerie's Northern Zone of Aerial Operations supported Blanchard's army group. The BEF had its own air component, and there was a separate Advanced Air Striking Force (AASF), part of Bomber Command, under Air Marshal Barratt. These arrangements testified to a difference in attitude between Allied air forces and the *Luftwaffe*. The latter was geared to winning air superiority and supporting ground operations, and the system of *Luftflotte* (air fleets) enabled the Germans to concentrate air resources to match priorities on the ground. They were to commit over 3000 aircraft to the battle, and although the French had 1200 available in May 1940 d'Astier was only able to use 746 to support Billotte. The Germans were superior in tactical bombers and ground attack aircraft, and although the Allies possessed more fighters, some were retained for the defence of the United Kingdom and others were hopelessly outclassed. Ironically, the programme to replace obsolete French aircraft got under way just as the campaign started.

The Allies intended to wheel forward into Belgium when the Germans attacked. The capture of a German plan encouraged Gamelin to organize an advance on to the River Dyle, covering Brussels. He later added the 'Breda variant', which would send 7th Army to assist the Dutch. On its right the BEF would hold the Dyle between Louvain and Wavre; 1st Army would cover the Gembloux gap and Namur; and 9th Army, with a high proportion of reserve divisions, would throw its left wing forward towards Namur while its right maintained contact with 2nd Army at the end of the Maginot Line. This plan would enable the Allies to meet the anticipated thrust into Belgium but, as Georges observed, it would be hard for them to react if the Germans attacked further south.

German Plans

'Case Yellow', the original German plan, looked very like Schlieffen's scheme a generation before. General von Bock's Army Group B would make the main thrust towards Ghent; General von Rundstedt's Army

1940
The Rival Plans

→ Planned German movements

} Allied troop positions

–·–·–·– Frontiers, 1940

0   10   20   30 Miles
0 10 20 30 40 50 Kms

Antw

Dunkirk •

Ghent •

BELGIUM

7th Army

Lille •

R. Scheldt

BEF

Mons •

Arras •

1st Army

9th A

No 1
Army Group

R. Aisne

R. Oise

FRANCE

R. Marne

• La Ferté-sous-Jouar

PARIS ■ • Vincennes

- AMSTERDAM

NETHERLANDS

Rotterdam

eda •

Albert Canal

Army Group
B

R. Rhine

• Louvain
USSELS

Eben •
Emael

GERMANY

• Liège

Gembloux
•   • Namur
Charleroi

R. Ourthe

Dinant •

A r d e n n e s

Army Group
A

Sedan

• Trier

LUXEMBOURG ■

2nd Army

Longwy

Maginot Line

Army Group
C

3rd Army

R. Meuse

• Châlons-sur-Marne

No 2
Army Group

N

W   E

S

Group A would mount a subsidiary attack towards Namur; and General von Leeb's Army Group C would cover the Maginot Line. The distinguished British military historian Alistair Horne has called this plan 'manifestly bad ... so conservative and uninspiring that it might well have been thought up by a British or French General Staff of the inter-war years.'

It was no more appealing to many Germans. Lieutenant-General Erich von Manstein, Rundstedt's chief of staff, objected that it would not produce 'a decisive issue by land', and Guderian maintained that the campaign would be won by striking 'to drive a wedge so deep and wide that we need not worry about our flanks'. Hitler, lobbied by the disaffected, favoured radical schemes, for he believed that the French army was undermined by the factionalism of the inter-war years and would not withstand a single massive blow.

OKH (Army High Command) was told to think again, and its new scheme, *Sichelschnitt* (sickle-cut) was altogether more ambitious. Bock's army group would still move into Holland and Belgium, wafting a matador's cloak to draw Allied eyes to the north. Leeb's men would continue to watch the Maginot Line. Army Group A became the centre of gravity for the offensive. It was to contain forty-five divisions in three armies – 4th, 12th and 16th – and its cutting edge was formed by the seven panzer divisions of Guderian's XIX, Reinhardt's XLI and Hoth's XV Panzer Corps, the first two making up Panzer Group Kleist. The panzers were to attack through the Ardennes, the hilly, wooded area where France, Belgium and Luxembourg meet, to smash the hinge of the Allied armies on the Meuse between Dinant and Sedan. This was enormously risky. Bock pointed out that: 'You will be creeping along, 10 miles [16 km] from the Maginot Line flank on your breakthrough and hoping that the French will watch inertly! You are cramming a mass of tanks together into the narrow roads of the Ardennes as if there were no such thing as air-power.'

The Balance of Forces

In raw numbers the two sides were evenly matched with 136 divisions available for the campaign, although the Allies, with 96 French, 19 British, 22 Belgian and 10 Dutch divisions were anything but a homogeneous force. They had just over 3000 armoured vehicles, slightly more than the Germans. Most German tanks were the lightly armed Panzers Mk I and II, stiffened by 349 Mk IIs, with a 37mm gun, and only 278 Mk IVs with a low-velocity 75mm gun. The French had 311 of the heavy B1 tank, and 260 of the Somua S65 – with its 47mm high-velocity gun arguably the best tank in the campaign – together with some 1800 lighter vehicles. The British fielded 100 infantry tanks, designed for infantry co-operation and sufficiently armoured to defeat most anti-tank weapons. The Mk I mounted either a .303 or an unreliable .5-inch machine-gun, while the 24 very heavily armoured Mk II Matildas carried a 2-pdr gun.

The Germans enjoyed no great material advantage. If they were better equipped with radios, which made it easier to fight a mobile battle, their 37mm anti-tank gun could not cope with heavier Allied tanks. They were able to use the 88mm anti-aircraft gun in the anti-armour role, although it had a high silhouette which made it vulnerable to shrapnel. The real German edge lay in training and organization. The British had no armoured division in France when the campaign began, and the French had three, with a fourth being formed. Most of their tanks were scattered amongst cavalry and light mechanized divisions or allocated to infantry support. Panzer divisions, in contrast, were flexible all-arms formations whose commanders had the experience of Poland behind them.

The Start of the Campaign

The campaign opened on 10 May with German air raids on airfields, roads and railways. Special forces attacked key points: the Belgian fortress of Eben Emael, on the Albert Canal, was taken by glider troops who landed on top of it. The Allied left wing swung into Belgium and reached the Dyle line; General Prioux's excellent Cavalry Corps of light mechanized divisions raced for the Gembloux gap, and 7th Army reached Breda only to discover that the Dutch had already been driven back on Rotterdam.

The panzers forged into the Ardennes despite resistance from Belgian Chasseurs Ardennais and French cavalry, and on the evening of 12 May Guderian's advanced guard reached the River Meuse at Sedan. Rommel's 7th Panzer Division did even better. It arrived at Dinant and, although the Meuse bridges were blown, reconnaissance troops crossed the weir at Houx, further north, and established a bridgehead. News of this reached Gamelin in Vincennes on the 13th, and there were growing suspicions that: 'The enemy seems … to be preparing to increase his pressure in the immediate future in the general direction of Sedan, where the centre of gravity of his offensive may be directed.' It was a little late for suspicions. That day, Guderian's three divisions crossed the Meuse on the heels of the heaviest aerial bombardment the world had seen. Billotte managed to move up a mechanized corps behind the broken front, but the French tried to contain rather than counter-attack and the moment passed. Guderian briefly considered his next step. One of his disciples reminded him of his dictum '*Klotzen, nicht Kleckern*', and he gave the order for a drive to the west.

Gamelin's grip on the battle weakened as the days went by. The Dutch began peace negotiations on 14 May. The BEF held firm in front of Louvain, and although Prioux's Cavalry Corps defended the Gembloux gap until 1st Army arrived it was badly mauled in the process. Corap, whose 9th Army had borne the brunt of the panzer attack, was replaced by General Giraud on the 16th, and it is symptomatic of the slowness of French reactions that when he reached his command post at Vervins, Giraud learned that there were German tanks at Montcornet, 12 miles (20 km) to the south.

The French premier, Paul Reynaud, quickly saw through the communiqués emanating from Vincennes, and on the 15th he telephoned Winston Churchill, his British counterpart, and announced: 'We are beaten;

A German Mk III tank clatters through a burning French town. The 25th Panzer Regiment, in Rommel's 7th Panzer Division, contained Mk III, Mk IV and some Czech 38(t) tanks. The campaign made Rommel's name *(right)* and he was sent to command German troops in Africa in February 1941.

we have lost the battle.' When Churchill flew to Paris the following afternoon he found things 'incomparably worse than we had imagined'.
Gamelin gave a 'clear and calm' exposition of the situation, but admitted
that he had no reserve to deal with the breakthrough. Churchill initially
agreed to send ten fighter squadrons, but on his return to London was persuaded that this would be unwise, for the Advanced Air Striking Force'
bases were already under threat. Eventually six Hurricane squadrons,
based in south-east England, were committed to the battle.

The German Advance

The panzer corridor opened out across northern France. Guderian's
advanced guards were at Marle on the evening of 16 May, 40 miles (64
km) from their starting point that morning and 55 miles (88 km) from
Sedan. The history of 1st Panzer Division describes the vacuum behind
the spearhead: 'Hardly a single German soldier [was] to be found except
for a few supply services, up to 25 or 30 miles [40 or 48 km] behind the
division. Munitions and petrol were brought up over a single very thin,
almost unprotected supply road. They were also, however, tanked up
from petrol dumps and public petrol stations captured from the French.'
Guderian passed an advancing column: 'The men were wide awake now
and aware that we had achieved a complete breakthrough. They cheered
and shouted remarks which often could only be heard by staff officers in
the second car: "Well done, old boy" and "There's our old man", and
"Did you see him? That was Hurrying Heinz", and so on.'

The speed of their advance even disconcerted some Germans. Rundstedt grew increasingly concerned at the danger of attack into the southern flank of the corridor, and ordered Kleist to check Guderian's rush. On
17 May Kleist berated Guderian for not obeying Rundstedt's order to
pause and allow the infantry to catch up: there was a row and Guderian
was relieved of his command. When Rundstedt heard the news he sent
Colonel-General List of 12th Army down to sort out the muddle. List
told Guderian that the orders came from OKH and were to be obeyed.
Guderian was to resume his command, and was authorized to carry out
'reconnaissance in force': his tanks were on the move again that evening.

A hint of what the Allies might have achieved came on the 17th when
de Gaulle's embryonic 4th Armoured Division thudded into Guderian's
flank at Montcornet. De Gaulle had only three battalions of tanks and a
battalion of infantry in buses, but jabbed hard into the corridor, just as
the German doubters had feared, and it was not until evening that the
French drew off, short of fuel and harried by aircraft.

Rommel was on a parallel route further north. He crossed the Franco-

Belgian border at Sivry late on the afternoon of 16 May, and drove on in bright moonlight, firing on the move to discourage opposition and hampered by pitiful columns of refugees. In Avesnes he clashed with French tanks and then, travelling with the leading elements of his panzer regiment, pushed on for the bridge over the River Sambre at Landrecies. Shortage of fuel and ammunition stopped the advance just east of Le Cateau, and Rommel drove back in an armoured car to bring up the rest of his division.

The Allied Response
Behind the spearhead were shoals of French troops, many armed and some inclined to fight. A broken-down Panzer IV – its gun still in working order – provided valuable protection just east of Maroilles, and at Marbais Rommel bluffed a column of forty trucks into surrender and led it to Avesnes. He took an hour-and-a-half's rest before sending fuel and ammunition forward, and followed the supply column and its escort as it broke through a toughly defended roadblock east of Pommeroeuil, observing that: 'Our guns seemed to be completely ineffective against the heavy armour of the French tanks.' Cambrai fell after the leading panzers struck across the fields to its north-west, throwing up such a cloud of dust that the French, unable to see that many of the vehicles were soft-skinned, offered no resistance.

On the 16th the Allied left wing began to withdraw from Belgium. Troops were brought up from the south-west in an effort to block the gap left by the destruction of 9th Army – whose new commander was captured near Le Catelet on 19 May – but the Germans were moving too fast for such tactics to work. Some French instincts were sound, and on 19 May Gamelin directed Billotte to attack towards the Somme, pointing out that there was 'a vacuum' behind German armour. An attack into the flanks of the corridor might have worked, but in practice the Allied command was too dislocated to seize fleeting opportunities.

Matters were not improved by the dismissal of Gamelin. On the 19th he was replaced by the trim seventy-three-year-old General Maxime Weygand, brought back from his post as commander-in-chief in Syria. He was exhausted, but as he enjoyed some sleep the clock ticked on remorselessly. On the 20th Guderian's German tanks tore across the First World War Somme battlefield, cutting up two British Territorial divisions, 12th and 23rd, which had been sent out as lines-of-communication troops and pitchforked into a battle for which they had neither equipment nor training. That evening, tanks of 2nd Panzer clattered alongside the Somme, past the old ford at Blanchetaque and a few miles from Crécy to reach Noyelles on the coast. The Allied armies were cut in half.

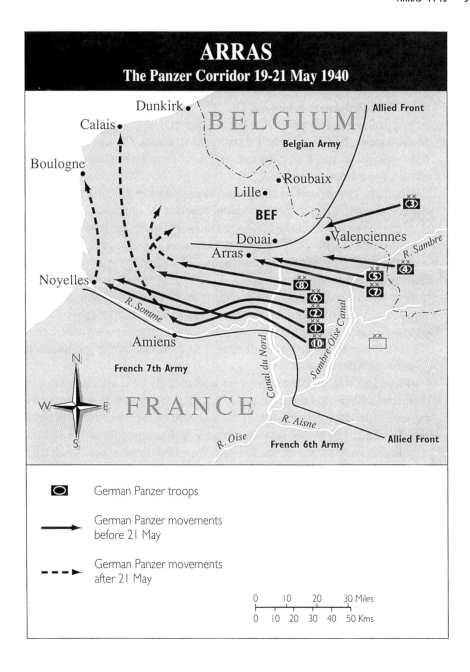

ARRAS
The Panzer Corridor 19-21 May 1940

German Panzer troops

German Panzer movements
before 21 May

German Panzer movements
after 21 May

0   10   20   30 Miles

0   10   20   30   40   50 Kms

The Move Towards Arras

The Germans were unsure of their next move, and it was not until late on 21 May that Guderian was ordered to swing north. This pause might have given the Allies time to react but the past week's fighting had not done much for inter-Allied relations. The BEF had seen relatively little action, although 3rd Division, under a fierce little major-general called Bernard Montgomery, had fought well in front of Louvain. On the 18th the BEF fell back on to the River Escaut, and two days later General Ironside, chief of the imperial general staff, visited Gort at his headquarters at Wahagnies. There had already been discussion over the BEF's future, and word that part might be evacuated had reached Billotte. Ironside repeated the Cabinet's view that the BEF should move southwards to avoid being cut off in the north. Gort disagreed. Seven of his nine divisions were in action. Withdrawal would expose the Belgians and leave a gap which the Germans would exploit. If Weygand organized an offensive Gort undertook to use his two unengaged divisions in a limited operation near Arras on the 21st. Ironside found Billotte and Blanchard and persuaded them to support Gort's attack, but had no confidence that they actually would. 'God help the BEF,' he wrote, 'brought to this state by the incompetence of the French command.'

Weygand flew north on the 21st and met Billotte and Belgian commanders at Ypres. Gort, whose headquarters moved that day to Prémesques, on the western edge of Lille, heard of the meeting too late and Weygand had left by the time he arrived. It was agreed that the Belgians should fall back on the River Lys and there would be a combined offensive, starting not before the 26th, into both flanks of the corridor. The plan's prospects, poor at its inception, diminished when Billotte was fatally injured in a road accident later that day: it took Blanchard three days to replace him.

While tired generals were haggling at Ypres, tanks were already burning around Arras. The Arras operation was the child of more modest circumstances than the offensive discussed at Ypres. As the situation on his right deteriorated, Gort had given his director of intelligence, Major-General Mason-MacFarlane, command of the improvised Macforce and responsibility for the BEF's right rear. On 18 May he appointed Major-General Petre of 12th Division to head Petreforce and hold the Arras area. On the 20th German tanks ripped through the belly of the BEF north of the Somme, and 70th Brigade, part of the unlucky 23rd Division, was caught on the move by 8th Panzer Division just south of Arras. After a hopeless fight the brigade lost all but 233 officers and men.

Gort extemporized another formation to support Petreforce. Major-

General Franklyn, commander of the uncommitted 5th Division, was given Frankforce – 5th Division, 50th (Northumbrian) Division, a good first-line Territorial formation, and 1st Army Tank Brigade – and told to relieve French or British troops on the River Scarpe east of Arras and then, as Franklyn put it: 'to make Arras secure, gaining as much "elbow room" as possible south of the town. To the best of my memory he used the term "mopping up". I certainly got the impression that I was only likely to encounter weak German detachments.' The official history uses much the same words. Frankforce was to 'support the garrison of Arras and block the roads south of Arras, thus cutting off German communications from the east.' Evidence of German tanks south of Arras was not passed on to Franklyn, who might have had reservations about tossing a force composed largely of infantry into a whirlpool of armour.

The British Troops

The need to reinforce Arras, hold the line of the River Scarpe and maintain a reserve meant that Franklyn had only Brigadier Churchill's 151st Brigade of 50th Division and the two battalions of the tank brigade available for the attack. The men of three infantry battalions – 6/, 7/ and 8/Durham Light Infantry (DLI) – were already tired. The BEF's first-line infantry was all motorized. The soldiers travelled on trucks, and each battalion had a platoon of lightly armoured Bren-gun carriers. French and German infantry covered the ground on foot like their fathers and grandfathers before them. This contributed to German nervousness, because the panzer corridor would not be secure until infantry regiments could revet its flanks, and on 21 May they were miles back, marching bare-headed and bare-armed along poplar-lined roads. The Durhams had gone into Belgium in trucks but had returned on foot and had been on the move for days in warm weather. They were well enough trained for infantry combat, but most had never seen a tank.

The Royal Tank Regiment (RTR) was the descendant of the Heavy Section Machine-Gun Corps which had manned the first tanks to enter battle on the Somme on 15 September 1916. Its men wore a white metal image of a First World War tank on their black berets, and the regiment's distinctive colours of brown, red and green symbolized passage through mud and blood to the green fields beyond. Although most British cavalry regiments had been mechanized by 1940, the Royal Tank Regiment regarded itself as the armoured warfare professionals *par excellence*. Its units were still called battalions and its sub-units were called companies as they had been in the First World War, and a sprinkling of its officers and senior NCOs were veterans of that conflict.

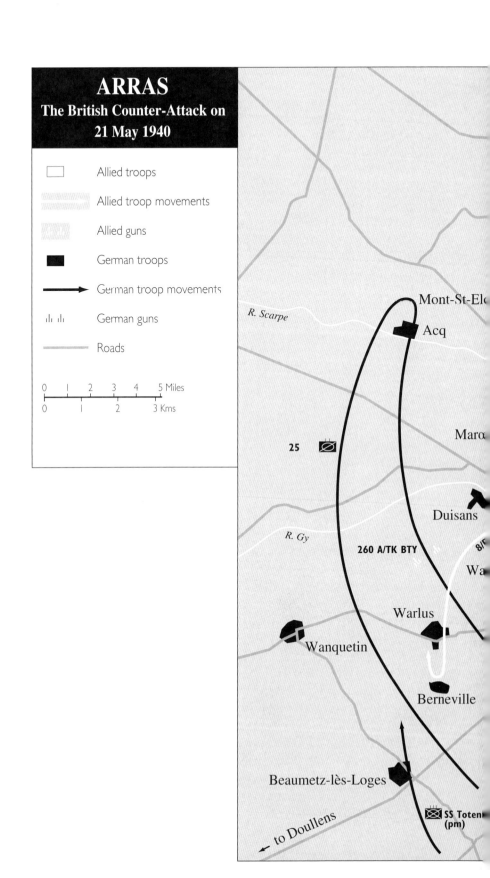

ARRAS
The British Counter-Attack on 21 May 1940

Allied troops

Allied troop movements

Allied guns

German troops

German troop movements

German guns

Roads

0   1   2   3   4   5 Miles
0   1   2   3 Kms

R. Scarpe

Mont-St-El

Acq

25

Marc

Duisans

R. Gy

260 A/TK BTY

Wa

Warlus

Wanquetin

Berneville

Beaumetz-lès-Loges

SS Toten
(pm)

to Doullens

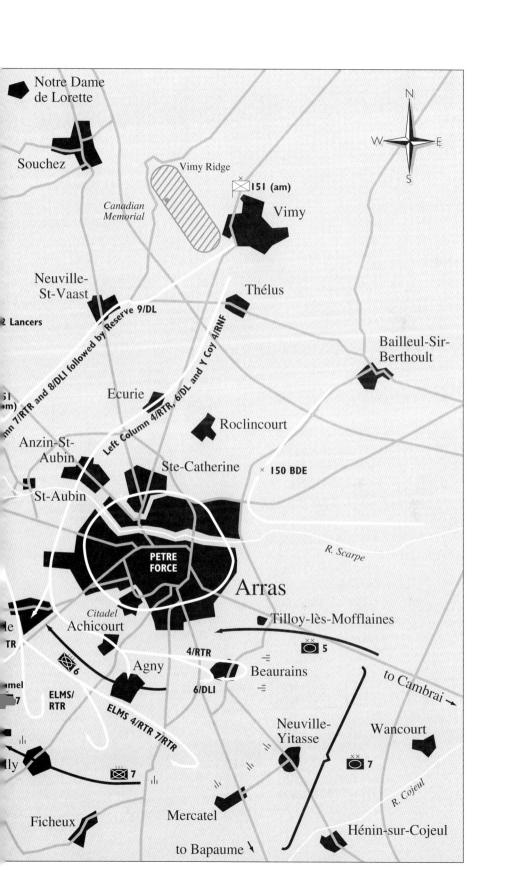

Brigadier Douglas Pratt's 1st Army Tank Brigade contained 4/ and 7/Royal Tank Regiment. Both had moved into Belgium at the opening of the campaign and out of it a week later: about one-quarter of the tanks were already out of action because of worn-out tracks or lack of petrol. Lieutenant-Colonel Fitzmaurice's 4/RTR had the Mk I Infantry tank with its .303 or .5 machine-gun, and Lieutenant-Colonel Heyland's 7/RTR had, in addition, some of the bigger Mk II Matildas with their 2-pdr guns and .303 machine-guns. Before the battle, seven of the Matildas were transferred to 4/RTR. In all, the brigade had 16 Mk IIs and 56 MKIs, as well as a dozen light tanks, so lightly armoured as to be of little use except for reconnaissance and liaison.

Artillery support was provided by 365th Field Battery Royal Artillery, with 18-pdrs and 368th Field Battery with the newer 25-pdrs. The former, part of 5th Division, had not worked with 151st Brigade before, and in the last-minute hurry there was no time for liaison between observation officers, the troops they were to support and the guns whose fire they were expected to control. There were two anti-tank batteries, 206th and 260th, with 2-pdr guns. Reconnaissance was furnished by 50th Division's motor-cycle battalion, 4/Royal Northumberland Fusiliers (RNF). No air support was available. The BEF's air component and the AASF were withdrawing to bases in England, and although the Air Ministry in London sent fifty-seven Battle light bombers against targets between Arras and the coast they had no effect on the action.

Arras was held by the Welsh Guards and improvised units including Cook's Light Tanks, a handful of vehicles collected from workshops. Welsh Guards companies covered the main approaches to the town, with battalion headquarters in the Palais St Vaast in its centre, and Cook's Light Tanks and the battalion's carrier platoon in reserve. There had been clashes on the 20th as reconnaissance units of 7th Panzer Division reached Beaurains on the southern outskirts of Arras and probed towards the town. On Rommel's left, 8th Panzer, with the SS Totenkopf Motorized Regiment just behind it, made even better progress and reached Hesdin, west of Arras, by dark. The Morris armoured cars of the 12th Lancers met 8th Panzer near Beaumetz-lès-Loges and 5th Panzer on the Cambrai road, and the lancers pulled back towards Vimy Ridge, establishing their headquarters in the ruins of the abbey at Mont-St-Eloi.

The Allied Attack

In view of all this it is puzzling that Franklyn was not given fresh orders. He already knew that a larger operation was envisaged, for he had met French commanders who had asked him to co-operate in it. He declined to do so, but the discussion was not without result because Prioux agreed to send the remnants of his 3rd Light Armoured Division – some seventy armoured vehicles – into action on Frankforce's right.

Franklyn entrusted the attack to Major-General Martel of 50th Division, telling him, at 6 a.m. on 21 May, that German infantry and tanks were moving south of Arras 'in numbers not believed to be great' and ordering him to clear the area. Martel announced that he proposed to do this with two mobile columns, and was told to attack as quickly as possible. Pratt thought that nothing could be done before 3 p.m., but Martel was persuaded to agree to 2 p.m.

The last leg of the move up to the assembly area around Vimy Ridge was wearisome, tanks completing a 31-mile (50-km) drive by dark to avoid air attack and infantry trudging up on to the ridge where some of them rested amongst preserved trenches which marked the Canadian capture of Vimy Ridge in 1917. Brigadier Churchill gave his orders in Petit Vimy, on the ridge's northern slope, at 9.45 a.m. No tank officer was present, and Lieutenant-Colonel Miller of 6/DLI was not sure which RTR battalion was to support his column: he met its commander only once, about three hours later. The tanks had established communications some days before but had preserved radio silence thereafter, and their

Men of the British Expeditionary Force on the march in June 1940. They are wearing khaki serge battledress and carrying 1937 pattern webbing equipment – not a happy combination in hot weather.

radios drifted 'off net' all too easily: few worked when the attack began. There was no radio link between infantry and tanks, and maps were in short supply. Second Lieutenant Tom Craig of 4/RTR tells how: 'I arrived at Petit Vimy in my Matilda exhausted and disorganized. I was given a map by my company commander and told to start up and follow him. The wireless was not working, there was no tie-up with the infantry and no clear orders.'

The columns set off at 11 a.m. with the aim of crossing the Arras–Doullens road, where the attack proper was meant to begin, at 2 p.m. The right column (7/RTR and 8/DLI) was to head for Boisleux-au-Mont on the River Cojeul by way of Maroeuil, Warlus and Wailly, while the left column (4/RTR and 6/DLI) made for Hénin-sur-Cojeul via Ecurie, Achicourt and Beaurains. Martel had allocated a company of 4/RNF to each column and kept the rest of the battalion, as well as 9/DLI, in reserve. As Martel's infantry began to tramp down the long, gentle slope towards Arras, Rommel was chivvying stray elements of his division around Vis-en-Artois, while 25th Panzer Regiment roared on to reach Acq, north-west of Arras, by late afternoon. Rommel's two rifle regiments, 6th and 7th, also by-passing Arras to the south, were approaching Mercatel and Agny.

The left-hand column met the Germans first. Although it had set off in good order, by the time it reached St Aubin it was evident that the British infantry could not keep up with the armour, and Lieutenant-Colonel Miller agreed that the tanks should go on ahead. They met elements of 6th Rifle Regiment in Dainville, which was cleared by Y Company 4/RNF with assistance from the tanks, and several prisoners were taken. Leaving 4/RNF to look after the prisoners, 4/RTR went on, crossing the Doullens road under sporadic shellfire. The level-crossing on the Dainville–Achicourt road was down, and it was some time before a strong-willed officer crashed through it. Some tanks negotiated the railway cutting and a few were marooned on the line. Just the other side of the railway 4/RTR ran into 6th Rifle Regiment. Second Lieutenant Peter Vaux described this:

We had come straight into the flank of a German mechanized column which was moving across our front. They were just as surprised as us and we were right in amongst them ... and for the first quarter of an hour or so there was a glorious 'free for all'. We knocked out quite a lot of their lorries: there were Germans running all over the place.

Miller, who had worked with tanks in the First World War, knew that infantry must be on hand to consolidate their success, and did his best to

Each British infantry battalion had a platoon of lightly-armoured Universal Carriers. These were usually fitted with a Bren light machine-gun, earning them the name Bren-gun carriers.

move on his 'very tired and footsore' men. German survivors had gone to ground in the villages and he sent his left-hand company to clear Agny. When he returned to battalion headquarters Major Jeffreys, the second-in-command, warned that 4/RTR was getting further away and suggested that the carrier platoon should be sent on to regain contact. Miller agreed and advanced towards Achicourt, startling a fine dog fox which Jeffreys hallooed away 'much to the delight of the men of B Company, many of whom were keen sportsmen from the Zetland country.' Many shaken Germans were taken prisoner, but Miller received a message from Martel telling him not to go beyond Beaurains as the right-hand column was making slower progress.

By now, 4/RTR was reaching the high-water mark of its advance. 'I do not know how many Germans we killed and how many German vehicles we set on fire,' recalled Peter Vaux. 'At that moment I didn't see why we shouldn't go all the way to Berlin.' But as the battalion passed through Beaurains the first tanks of 5th Panzer Division appeared at Tilloy on the Cambrai–Arras road. One tank 'with a proper gun in its turret' was close enough to 4/RTR for the commanding officer to send

Vaux on a fruitless mission to ask help from a French Somua, which was busily engaged in shelling Beaurains cemetery.

When Vaux returned to the Beaurains–Tilly road and looked westwards towards Telegraph Hill, a low ridge topped with a wood, he saw over twenty tanks from A and B Companies in the field in front of him. The commanding officer's light tank – he had transferred into it in order to get about more easily – was ahead of the others, identifiable by its flag. Vaux failed to reach Lieutenant-Colonel Fitzmaurice on the radio, and was then called forward by the adjutant. They both fired on anti-tank guns in a nearby potato clump, but Vaux realized that most enemy fire was coming from the ridge and drove forwards. As he did so he could see that the British tanks were all knocked out, crews lying beside them or crawling back through the grass. He machine-gunned the wood but was soon signalled back by the adjutant. As he returned he saw that the CO's tank had its side blown in, and 'although I didn't know it the Colonel and Corporal Moorhouse, his operator, were dead inside it.'

The damage had been done by the 105mm guns of Rommel's 78th Artillery Regiment, its 4th and 5th Batteries astride the wood on Telegraph Hill and 6th Battery south of Tilloy. Just north of the Neuville-Vitasse–Mercatel road, 1st Battery, assisted by the fire of 88mms north of Mercatel, prevented the British from outflanking Telegraph Hill to their right. Major Stuart Fernie had taken effective control of the battalion, and an officer met him on the sunken road running diagonally from Agny to Beaurains 'still in his smart service dress with his floppy jacket, on the ground, organizing the chaps since there was no wireless.'

One of those he organized was an ex-circus strong-man, 'Muscle' Armit, who held the short-lived rank of Warrant Officer Class III, Platoon Sergeant-Major. Fernie told Armit (wrongly, in the event) that the CO had been killed by anti-tank guns firing from Mercatel and ordered him to go and get them. Armit drove south, met six 37mm guns and destroyed two of them. His gun was damaged, and his tank was hit several times as he tried to repair it. He managed to reverse into cover, although he had a tense moment after he ignited a smoke discharger in the turret and then found that the hatch would not open for him to throw it out. Having repaired the gun he returned to the fray. 'They must have thought I was finished,' he reflected, 'for I caught the guns limbering up … and revenge was sweet.'

The German artillery was not only within range of Martel's batteries but could also have been hit from positions north of the River Scarpe, but British artillery fire was never effective. Miller called down the fire of his own battery, passing information to the guns by messenger because the radios had failed, but was picking his targets from the map and could not observe the fall of shot. At 8.15 p.m., with Beaurains under artillery fire and repeated air attack, Miller decided to withdraw. His two forward companies – D, in the centre of Beaurains, and C, in an orchard on the south-east edge of the village – moved back through the junction where the D919 crosses the Achicourt–Beaurains road. Y Company 4/RNF had been ordered to hold it until ordered to withdraw. The order never came, and the company fought on until well after dark when it was overwhelmed.

Miller and Fernie waited at a crossroads east of the junction as survivors of C and D Companies emerged from the flames of Beaurains. It was pitch dark when a tank approached from the east. The adjutant of 4/RTR flagged it down with a map-board to speak to the commander, who turned out to be an officer of 5th Panzer Division. There was a confused battle as the British withdrew. 'It was dark with the moon just rising,' wrote Peter Vaux. 'There was flames, smoke, our vehicles, the carriers of 6/DLI, soldiers of 6/DLI on foot; there were German soldiers, some doubtless prisoners, but others were on motor cycles – so God knows what they were doing there.' Miller eventually found brigade headquarters in Ecurie and then set about getting his exhausted men, so tired that they collapsed as they marched and slept where they fell, back on to Vimy Ridge.

The right column had also set off at 11 a.m. that morning, although without its motor-cyclists from 4/RNF who were not ready to start. Some light shelling was encountered just short of Maroeuil, and when the infantry, well behind the tanks, crossed the main road near Duisans they were heartened to see the wreckage of a 150mm battery of 8th Panzer Division which had been shot up by the 12th Lancers. The survivors had taken refuge in Duisans, which was cleared by C Company 8/DLI with the help of French tanks. Numerous prisoners were taken and handed over to the French who stripped them to their underwear and held them in the square in front of the church.

The Allied commanding officers of tanks and infantry met in Maroeuil at about 12.45 p.m., but soon afterwards 7/RTR's liaison officer, accompanying the Durhams in his scout car, lost radio contact with his own headquarters. Infantry and armour never regained touch thereafter, and Pratt cautioned Martel: 'This is going to be a shambles. The infantry are miles behind. We are going forward against strong opposition … We will be absolutely smashed and we must stop this mess, get things together and try later.' Martel, commanding from an open-topped car, told him that the attack had to go on.

Lieutenant-Colonel Heyland's 7/RTR lost direction in Duisans, edging south-east towards Wagnonlieu and Dainville and becoming entangled with the rear elements of 4/RTR. This may have happened because there were so few maps that tank commanders were told to follow a line of pylons which took them too far east, or it may be that the CO, aware that time was slipping away, decided to head straight for Wailly.

Had 7/RTR followed its intended route it would have met 25th Panzer Regiment which was heading north between Warlus and Wanquetin at exactly this time. The German regiment had far more tanks, but would have found it hard to deal with the Mk IIs of 7/RTR. As it was, 25th Panzer continued virtually unopposed, destroying a scout platoon of 4/RNF as it plunged onwards. The German tanks were spotted by the 12th Lancers at Mont-St-Eloi, and by X Company 4/RNF which had moved late but was now watching the open ground south and west of Duisans. It relayed the news to brigade headquarters and was ordered to fall back, and as it retired it passed through 260th Anti-Tank Battery Royal Artillery, its guns guarding against the reappearance of 25th Panzer.

It was with difficulty that 7/RTR swung round towards Wailly: few radios worked and orders had to be taken by officers in light tanks. The CO and the adjutant were both killed, the former by machine-gun fire as he stood outside his tank organizing the attack, and the advance became disjointed with tanks making for Wailly, Mercatel and Ficheux.

Rommel's Progress
Rommel usually travelled with 25th Panzer Regiment, often in the tank of its commander, Colonel Rothenburg. On 21 May he had intended to move with the tanks but 'the infantry regiments were so slow … that I drove straight off back to chase up the 7th Rifle Regiment and get it to hurry up.' He could not find it, but met part of 6th Regiment near Ficheux and drove alongside it towards Wailly. East of the village he came under fire from the north, and saw a German battery (2nd Battery 78th Artillery Regiment) in action nearby. He left his vehicle and ran into Wailly with his aide-de-camp, Lieutenant Most, behind the gun-line, recording 'chaos and confusion amongst our troops in the village … they were jamming up the roads and yards with their vehicles

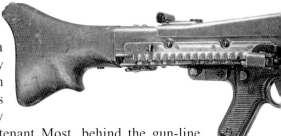

instead of going into action with every available weapon to fight off the oncoming attack.' He called up his vehicle and drove on to a prominent hillock west of Wailly where he found some anti-aircraft and anti-tank guns in hollows in a thin wood.

His position was desperate. Some British tanks (D Company 7/RTR) had crossed the Wailly–Berneville road and had already knocked out a Panzer III, while others (B Company 7/RTR) were moving up from the Doullens road. Rommel saw nearby gunners take to their heels. 'With Most's help,' he wrote:

I brought every available gun into action at top speed against the tanks ... With the enemy so close only rapid fire from every gun could save the situation ... Soon we succeeded in putting the leading enemy tanks out of action. About 150 yards [137 metres] to the west of our small wood a British captain climbed out of a heavy tank and walked unsteadily towards us with his hands up. We had killed his driver.

Rommel dealt first with the attack from the north before engaging the tanks moving in from the west. 'The worst seemed to be over and the attack beaten off,' he noted, 'when suddenly Most sank to the ground behind a 20mm anti-aircraft gun close beside me. He was mortally wounded and blood gushed from his mouth.'

The Battle Continues
Lieutenant-Colonel Beart's 8/DLI had marched on without its tanks. Beart left B and C Companies in Duisans and continued to Warlus with A and D, sending A on through the village towards Berneville, where it came under fire from Germans on the Doullens road. D Company moved through the village to woods at its south-eastern edge. Here it was viciously dive-bombed by German Stukas. Although, as was so

In 1934 the Germans introduced the MG 34, the first real general purpose machine-gun, which could be used on a variety of ground mounts or fitted to vehicles. The MG 42, shown above, was a wartime development which had a higher rate of fire (theoretically up to 1200 rounds a minute), giving it a distinctive buzz-saw sound.

often the case with these terrifying but primitive aircraft, few casualties were caused 'everyone was absolutely shattered. After a few minutes the officers and some of the NCOs collected themselves and said "Right, we must get on with it", but it was very difficult to get some of the men moving – we had to kick them into position and the effect was very considerable.'

Some German tanks appeared from the south-east while the air attack was in progress but three French tanks, with battalion headquarters in the area of the water tower, helped to drive them off, and other enemy tanks which threatened the Durhams' left flank were checked by the fire of part of the brigade anti-tank company. A Company had lost its commander and sergeant-major in Berneville and joined D Company, whose commander had been wounded, in Warlus. Beart pulled his men into a tight perimeter as shells ignited several houses. The French tanks left, their commander announcing that he had tasks to undertake elsewhere. Messages could not be got through to the battalion second-in-command in Duisans, and the Durhams faced the prospect of an unpleasant night.

The reappearance of 25th Panzer Regiment worsened the battalion's prospects. The regiment was cooking chickens at Acq: they were almost ready when orders arrived to return to Dainville to fall on the British rear. On the way the Germans ran into 260th Anti-Tank Battery and broke through, losing tanks in the process. They then brushed 'strong armoured forces' (probably the remnants of 7/RTR retiring northwards), losing still more tanks because of what a German officer called 'the bigger calibre and range of your tanks and stronger armour'. The regiment spent the night on the battlefield, severing communications between the two portions of 8/DLI.

Second Lieutenant Potts, 8/DLI's mortar officer, rode through the cordon on his motor bike and found brigade headquarters at 2.30 a.m. on 22 May. He received orders to withdraw and took them to the companies in Duisans but could not get through to Warlus. Just when things seemed blackest, six French tanks and two armoured personnel carriers reached Warlus. Survivors were loaded on to all available vehicles, and the little column broke out of Warlus in a squall of firing. It found Duisans deserted, and reached Vimy Ridge at 6 a.m.

The Aftermath
The day cost Rommel's division 30–40 tanks and 378 officers and men, and the British took 400 prisoners from 7th and 8th Panzer Divisions and the SS Totenkopf. According to 7th Panzer, it destroyed 43 British tanks, and credited 25 of these to 78th Artillery Regiment. The RTR battalions

lost over half the tanks engaged, and the infantry returned to Vimy Ridge with perhaps half the soldiers who had left it. Not all the missing ended up as prisoners of war: some resourceful members of 4/DLI made their own way to Boulogne, assisted in the defence of the port and were safely evacuated.

The action enabled the British to tighten their grip on Arras, although Gort reluctantly authorized its abandonment late on the 23rd as part of a general withdrawal. Despite instructions from Weygand and Churchill, he saw that the projected counter-attack into the panzer corridor would never get under way. Withdrawal on Dunkirk further soured Allied relations and led some Frenchmen to argue that it was only British dereliction that had thwarted a promising plan. The Belgians, who had fought far harder than contemporaries or most historians have admitted, agreed to cease-fire terms on the 27th, persuading Gort to increase the pace of his withdrawal. Another bout of misunderstanding resulted in much of the French 1st Army fighting on in Lille, and it was only on 29 May that Weygand agreed that French troops could be evacuated from Dunkirk. Although Gort had prophesied that 'a great part of the BEF and its equipment will inevitably be lost even in the best of circumstances', 338 000 men, one-third of them French, were taken off by the time the operation ended on 4 June.

Evacuation was assisted by the fact that German armour was ordered to halt on 24 May, and it was not until the 26th that it was allowed to move again. Liddell Hart traces the halt order to shock created by the Arras counter-attack. Few historians would wholly agree with him. The attack certainly inspired what the war diary of Guderian's corps called 'nervousness throughout the group area', and General von Kluge of 4th Army admitted that 21 May was 'the first day on which the enemy has achieved some success'. There were many other reasons for a pause, not least the erosion of German armour by battle and breakdown. Yet the Arras action certainly helped to delay the German advance on Dunkirk. It not only alarmed the German High Command – the fact that 7th Panzer's situation map showed five British divisions is a measure of the concern – but it also bought time for the defence of Boulogne and Calais, which slowed down the drive on Dunkirk. The defence of Calais remains deeply controversial. The town was entrusted to the three rifle regiments of Brigadier Claude Nicholson's 30th Brigade, ordered to fight on to the end in the interests of Allied solidarity. They fought on until 26 May, and the bombardment which reduced the old town to smoking rubble destroyed many buildings which might have been familiar to Henry V's men on their way home from Agincourt.

A View of the Field

Thousands of British visitors, making the last sprint for Calais, follow the A26 which slides along the southern flank of Vimy Ridge, with the Canadian memorial to the missing of the First World War to the north and the spur of Notre Dame de Lorette to the south. An old French aphorism declared that he who held the Lorette feature held France and, although cruising the autoroute does not make the fact immediately apparent, this is vital ground. On the northern edge of Vimy Ridge the chalk downs of Artois drop abruptly on to the Flanders plain. It is a sharp geographical divide, and we should not be surprised that for centuries the northern frontier of France has run within sight of the ridge. It is a linguistic frontier too, and not far to the north Courtrai is rendered as Kortrijk and Ypres as Ieper.

In the summer of 1711 Marshal Villars held the lines of *Ne Plus Ultra* (so-called because the Duke of Marlborough was to be held there 'and no further' into France) which stretched from Cambrai to the coast. Here they ran along the River Scarpe south of the ridge, with Arras as their buttress. Marlborough unbalanced Villars first by marching from the eastern end of the lines to Vimy, the French moving parallel on their side of the lines. Then he quietly slipped his guns and baggage away behind the ridge before dashing eastwards with his infantry and cavalry – 'My Lord Duke desires the foot to step it out' – to beat the exasperated marshal to the eastern end of the lines, breaching them before the French could arrive.

A German staff car passes an abandoned infantry tank Mk I of 7/RTR. The tower and dome in the background mark the French National Cemetery of Notre Dame de Lorette.

The Town of Arras

Arras, the capital of Artois, was the birthplace of the French revolution-ary leader Maximilien Robespierre. It formed an important route-centre in Roman times, with roads running out from it like spokes from the hub of a wheel. The medieval town grew up around the Benedictine abbey of St-Vaast, which is now a museum of fine arts. Its considerable wealth came from the textile industry, and the words 'arras' in English and *arazzi* in Italian came to mean tapestries in general, so pervasive was the influence of those which really originated in Arras. The town's two great cobbled squares, the Grand Place and the Place des Héros, are fine exam-ples of Flemish architecture, and were sensitively restored after damage suffered in the First World War when the front line ran just east of the town. In fact the line was so close that it could be safely reached from the town, and the *hôtel de ville* gives access to the *boves*, a complex system of tunnels begun in the tenth century and developed since. They were extensively used by the British in the First World War, and contain familiar graffiti.

Arras was fortified by the military engineer Sébastien de Vauban, and although most of the ramparts disappeared to make way for the wide boulevards circling the town, the citadel, finished in 1670, survives at its south-west corner. It is still in military hands and is not open to the public, but a lane leading off the Boulevard Charles de Gaulle between the citadel and the British First World War memorial takes the visitor into the ditch girdling the fortifications. Fortress ditches were convenient spots for military executions: secure accommodation was on hand nearby and lofty ramparts could absorb stray bullets. In 1940–4 the Arras area, and in particular the mining belt to its north, produced fierce opposition to the Germans, and many members of the Resistance were shot here in the ditch. A post marks the place of execution, and plaques on the ram-part walls commemorate the dead. The nearby British Memorial to the Missing commemorates the First World War dead of the Royal Flying Corps, amongst them Major Edward 'Mick' Mannock VC, DSO and two bars, MC and bar.

Vimy Ridge

The Arras operation began on Vimy Ridge, which is an ideal spot at which to begin any study. The Germans had taken the place during the 'race to the sea' in 1914, and in October they seized Neuville-St-Vaast, Carency and Notre Dame de Lorette to establish a line running through the abbey at Mont-St-Eloi. In May 1915 the French managed to wrest Lorette from the Germans and to win a toehold on the southern slopes of

Vimy Ridge, but at an appalling cost. The cemetery at Lorette contains the graves of 20 000 Frenchmen and the ossuary the bones of another 20 000. General Frido von Senger und Etterlin was there as a young man, and remembered 'a big burial ground for the bones of those dismembered bodies that nobody could put together'. He was back in 1940 and, like so many older combatants, was struck by the absurd familiarity of the land-scape. He even tracked down his former landlady: 'Unbelieving, she gazed on me, claiming to recognize again the Lieutenant von S., if that was indeed the man who stood before her.' Above the ossuary stands a lighthouse-like tower which gives a wide if distant view of the 1917 and 1940 battlefields.

Vimy Ridge was attacked by the Canadian Corps on Easter Monday, 9 April 1917. The Canadians had made good use of the tunnels beneath the ridge, some of them ancient when the battle was fought and others dug by tunnelling companies of the Royal Engineers. There were twelve main tunnels in the Canadian sector with a network of smaller tunnels and dug-outs running off them. The main shafts were $6\frac{1}{2}$ feet (2 metres) high, at least 3 feet (1 metre) wide, and were lit by electricity. Grange Tunnel,

This particular 88mm gun was captured in Normandy in 1944. Its shield marks it out as an anti-tank variant of this very successful anti-aircraft and anti-tank weapon.

one of the longest, is open to the public during the season, and visitors are shown round by well-informed young Canadians.

The Canadians had taken great care to prepare the assaulting troops. Over 40 000 maps were issued, and troops were briefed on the details of German defences so they would be able to use their initiative if there was an unexpected hitch. The Germans were handicapped by the fact that the steep rearward slope of the ridge made it impossible for them to defend in depth, and the Canadian assault was an almost complete success. Preserved trenches, their sandbags filled with cement, mark the Canadian start line. They are rather neater than anything that might have been seen hereabouts in 1917 but give an excellent feel for the dogtooth layout of a First World War trench system. The Canadian memorial stands in the centre of the German line and bears the names of 11 285 Canadians who were declared 'missing, presumed dead' in France.

The memorial was only four years old when the Durhams assembled on the ridge in 1940. Their advance took them past cemeteries full of First World War dead. It must have been strange for the veterans amongst them: the forty-seven-year-old Lieutenant-Colonel Harry Miller of 6/DLI had fought in the area in his youth. The memories and memorials in the area are largely from the First World War. There is a memorial to a North African Division – 'Without fear and without pity' – on the ridge, and others, with a little museum, in Neuville-St-Vaast. The ruins of the abbey at Mont-St-Eloi are in view as one descends the slope, but they were ruined long before the 12th Lancers established their headquarters there.

The 1940 Campaign

It is not until we reach Duisans, on the route of the right-hand column, that there is evidence of the 1940 battle. German prisoners were kept in the square in front of the church, and the church itself bears the scars of shrapnel and small-arms fire.

The left-hand column's route is all but swamped by the southwards expansion of Arras. The once-distinct villages now tend to merge with one another and the construction of new roads has not been kind; the route is better driven than walked. However, the D60, which leaves Dainville and crosses the Doullens road, takes us towards Achicourt just as it did 4/RTR and 6/DLI, and ½ mile (1 km) along it is the level-crossing which caused so much trouble in 1940.

It takes adroit map-reading to strike through Achicourt and Beaurains, and it is easiest to sidestep them to the south. Stay on the D60 through Agny and zigzag, still on the same road, to meet the new by-pass connecting the N17 to the N39 Arras–Cambrai road. This goes just west of Telegraph Hill (which was held by the 4th and 5th Batteries of Rommel's 78th Artillery Regiment), and there is convenient parking on the Beaurains side exactly half-way between the N17 junction and the turn-off for Tilloy. Looking eastwards one has Peter Vaux's view of 4/RTR's last attack; the field across the road was strewn with knocked-out British tanks, and the wood on the crest-line was the one he machine-gunned. It still contains defences – a German pillbox which pre-dates the British Arras offensive of April 1917, a hopeless business enlivened only by Canadian capture of Vimy Ridge.

The right-hand column may have been less successful but its route today is more congenial. From Duisans a track leads directly along 8/DLI's line of march to Warlus, and for the car-bound the road through Agnez-lès-Duisans deviates only slightly from this route. The road crosses a gentle ridge half-way to Warlus, and it was on this that 260th Anti-Tank Battery stood, engaging 25th Panzer Regiment as it returned from the north-west. Warlus has changed little, and its water tower still stands on the road to Berneville. It was here that Lieutenant-Colonel Beart had his headquarters at the time of the Stuka attack: it is a rather bare place in which to be dive-bombed. When I was last there a rusty and battered British fuel can, known for telling reasons as a 'flimsy' and later replaced by the more robust jerry-can copied from the Germans, lay by the fence.

The general line of 7/RTR's advance can be followed from Maroeuil to Wagnonlieu and thence to the Doullens road. The wooded hillock occupied by Rommel himself is obvious from many viewpoints on this side of the road. It is surmounted by a handful of trees for which 'bushy-topped' is the only apt description: they look almost tropical. Tanks from D Company 7/RTR made straight for Warlus on the axis of the minor road which heads due south from Dainville. Others, from B Company, moved parallel with the Doullens road and then turned south-east, advancing on Rommel's position. There were others which rattled straight across the ridge towards Agny, some swinging down towards Wailly and others keeping course for Mercatel, where they encountered those deadly 88mms – the first of the many British tanks to do so during the war.

Some heavily-armoured Mk IIs bit deep into the German stop-line. Two of 7/RTR's MK 11s, commanded by Major King and Sergeant Doyle, may have got as far as the Bapaume road. They overran a 37mm battery, knocked out four tanks (they were encouraged to see that their 2-pdrs went clean through them), crashed through a barrier of farm carts and fired on another anti-tank battery. Then, turrets jammed by shell-splinters and external stowage boxes blazing, they took on an 88mm. King kept the gunners' heads down with his machine-gun and Doyle destroyed it with his main armament.

Rommel's position is on a prominent ring contour with the spot height 111 on the IGN 1:50 000 map. It is on a network of tracks, but is best approached by parking alongside the village cemetery to the north-west of Wailly: the crew of a British tank rest there. Walk up through Belloy Farm to turn right along the (usually muddy) track just beyond the farmyard. There are fewer trees now than there were in 1940, but the shallow workings of what seems to be an old quarry would have offered good protection to guns. On this piece of dominant ground Rommel demonstrated, neither for the first nor the last time, the value of forward command. But the fate of Lieutenant Most shows that it was a style replete with risks, and as we look out to the north and west, and imagine those Matildas trundling up the slope, we can see just how close Rommel came to being a promising panzer commander who was cut off in his prime.

CHAPTER 10

Dunkirk
1940

Background

The Commander-in-Chief did not mince his words. 'I must not conceal from you,' he warned the Secretary of State for War, 'that a great part of the BEF and its equipment will inevitably be lost even in the best circumstances.' Viscount Gort gave this chilly prognosis on 26 May 1940, as his British Expeditionary Force fell back across Belgium and northern France. Gort had earlier suggested that the BEF was making 'the retreat with which all British campaigns start'. As the campaign reached its climax he must have feared that the retreat would end in disaster.

Yet only 10 days later most of the BEF was safe. A total of 338,000 men – 120,000 of them French – had been evacuated from Dunkirk and the open beaches to its east. The Royal Navy had played its part, with destroyers like *Grafton, Javelin, Shikari* and *Wolfhound* as had Allied warships like the French *Bourrasque* and the Polish *Blyskawicz*. Passenger steamers, like *Lochgarry, Mona's Queen* and *Royal Daffodil* also made their valuable contribution. Then came a host of smaller craft: their types a naval architect's catalogue; their names a blend of the utilitarian and the whimsical.

There was the Isle of Wight Ferry *Fishbourne*; the eel boat *Johanna*; the motor cruiser *Silver Queen;* the London fire float *Massey Shaw;* the wherry *Medora;* the Belgian fishing boat *Lydie Suzanne,* the Margate lifeboat *Lord Southborough* and over five hundred more. Some survived, but many did not. The Thames estuary cockle-boat *Renown* spent a day under fire, ferrying troops out to larger craft. On her way home her engine broke down, and she asked for help from her sister ship *Letitia*, herself under tow. 'They made fast to our stern,' reported *Letitia*'s skipper:

That was at 1.15 am, and tired out, the engineer and seaman and signaller went to turn in, as our work seemed nearly done…at about 1.50 a terrible explosion

Above: The shriek of the *Stuka* dive-bomber was an abiding memory for Dunkirk survivors. Many came back to England, like those in the main photograph, on the decks of warships.
Left: The Victoria Cross, Britain's highest award for gallantry in battle, was won by Captain Ervine-Andrews, who helped defend the Dunkirk perimeter while evacuation went on.

Overleaf: Charles Cundall's dramatic painting shows most of the evacuation's key features. In the foreground small craft ferry troops to larger vessels. In the centre an improvised jetty helps men reach a coaster. In the background, burning oil tanks west of the port cast a pall of smoke over the scene.

took place, and a hail of wood splinters came down on our deck. In the pitch dark you could see nothing, and after the explosion we heard nothing. And we could do nothing, except pull in the tow-rope which was just as we passed it to the *Renown* about three-quarters of an hour before, but not a sign of *Renown.*

Though contemporaries exaggerated the contribution made by the little ships, they were an inseparable part of this tale of unlooked-for deliverance. The weather was unexpectedly calm; the German high command halted its tanks with victory within its grasp, and, terrifying though the *Luftwaffe* was, its attacks were less conclusive than its commanders hoped. It is small wonder that a relieved nation hailed the miracle of Dunkirk.

Britain Before the Second World War
The three and a half centuries since the Battle of the Boyne had seen Britain rise to become an imperial power. In the eighteenth century industry and agriculture burgeoned: the domestic market for manufactured goods grew, and exports tripled in the second half of the century. Britain emerged victorious from a long struggle with Revolutionary and Napoleonic France, and by the middle of the nineteenth century was at her apogee. The Royal Navy brooked no competition, and under its protection trade flourished and the largest empire the world had ever seen prospered.

There was a price to be paid for all this. Industrialization condemned much of the population to life in reeking, overcrowded cities, and it took decades for liberal politicians and medical reformers to improve matters. Periodic agricultural depressions brought misery to the countryside, and in Ireland failures of the potato crop – the staple diet for much of the population – resulted in famine. A series of reform bills widened suffrage, but it was not until after the First World War that women were able to vote.

The 1914–18 war itself did extraordinary damage to the old Britain. It was not simply that its human cost was horrifying: Britain lost 700,000 men killed, and tens of thousands of others were physically crippled or mentally scarred. The whole country was impoverished by the war, and industrial stagnation and mass unemployment cast a shadow over the inter-war period.

Yet the picture was not universally bleak. The working class, though blighted by the Depression, maintained its own cohesive character, and a growing middle class filed out into the orderly suburbs. Public entertainment, in music hall and cinema, on football field and cricket pitch, not only furnished 'opium for the people' but also helped give a sense of common values. The monarchy remained a powerful symbol of national unity. Even the crisis of 1936, when Edward VIII abdicated to marry Mrs Simpson, left it essentially untouched.

The coalition government under David Lloyd George, 'the man who won the war', was returned to power in 1918. It was swamped by a sea of troubles. The national debt rose alarmingly, leading to demands for better management of public expenditure. In Ireland, the nationalist Sinn Fein party won the majority of seats, and its MPs withdrew from Westminster to establish an unofficial parliament in Dublin. After a bitter campaign against the Irish Republican Army, Lloyd George negotiated with Sinn Fein leaders, and in 1922 the Irish Free State came into being, leaving just the six counties of Northern Ireland as part of the United Kingdom. Rising unemployment and harsh treatment of strikers reflected the government's failure at home; and growing disillusionment over the consequences of the Treaty of Versailles, which ended the First World War, testified to the unpopularity of its foreign policy.

Though the Conservatives won the 1922 election, the Labour Party, under Ramsay MacDonald, grew in strength. In 1924 MacDonald became the first Labour prime minister, but his minority government, at the mercy of its Liberal allies, proved short-lived. The Conservatives, under Stanley Baldwin, won the 1924 election, but in 1931 MacDonald was prime minister once again.

The collapse of the American stock market in October 1929 sent shock-waves across the whole of the western world; and in 1931 MacDonald's goverment could not reconcile conflicting demands to reduce spending and maintain social benefits. MacDonald stayed on as the head of a National Government consisting mainly of Conservatives and Liberals; an election later that year brought the National Government back with a huge majority.

MacDonald himself, his power base gone, was succeeded by Baldwin in 1935, and in 1937 Neville Chamberlain became prime minister at the head of a largely Conservative National Government. In domestic terms Chamberlain's solid managerial conservatism seemed to have much to offer; it was foreign policy that became his downfall.

The Lead-up to the Second World War
The Versailles settlement was a compromise. It was deeply humiliating to Germany which was stripped of territory and allowed an army of only 100,000 men. Yet the Europe it created was inherently unstable: states like Poland and Czechoslovakia could not realistically defend themselves

against major aggressors. The League of Nations initially seemed to offer the hope of creating collective security, but the United States declined to join and the League's voice soon counted for little.

The rise of extremist politics in Europe was bound up with the growing economic crisis. Benito Mussolini had taken power in Italy before the storm broke, but in Germany the rise of Adolf Hitler was made possible by mass unemployment and hyper-inflation. Some British politicians admired the achievements of Mussolini's Italy and Hitler's Germany, and argued that Germany formed a bulwark against Communist Russia. They also maintained that some of Hitler's early expansionist moves were only correctives to Versailles. When Spanish nationalists, under General Franco, rose against the republican government in 1936 the British Cabinet remained rigorously non-interventionist.

Chamberlain's attempts to maintain a working relationship with the dictators at first seemed to chime with popular opinion, but news from Spain and Germany helped change the mood. In September 1938, with war looming over the German threat to Czechoslovakia, Chamberlain went to Munich, came to an accommodation with Hitler, and returned to announce 'peace in our time'. Initial enthusiasm evaporated when Hitler invaded Prague, and Chamberlain was compelled to offer Poland security guarantees he had no means of honouring. When Hitler invaded Poland on 31 August 1939 a British ultimatum did not deter him, and when it expired, at 11 a.m. on 3 September, Britain found herself at war with Germany.

Shortages of British Troops and Arms

There had been over 3.5 million troops in the British establishment in 1918 (at the end of the First World War) but only 370,000 in 1920, and numbers fell further as the Treasury's axe bit. From 1919 successive governments followed the 'Ten Year Rule', declaring that defence planning must proceed on the assumption that there would be no major war for the next 10 years. The recent world war was officially described as 'abnormal', and both the forces and the domestic armaments industry were allowed to wither.

Hitler's repudiation of Versailles brought only a gradual response. As late as December 1937 the dispatch of an expeditionary force to support a European ally was accorded the lowest priority, well below the defence of the United Kingdom against air attack, the reinforcement of imperial garrisons and the sending of a force to an unspecified eastern theatre. However work had already been begun on new fighter aircraft, and British investment in radar – R(adio) D(etecting) A(nd) R(anging) – would pay dividends. In March 1939 the government announced the doubling of the part-time Territorial Army, and the following month it introduced limited conscription.

The future Field-Marshal Montgomery, shortly to command a division in the BEF, was scathing. 'In September 1939,' he wrote:

the British Army was totally unfit to fight a first class war on the continent of Europe. It must be said to our shame that we sent our Army into that most modern war with weapons and equipment which were quite inadequate, and we had only ourselves to blame for the disasters which early overtook us in the field when fighting began in 1940.

Numbers were scarcely impressive. The expeditionary force sent to France initially numbered four divisions, and was to rise to 13 by May 1940 when the French had 103 divisions and the Belgians 20. Equipment was patchy. Although the entire force was motorized, many vehicles had been commandeered from their civilian owners and breakdowns were frequent. The new Bren light machine-gun was on general issue, and the excellent 25-pdr field-gun was beginning to come on stream. There were relatively few armoured vehicles and initially only a single tank brigade which could take on German armour on anything approaching equal terms. And, partly because of inter-service rivalry in the inter-war years, the BEF's Air Component was weak even in May 1940, with four fighter, two bomber, two bomber reconnaissance and four army co-operation squadrons.

The paucity of tanks and aircraft did not simply reflect pre-war parsimony. The RAF placed greater emphasis on the air defence of the UK and the build-up of its strategic bombing force than on co-operation with the army. The army itself had flirted with the development of experimental mechanized units in the late 1920s but had failed to keep up the momentum. One leading advocate of mechanization, Major-General J. F. C. Fuller, described by Brian Bond as 'an eccentric genius with remarkable abilities', flared into prominence only to be retired prematurely in 1930. Another, Captain Basil Liddell Hart, successively military correspondent of the *Daily Telegraph* and *The Times,* sketched out ideas for an 'expanding torrent' of armour and was influential as adviser to Leslie Hore-Belisha, Secretary of State for war 1937–40. However, the army's leadership eventually decided in favour of gradual wholesale mechanization and motorization, rather than concentrating on specialist tank formations, and Liddell Hart was to write damningly of Britain's surrender of her lead in armoured warfare.

The French Army

The French also favoured caution. In their case, the size of their army and its limited resources (the Maginot Line, a fortified barrier covering parts of the Franco-German border, had made great demands on their defence budget) meant that in 1940 most French infantrymen still marched on foot like their fathers before them.

France had her share of forward thinkers: Colonel Charles de Gaulle had been struck off the 1936 promotion list because his book *Vers l'armée de métier* had recommended the establishment of a mechanized force composed of professional soldiers. France also produced some good tanks, and by May 1940 had six armoured or mechanized divisions and was forming a seventh. But her army remained firmly wedded to doctrine based on the tactics of the First World War: artillery conquered and infantry occupied. Most tanks were allocated to infantry support, and their design, armament and limited communications reflected this preference.

Germany Takes the Lead in Armoured Warfare

The *Reichswehr*, the 100,000-man army permitted Germany by the Treaty of Versailles, was largely officered by men who were militarily and politically conservative. However, they and their NCOs were trained to take responsibilities well above their formal ranks, making the *Reichswehr* a kernel for subsequent expansion; and collaboration with the Soviet Union enabled the Germans to familiarize themselves with tanks and aircraft forbidden them by Versailles.

The German army, too, contained advocates of mobility. Heinz Guderian was convinced that all arms formations, all of whose elements enjoyed the same cross-country mobility as tanks, would achieve 'decisive importance' in a coming war. The German army expanded rapidly after 1933, and in 1936 the first three panzer (armoured) divisions were formed. Many senior officers regarded them with suspicion, and feared that selective mechanization would consume resources better spread across the army as a whole.

Nevertheless Hitler's support helped advocates of mechanization, and the Germans gained experience of armour during the Spanish Civil War, when 'volunteers' fought for Franco. The invasion of Poland in 1939 helped develop panzer tactics still further. Guderian's slogan '*Klotzen, nicht Kleckern*' – 'Smash, don't tap' – applied, and divisions were concentrated into panzer corps so that tanks could be used en masse. The *Luftwaffe* prevented hostile aircraft from intervening, and lent powerful support to the ground battle, acting as 'flying artillery.' The Junkers 87

Stuka dive-bomber, with its gull-wing silhouette and banshee shriek, was particularly unnerving.

Campaign and Battle

Although Britain and France had declared war in response to Hitler's invasion of Poland, there was little they could do to help the Poles. The French launched a half-hearted offensive into the Saar, and then settled down to build up their forces for a long struggle. The BEF established itself in north-west France, with its headquarters in Arras.

The Allied Commanders

General Lord Gort, Commander-in-Chief of the BEF, was a descendant of Colonel Charles Vereker, MP for Limerick and commander of its militia, who in 1798 had distinguished himself against French troops who had landed to support the Irish rebels. Gort was born in 1886, commissioned into the Grenadier Guards in 1905 and won the Victoria Cross as an acting lieutenant-colonel in September 1918. Chief of the Imperial General Staff at the outbreak of war, Gort had, as his biographer puts it, 'done his conscientious best in work and surroundings that were uncongenial and with a Secretary of State [Hore-Belisha] he found even more so.'

The official history of the campaign declares that Gort 'was not an intellectual man nor had he the mind of an administrator: by temperament and training he was a fighting soldier…' He had a guardsman's respect for precision. One of his first conferences discussed which shoulder the steel helmet should be slung from when it was not worn on the head, and shortly before his evacuation – characteristically he took no more kit than a private soldier – he cut the medal ribbons from uniforms he left behind. When faced with the campaign's sternest decision 'he stood unmoved and undismayed', with a moral courage equal to his physical valour.

The BEF was part of General Billotte's No 1 Army Group, but in practice Gort received orders from General Georges, Commander-in-Chief North-East Front. The War Office directive emphasized that Gort was to 'carry out loyally' instruction issued by Georges, but 'if any order given by him appears to you to imperil the British Field Force…you should be at liberty to appeal to the British government before executing that order.' Georges' headquarters were at La Ferté-sous-Jouarre, about 40 miles (64 km) east of Paris. His own superior, the French Commander-in-Chief, General Maurice Gamelin, was based at the Château de Vincennes on the eastern edge of Paris.

The air chain of command was almost equally long. From January 1940 Air Marshal A.S. Barratt commanded both the BEF's Air Component and the Advanced Air Striking Force. He had previously been based at Coulommiers, east of Paris, with the Commander-in-Chief of the French Air Force, but now established a forward headquarters at Chauny, with General d'Astier de la Vigerie, whose Northern Zone of Aerial Operations was to support Billotte's army group. The Air Ministry ordered Barratt to use his aircraft 'in accordance with the day to day needs of the Allied situation on the Western Front as a whole', but to give Gort 'full assurance' regarding his own air support. It was, as the official history recognizes, a 'somewhat ambiguous directive'.

Planning the Campaign
Belgium had become neutral in 1936, and was not prepared to countenance planning with the British and French, but let it be known that, if attacked, she proposed to fight a delaying battle on the Albert Canal. This had been strengthened by forts, notably the mighty Eben Emael, and its defence would buy time in which the Allies might come to Belgium's aid.

Gamelin planned to meet an attack by holding fast along the Maginot Line and wheeling forward on his left to take up a position on the River Escaut (Scheldt) between Antwerp and Ghent. This plan would result in the Allies holding a long line but defending little of Belgium. Gamelin was considering modifying it when a copy of a German operations order fell into Belgian hands. It revealed that the Germans were indeed planning to move into central Belgium, and encouraged Gamelin to opt for the Dyle Plan, which took his left wing forward of Brussels, with the Breda variation, which would send a French army up to help the Dutch. The revised plan would throw 30 Allied divisions, including most of the armoured, motorized and light mechanized divisions, deep into Belgium.

By this stage the Germans had changed their minds. Their original plan, Case Yellow, had pushed the weight of the attack into Belgium, where Army Group B was to head for Brussels. Army Group A was to launch a subsidiary attack towards Namur, while Army Group C covered the Maginot Line.

Amongst the critics of this project were Hitler himself and Lieutenant-General Erich von Manstein, Chief of Staff of Army Group A. The latter argued that the attack should force 'a decisive issue by land', and the new plan, *Sichelschnitt* ('Sickle-cut'), went a long way towards meeting his suggestions. Army Group B was reduced in size, and would now form the 'matador's cloak' which would draw the Allies to the Low Countries. General von Rundstedt's Army Group A, with 45 divisions, would penetrate

General Lord Gort, Commander-in-chief of the BEF, studying a map with his Chief of Staff, Lieutenant-General Pownall, before the opening of the campaign. Gort had won a VC in the First World War, and in 1940 he showed considerable moral courage.

the hilly and wooded Ardennes. It would contain seven panzer divisions, in Guderian's XIX, Reinhardt's XLI and Hoth's XV Panzer Corps (the first two comprising Panzer Group Kleist) which would hit the Allied front between Sedan and Dinant on the River Meuse, the hinge between the static armies in the Maginot Line and the mobile force clattering forward into Belgium.

It was high risk. The attackers would be vulnerable to air attack as they wound through the Ardennes, and there was no guarantee that they would succeed in crossing the Meuse. But the potential pay-off was also high. If the Germans broke through and moved fast it would be hard for the Allies to regain the initiative.

Churchill Comes to Power
In April 1940 the Germans invaded Denmark and Norway. The Allied response was hopelessly uncoordinated, and its political backdraught blew Chamberlain from power. He was replaced by Winston Churchill, whose political career to date had been controversial. Churchill had been in both the Liberal and Conservative parties, and had held high office. As

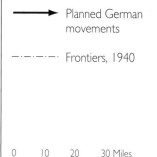

DUNKIRK
1940: The Campaign

→ Planned German movements

—·—·—·— Frontiers, 1940

0   10   20   30 Miles
0   10 20 30 40 50 Kms

Nieuport

Dunkirk

Gł

Calais

R. Yser

Ypres

7th Army

Menin

St Omer Cassel Halluin

Boulogne

Premesques Lille

R. Lys

BEF

Maulde

Arras

1st A

Abbeville

R. Escaut

R. Somme

N

Amiens

Army

St Quentin

Chauny

R. Aisne

R. Oise

La Ferté-
sous-Jou:

PARIS ■

Vincennes

Coulommiers

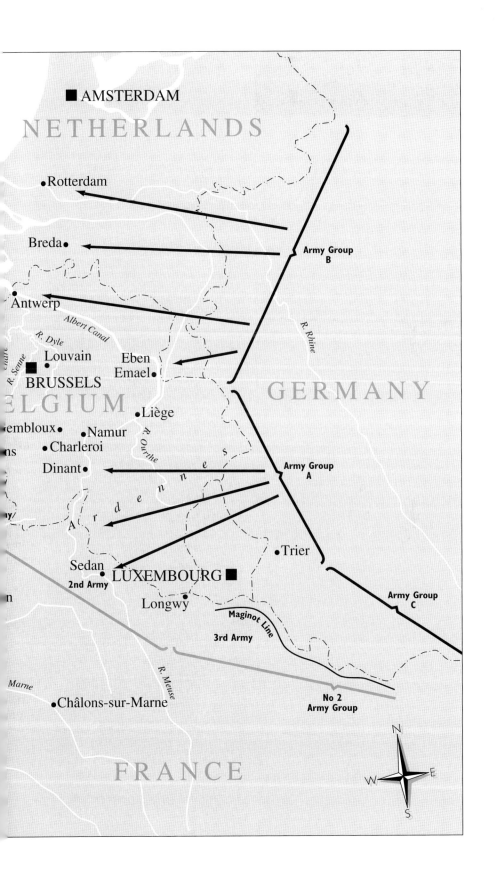

AMSTERDAM

NETHERLANDS

Rotterdam

Breda

Army Group
B

Antwerp

Albert Canal

R. Dyle

R. Schelde

R. Senne

Louvain

Eben
Emael

BRUSSELS

GERMANY

BELGIUM

Liège

embloux

Namur

R. Ourthe

Charleroi

ns

Dinant

Army Group
A

Ardennes

y

A

Trier

Sedan

LUXEMBOURG

2nd Army

Longwy

Army Group
C

Maginot Line

3rd Army

n

Marne

R. Meuse

Châlons-sur-Marne

No 2
Army Group

FRANCE

N
W   E
S

First Lord of the Admiralty on the eve of the First World War he did much to prepare Britain for a conflict he regarded as inevitable. Blamed for the failure of the Gallipoli expedition in 1915, he resigned and fought on the Western Front before returning to serve in Lloyd George's coalition government. Chancellor of the Exchequer under Baldwin, he then spent 10 years in the political wilderness, attacking appeasement and inaction in the face of the threat from Germany. He was brought back into the government on the outbreak of war, and his pugnacious manner made him a popular choice as Chamberlain's successor.

Churchill was not always an easy man to deal with. He often intervened directly in the conduct of operations, and did not always grasp tactical realities. 'A scandalous (i.e. Winstonian) thing to do, and in fact quite impossible to carry out,' complained Gort's Chief of Staff, Lieutenant-General Henry Pownall of one proposed manoeuvre. For all this, Churchill was the man of the hour, an inspirational war leader at a time when Britain's fortunes were approaching their nadir.

The German Advance

The Germans attacked on 10 May. Their aircraft wreaked havoc in France and the Low Countries (Belgium and the Netherlands), attacking airfields and strafing troops on roads and railways. Half the Belgian aircraft were destroyed before they could get airborne, and some French airfields suffered severely. Special forces, some in Allied uniforms, attacked key points. Eben Emael was blinded by a glider assault group that landed on top of it, and surrendered the next day. General von Rundstedt's men plunged into the Ardennes, brushing aside Belgian *Chasseurs Ardennais* and a French cavalry screen, and reached the Meuse on 12 May.

The Allies, meanwhile, advanced into Belgium as planned. However, when the French 7th Army reached Breda it found that the Dutch had already been pushed back to Rotterdam. Things went from bad to worse on 13 May. Guderian crossed the Meuse at Sedan, and Major-General Erwin Rommel's 7th Panzer Division, which had gained a foothold on the far bank on the previous day, established a solid bridgehead near Dinant. A French mechanized corps, brought up behind the Sedan front on 14 May, was ordered to contain the breakthrough rather than counter-attack; and while it struggled with Guderian's flank guard the panzers swung westwards, making for the Channel coast.

When his army advanced, Gort had moved forward to keep in better touch with his corps commanders, Lieutenant-Generals Barker (I Corps), Brooke (II Corps) and Adam (III Corps). The next day, 15 May, saw him just west of Brussels, with the BEF in action on the River Dyle from Louvain to Wavre, the Belgians on its left and the French 1st Army on its right.

There was more bad news. The Dutch surrendered that day after the *Luftwaffe* had bombed the undefended city of Rotterdam, and the Germans forced back part of the French 1st Army, compelling Gort to withdraw his right flank to conform. He was concerned that further withdrawal would leave his left flank forward of the main allied line at Louvain, and pressed Billotte for direction. The response was an order that the Allies would fall back on the River Senne that night, onto the River Dendre on 16 May and then onto the River Escaut on 17 May.

Things were worse elsewhere. Paul Reynaud, the French premier, had telephoned Churchill early on 15 May to announce: 'We are beaten: we have lost the battle.' Churchill flew to France and was shocked to hear Gamelin admit that there was no strategic reserve with which to counter the breakthrough. Pownall was equally aware of the danger. 'The news from the far south is very bad,' he wrote on 16 May. 'German mechanised columns are getting deep into France towards Laon and St Quentin. I hope to God the French have some means of stopping them and closing the gap or we are *bust*.'

Allied air power did its unavailing best. Battle and Blenheim bombers attacked German crossings at Sedan with extraordinary courage: in all, 45 out of 109 aircraft were lost. The Hurricanes of the Air Component were reduced to 50 serviceable aircraft after two days of fighting. Gort asked Anthony Eden, the newly appointed Secretary of State for War, for reinforcements, and promptly received another three squadrons which were sent to help the French.

On 17 May Gort cobbled together a force under Major-General Mason-MacFarlane, Director of Military Intelligence at General Headquarters (GHQ), to protect the right flank of the BEF: it was known as 'Macforce', and was the first of several improvised detachments. This was a wise precaution, although the French 1st Army, under heavier pressure than the BEF, held together better than Gort had expected. It had the disadvantage, however, of depriving Gort of the head of his intelligence staff. 'Had he remained in charge,' comments the official history, 'Lord Gort might not so often have been without adequate information.'

During the withdrawal to the River Escaut, Gort was visited by Billotte, who told him of the measures being taken to contain the breakthrough, 'though clearly,' wrote Gort, 'he had little hope that they would be effective.'

'I am completely done in,' admitted Billotte to a British liaison officer, 'and I can't do a thing against these panzers.'

If the gap could not be closed Gort had two alternatives. He could fall back southwards on his lines of communication, keeping in touch with the French but abandoning the Belgians. Alternatively he could retire to the coast for evacuation, a process that would result in the loss of equipment, and would abandon the French at a time when they needed all possible support.

Gort Considers Evacuation

Given that there were now no French troops between the Germans and the coast, the southern option seemed increasingly unrealistic; and Gort thought it prudent to consider what withdrawal to the coast might entail. Pownall discussed this on the telephone, in guarded language, with the Director of Military Operations at the War Office, whom he found 'singularly stupid and unhelpful'.

The Appointment of Ramsay

The War Office was actually more helpful than it seemed. That day, 19 May, a conference there discussed the temporary maintenance of the BEF through the Channel ports of Dunkirk, Calais and Boulogne, and the evacuation of personnel from them. At this juncture the army was considering only the evacuation of non-combatants and some key specialists, and announced that 'the hazardous evacuation of very large forces' was considered to be 'very unlikely'. The meeting decided that Vice-Admiral Dover would be responsible for the evacuation, and the available shipping would be placed at his disposal.

Vice-Admiral Bertram Ramsay was in command at Dover. He knew it well, for during the First World War he had served in the Dover patrol. After the war he commanded the battleship *Royal Sovereign* before becoming Chief of Staff, as a rear-admiral, to Admiral Sir Roger Backhouse, Commander-in-Chief Home Fleet. It was not a happy relationship. Backhouse was what we might term a workaholic, and personally controlled everything, whereas Ramsay believed in the proper delegation of staff duties. He quickly asked to be relieved of his appointment and went onto half pay. In 1938, after declining an appointment commanding the Yangtse gunboat squadron, he was placed on the retired list.

Ramsay was comfortably off and enjoyed a happy family life, so retirement was no burden, and in any event he was almost immediately commissioned to write a report on Dover. He revealed that it was in a

The perceptive and hard-working Vice-Admiral Bertram Ramsay was responsible for naval aspects of the evacuation. He served as Allied Naval Commander-in-Chief for the Normandy landings in 1944, but was later killed in an aircraft accident.

state of considerable neglect. Some money was made available to rectify the worst of its defects, and Ramsay was given the dormant appointment (to be taken up when war broke out) of Flag Officer in Charge, Dover. He was soon promoted and freed from the authority of the Nore Command becoming Vice-Admiral Dover, and reporting direct to the Admiralty.

Ramsay's headquarters were in tunnels beneath Dover Castle. These had been begun during the Napoleonic Wars, and were expanded as the Second World War went on. In 1940 the section known as Admiralty Casemates was divided into a number of offices, and Ramsay himself had a 'cabin' looking out onto Dover harbour. One of the chambers had previously contained dynamos and this room may have given the evacuation its codename, Operation Dynamo.

Large-scale Evacuation is Planned

As the situation worsened there were further conferences, and on 21 May the 'emergency evacuation across the Channel of very large forces' was considered. Several key decisions were made at this stage. All sea movement would be controlled by Ramsay, assisted by liaison officers from War Office Movement Control and the Ministry of Shipping. Air cover would be arranged direct with Fighter Command. Because the beaches around the Channel ports shelved very gently, Ramsay recognized that: 'It would be necessary to have a very large number of small boats to carry troops from the beaches to the off-shore ships.' However, only a limited number of troops could be lifted off the beaches and, if at all possible, the ports themselves would be used as well.

The Admiralty already had a Small Vessels Pool which maintained small craft at harbours and naval bases. On 14 May it had arranged for the BBC to broadcast an appeal for 'all owners of self-propelled pleasure craft between 30 and 100 feet [10-30 m] in length to send all particulars to the Admiralty within 14 days'. The call had been prompted by the fact that the danger of magnetic mines meant that boatyards were busy building wooden minesweepers, and the Small Vessels Pool needed more little ships.

Allied Uncertainty

While the staff of the Small Vessels Pool were cataloguing motor yachts and cabin cruisers the BEF's plight worsened. On 20 May it was on the Escaut line, with the Germans probing its defences and growing uncertainly about both flanks. Arras still held out but was almost surrounded, and Gort assembled 'Frankforce' with a view to attacking in order to gain more elbow-room around the town.

To the south, in what had once been the rear areas between the BEF and its base at Le Havre, were two under-equipped Territorial divisions, 12th and 23rd, which had been sent out to perform labour duties and were not fully trained as fighting infantry. They were ordered to hold several towns north of Amiens, but by nightfall on 20 May German armour had burst clean through and the divisions had practically ceased to exist.

That day Gort was visited by General Ironside, Chief of the Imperial General Staff, who brought with him a written order from the War Cabinet. Gort was to move south towards Amiens, attacking any Germans he met en route, and the Belgians were to be advised that their best hope was to move between the BEF and the coast. Gort demurred. Seven of his nine divisions were in action on the Escaut. How could he disengage and then swing southwards to attack an enemy of substantial if uncertain strength? He was still prepared to conduct the Arras operation, but convinced Ironside that any major attack from the north could succeed only if the French made a serious effort from the south.

That was precisely what the French proposed to do. Gamelin had been replaced by General Maxime Weygand, a trim 73-year-old then serving in the Lebanon. After an exhausting journey to Paris Weygand snatched some sleep and then, on 21 May, flew north to confer with Billotte, Gort and the Belgians in the Belgian town of Ypres. There were three meetings that day: Gort, who heard of the conference late, arrived for the third, by which time Weygand had already left.

Weygand's intentions were quite clear. The BEF and the French 1st Army would attack southwards while French forces, assembling south of the Somme, struck north to meet them. The Belgians would withdraw to the River Yser to cover the Allies' left and rear. This scheme was not cordially received. At the first meeting the Belgians opposed withdrawal from the River Lys, arguing that successive retreats were 'the bane of discipline'. Billotte then arrived and pointed out that the 1st Army was already so hard-pressed that it could barely defend itself, let alone launch a counter-attack: this should be left to the BEF.

Only then, after Weygand had departed, did Gort appear. He observed that he was already counter-attacking at Arras, and that a further attack would only be possible if some of his divisions in the line could be relieved to form a reserve. It seems to have been agreed that the Belgians would hold the line of the Lys and relieve one British division, while the 1st Army would relieve another two. None of this could happen before the night of 23 May, and the earliest Gort could attack was 26 May. The confusion deepened when Billotte's car hit a truck on its way home. The General was mortally injured, and his successor, Blanchard of 1st Army, was not confirmed in his appointment until early on 25 May.

Gort left Ypres for a new command post in a modest château at Premesques, just west of Lille. Churchill, who had again visited Paris, where he had been favourably impressed by Weygand, sent Gort a telegram on the evening of 23 May, ordering him to attack southwards with about eight divisions, with the Belgian cavalry corps covering his right flank. Pownall was livid. 'Here are Winston's plans again,' he wrote the next day:

Can nobody prevent him trying to conduct operations himself as a super Commander-in-Chief? How does he think we are to collect eight divisions and attack as he suggests… He can have no conception of our sitiuation and condition. Where *are* the Belgian Cavalry Corps? How is an attack like this to be staged involving three nationalities at an hour's notice? The man's mad.

There were more misunderstandings the following day, and it was becoming clear to Gort that neither the Allied chain of command nor his own government really understood how serious the situation was. The 1st Army Group was encircled and outnumbered. The BEF was now on its old positions on the French frontier between Maulde and Halluin, with the Belgians on the Lys to its left; and, round to its right rear, a thinly held line along the canals to Gravelines and the sea. The *Lufwaffe*'s superiority grew more marked by the day, and the BEF's Air Component was now largely operating from England.

On 25 May Lieutenant-Colonel Gerald Templer – himself a future field marshal – had to go through Gort's room to reach Pownall's office. He saw the Commander-in-Chief standing:

in a very typical attitude – with his legs apart and his hands behind his back. He was staring – quite alone – at a series of maps of Northern France and the

Channel ports, pinned together and covering most of the wall of his small room…Though I had no precise idea of the problem which was then facing him, all my heart went out to him in his loneliness and tribulation.

By 6 p.m. Gort's mind was made up. He cancelled the British contribution to the planned offensive, and swung a division up to cover the area north-west of Menin, where the Belgians were in growing difficulties. He told Eden of his decision, and the Secretary of State's reply on 26 May acknowledged that his own information 'all goes to show that the French offensive from Somme cannot be made in sufficient strength… In such conditions the only course open to you may be to fight your way back to the West where all beaches and ports east of Gravelines will be used for embarkation'. Gort warned that even if all went well a great part of the BEF would be lost, but later that day the War Office authorized him 'to operate towards coast forthwith in conjunction with French and Belgian Armies.'

German tanks had reached the coast near Abbeville on 20 May, and on the following day began to thrust north-eastwards, placing the Channel ports in an increasingly perilous situation. Boulogne was belatedly gar-risoned by 20th Guards Brigade, snatched from training in Surrey on 21 May. After a brave defence the brigade was embarked on destroyers on the night of 23/24 May.

The Defence of Calais

The defence of Calais, in contrast, featured what the official history calls 'some of the failings which have been matched too often in the conduct of our military excursions'. The garrison began to arrive on 22 May, and eventually consisted of 3rd Royal Tank Regiment, Queen Victoria's Rifles, a good Territorial motor-cycle battalion sent without its machines, transport or 3-inch mortars, and two regular battalions of 30th Brigade, 1st Rifle Brigade and 2nd King's Royal Rifle Corps, together with assorted gunners and base details.

Brigadier Claude Nicholson was given a series of conflicting instruc-tions. First the tanks were to proceed south-westwards to Boulogne; then south-eastwards towards St Omer. Then they were to convoy rations for the BEF north-eastwards to Dunkirk. By this stage Calais was encircled and only three tanks got through. The remainder joined the infantry in defence of the town.

Nicholson was first told that evacuation was agreed in principle, but then informed that the garrison came under overall French command, so there could be no evacuation. The harbour was now 'of no importance to the BEF', and he should simply choose the best position from which to fight to the end. This did not appeal to Churchill, and on his instructions Eden sent a more inspirational message which concluded: 'HM Government are confident that you and your gallant regiments will perform an exploit worthy of the British name.'

Nicholson duly fought on, declining an invitation to surrender, and the Germans eventually over-ran Calais on 26 May. Both Churchill and Eden had found it a painful decision. 'I had served,' wrote Eden, 'with one of the regiments and knew personally many of those whose fate I now had to decide.'

Churchill was sure that, but for the defence of Calais, Dunkirk could not have been held, but historians have been less than convinced. 'For all the gallantry displayed by the defenders of Boulogne, Calais and the Canal line,' wrote Brian Bond, 'it is hard to escape the conclusion that there was no military solution to 1st Army Group's problem... Only remarkable blunders on the German side can explain why the total disaster...was averted.'

The German Armoured Advance

The German high command had never subscribed unequivocally to Guderian's view of war, and the sheer pace of the armoured advance after the Meuse crossing dismayed some generals, notably Kleist, commanding the panzer group of which Guderian's corps formed part, and Kluge of 4th Army. Hitler, too, had his doubts, and as early as 17 May General Halder, Chief of the General Staff, recorded how: 'He mistrusts his own success; he's afraid to take risks; he'd really likely to stop now.' Once he had reached the Channel coast Guderian planned to send a division apiece to Boulogne, Calais and Dunkirk, but one was temporarily taken from him and parts of the others had to hold the Somme bridgeheads until follow-up troops arrived. Nevertheless, by 24 May 1st Panzer Divison had secured crossings over the Aa Canal, only 15 miles (24 km) from Dunkirk.

After cautious braking came an emergency stop. Hitler and Rundstedt met at Charleville on the same day. Hitler first confirmed Rundstedt's earlier decision that the armour should halt on the canal line, a view based on the fact that the Flanders coast was poor tank country, and mopping up could be better undertaken by infantrymen of Bock's northern army group. The Arras battle of 21 May, when even the supremely confident Rommel supposed that he was being attacked by five divisions, rather than by less than one, also produced what the German historians, Jacobsen and Rohwer term 'a certain psychological effect'.

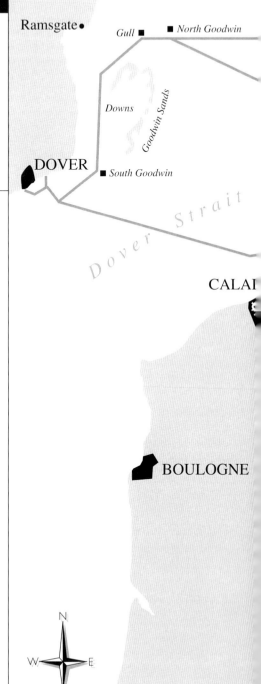

Canals or canalised rivers
(much simplified)

Sea routes

■   Lightships

| 0 | | 10 | | 20 Miles |
| 0 | 10 | | 20 Kms | |

• Margate

Ramsgate •   *Gull* ■   ■ *North Goodwin*

Downs   *Goodwin Sands*

DOVER   ■ *South Goodwin*

Dover   Strait

CALAI

BOULOGNE

N
W   E
S

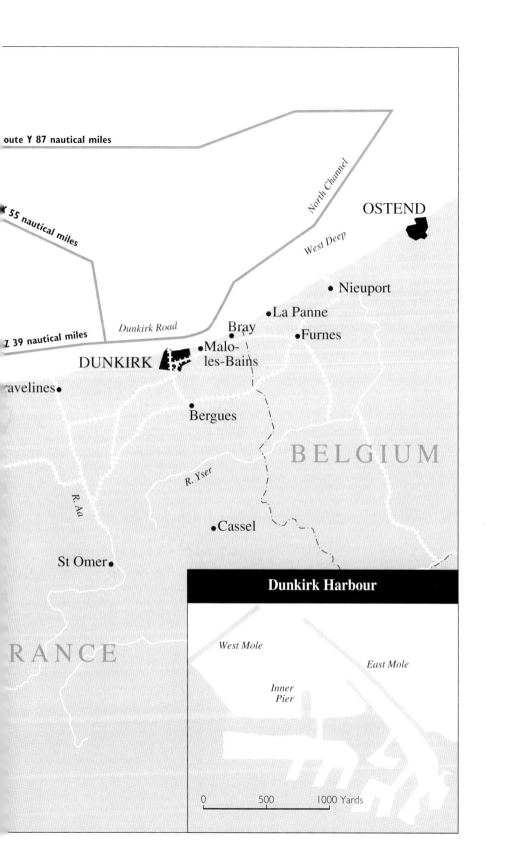

oute Y 87 nautical miles

55 nautical miles

North Channel

OSTEND

West Deep

• Nieuport

Z 39 nautical miles

Dunkirk Road

•La Panne

Bray

•Furnes

DUNKIRK

•Malo-
les-Bains

ravelines•

Bergues

BELGIUM

R. Yser

R. Aa

•Cassel

St Omer•

Dunkirk Harbour

West Mole

East Mole

Inner
Pier

RANCE

0   500   1000 Yards

Hitler went further, announcing that he wished to preserve the panzer divisions for the next phase of the campaign, an attack on the French south of the Somme. He was also influenced by the views of Hermann Goering, head of the *Luftwaffe*, who was confident that air power could deal with the Allies in the Dunkirk perimeter. By midday on 26 May it was clear that the halt order could no longer stand. However, by this stage the advance had lost much of its momentum, and Operation Dynamo was well underway.

Operation Dynamo Begins

In 1940 Dunkirk was the third-largest port in France, with substantial harbour facilities and, to its south, a large complex of oil storage tanks. It had been fortified in the seventeenth century by the great military engineer Vauban, and the fortifications had been improved in the nineteenth century. Although Dunkirk had officially lost its fortress status, many of the old defence works still offered protection even against modern weapons, and the French maritime commander, Admiral Abrial, had established his headquarters in Bastion 32, just east of the harbour.

East of Dunkirk ran the beaches, broad stretches of gently sloping sand. At popular resorts, Malo les Bains and Bray Dunes in France and La Panne across the border in Belgium, there were sea walls, but elsewhere the beaches rose into sand dunes, held together by coarse grass. The low-lying meadowland behind the coastal strip was intersected by canals, the chief of which ran from the little town of Bergues to Furnes.

The Bergues–Furnes canal formed a convenient defensive perimeter. The sector from Bergues through Furnes and on to Nieuport, about 20 miles (32 km) in all, was to be held by the British, while the French defended the western flank. Gort ordered Lieutenant-General Sir Ronald Adam to organize the bridgehead. It was divided into three corps sectors – II Corps to the east, I Corps in the centre and III Corps to the west. There were ration and ammunition dumps in each sector, and as retreating troops arrived they were directed to a collecting area outside the perimeter and then sent to the appropriate corps area where they were allocated a sector to defend and an evacuation beach. Vehicles were to be disabled outside the perimeter, but this order was not always obeyed and the situation inside the perimeter was a good deal more chaotic than these arrangements might suggest.

Although the Admiralty ordered Ramsay to commence Dynamo at 6.57 p.m. on Sunday 26 May, he had already sent out vessels that afternoon. The first, the Isle of Man steam packet *Mona's Queen*, berthed in the harbour under air attack but took 1420 men aboard. On her way home

The accurate and reliable Bren light machine-gun had come into service just before the war. Each British infantry battalion had a platoon of Bren-gun carriers, open-topped light armoured vehicles, armed with Brens or other weapons. This Bren is firing in the anti-aircraft role. Although this was not enormously effective, it sometimes discouraged pilots from pressing home their attacks and gave men the feeling that they were able to hit back.

she was shelled by shore batteries around Gravelines and then machine-gunned from the air. Her experience suggested that the quickest route from Dover to Dunkirk, Route Z, only 39 nautical miles (72 km), was no longer practicable now that the Germans held the coast. A more northerly approach, Route X, was 55 nautical miles (102 km) long, but was known to cross minefields, and was not swept for several days. An even wider approach, Route Y, presented less risk of mines and could be used more quickly, but it lengthened the distance to 87 nautical miles (161 km).

To the Beaches

Heavy air attacks on Dunkirk did so much damage that the Senior Naval Officer ashore, Captain W.G. Tennant, concluded that it was no longer possible to use the harbour. He signalled Ramsay: 'Please send every available craft to beaches East of Dunkirk immediately. Evacuation tomorrow night problematical.' Soon the anti-aircraft cruiser *Calcutta*, nine destroyers, four minesweepers, 17 drifters and numerous *schuyts* (inevitably known as skoots) – Dutch coastal vessels with naval crews – were working the beaches with their boats.

As Ramsay was to report: 'A moderate surf on the beaches reduced the rate of embarkation, exhausted the boats' crews, the majority of whom were "hostilities only" ratings, rendering the whole operation slow and difficult.' Only 7669 men were landed in England on 27 May: unless there was radical improvement, most of the BEF would be captured while awaiting evacuation.

That was not the end of the day's miseries. At midnight the Belgians surrendered. Paul Reynaud, the French premier, railed bitterly against King Leopold, calling it 'an event without precedent in history'. However it is now clear that the Belgians had fought hard against overwhelming odds, and had given warning of the seriousness of their plight. The surrender opened a gap at the north-east end of the perimeter, but it was plugged by brilliant improvisation, some of it by Major-General Montgomery of 3rd Division, fast making his name as a man to watch.

The BEF fell back onto the Dunkirk perimeter like a collapsing balloon, leaving the River Lys on 28 May and the Yser, the last major obstacle south of the Bergues–Furnes Canal, on the following day. Devoted rearguards covered its withdrawal. The garrison of Cassel, on a lofty hill overlooking the Flanders plain at the junction of five major roads, held out until orders to retire reached it on 29 May. There were Germans all around, and most of the force was killed or captured in a series of bitter little fights on the way to Dunkirk. The orders never reached a handful of Gloucesters, under Second Lieutenant Roy Cresswell, holding a bunker on the road north from Cassel. They held out till the evening of 30 May. By that time there had been a fire in the bunker and there were Germans on its roof: it was only when a captured British officer was brought up to point out that everyone else had gone that they surrendered.

The Evacuation Begins

Gort's headquarters moved to La Panne on 28 May. Lieutenant-General Adam, his task now completed, was evacuated, and Gort laid down that the corps would be evacuated in reverse numerical order, I Corps leaving last. Late that day he received a personal message from Churchill telling him that if further evacuation became impossible he 'would become the sole judge of when it was impossible to inflict further damage upon the enemy' and could surrender.

By then the picture was less bleak. Two long moles or breakwaters ran out to sea at the entrance to Dunkirk harbour. The eastern mole was by far the longer. Although it could be used a a temporary mooring, it was made of timber latticework and had not been designed to bear the impact of

The eastern mole at Dunkirk, shown clearly on the left of the photograph, had not been designed as a mooring for large vessels. However, on 27 May a passenger steamer proved that the mole could be used, and thereafter it played a crucial part in the evacuation. These troops have boarded the destroyer HMS *Vanquisher* by ladder because of the low tide, though some soldiers, already tired, hungry and frightened, found the process difficult. Despite the remarkable contribution of the 'little ships', the majority of men evacuated from Dunkirk were taken off the mole by destroyers or passenger ships.

large vessels. Its top was 10 feet (3 m) wide, and there was a 15-foot (4.5 m) rise and fall in the tide beneath it. German pilots had not so far attacked it, and for the moment it was screened from their view by the pall of smoke drifting from burning oil storage tanks. Late on 27 May Captain Tennant ordered *Queen of the Channel* to go alongside. She got away with about 1000 men, and proved that the mole could be used. German bombers sank her in mid-Channel, but most of the men aboard her were rescued by *Dorrien Rose*.

Losses amongst shipping were heartbreaking. The destroyer *Wakeful*, with 650 troops on board, was hit by a torpedo and went down in seconds. *Grafton,* another destroyer, was torpedoed while picking up survivors and, though sinking, opened fire on a nearby vessel which she took to be an enemy torpedo boat. The drifter *Lydd* drew the same conclusion and rammed the ship, sinking her, only to discover that she was the drifter *Comfort:* only one of her crew and four of the soldiers she had rescued from *Wakeful* survived.

On 29 May the *Luftwaffe* struck hard at the mole. Of the 11 British ships alongside, *Grenade, Fenella, Crested Eagle, Polly Johnson* and *Calvi* eventually sank, and *Jaguar* and *Canterbury* returned home safely but could take no further part in the operation. The destroyer *Grenade*'s end was especially awesome. Captain John Horsfall of the Royal Irish Fusiliers was leaving the mole aboard a drifter and saw *Grenade* 'glowing white down her length in the darkness, with showers of sparks shooting up into the starry sky above her. She was barely afloat.' Ramsay was mistakenly informed that the mole was now unusable, and for a time all ships were directed to the beaches. But, despite the terrible losses, 47,310 men were landed in England that day.

Destroyer losses persuaded the Admiralty to withdraw modern destroyers from Dynamo, leaving Ramsay with only 15 old ones. It soon became clear that the remaining destroyers and all other available shipping had a daily lift capacity of only 43,000 men (well below the target of 55,000), and some of the modern destroyers were soon returned to Ramsay.

By now the navy's side of the operation was working smoothly. Naval officers, with small parties of sailors, served as beachmasters, supervising embarkation arrangements from the shore. Captain Tennant, sharing Admiral Abrial's headquarters in Bastion 32, was ably assisted by Commander John Clouston, pier master at the eastern mole, who set up a control post at the base of the mole. Clouston, a big, confident Canadian, was one of the heroes of the evacuation. He hastened the laggards, checked the panic-stricken, and regulated the incessant flow along the mole. John Horsfall wrote approvingly of the activities of the naval staff. 'They heeded nothing and simply got on with their job,' he declared, 'showing patience, courtesy and affability to all comers. They were sorely tried and I doubt that many of our own officers would have achieved those three marks of virtue consistently just then.' Senior naval officers offshore – Rear Admiral Wake-Walker for Dunkirk itself – controlled the shipping, using megaphones to marshal vessels around the mole or off the beaches.

The Waiting Troops
The army's arrangements were, of necessity, more haphazard. Some officers were issued with neat slips entitling them to embark a given number of officers and men from a specified beach. Unfortunately there were no routes signed to the beaches, and once there it became apparent that staff officers' logic did not apply to tens of thousands of waiting men. On 28 May the commanding officer of HMS *Gossamer* reported: 'There appeared to be a large wood close to the shore but on approaching nearer this was seen to be a mass of troops on the sand.'

Troops formed great lines stretching out into the water. Sometimes formal discipline prevailed, but more often it did not, and there was a powerful collective sense of natural justice which dealt harshly with queue-jumpers. A Royal Artillery officer who wrote under the pseudonym 'Gun-Buster' gives a graphic description of the apparently endless wait:

We tacked ourselves onto the rear of the smallest of the three queues, the head of it was already standing in water up to the waist. Half an hour passed. Suddenly a small rowing boat appeared. The head of the queue clambered in and were rowed away into the blackness. We moved forward, and the water rose to our waists.

Our only thoughts now were to get on a boat. Along the entire queue not a word was spoken. The men just stood there silently staring into the darkness, praying that a boat would appear and fearing that it would not. Heads and shoulders only showing above the water. Fixed, immovable, as though chained there…

When a boat appeared at last he was too exhausted and weighed down by sodden clothing to climb in, but powerful arms hauled him aboard. Then, he wrote: 'I felt that my job was over. Anything else that remained to be done was the Navy's business.'

The behaviour of troops during the evacuation varied dramatically. At one end of the scale there were sullen or drunken stragglers in the rubble of Dunkirk, terrified men cowering amongst the dunes, and instances of raw panic on the beaches themselves. At the other extreme, some foot guards impressed observers by swinging down to the mole in step. A surviving photograph shows a detachment of Grenadier Guards marching past the station on Dover docks after their return to England, rifles smartly at the slope.

It was easiest for soldiers in formed units, with the discipline and cohesion that spring from mutual regard, to remain steady in a world turned upside down. John Horsfall's men moved in single file along the mole under sporadic air attack:

chattering like monkeys. Sometimes [Company Sergeant Major] Good or one of the NCOs would bellow at them, but inevitably this drew repartee, probably [Fusilier] Given's, in the dark. There were variants as some warrior took a toss, and one heard the clatter of ironmongery or fragmented rock dropping into the water below…

In several places the mole was demolished, and it was a slow business dropping down into the void beneath, one by one, and swinging over the gap – or clambering in the black dark over unstable wreckage.

The commanding officer of a Territorial battalion of the King's Own Royal Regiment reminded his officers that they wore a distinguished cap-badge and urged them to 'set an example to that rabble on the beach', and the battalion marched down in good order.

Most of the waiting troops had long since run out of food and water, and on the night of 29/30 May some big lighters full of supplies were towed across the Channel and beached so that their contents could be unloaded as the tide receded. They then formed makeshift piers which made it easier for men to board the small craft which would ferry them to larger vessels. Commander Hector Richardson, Senior Naval Officer at Bray-les-Dunes, suggested that trucks could be manhandled out into the sea and then connected by planks to form improvised jetties – a military police officer had the same idea at La Panne – and these also helped.

The Little Ships
There were still too few small craft to get men off the beaches, and the ships' lifeboats, whalers and cutters were not ideal for the task: their keels dug deep into the sand as troops piled aboard, and sometimes they were overturned by the sheer weight of men clambering in. Allan Barrell, owner of *Shamrock*, one of the first civilian small craft to appear, was shocked to see 'what looked like thousands of sticks on the beach…turn into moving masses of humanity'. He went in as close as he dared to ferry soldiers, 80 at a time, to waiting destroyers. 'Navigation was extremely difficult,' he wrote:

owing to the various wreckage, upturned boats, floating torpedoes and soldiers in the water trying to be sailors for the first time, they paddled their collapsible little boats out to me with the butts of their rifles, and many shouted that they were sinking…

Eventally *Shamrock*'s propeller fouled what her skipper thought to be 'a human obstruction…I was too weak to dive under the thick black oil which surrounded us, so rather than be left sitting on our useless craft I asked to be taken on HM ship. This was the last straw, having to leave my vessel which constituted my life savings…'

Responding to the need to lift men off the beaches in greater numbers, Ramsay stepped up the flow of little ships. Many had started their journey at Tough Brothers' boatyard in Teddington where many Thames craft were collected, but the Small Vessels Pool had cast its net wide and boatyards from Cowes to Canvey Island played their part. Some owners were co-operative, and crewed their boats themselves; some never discovered that their vessels had been commandeered until long after they had gone, and a few raised bureaucratic objections. The small craft gathered at Sheerness, where their engines were checked over and they were given crews. Many of the latter were volunteers, shipwrights, marine engineers and yachtsmen, and there was a good leavening of Royal Naval Volunteer reserve officers and ratings. From Sheerness they went to Ramsgate, where they were given charts and water and sent off in convoys across the English Channel, usually escorted by an armed tug or skoot.

Some never completed the journey: they had been built for quieter times in the upper reaches of the Thames; and the Channel, even when miraculously calm, was too much for them. Others were hit by German guns (now ranging, with increasing accuracy, onto the beaches) or attacked from the air. Many of their crews found it a shocking experience, but most kept at their task. The skipper of the cockle-boat *Letitia* admitted that he turned back when a shell burst in front of his boat, but the young signaller 'who had only been "out" for about six weeks, and who had never been under fire, said "We've got to go in again" so we went in.' On 30 May 53,823 men were landed in England, almost 30,000 of them from the beaches. The author David Divine was right to hail this as 'the triumph of the little ships'.

The End of the British Evacuation
It was not only the crews of the little ships who felt the strain. There were difficulties in England when the crews of some steamers were reluctant to return to Dunkirk, and some were replaced by Royal Naval personnel or

other volunteers from the Merchant Navy. There was even something approaching a collapse of morale aboard a destroyer which had been damaged and lost her captain, but Vice-Admiral Sir James Somerville, temporarily assigned to assist the tired Ramsay, spoke to her crew and gave them a night's rest: she went back to Dunkirk the next day.

As the evacuation reached its climax – 68,014 men, the highest daily total, were rescued on 31 May – the Germans pressed hard at the perimeter. In one of the many hard-fought battles that day Captain H. M. Ervine-Andrews of the East Lancashire Regiment was awarded the Victoria Cross, the only one won at Dunkirk. His company held a sector of the canal just east of Bergues quite literally to the last round, and he then brought the last of his men to safety, wading up to their necks down a side canal.

It was Gort's intention to stay till the end, but Eden, on Churchill's instructions, ordered him to hand over command to a selected corps commander and to leave for England. 'This is in accordance with the correct military procedure,' ran the order, 'and no personal discretion is left to you in the matter.' Gort considered appointing Barker of I Corps, but it became clear that the strain had told heavily upon him, and Major-General the Hon. Harold Alexander of 1st Division was selected. Gort told him:

to operate under the orders of Admiral Abrial, and to assist the French in the defence of Dunkirk. At the same time he was to occupy himself with arrangements for the evacuation of his command, and I stressed the importance of the French sharing equally in the facilities which were provided for evacuation.

Gort's headquarters closed at 6 p.m. on 31 May, and he was ferried out to the minesweeper HMS *Hebe.*

The French Evacuation

The instructions given to Alexander highlighted one of the dilemmas of the evacuation: the degree of French involvement. The message of 26 May which gave Gort permission to operate towards the Channel coast implied that the French premier had been informed of the change of policy, but it is clear that neither General Blanchard nor Admiral Abrial were told that evacuation was intended, an omission blamed by the British official history on the French High Command.

The following day, after a conference at Cassel, Gort asked Weygand's representative, General Klotz, what he knew of a plan to evacuate 30,000 men a day. 'I've never heard of it,' replied Klotz. It was only on the afternoon

This German photograph shows the base of Dunkirk's eastern mole after the evacuation, with abandoned British transport in the foreground. Commander Clouston's control post was in the centre right: this area is now a car park, and also houses a substantial German pill-box. Sunken ships can be seen near the mole.

of 29 May that Weygand authorized the evacuation of French troops, and by then much damage had been done.

'The French staff at Dunkirk feel strongly that they are defending Dunkirk for us to evacuate, which is largely true,' reported Captain Tennant.

Churchill had stressed, also on 29 May, that: 'It is essential that the French should share in such evacuations from Dunkirk as may be possible... Arrangements must be concerted at once, so that no reproaches, or as few as possible, may arise.' Yet when the Allied War Council met in Paris on 31 May he was nonplussed to hear that 150,000 British but only 15,000 French soldiers had so far been rescued. He refused to accept that the British should be evacuated first, and declared that the Allies should fight and then evacuate arm in arm – '*Bras dessus, bras dessous*!' A signal summarizing the meeting's conclusion was sent to Abrial. It decreed: 'The British troops will remain as a rearguard for as long as possible... The evacuation from Dunkirk will be carried out under your orders.'

In the event, Alexander, more concerned than Abrial about the tenability of the perimeter, withdrew his rearguard sooner than the Admiral wished, giving rise to further complaints that the British were saving themselves at the expense of the French. The last of the BEF got away late on 2 June. Tennant intended to signal Ramsay 'Operation completed. Returning to Dover,' but an enterprising signaller sent the more succinct: 'BEF evacuated.'

It was true of the BEF but not of the French. Confused instructions meant that many ships had sailed without being able to find French soldiers to fill them. When Weygand complained that the French were being sacrificed, Churchill replied that the navy would make one last try. Just after 10 a.m. on 3 June Ramsay signalled: 'We cannot leave our Allies in the lurch, and I call on all officers and men detailed for further evacuation tonight to let the world see that we never let down our Ally...'

The last foray was shot through with poignancy. Rear Admiral Wake-Walker sailed in MTB 102, flying an admiral's flag which had started life as a Southern Railways tea-cloth and had been suitably converted by one of her crew when she had acted as 'flagship' previously. HMS *Whitshed*'s harmonica band played as she drew out of port, and HMS *Malcolm*'s officers still sported their mess jackets for the end-of-evacuation party. The tug *Sun IV* – no less than 10 of her fellow *Suns* had taken part in the evacuation – set off towing 14 launches, skippered by the tugboat company's managing director.

Because the beach parties had been withdrawn – Commander Clouston, tragically, had been lost after the RAF crash boat taking him home was sunk – a berthing party had to be landed and it took longer than planned to get ships alongside. There were the usual linguistic difficulties, but over 26,000 men were rescued. There was no room for them all. As General Lucas of the French 32nd Division prepared to embark there were 1000 soldiers drawn up four deep, standing to attention with the flames flickering on their steel helmets. Lucas and his staff walked to the edge of the pier, turned, and gave a final salute. The last vessel out was MTB 107, commanded by Lieutenant John Cameron 'a settled barrister of 40' and future Scots law lord. He circled the outer harbour, littered with wrecked shipping, with French troops still standing on the mole. 'The whole scene,' he recalled, 'was filled with a sense of finality and death; the curtain was ringing down on a great tragedy.'

'A Miracle of Deliverance'

It did not seem a tragedy in England. The survivors were stunned by the warmth of their reception. Tom Collins of the Royal Artillery remembered:

Unwashed, unshaven, very prominent in our rags and tatters, we were welcomed it seemed by people from all walks of life; but those who were top of the league in my book were the crew who brought us back, the medical men who attended the sick and wounded – and the W(omen's) V(oluntary) S(ervice), who gave every man a mug of tea, a piece of cake and a cigarette. After we settled down in the waiting train…a soldier got to his feet and said, 'Boys, I'm thanking God I'm home. Now let's give a thought for the boys we left behind.' And we, all strangers from different units, held a minute's silence in that compartment; and as we travelled through the green fields, I thought that England wasn't such a bad place after all.

Churchill warned Parliament: 'We must be very careful not to assign to this deliverance the attributes of a victory. Wars are not won by evacuations.' Yet even he called it a 'miracle of deliverance', and somehow miracle seemed the right word. It was admittedly costly. Fighter Command lost 106 aircraft during the period of the evacuation. And, as David Divine put it, 'the price of admiralty was, as always, heavy.' Of the 693 British ships which took part in the operation, six destroyers, eight personnel ships, a sloop, five minesweepers, 17 trawlers, a hospital ship and 188 smaller vessels had been sunk and an equal number damaged.

Above all, Dunkirk was a sailor's triumph. During a difficult night's work off Dunkirk Coxswain H. Knight was hailed by a naval officer: 'I cannot see who you are: are you a naval party?'

'No, sir,' replied Knight, 'we are members of the crew of the Ramsgate lifeboat.'

'Thank you,' replied the officer. 'And thank God for such men as you have this night proved youselves to be.'

A View of the Field

Dover Castle

It is possible to get a good feel for Operation Dynamo without even leaving England. Dover is a giant among castles, with the longest recorded history of any in Britain. It is now in the care of English Heritage, and substantial parts of the tunnels beneath it are open to the public. These include the Admiralty Casemates, which housed Ramsay's headquarters in 1940. A telephone exchange, similar to that which received so many of the crucial messages, retains all its equipment, and there is an anti-aircraft control room which postdates the battle. There is a good exhibition devoted to Hellfire Corner (as south-east Kent was known during the Second World War). The balcony outside Ramsay's cabin is now unsafe, but the main entrance to the tunnels is on another balcony which, on a fine day, gives a good view of the French coast. During the evacuation Dunkirk was visible from here, marked by a pillar of smoke by day and fierce fires at night.

Ramsgate Maritime Museum

Several of the little ships have survived. Perhaps the most evocative is *Sundowner*, now the property of Ramsgate Maritime Museum. Built in 1912 as an Admiralty steam launch, in 1930 she was converted to a private motor yacht for her new owner Commander Charles Lightoller, senior surviving officer of the ill-fated *Titanic*.

On the evening of 30 May 1940 Lightoller was told that the Admiralty intended to requisition *Sundowner* for the evacuation, and was asked to take her to Ramsgate where a naval crew would take over. Lightoller demurred – 'they had another guess coming' – and decided to go to France himself, with his eldest son Roger and an 18-year old sea-scout Gerald Ashcroft as crew. They left Southend for Ramsgate at 3.15 a.m. on 1 June, paused there briefly, and set out across the Channel.

On their way they narrowly missed a mine, and then stopped to take on five men from the 25 foot (7 m) motor cruiser *Westerly*, broken down and on fire. Despite being bombed and machine-gunned, Lightoller reached the mole, where he went alongside a destroyer and took 122 soldiers aboard. Another of Lightoller's sons, an RAF pilot lost the day war broke out, had discussed tactics with his father, and Lightoller knew that an air-craft diving to attack must pull up out of its dive to make its guns bear. When attacked on the way home he waited until the aircraft was on the point of pulling up, and then turned the yacht sharply: 'This of course threw his aim off completely.' *Sundowner* returned home intact, but Lightoller discovered that many of his passengers had been unwell, and there was 'a nice clearing up job for the three of us'. Although *Sundowner* can only be visited by arrangement, she can be seen at her berth in front of the museum.

Lowestoft Yacht Harbour

Motor Torpedo Boats (MTBs) were high-speed craft armed with torpe-does. They were once judged to pose such a threat to battleships that destroyers – 'torpedo boat destoyers' in full – were initially designed to combat them. MTB 102 (believed to be the only surviving Royal Navy vessel which took part in the evacuation) was built as an experimental craft by Vosper Ltd and then bought into the service. She can now be seen in a heritage berth in Lowestoft yacht harbour. In 1940 she was commanded by Lieutenant Christopher Dreyer, made seven crossings to Dunkirk, and for the last two nights of the operation she acted as Rear Admiral Wake-Walker's flagship.

After the war she was sold off and converted to a private motor cruiser. In 1973 a Norfolk Scout Group found her in the process of being converted to a houseboat, and in 1976 she was refurbished to appear in the film *The Eagle Has Landed*. In 1985, 1990 and 1995 she participated in the Association of Little Ships' crossing to Dunkirk: on the last occasion Commander Dreyer took her into the harbour.

Dunkirk

Although Dunkirk was badly damaged by bombing it is not hard to trace the key events of 1940. The evacuation is commemorated by a war memorial on the Digue des Alliés on the north-east edge of the town. Bastion 32, Admiral Abrial's headquarters, lies beneath the modern art museum on the Canal Exutoire, just to its south. It is not open to the public, and its rather run-down exterior, approached via the Rue des Chantiers de France, gives little clue to its former importance. A small museum on the nearby Rue Militaire was open at weekends when this book went to press but has an uncertain future.

The Rue Militaire leads, past another bastion peppered with shrapnel, to a narrow bridge over the Canal Exutoire. A small car park and German bunker stand in the area of Commander Clouston's control post, and the eastern mole juts out to sea beyond it. Its landward end has been reinforced since 1940, and concrete tetrahedrons now protect it from the sea. At its far end, no longer approachable on foot, but easily seen from the Ramsgate ferry, the mole retains its distinctive 1940 latticed silhouette.

The beaches between Dunkirk and La Panne (now De Panne) have changed little, though there are several German concrete bunkers. There are still dunes behind them for much of their length. The Bergues–Furnes Canal (Canal de la Basse Colme) runs through low-lying meadows about 6 miles (10 km) inland: Captain Ervine-Andrews' VC-winning action was fought just north of Hoymille. Bergues itself is a pleasant little town, still girt about with Vauban's ravelins and bastions, redolent of an era when war moved at a slower pace.

CHAPTER 11

The Blitz
1940–41

Background

'When we got there,' wrote Alf Tyler of Civil Defence Rescue:

…one of the bombs had made a direct hit on an Anderson shelter situated at the end of a short garden belonging to one of the small terraced houses. A warden said that the family of six had been in the shelter, now blown to pieces with its occupants, parts of bodies were scattered over a large area, one large piece was on a slated roof…the dinner was still on the table in the back room, the family having left it to go down the garden into their shelter.

This 'incident', to use the official euphemism, from a single bombing raid on the northern suburbs of London on 15 September 1940, speaks volumes about the arbitrary brutality of the Blitz: it was indeed a people's war.

The German Occupation of France
After the evacuation from Dunkirk the campaign in France was soon over. Although there was some gallant fighting on the part of the French, the Germans rapidly crossed the Somme and pushed southwards. The 51st Highland Division, serving under French command, was trapped and forced to surrender at St Valéry-en-Caux, and a British force was evacuated from Normandy after a predictably confused campaign.

The French government left Paris on 12 June and established itself in Bordeaux. The premier, Paul Reynaud, was replaced by the aged Marshal Pétain, hero of the First World War battle of Verdun. And on 22 June French representatives concluded an armistice at Rethondes in the Forest of Compiègne, on the same spot, and in the same railway carriage, that the armistice of November 1918 had been signed.

This Anderson shelter was hit on the first raid on London on 24–25 August 1940: although buckled, it withstood the blast. Gallantry by members of fire, rescue and bomb-disposal teams could be rewarded by the George Medal *(right)* and George Cross.

Just as the 1918 armistice had been a national humiliation for Germany, so that of 1940 degraded France. It left the Germans in occupation of northern and south-western France, and the French government, now situated in the little spa town of Vichy, controlling only the unoccupied Zone of the Centre and South-East. The French army was reduced to 100,000 men, and French prisoners of war remained in German hands.

Charles de Gaulle, a temporary brigadier-general who had commanded an armoured division with some success, reached London after the fall of Reynaud and on 18 June broadcast an appeal urging Frenchmen to continue the fight. His Free French movement had a slow and painful start, but was to ensure that France never fully dropped out of the war, and was eventually able to assist in her own liberation.

The Planning of Operation Sealion

The French collapse left many British people feeling curiously stimulated. 'I feel happier now that we have no allies to be polite to & pamper,' wrote King George VI, and a reader assured the magazine *Picture Post* that: 'A nation without allies is a nation with no one to let them down.' Churchill had already made it clear that Britain would fight on alone. 'Even though large tracts of Europe and many old and famous states have fallen or may fall into the grip of the Gestapo and the odious apparatus of Nazi rule,' he proclaimed on 4 June, 'we shall not flag or fail. We shall go on to the end.' Two weeks later he was more specific, and warned the House of Commons that: 'Hitler knows that he will have to break us in this island or lose the war.'

At first Hitler was less convinced. He seemed indifferent to the notion of an invasion of England when it was mentioned at a conference on 20 June, but soon appeared to warm to the idea. On 2 July the German armed forces were informed that invasion would be considered under certain conditions, the most important being German acquisition of air superiority. Führer Directive No. 16 of 16 July 1940 laid down guidelines for the invasion, codenamed Operation Sealion. The navy set to work assembling barges and landing craft, and the army prepared plans for a landing between Brighton and Folkestone. It is one of history's strange coincidences that the 26th Infantry Division was to land near Pevensey, not far from the spot where Duke William's men had come ashore in 1066.

Sealion never looked easy. It hinged, as German planners were quick to recognize, upon command of the air. The German navy, far smaller than that of the British at the outset of the war, had suffered heavy losses during its campaign in Norway, and would have found it difficult to escort the invasion fleet and to keep a logistic lifeline open during the early stages of a campaign in southern England. 'The navy,' admits one German historian, 'unquestionably gave Sealion no chance of succeeding.'

However the land battle would have taxed the British most severely. Although the majority of the BEF had been evacuated from Dunkirk, its equipment had been left behind. Alan Brooke, now Commander-in-Chief of Home Forces, warned that Britain's exposed coastline was twice the length of the front the French had tried to hold with 80 divisions and the Maginot Line. He had 22 divisions, 'of which only half can be looked upon as in any way fit for any form of mobile operations'. It is hard to disagree with Ronald Wheatley, in his study of Sealion, that: 'Had Britain not been an island, she would have been overrun as surely as were Poland and France.'

The difficulties confronting Sealion have persuaded some historians that Hitler never took it seriously, and privately hoped that his preparations, and the air offensive which accompanied them, would persuade the British to sue for peace, thus making invasion unnecessary. We simply cannot be sure. Two things are, however, certain. The first is that the Germans strenuously attempted, in the Battle of Britain (mid-June to mid-September 1940), to gain the air superiority which was a prerequisite for Sealion. The second is that they then, from August 1940 to mid-May 1941, turned their attention to cities in an attack known, from abbreviation of the German word *Blitzkrieg* (meaning 'lightning war') as the Blitz.

In one respect the two campaigns were not distinct, for bombing attacks began in an attempt to reduce aircraft production and thus cripple the RAF, and became an assault on cities only when it became clear that the Battle of Britain had been lost. In another, though, their character was very different. It is no mere cliché to say that the Battle of Britain was fought by the few, the pilots of the RAF's Fighter Command. The Blitz was the business of the many: not only of the firemen, rescue workers, wardens, ambulance crews, policemen and anti-aircraft gunners, and the others, volunteer or professional, who played an active role; but also of the tens of thousands of civilians who had to tolerate blacked-out streets, air-raid warnings, the nightly terror of bombing raids and the bewilderment of seeing a familiar townscape changed for ever.

The German Air Attack Begins

Air attack on the United Kingdom came as no surprise, and Stanley Baldwin had glumly prophesied that 'the bomber will always get through'. In 1917 the Smuts report on the relatively modest German bombing of Britain in the First World War warned that: 'the day may not be far off when aerial operations and their devastation of enemy lands and destruction of industrial and populous centres on a vast scale may become the principal operations of war...' Theorists like the Italian Giulio Douhet and the American Billy Mitchell had pointed to the value of air power, and Douhet specifically recommended the strategic use of bombing to shatter civilian morale.

Sir Hugh Trenchard, the RAF's Chief of Staff from 1919 to 1929, argued in favour of devoting most of the RAF's resources to Bomber Command for just this reason, and the National Government favoured the development of a bomber deterrent whose existence would dissuade potential adversaries from attacking Britain. This was an unwise policy. Not only did Bomber Command have little effect in deterring Hitler, but at the outbreak of war it was hard-pressed to reach well-defended targets in daylight or to find them at all in darkness. The *Luftwaffe*, whose leaders had been far less impressed by theories of strategic bombing, developed primarily as a ground support air force, a role it carried out brilliantly in the campaign in France. In 1940 it was not well-suited to launch a bomber offensive; and lack of clear direction, for which Hermann Goering, its commander-in-chief, must be held largely responsible, made matters worse.

Goering was born in Bavaria in 1893 and commissioned into the infantry on the eve of the First World War. In October 1914 he began flying, and by the war's end he had 22 kills to his credit, had been awarded Germany's highest decoration for bravery, the *Pour le Mérite*, and had commanded the crack Richthofen squadron. He joined the Nazi Party in 1922 and commanded Hitler's Bodyguard, but was wounded in the Munich putsch of 1923, became addicted to the morphine given to ease his pain, and spent some time in mental hospitals. Elected to the *Reichstag* in 1928, he became its president in 1932, and in the following year, when Hitler became chancellor, he began to enjoy a series of important posts, not least Minister of Aviation. As such he was one of the founding fathers of the *Luftwaffe,* and deserves some of the credit for its performance in 1939–40. His promotion to the unique rank of *Reichsmarschall* in July 1940 saw him at the apogee of his success. Thereafter, overweening personal vanity and an appetite for power which far exceeded his real abilities turned him into an overdressed buffoon, albeit a deadly one.

Goering's adversary in the summer of 1940 could scarcely have been a more different personality. Air Chief Marshal Sir Hugh Dowding, Commander-in-Chief of Fighter Command, was a lonely and aloof figure with the less than flattering nickname 'Stuffy'. Dowding had been an

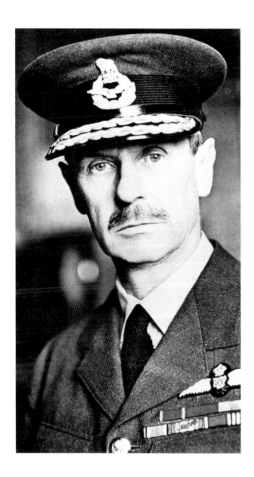

The rival commanders in the Battle of Britain could scarcely have been more different. Air Chief Marshal Sir Hugh ('Stuffy') Dowding *(above)* was chilly and austere, and had thought deeply about the air defence of Britain long before war broke out. *Reichsmarschall* Hermann Goering *(right)*, in contrast, was a flamboyant showman with a taste for self-designed uniforms. In fact Dowding fought the better battle, and Goering's failure to plan a coherent campaign contributed greatly to the German defeat.

artillery officer before joining the RAF, and from 1930 to 1936 he served as the Air Council's Member for Research and Development, encouraging the development of the Spitfire and Hurricane fighters. He was appointed to head Fighter Command in 1936, and at once set about remodelling Britain's air defences.

British Use of Radar

Dowding inherited an early warning system based on experience gained from the First World War: listening posts on the coast telephoned warnings to a control room, which ordered aircraft to take off and deal with the intruders. As aircraft became faster this scheme had obvious limitations, but the development of radar (in fact known as RDF, for Radio Direction Finding, during the Battle of Britain) changed this at a stroke. The first radar stations (known as Air Ministry Experimental Stations to preserve secrecy) came into service in 1937, and were expanded to form Chain Home, a network of 20 stations capable of detecting high-altitude long-range targets. The 12 sites of Chain Home Low, which picked up aircraft coming in beneath the coverage of Chain Home, became operational only in July 1940.

Dowding had consistently argued, often in the face of very heavy political pressure, against the diversion of key fighter resources to the campaigns in Norway and France. The fact that Fighter Command maintained a winning margin in 1940 is due, in no small measure, to his efforts. Dowding's aircraft, most of them Hurricanes and Spitfires, in a ratio of about 5:3, were deployed on RAF sector stations which had smaller satellites. Sectors were combined to form groups, and in August 1940 there were four of these. Air Vice-Marshal Park's No. 11 Group, with its headquarters at Uxbridge, was responsible for London and the South-East. From Watnall, near Nottingham, Air Vice-Marshal Leigh-Mallory commanded No. 12 Group, covering the Midlands and the Eastern Counties. Northern England, Scotland and Northern Ireland were the responsibility of Air Vice-Marshal Saul's No. 13 Group; and Wales and the West Country that of Air Vice-Marshal Brand's No.10 Group, activated only in June 1940.

Initially radar warnings of air raids were passed to Fighter Command Headquarters at Bentley Priory, near Harrow. Here the information was filtered and relayed to the appropriate group headquarters. Groups decided which of their sectors should deal with the raid and how many aircraft to allocate to it. Sectors sent orders to their aircraft to take off, and then directed them so as to put them in the best position to engage the enemy. Once raiders had crossed the coast their progress was relayed, not by radar, but by posts of the Royal Observer Corps.

The British Defence

The army's anti-aircraft command, under Lieutenant-General Sir Frederick Pile, had 1200 heavy and 580 light guns available when the Battle of Britain began. These formed seven anti-aircraft divisions, their

Top: It is hard to overstate the contribution made by radar to the British defence. These are the 300-foot masts of a typical 'Chain Home' radar station. Information from radar was relayed to sector control rooms by Headquarters Fighter Command at Bentley Priory *(above)*. Symbols representing hostile and friendly squadrons are moved across the map while officers in the gallery look on and consider the appropriate response.

guns deployed on sites across Britain. Royal Artillery liaison officers were stationed at RAF group headquarters, and telephoned gun operations rooms to warn them of the approach of hostile aircraft. Heavy 3.7-inch guns could aim at individual targets, but usually fired a barrage of shells, fused to burst at the estimated height of the aircraft, into the attackers' path. Finally, nearly 1500 gas-filled barrage balloons were flown on the expected flight path of intruders in the hope that aircraft would collide with their steel cables, or alternatively keep high in order to avoid them.

Although the government had not abandoned the notion of 'business as usual' (which decreed that rearmament must not be allowed to interfere with normal trade) until 1938, it had already begun to take key defensive steps. In 1937 Parliament passed the Air Raid Precautions (ARP) Act, which formed the basis for civil defence measures. There would be a warden post for every 500 people, manned by three volunteer wardens: chief wardens would supervise local groupings of warden posts. A Civil Defence Rescue Service was established, and steps were taken to form an Auxiliary Fire Service. In November 1939 the latter amalgamated with the London Fire Brigade to form a force whose more than 25,000 personnel – men, women and youths – crewed 3000 firefighting appliances.

In December 1938 the government announced that the Anderson air-raid shelter would be supplied free to low-income families living in likely target areas. Official booklets advised householders on how to protect their homes against bomb and gas attack, and gas masks were issued to adults and children alike. Many large public shelters were initially badly planned – some lacked seats and lavatories – but their design soon improved.

At first the London Underground was used as an unofficial shelter, and the authorities eventually bowed to the inevitable and provided bunk beds, medical cover and even libraries to entertain Londoners during the long nights below ground. The Women's Voluntary Service, whose soup-kitchens played such a vital part in sustaining civilian morale during the Blitz, furnished 7 tons (7 tonnes) of food and 2400 gallons (10,900 litres) of tea, coffee and cocoa each night. Few shelters were totally safe, and even the Underground had its share of misfortunes: on 14 October 1940 Balham Station suffered a direct hit and 68 people were killed; and on 12 January 1941 a bomb blew up the booking hall at Bank Station, killing at least 55 people.

The Balance of Forces
At the beginning of the Battle of Britain the balance of forces seemed to favour the Germans. Britain was within range of three *Luftflotten* (Air

Fleets): Field-Marshal Kesselring's *Luftflotte 2*, based in northern France and the Low Countries; Field-Marshal Sperrle's *Luftflotte 3*, in southern France; and General Stumpff's *Luftflotte 5* in Norway and Denmark. The fact that the bombers of *Luftflotte 5* were based too far from Britain to enjoy single-engine fighter cover meant that they made only a marginal contribution to the battle. Nevertheless the *Luftwaffe* had a daily fighting strength (two-thirds of the total strength of units engaged) of around 750 long-range bombers, 250 dive-bombers, more than 600 single-engined and 150 twin-engined fighters. Dowding could expect to fly perhaps 600 of his 900 fighters on any given day.

There was no clear technological edge. The Messerschmitt 109 was arguably the best fighter on either side, but its advantages were by no means decisive and its short range limited the time it could spend in British airspace. The twin-engined Messerschmitt 110 was too cumbersome to take on Spitfires and Hurricanes on equal terms, and the Junkers 87 *Stuka* dive-bomber, for all its formidable reputation, fared ill in air-to-air combat and bore only 1100 lb (500 kg) of bombs. Bombers like the Heinkel 111, Dornier 17 and Junkers 88 carried heavier loads. Even so, the 6600 lb (3000 kg) of bombs borne by the Junkers 88 was less than half the load carried by the Lancaster, workhorse of the RAF's subsequent bombing campaign against Germany.

Radar provided Fighter Command with an important advantage: indeed, it is hard to see how the battle could have been won without it. But in the summer of 1940 the system was in its infancy, operators were learning on the job and there was little margin for error. As Dr Malcolm Smith has shown, it took only six minutes for German aircraft to cross the Channel at Dover, and another 10 minutes to be over No. 11 Group's sector airfields. Radar could pick up bomber waves south of the French coast, but it took four minutes for the news to reach airfields and another 13 for Spitfires to reach 20,000 feet: even then there was a danger that they might find Me 109s, flying top cover for the bombers, immediately above them.

Campaign and Battle

The Battle of Britain began with a preliminary skirmish. There was, as we have seen, widespread recognition in the German high command that the success of Operation Sealion depended on winning air supremacy. Goering believed that this would take him about a month, and although his *Luftflotten* were prepared to launch the attack from mid-July it would take much longer for naval preparations to be complete. In the meantime

BRITISH FIGHTER FORCES
9th July 1940

━━━ Boundaries of Fighter groups

──── Boundaries of Fighter sectors

The figures show the numbers of fighters in each sector, on the basis of a 'tactical strength' of twelve aircraft a squadron. Types shown are:

⑫ Hurricanes and Spitfires

[12] Blenheims

◆12◆ Defiants

■ Chain Home radar station

▪ Chain Home Low radar station

```
0          50         100 Miles
├────┬────┬────┤
0    50   100 Kms
```

Atlantic Ocean

Gl

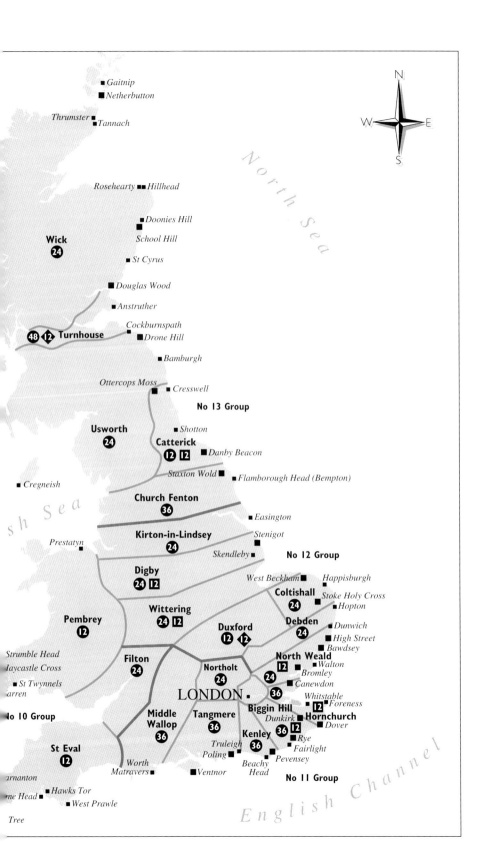

■ Gaitnip
■ Netherbutton

Thrumster ■
■ Tannach

North Sea

N
W   E
S

Rosehearty ■ ■ Hillhead

■ Doonies Hill
■ School Hill

Wick
24

■ St Cyrus

■ Douglas Wood

■ Anstruther

Cockburnspath
48 12 Turnhouse
■ Drone Hill

■ Bamburgh

Ottercops Moss
■ ■ Cresswell

No 13 Group

Usworth
24
■ Shotton
Catterick
12 12 ■ Danby Beacon

Staxton Wold ■
■ Flamborough Head (Bempton)

■ Cregneish

sh Sea

Church Fenton
36
■ Easington

Kirton-in-Lindsey
24
Stenigot

Prestatyn ■
Skendleby ■
No 12 Group

Digby
24 12
West Beckham ■   ■ Happisburgh
Coltishall
24
Stoke Holy Cross ■
■ Hopton

Wittering
24 12
Debden
24
■ Dunwich
■ High Street
■ Bawdsey

Pembrey
12

Duxford
12 12

Strumble Head ■
Maycastle Cross ■
Filton
24
Northolt
24
North Weald
12 24
■ Walton
■ Bromley
■ Canewdon
36

■ St Twynnels
arren

LONDON ■

Whitstable
■ ■ Foreness
12

No 10 Group

Biggin Hill
Dunkirk ■
Hornchurch
■ Dover

St Eval
12
Middle
Wallop
36
Tangmere
36
Kenley
36 12
■ Rye
■ Fairlight
Pevensey ■

arnanton
ne Head ■
■ Hawks Tor
■ West Prawle
Worth
Matravers ■
■ Ventnor
Truleigh
Poling ■
Beachy
Head
No 11 Group

Tree

English Channel

there was much to be said for attacking ports and shipping, which would both weaken Britain (by depriving it of supplies) and begin to whittle away at Fighter Command.

However the attacks on shipping proved inconclusive. Several merchantmen and warships were sunk, and Channel traffic was temporarily interrupted. The *Luftwaffe* lost about 300 aircraft between 10 July and 12 August, but had more than made up this loss by 14 August. The RAF, in contrast, lost 150 aircraft, but another 500 fighters were produced during the same period, so that its relative strength actually improved.

'Eagle Day'

The air campaign proper was to begin with *Adler-Tag*, or 'Eagle Day'. Hitler had made it clear that the attack was to be 'directed primarily against the flying units, ground organisation and supply installations of the Royal Air Force, and against the air armaments industry'. Goering was less single-minded, and did much to confuse senior commanders by lecturing them on tactical detail rather than setting clear objectives. He was at first eager to free his high-performance fighters for independent sweeps over Britain and ordered the *Luftflotte* commanders to minimize the numbers allocated to bomber escort: this in turn induced them to weaken their strike forces so as to ensure the aircraft they sent were properly escorted.

Adler-Tag was eventually scheduled for 13 August. On the previous day there had been preliminary raids on No. 11 Group's forward airfields at Manston, Lympne and Hawkinge, attacks on south coast radar stations, on naval installations at Portsmouth and Gosport and shipping in the Thames Estuary. Although the airfields were damaged but usable, the radar station at Ventnor on the Isle of Wight was put out of action.

Unfortunately for Goering, the weather on 13 August was poor: low cloud cover meant that the high-level fighter sweeps would have been unable to intervene against British fighters attacking bombers and their immediate escorts. The morning's raids were to have been cancelled because of the weather but some were in fact launched, and more followed in the afternoon. A series of badly co-ordinated efforts resulted in the Germans losing 45 aircraft to the RAF's 14, only seven of whose pilots were lost.

The Fate of the Pilots

Pilots were often uninjured by the fire which hit their aircraft and could escape if they managed to bale out in time. This was not always straightforward, as Flying Officer Hugh 'Cocky' Dundas discovered when his Spitfire was hit above the Kent village of Elham, near Hawkinge:

White smoke filled the cockpit, thick and hot, and I could see neither the sky above nor the Channel coast 12,000 feet [3660 m] below… I stood up on the seat and pushed the top half of my body out of the cockpit. Pressed hard against the fuselage, half in, half out, I struggled in a nightmare of fear and confusion to drop clear, but could not do so… Try again; try the other side. Up, over – and out. I slithered along the fuselage and felt myself falling free. Seconds after my parachute opened, I saw the Spitfire hit and explode in a field below. A flock of sheep scattered outwards from the cloud of dust and flame.

Because most of the fighting took place over southern England or the Channel, RAF aircrew who baled out and landed safely were soon back at their bases. Some even found themselves back in action the same day. Michael Constable Maxwell, shot down for the third time on 30 August, crash-landed near Herne Bay. He had an unpleasant train journey, hatless and dishevelled, back to his base at North Weald in Essex, where he found that his brother had been shot down. The taxi-driver who drove him across London declined a tip, saying that he would be ashamed to take one from a man who had just risked his life for him. Baled-out German aircrew, in contrast, were captured. This meant that attrition of pilots was always higher for the Germans, no small matter at a time when it took far longer to train a pilot than to produce an aircraft.

German Miscalculation

Bad weather on 14 August forced the Germans to postpone attacks till the next day. This time *Luftflotte 5* was to play a leading part. The Germans believed that the fighting on 13 August had caused heavier losses in Nos. 10 and 11 Groups than was in fact the case, and that Dowding would accordingly shift squadrons from the Midlands and the North to defend the South. Both sides consistently over-estimated the number of aircraft they shot down: several pilots might claim the same kill, and anti-aircraft gunners lodged their own claims. Even now it is hard to be certain of combat losses, for accidents – to which battle damage was often a contributory cause – also eroded fighting strength.

The *Luftwaffe's* miscalculation was disastrous, and the defenders took full advantage of it. Air Vice-Marshal Saul's fighters intercepted German aircraft making for Yorkshire and Tyneside, shooting down eight bombers and seven of their escorts without loss. Further south, Air Vice-Marshal Leigh-Mallory's interception was less successful, but another eight bombers were shot down. The Germans did rather better against Nos. 10 and 11 Groups, hitting several airfields and Short's aircraft factory at Rochester. Nevertheless, although the Germans had flown almost 1800 sorties (the highest daily rate they were to achieve during the battle), they had lost 75 aircraft and destroyed only 34.

Goering remained confident: his intelligence staff believed that Dowding would be reduced to about 300 operational aircraft for 16 August. In fact they both over-estimated casualties inflicted and under-estimated aircraft production, for Dowding's 47 Hurricane and Spitfire squadrons had sufficient aircraft to fly at their normal tactical strength of 12 aircraft apiece. There were reserves in 'Group Pools', as well as aircraft in Operational Training Units and squadrons re-equipping or working up, and 230 more in the Aircraft Storage Units which topped up fighting squadrons.

However at this stage Dowding's victory was by no means assured. Over half Fighter Command's losses had occurred in the past 10 days, the supply of trained pilots was dwindling faster than the stock of aircraft, and a continuation of such attrition must eventually wear out the RAF. If they chose to do so the Germans could outnumber British fighters by about two to one, and much of Fighter Command's tactical advantage sprang from its system of early warning and control, which in turn hinged on the vulnerable radar stations. Goering never fully grasped their importance, and though Kesselring and Sperrle (commanders of *Luftflotten 2* and *3*) did attack them from time to time, there was no concerted plan for doing so.

Nor did Goering's decision to use more fighters to escort bombers improve matters. While visiting his aircrew he asked them just what they needed to beat the RAF. Major Adolf Galland, a fighter group commander who was to achieve 103 victories in combat, replied that re-equipping his squadrons with Spitfires would help. He was not being entirely facetious, for if the Me 109 had the edge in the 'free-hunting' fighter sweeps at which Galland excelled, the slower and more manoeuvrable Spitfire might have been better for escort duties.

On 16 August Kesselring and Sperrle pushed home more attacks, hitting the radar station at Ventnor yet again and inflicting severe damage on the airfield at Tangmere, near Chichester, where 14 aircraft were caught on the ground. Other airfields were also hit, and 48 training aircraft were destroyed at Brize Norton in Oxfordshire. After a day's respite the *Luftwaffe* struck again, hitting more airfields but losing 71 aircraft in the process. Goering's first attempt to achieve air superiority over southern England had conspicuously failed.

Night Bombing Begins
On 19 August Goering decided on a change of tactics. Targets like airfields, which the British would have no option but to defend, would be

attacked by smaller concentrations of bombers with powerful escorts. The remaining bombers would mount sporadic, unescorted raids at night or in bad weather to keep the defenders fully stretched. *Luftflotte* commanders were ordered to prepare for attacks on cities, but not to launch them without specific orders. In all, this was a much wiser policy, and had Fighter Command been as close to collapse as Goering believed it might very well have worked.

Bad weather delayed resumption of the fighting till 24 August, when Kesselring, now heavily reinforced, had some 1000 aircraft available against Air Vice-Marshal Park's 200 of No. 11 Group. The weight of numbers told, and Dowding's fighters found it hard to get at German bombers with their close escorts and top cover. Manston, defended by outclassed Defiant fighters, was so badly damaged that it had to be abandoned as a permanent base, and bombers also managed to reach Hornchurch and North Weald. Portsmouth was hard hit, though most of the bombs aimed at the dockyard fell on the city.

That night bombers ranged widely across England and Wales, and in the process several bomber crews, with little idea of their whereabouts, bombed London. Goering was furious, for attacks on London were strictly prohibited. 'An immediate report is required identifying those crews who dropped bombs within the perimeter of London,' he thundered. '*Luftwaffe* High Command will itself undertake the punishment of each aircraft captain involved. They will be posted to infantry regiments.' Damage was relatively light: nine people were killed, 58 injured, and 100 inhabitants of Bethnal Green were rendered homeless. Churchill had already declared that if London was hit 'it seems very important to be able to return the compliment the next day upon Berlin', and on the night of 25 August Bomber Command mounted its first attack on the German capital, paving the way for further escalation.

On 25/26 August the pattern of raids was much the same, with heavily escorted bombers attacking airfields. The pressure helped generate friction between Nos. 11 and 12 Groups. Leigh-Mallory's aircraft were often ordered south to guard 11 Group's airfields, and on 26 August their failure to intercept a raid on Debden caused resentment. There was also a dispute over tactics. While the basic *Luftwaffe* tactical unit was the *gruppe* of 30 aircraft, that of the RAF was the 12-aircraft squadron. In the early stages of the battle uncertainty over the strength of incoming raids and the short warning time meant that squadrons were sent off individually, and it took time for multi-squadron operations to be mounted. Eventually No. 12 Group created the 'Big Wing' of five fighter squadrons, based at Duxford, near Cambridge. The scheme remained controversial. Its

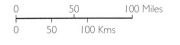
Atlantic Ocean

Be

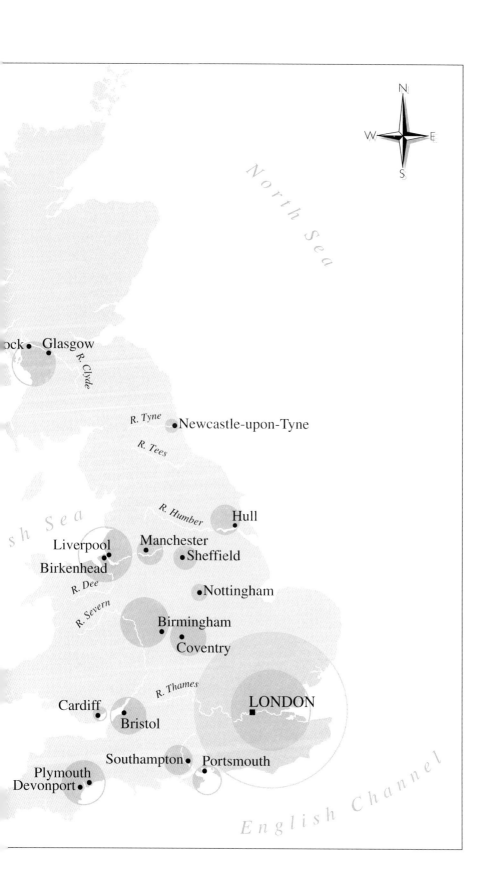

advocates, like Squadron Leader Douglas Bader, who had returned to flying after losing both legs in an accident in 1931, argued that simultaneous attack by many aircraft was more effective, but opponents pointed out that it took a long time to get a 'Big Wing' into the air.

Goering's change of tactics had resulted in the *Luftwaffe* losing 99 aircraft to the RAF's 69 in three days of fighting, encouraging him to believe that he might yet achieve the 'specially favourable initial situation' upon which Sealion depended. On 29 August, after another satisfactory exchange on the previous day, Kesselring's fighter commander reported that he had achieved 'unlimited fighter superiority', and this note of confidence helped persuade Hitler to agree to postpone his decision on Sealion till 10 September with a view to mounting the invasion 11 days later.

In the meantime Sperrle was authorized to mount night attacks on Liverpool, and General Stumpff's *Luftflotte 5* joined in with raids on Tyneside and Hartlepool. The results were so derisory that it was never clear to the defenders what the attacks were trying to achieve. They did, however, show that Fighter Command could do little against night attack: indeed, Dowding had already warned that without special equipment he could hope for nothing more than 'the occasional fortunate encounter'.

The daylight battle followed the now-familiar pattern of well-escorted raids on airfields, with increasing damage to No. 11 Group's bases and a rate of exchange which reflected the difficulty of breaking through to reach the bombers. The key sector airfield of Biggin Hill was hard hit, its operations room destroyed and two of its three squadrons withdrawn, and a continuation of such attacks would have made it impossible for Park to defend London from airfields south of the capital. Although the rate of exchange between 30 August and 6 September, at 185 to 225, still favoured Fighter Command, Dowding knew that his tired pilots could not shoulder the burden much longer.

Thanks to Goering they did not have to. On 4 and 6 September some raids were directed, not against Park's crucial airfields, but against aircraft factories, a reflection of Goering's failure to grasp the essentials of the campaign. On 2 September he issued a new directive shifting the weight of the *Luftwaffe*'s attacks from airfields to cities. He was influenced by Hitler's desire to punish Britain for the RAF's raid on Berlin on 25 August, and also felt that, in order to meet attacks on London, Dowding would be forced to throw in what the Germans believed were his last reserves.

The Bombing of London Begins
London was to be bombed round the clock, *Luftflotte 2* attacking by day and *Luftflotte 3* by night. Although Hitler, in an address at the *Sportpalast*

in Berlin on 4 September, had announced that the *Luftwaffe* would now reply to British provocation – 'If they declare that they will attack our cities on a large scale, we will erase theirs!' – he was reluctant to order wholesale bombing of civilian targets. Goering's chief of staff argued in favour of striking residential areas in order to provoke mass panic, but Hitler believed that attacks on military and economic targets were more effective. In practice it mattered little, for at this stage in the war bombing was so inaccurate that attacks directed against military targets would inevitably cause damage across a wide area around them.

The Germans were doing their best to improve the accuracy of their bombing with radio navigation aids. *Knickebein* used narrow radio beams, originating in Occupied Europe, which were set to intersect over a

A Heinkel 111 over Wapping on the evening of 7 September 1940, 'Black Saturday'. This area, with the characteristic loop of the Thames, was known to the Germans as *Zielraum* (target area) G. Bomber crews were given specific targets like docks or gasworks and attacked them if visibility permitted: otherwise they simply bombed a designated target area.

target. The more sophisticated *X-Gerät,* first used in mid-November, also employed signals which crossed the bomber's path en route to the target, enabling bomb-aimers to work out the time at which their bombs should be released. A combination of deciphering at Bletchley Park, which produced ULTRA (above even Top Secret) intelligence from German high-level communications, the interrogation of captured aircrew, and painstaking work by Dr R. V. Jones, head of scientific intelligence in the Air Ministry, enabled the British to learn the secrets of these radio aids. *Knickebein* could be 'bent' or jammed, and the location of the beams gave advance warning of a raid, sometimes enabling fighters to be positioned to intercept it.

'Black Saturday', 7 September, was the first day of the offensive against London. There were minor attacks on Dover and Hawkinge in the morning. In the afternoon growing numbers of German aircraft formed up south of Cap Gris Nez, where Goering and a galaxy of senior *Luftwaffe* officers had assembled to watch the attack. Just after 4.15 almost 1,000 aircraft, stacked up at heights from 14,000 (4270 m) to 23,000 feet (7000 m), crossed the coast. Twenty British squadrons went up to meet them, bringing about the largest aerial battle yet seen.

There was no stopping the bombers, which pressed home their attack and dropped 300 tons (305 tonnes) of high explosive on London. About 2000 civilians were killed or seriously injured, and wide areas of ware-houses and factories in the East End were soon ablaze. Sub-Officer Cyril Demarne's fire station was in West Ham, in the epicentre of the attack.

Flames erupted from the great factories and warehouses lining the River Thames from Woolwich to Tower Bridge. In the crowded dockland streets, massive ware-houses and tiny dwellings alike came crashing down under the impact of high explosive, burying their occupants and any luckless passer-by…

Two hundred acres of tall timber stacks blazed out of control in the Surrey Commercial Docks. The rum quay buildings in West India Docks, alight from end to end, gushed flaming spirit from their doors. An army of rats ran from a burning Silvertown soap works…

When the bombers came back after dusk they needed no navigational aids: they were guided by the blazing East End and fires downstream at Thameshaven. They dropped another 300 tons (305 tonnes) of explosive and thousands of smaller incendiary bombs, and when the last of them left, before dawn on 8 September, London was still burning, with three of its main-line railway termini closed. 'Londoners emerged from their shelters to face scenes of devastation,' recalled fire officer Cyril

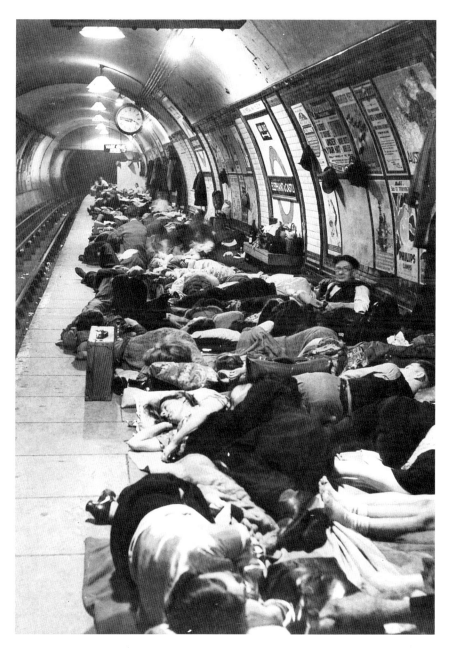

Thousands of Londoners spent the nights of the Blitz sleeping – or reading, chatting and playing cards – in the Underground The practice was not encouraged at first, but, recognizing that it was impossible to keep people out, the authorities did what they could to make things more comfortable. This crowded platform is at Elephant and Castle. Even the Underground was not totally safe: there were occasional accidents, and at least two stations, Bank and Balham, received direct hits.

Demarne. 'They were faced for the first time by problems that would confront them for fifty-seven mornings in succession.'

Thousands of London's children had been evacuated to the country-side on the outbreak of war. Despite official attempts to ensure that they remained in comparative safety, many had returned by the time the Blitz began. A study based on the Government's Mass Observation concluded:

Of those who stayed put with their parents, a few were continuously nervous, and a few constantly exhilarated. The greater part adjusted as well as their parents or mildly better. At no stage did they present a special problem as compared, say, with old ladies, or stray pets.

Fighter Command's failure to prevent the bombers from reaching London on 7 September placed Dowding under pressure to ensure that his most experienced squadrons were available for the capital's defence. When the Germans came again in strength, on the afternoon of 9 September, few of them were able to reach London, and they lost 28 aircraft to the RAF's 19. The battle swung in favour of the Germans again two days later. Bombs fell in the grounds of Buckingham Palace, and after another more dam-aging raid on the palace on 13 September the Queen remarked: 'I'm glad we've been bombed. It makes me feel I can look the East End in the face.' For the next two days losses were roughly equal and bombers were able to reach their targets. It seemed very much as though the *Luftwaffe* had the edge at last.

The Climax of the Battle of Britain
Sunday 15 September dawned fine, but soon became cloudy. Basil Collier catches the almost Agincourt-like mood of preparation:

At Park's sector stations and their forward aerodromes and satellites from the Sandlings to west Sussex, the pilots who would bear the burden of the daylight fighting were up early. At Debden and Martlesham on the borders of Suffolk and Essex, at North Weald in Epping Forest, at Hornchurch above Erith Reach, at Northolt and Hendon in the northern suburbs, at Croydon, Biggin Hill and Kenley, at Tangmere and Westhampnett below the hanging woods of Lavant Down, veterans of twenty-five began to move at dawn from messes and billets to dispersal huts.

Kesselring intended to hurl his full strength against London in two attacks, and the first of them reached the English coast at 11.30 that morning. Park already had 11 of his 21 Hurricane and Spitfire squadrons airborne to meet the bombers, which were mercilessly harried on their way to London. There the Duxford Wing joined in, though views on its effectiveness varied. After a brief pause the second wave rolled in, and it too was met as it approached. Squadron Leader Bob Stanford Tuck, newly promoted and given his own squadron, tells how:

We found a big bunch of mixed bombers, flying in formations of anything from thirty to sixty, with escorting fighters above them. As I led my new squadron in, I saw three of these parties nearing London. As the boys waded into the bombers, I went for some of the fighters. I picked off an Me 110 which I shot down over Barking, and one of his pals nearly got his own back when he put a bullet through my windscreen.

Twenty-six of Fighter Command's aircraft were shot down that day, but The *Luftwaffe* lost a total of 60 – not all to British guns and fighters – and others struggled back across the Channel with dead and wounded crewmen aboard. Few German bomber crews now believed bland assertions that it would never be possible to prevent the occasional fighter from appearing. The attainment of air superiority seemed as far away as ever, and on 17 September Hitler postponed Sealion until further notice: the Battle of Britain had been won.

The Blitz Goes On
The effective cancellation of Sealion changed the tempo of the fighting but did not end it. Goering ordered that the night bombing of London would continue, 'harassing attacks' would be launched in daylight, and pressure on aircraft factories would be stepped up. The Italian Air Force belatedly joined the battle on 25 October, when 16 of its bombers attacked Harwich. On 11 November 40 CR 42 biplanes escorted 10 bombers in another attack on Harwich, and although the fighters defended their charges bravely they were hopelessly outclassed: three bombers and three fighters were shot down without loss to the British, and daylight bombing raids were abandoned. A final daylight Italian fighter sweep on 23 November was also driven off with loss.

Two days later Dowding, who had remained on duty at the personal request of the Chief of the Air Staff despite being over the age limit for retirement, slipped into civilian life and was replaced by Air Marshal W. S. Douglas. The new Commander-in-Chief declared that 'it does not matter where the enemy is shot down provided he is shot down in large numbers', and made arrangements to set up more 'Big Wings'. However the Germans had suspended the daylight attacks which justified the use of large wings, and the task immediately facing Douglas was to deal with the night bomber offensive.

Steps were taken to form more night-fighter squadrons, to equip airfields with special equipment for night flying, and to produce more radar sets capable of permitting ground controllers to direct a night-fighter onto its target or, better still, to be fitted in aircraft. Other expedients were adopted, such as drifting balloons containing explosive charges; and a variety of deception measures were designed to encourage bombers to attack empty countryside.

Hardly any of General Pile's anti-aircraft guns were equipped with fire-control radar, and few had been able to fire during the first raids on London. By 11 September, though, there were some 200 guns defending the capital. They produced a vigorous barrage as soon as the raiders appeared, and searchlights lit up the sky. All this had little practical effect beyond forcing the attackers to remain high, but it was a fillip for civilian morale to feel that Britain was hitting back.

Britain was certainly being hit. London was bombed night after night, and during the second week in October there were almost 1400 killed in the capital. Terrible damage was caused by 2200 lb (1000 kg) parachute mines, provoking Churchill to order ministries that: 'No disclosure should be made of the severity of effect, in the public estimation, of these mines.'

One six-year-old girl described the weapon's effect with dreadful simplicity. 'There was a parachute and a landmine,' she said. 'The parachute was stuck on the school railings and a man pulled the parachute and the school blew up to pieces and so did the man.'

On the bright moonlit night of 15 October London was heavily bombed, while other raiders struck Birmingham and Bristol. Much of London's railway network was put out of action and both Becton Gas Works and Battersea Power Station were hit. There were more than 900 fires – firefighting was badly disrupted by ruptured mains – whose glare could be seen in mid-Channel by German aircrew. Although the RAF sent up 41 fighters, only one bomber was shot down.

In November London gained a brief respite, albeit at the expense of provincial cities like Birmingham, Bristol, Liverpool, Plymouth and Southampton. On the night of 13/14 November *X-Gerät* was used for the first time, against Coventry. Although Bletchley Park had deciphered messages announcing that a large operation was planned, it was not immediately clear what its targets were to be. The radio guidance beams were found to intersect over Coventry on the afternoon of 13 November, but attempts to jam them failed and, although Fighter Command was warned of the attack, 449 of the 509 bombers dispatched to Coventry reached it. Twelve armaments factories were destroyed: so too was the city's fourteenth-century cathedral. There is little real evidence for the assertion that Coventry was sacrificed to protect the security of ULTRA, though its ravaging probably did accelerate the planned replacement of Dowding.

On the night of 29/30 December London suffered the most spectacular attack of the Blitz. The square mile of the City was hit by a hail of incendiaries which caused six enormous fires, destroying the Guildhall and eight Wren churches. St Paul's Cathedral escaped by a miracle. One eyewitness found it 'a hauntingly beautiful picture' as buildings collapsed to reveal Wren's masterpiece rising in its glory amongst the smoke and flames. Because the Thames was low, fireboats could do little to help, and burst water mains impeded the work of their land-based colleagues. Casualties were lighter than might have been expected, possibly because it was a Sunday night, and the City was virtually empty, but 163 people were killed (16 firemen amongst them) and another 509 injured.

The survival of Sir Christopher Wren's masterpiece, St Paul's Cathedral, was little short of miraculous. On the night of 29/30 December, when much of the City of London burned, it was ringed by fires and hit by an incendiary bomb, but damage was slight. The image of the Cathedral's great dome rising proudly from the debris around it came to typify the spirit of London in the Blitz.

Anti-aircraft guns fired 4000 rounds that night and 29 aircraft took off to intercept the bombers, but none were shot down. Indeed, the night bombing raids of 1940–41 were cheap for the *Luftwaffe*. However the strain of operating in difficult weather and with tired crews, together with the need to repair and overhaul heavily used aircraft, helped reduce the combat strength of *Luftflotten 2* and *3* from about 800 bombers in September 1940 to 551 on 4 January 1941. In the first three months of 1941 night-fighters and anti-aircraft guns became somewhat more effective, leading the official history to suggest that 'while the menace of the night-offensive had not yet been overcome, at least its measure had been taken.'

The End of the Blitz
The campaign was already drawing to a close. On 6 February 1941, prompted by Grand Admiral Raeder, Commander-in-Chief of the Navy, Hitler gave attacks on ports the highest priority, and between February and May 46 raids were mounted on ports in England, Wales, Scotland and Northern Ireland, and only seven against the cities of London, Birmingham, Coventry and Nottingham. Some of these later raids were exceptionally heavy: Belfast, for example, was hit by 400 tons (406 tonnes) of high explosives and thousands of incendiaries in just two nights. But Hitler now had other priorities. His bomber squadrons were diverted to take part in the campaign in the Balkans and then shifted eastwards on a massive scale to prepare for Hitler's assault on the Soviet Union in June. The Blitz ended in mid-May, and Britain licked her wounds.

Materially these were serious. More than 43,000 civilians had been killed, 139,000 injured and tens of thousands made homeless. Great tracts of Britain's ancient cities and thriving industrial centres had been devastated. Port facilities and factories had been destroyed, transport severely interrupted and public utilities badly mauled. Resources of manpower and equipment, many of which could have been used elsewhere, had been diverted to military and civil defence. All this had been achieved for a cost of about 600 German bombers.

Yet the Blitz had not broken British will to resist. The American reporter Quentin Reynolds told his listeners:

I have watched the people of London live and die ever since death in its most ghastly garb began to come here as a nightly visitor... It is true that the Nazis will be over again tomorrow night and the night after that and every night. They will drop thousands of bombs and they'll destroy hundreds of buildings and they'll kill thousands of people. But a bomb has its limitations. It can only destroy buildings and kill people. It cannot kill the unconquerable spirit and courage of the people of London.

Of course it was not that simple. The government's own Mass Observation reports revealed that sometimes even the Londoners lost their cheerfulness, and in smaller cities, where the concentration of bombing was far greater, public morale became a matter of concern.

Quentin Reynolds lived through the London Blitz, but admitted: 'Nothing I had seen prepared me for the sight of Plymouth.' In April 1941 this West Country port was hit by over a hundred bombers a night for five nights: 1000 of her citizens were killed and another 40,000 made homeless. Lady Astor, one of the local MPs, was furious that the official report did so little justice to the city's sufferings: 'the raid did not last long, but in one of the towns…a number of fires were started, some of them large.'

Following her complaint, a Regional Information Officer visited Plymouth to compile a report. He admitted that 'the terrible strain and steady casualties' had sapped the morale of the volunteer firemen. 'The centre of both Plymouth and Devonport have been totally destroyed,' he wrote, 'and the damage is in millions… It would be wrong to assume that the people are broken. Equally it would be suicidal to ignore the implications and symptoms of the actual state of affairs…'

Herbert Morrison, the Minister for Home Security, recognized that 'people cannot stand this intensive bombing indefinitely and sooner or later the morale of other towns will go even as Plymouth's has gone'. Liverpool, too, was hard hit, and a Mass Observation report of May noted: 'The general feeling – it is difficult exactly to express it, but the residents spoken to felt it too – that there was no power or drive left in Liverpool.' Britain was fortunate that the *Luftwaffe* was not better equipped for strategic bombing, and that its commanders applied the power they had in a less than focused way.

Air Chief Marshal Arthur Harris of Bomber Command was not slow to learn the lessons of the Blitz. The raid on Coventry, he wrote, served to 'teach us the principle of concentration, the principle of starting so many fires at the same time that no fire fighting services, however efficiently and quickly they were reinforced by the fire brigades of other towns, could get them under control.' One night (probably 29 December 1940) he stood on the Air Ministry roof with Sir Charles Portal, Chief of the Air Staff, and 'watched the old city in flames...with St Paul's standing out in the midst of an ocean of fire'. As they turned to go, Harris said: 'Well, they are sowing the wind'.

A View of the Field

As a boy I made frequent visits to a London which still had large, empty bomb sites, relics not only of the Blitz proper but also of the 'Little Blitz' of January-March 1944, a reprisal for the bombing of Germany, and of the V1 (flying bomb) and V2 (long-range rocket) campaign of 1944–45. These have all disappeared, and the buildings which have filled them are often dreary and soulless. The first bomb to fall on the City of London is commemorated by a plaque on St Giles' Church, off Wood Street, in the Barbican, an area badly damaged during the Blitz. St Clement Danes in the Strand was destroyed by fire on 10 May 1941, but restored and, in 1958, re-dedicated to the memory of the RAF, Commonwealth and Allied air forces. The ruins of St Michael's Cathedral in Coventry were preserved when the new cathedral was built in 1954-62, and a statue showing St Michael triumphing over the devil stands on the steps to the porch linking the old and new cathedrals.

Graves and Cemeteries
Some German aircrew killed during the Battle of Britain and the Blitz are buried in civilian cemeteries, but the majority now rest in the German military cemetery at Cannock Chase, Staffordshire. Of the civilians killed in the Blitz, some were buried in individual marked graves, and others, like Fred and Dorothy Gill, the first civilians killed on the mainland, who perished when a mine-laying Heinkel crashed onto their house in Clacton-on-Sea in May 1940, have unmarked graves in town cemeteries.

There are a number of mass graves, like that in Abney Park Cemetery, Stoke Newington, the result of a direct hit on a block of flats in Coronation Avenue. A bomb brought the building down onto the shelter beneath it, and those who survived the explosion and fall of debris were drowned by water and effluent which poured into the shelter from fractured pipes. It took rescue services a week to remove the bodies.

The dead of the Blitz are listed in a multi-volume Book of Remembrance in Westminster Abbey, in an alcove on the right just inside the west door: a page is turned each day. It underscores the sheer capriciousness of death from the sky. There are infants and grandparents, firemen and air raid wardens, dockers from the East End and the gilded youth of Mayfair. The RAF chapel, at the Abbey's east end, contains its own Book of Remembrance for the dead of the RAF, reminding us of the part played in the Battle of Britain by Czech and Polish pilots. A small hole, low down in the abbey wall at the far left-hand end of the chapel, is bomb-damage, deliberately glazed but not blocked up.

Museums

The Imperial War Museum's Blitz Experience, a reconstruction of a London street and air-raid shelter, captures the mood of the Blitz very well. The Royal Air Force Museum at Hendon has a Battle of Britain Hall which contains a series of tableaux whose life-size figures represent various aspects of the Blitz, amongst them an East End street scene, a 3.7inch gun site and a radar station. Upstairs, not far from figures of Dowding and Goering, is a reconstruction of No. 11 Group's operations room. The aircraft exhibited include most of the types that participated in the Battle of Britain and the Blitz. They include, most poignantly, the remains of a Hurricane shot down on 31 August but not recovered till 1973.

The Airfields of 1940

The airfields of 1940 have suffered a variety of fates. Duxford, near Cambridge, which housed the first of the 'Big Wings', is now a satellite of the Imperial War Museum. It is a unique combination: a historical airfield which houses Europe's largest and most popular aviation museum. History is quite literally in the air, for some 40 of its 140 or so aircraft, including Spitfires, Hurricanes and Messerschmitts, still fly from time to time. The sector operations room has been carefully restored to its September 1940 condition. Remove the parked cars and the airfield reverts to its Second World War appearance.

A few airfields, like Manston and Middle Wallop, are still used by the services. Some house civilian flying clubs, and others have disappeared altogether. The M11 has clipped the western edge off North Weald, but its hangars still remain. There is an aviation museum at Tangmere, just east of Chichester, open during the summer months. The front-line fighter base at Hawkinge, north of Folkestone, now houses the Kent Battle of Britain Museum, and both RAF and *Luftwaffe* aircrew are buried in Folkestone New Cemetery, on the edge of the airfield. Only 3 miles (5 km) to its south the Battle of Britain Memorial looks out across the Channel, that moat crossed by Duke William almost nine hundred years before Spitfires and Messerschmitts laced the skies above it with their vapour trails.

CHAPTER 12

Operation Goodwood
1944

Background

'The battle of Normandy,' maintained Stephen Badsey, 'was the last great set-piece battle of the Western World.' An historian should never say never, but we may hope that three months of fighting amongst seaside villas, half-timbered *manoirs* and apple orchards mark the end of a barbarous dynasty of battles which had ruled Europe for centuries before Agincourt was fought. Without the great sea-borne landing of D-Day, 6 June 1944, there could have been no Allied invasion of occupied Europe: but winning a beachhead was only the campaign's first act. Surging out of it to make Normandy a stepping stone to Hitler's defeat was always the Allied aim, and for many combatants it was not the break-in but the break-out which curdles memories of this land of cream and Calvados.

Operation Goodwood was the British army's major contribution to the break-out. Historians remain divided as to whether it was meant to achieve a break-out itself, or to attract German armour from the American sector. Alexander McKee called it 'the death ride of the armoured divisions' with good reason. It was one of the largest ever British mechanized battles, and over 400 tanks were lost, more than the army's tank strength at the time of writing.

The war had been transformed from European conflict to global struggle by the entry of America, Russia and Japan and the spread of hostilities from the deserts of North Africa to the island-speckled immensity of the Pacific. There was broad agreement that Britain and the United States would enter occupied Europe, although it was less easy to agree on the time or method of invasion. At one extreme, the Russian leader Josef Stalin

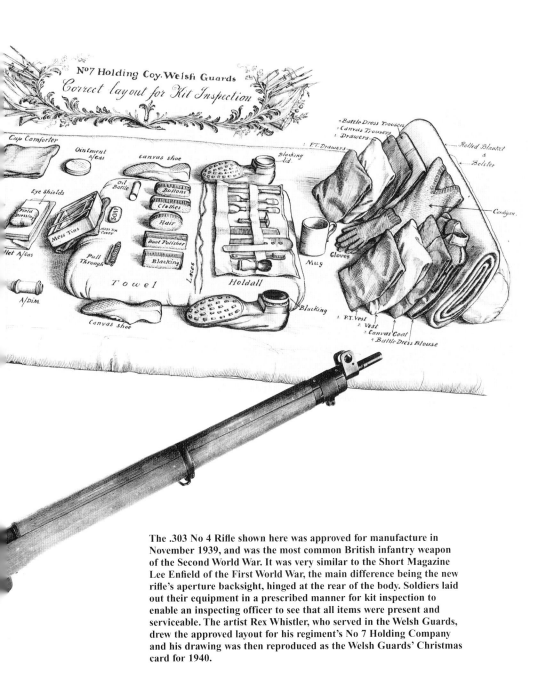

The artwork is labelled:

No 7 Holding Coy. Welsh Guards
Correct layout for Kit Inspection

Cap Comforter · Ointment A/Gas · Canvas shoe · Blacking Lid · Battle Dress Trousers · Canvas Trousers · Drawers · P.T. Drawers · Rolled Blanket & Bolster · Eye Shields · Oil Bottle · Buttons · Clothes · Soap · Hair · Field Dressing · Mess Tins · Mess Tin Cover · Boot Polisher · Cardigan · Pull Through · Blacking · Laces · Holdall · Mug · Gloves · Towel · A/DIM · Canvas Shoe · Blacking · P.T. Vest · Vest · Canvas Coat · Battle Dress Blouse

The .303 No 4 Rifle shown here was approved for manufacture in November 1939, and was the most common British infantry weapon of the Second World War. It was very similar to the Short Magazine Lee Enfield of the First World War, the main difference being the new rifle's aperture backsight, hinged at the rear of the body. Soldiers laid out their equipment in a prescribed manner for kit inspection to enable an inspecting officer to see that all items were present and serviceable. The artist Rex Whistler, who served in the Welsh Guards, drew the approved layout for his regiment's No 7 Holding Company and his drawing was then reproduced as the Welsh Guards' Christmas card for 1940.

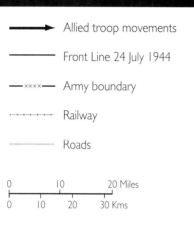

NORMANDY
Operation Goodwood and the Normandy Break-out Battles
June-July 1944

→ Allied troop movements

─── Front Line 24 July 1944

─×××× Army boundary

·····› Railway

─── Roads

0	10		20 Miles
0	10	20	30 Kms

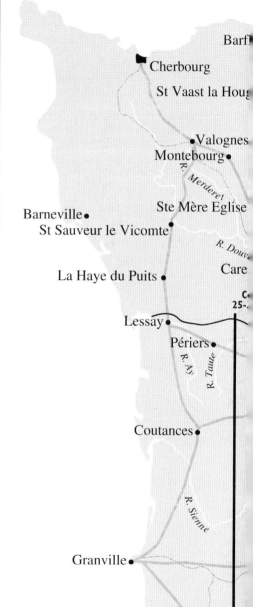

Cap de la Hague

Barf

Cherbourg

St Vaast la Houg

•Valognes

Montebourg•

R. Merderet

Ste Mère Eglise

Barneville•

St Sauveur le Vicomte•

R. Douv

La Haye du Puits •

Care

C
25-

Lessay•

Périers•

R. Ay

R. Taute

Coutances•

R. Sienne

Granville•

Avranches•

English Channel

Martin de Varreville

St Laurent

Isigny

R. Aure
Trevières

Port en Bessin

Arromanches

Courseulles

Douvres

Bayeux   R. Seulles

St Jean de Daye

Charnwood
7-8 July

First
Canadian
Army

Ouistreham

Cabourg

Amercian First Army

British Second Army

R. Drome

Ranville

Goodwood
18-20 July

Epsom
25-30 June

Tilly

Caen

Troarn

St Lô

12-13 June

Noyers

Caumont

Villers Bocage

Evrecy

Bourguébus

Vimont

Mézidon

Torigni

R. Odon

Aunay

Bretteville sur Laize

Tessy

Mt Pinçon

R. Dives

rcy

R. Vire

Le Bény Bocage

Thury Harcourt

edieu

Vire

Condé

Falaise

R. Orne

Tinchebray

Flers

Argentan

R. Sée

urgently demanded the opening of a second front to divert German resources from the east. At the other, Winston Churchill was inclined to fight where British forces were already deployed because he saw the losses of the First World War as a warning of what might happen if a campaign in France turned sour. The Americans were initially persuaded to acquiesce in British-inspired Mediterranean strategy, but the Allied conference in Washington in May 1943 set a target date for an invasion one year ahead. Six months later in Tehran, the Western Allies committed themselves to Operation Overlord, the invasion of France, and at Cairo, in December 1943, the American General Dwight D. Eisenhower was appointed Supreme Allied Commander for the operation.

The German Position

The Germans had long expected invasion, and although a Canadian descent on Dieppe in August 1942 taught the Allies valuable lessons, it lent impetus to work on the Atlantic Wall, the defences along the French and Belgian coasts. The area was the responsibility of Field Marshal Gerd von Rundstedt, Commander-in-Chief West, and his two army groups. Army Group G held southern France; Army Group B defended Normandy and Brittany with 7th Army, and northern France, Belgium and Holland with 15th Army. The armoured reserve, Panzer Group West, was held back near Paris.

Rundstedt's chain of command was tangled. Field Marshal Erwin Rommel of Army Group B was also Inspector-General of the Atlantic Wall and enjoyed direct access to Hitler. Rommel had authority over three divisions in Panzer Group West, but the remainder could not be moved without Hitler's authority. Aircraft were controlled by *Luftflotte* 3, whose commander answered to Reichsmarschall Hermann Goering. Anti-aircraft guns, including dual-purpose 88mms, were the responsibility of the *Luftwaffe*, as were *Luftwaffe* field divisions, composed of redundant pilots and ground crew. The Waffen-SS maintained divisions of its own, often better equipped than their army counterparts and enjoying a great measure of independence.

The Eastern Front was Germany's overriding priority, and it burnt up troops like kindling. Most divisions in France were not fit for service in the east, many filled with unfit or over-age soldiers who could carry out only static duties: some contained 'Ost' battalions of Russian prisoners of war. The German army had become a two-tier structure as General Heinz Guderian's opponents had feared, its infantry divisions relying on horse-drawn transport. There was a conflict of opinion as to how invasion should be met. Conventional wisdom, to which most senior officers subscribed, favoured identifying the real Allied thrust (there might easily be feints) and sending massed armour against it. Rommel, who knew what Allied air-power could do, believed that the invasion had to be stopped on the beaches. Its first day would be the longest, for Allies and Germans alike.

The Allied Plan

Rommel's opponents would not have disagreed. Planners on the staff of COSSAC (Chief of Staff to Supreme Allied Commander) had decided in favour of landing in Normandy rather than the Pas de Calais, which was closer but more obvious and better defended. When General Sir Bernard Montgomery, who was to command all ground forces for the invasion, saw the COSSAC plan he demanded something bigger: five divisions were to land on a 50-mile (80-km) front, with airborne landings protecting their flanks. Montgomery briefed senior commanders on 7 April 1944. General Omar Bradley's US 1st Army would land in the west on Utah and Omaha beaches, covered by 82nd and 101st Airborne Divisions. Lieutenant-General Sir Miles Dempsey's British 2nd Army was to go ashore on Gold, Juno and Sword beaches in the east, with 6th Airborne Division securing its left flank. The Canadian 1st and US 3rd Armies would be landed later to form two army groups, Montgomery's 21st and Bradley's 12th, at which stage Montgomery would relinquish the role of overall land force commander.

Montgomery's intentions for the development of the campaign loom large in the story that follows. On 7 April his briefing map showed coloured phase lines which may be regarded as illustrative of rates of advance, useful as planning tools. However, Carlo d'Este has argued that they help to cast doubt on what was long regarded as Montgomery's master-plan for the campaign: drawing German reserves to the British sector so as to allow the Americans to break out. The briefing made no mention of a holding operation in the British sector, and a document issued a month later described 'co-ordinated thrusts towards both the Loire and the Seine, so timed as to keep making the enemy move his reserves against first one and then the other.' It was an essentially opportunistic scheme which relied on seizing and maintaining the initiative and then, as d'Este puts it, 'expanding the initial bridgehead and … seizing port facilities in whatever direction proved most advantageous.'

It would be imperative for the Allies to build up forces in Normandy more quickly than their enemy. An elaborate deception plan, Operation Fortitude, encouraged the Germans to believe that an American army group in south-east England was about to invade the Pas de Calais: long

This self-portrait of the artist Rex Whistler *(above)* in his Welsh Guards' uniform, was painted in May 1940 just as he left civilian life to join up with his new regiment. Whistler, who had studied art at the Slade in London, had a particular flair for book illustration, murals and theatre design. The elegance of the conservatory at York Terrace, overlooking Regent's Park, sharply contrasts with the rather more basic conditions of the wartime officers' mess shown in Whistler's humorous sketch *(right)*, but officers and men alike suffered far worse conditions than just the poor lighting portrayed here during wartime. Like much of the young talent of this period, Whistler was killed in 1944, aged 39, while serving with the Guards' Armoured Division during Operation Goodwood. Another Normandy casualty was the poet Keith Douglas, a Yeomanry officer, whose work stands comparison with that of the best of the First World War poets.

after the invasion the German High Command braced itself for the blow that never came. The Allied air forces, under Air Chief Marshal Sir Trafford Leigh-Mallory, gained superiority in the skies, crippled the French railway system and denied the Germans air reconnaissance. The Allies had an added advantage in secret information graded 'Ultra' that came from codes broken at Bletchley Park in Buckinghamshire. This gave warning of German moves and made possible the location of units whose radio traffic gave them away. When headquarters Panzer Group West at last arrived in Normandy after negotiating roads swept by fighter-bombers, it was identified by Ultra and devastated by a bombing raid which wounded its commander and killed most of his staff. It was out of action for two weeks.

Campaign and Battle

D-Day was an unquestionable but not unqualified success. The Americans ran into heavy opposition on 'Bloody Omaha', and the advance inland went more slowly than expected. Michael Carver, who commanded an armoured brigade in Normandy, went to the heart of the matter when he spoke of: 'The emphasis placed before the campaign on the expected fierceness of the battle on the beaches. There was a tendency to build up a climate of feeling that, once ashore, it would all be fairly easy and merely a matter of build-up.'

Over the next fortnight the Allies strengthened their hold on the fore-shore, taking Bayeux on 7 June and going on to link up the beachheads. Caen, a D-Day objective, remained in German hands. On 12 June, 7th Armoured Division turned the flank of its defenders by taking Villers Bocage but was rebuffed by a well-handled German counter-attack. The Americans, too, had their share of unpleasant surprises: a drive towards St Lô petered out in country that might have been made for defence. Bradley's men crossed the Cotentin peninsula to reach the Atlantic coast on 17 June, cutting off three German divisions and isolating Cherbourg.

In the second half of June the battle solidified. The Allies had bare numerical superiority, but command of air and sea meant that they could reinforce the half-million men already ashore. The Germans endured constant abrasion from the air. For example, 2nd Panzer Division left Abbeville for Normandy by rail on 9 June. It was so frequently attacked that the tanks had to finish the journey by road, and it was not until 18 June that 80 of the 120 tanks which had started reached the front at Caumont. Air-power was no respecter of persons. It killed tough old General Erich Marcks of LXXXIV Corps, whose wooden leg delayed his escape from his car when fighter-bombers swooped, and on 17 July Hurricanes strafed another German staff car near Livarot: its driver was killed and the passenger badly injured. He was Field Marshal Rommel.

Rommel had lost confidence in victory, his faith shaken as much by Hitler's wild schemes for counter-attacks as by Allied material superiority. On 23 June he told his wife that: 'Militarily things aren't at all good. The enemy air force is dealing extremely heavily with our supplies and at the moment is completely strangling them. If a decisive battle develops, we'll be without ammunition ... We must be prepared for grave events.' In fact, a decisive battle in the east began that day when the Russians launched Operation Bagration, which led to the destruction of Army Group Centre and the loss of 350 000 men. Rundstedt was no more optimistic. On 1 July he assured the chief of Armed Forces High Command (OKW) that the situation was impossible. 'Make peace, you idiots,' said Rundstedt. 'What else can you do?' He was dismissed on 2 July and replaced by Field Marshal Gunther von Kluge.

'A Greater Sense of Urgency'

Allied air commanders, however, were concerned at the lack of progress: on 16 June Air Marshal Sir Arthur Coningham of the 2nd Tactical Air Force demanded 'a greater sense of urgency from the army and a frank admission that their operations were not running according to plan.' Eisenhower's deputy, Air Chief Marshal Sir Arthur Tedder, was worried by the army's failure to take the Caen-Falaise plain which could provide bases for aircraft operating from England. The landing schedule was running late. Cherbourg was still in German hands, and a gale which raged for four days from 19 June destroyed the American Mulberry artificial harbour and damaged the British one.

Montgomery did his best to break the deadlock, maintaining pressure on both sides of the bridgehead. On 18 June he directed that Cherbourg was to be taken by the Americans, and Caen by the British, before 23 June. Cherbourg eventually fell on 26/27 June; the port was so thoroughly wrecked that it could not operate at full capacity until the end of September. An American drive southwards floundered through *bocage* countryside, its chequerboard of fields blanked off with banks and hedges, and had spent itself by 11 July. On 26 June the British launched Operation Epsom, an attempt to outflank Caen from the west. It punched a salient into German lines, left Caen dangerously exposed, but did not take the city. A direct assault, Operation Charnwood, also made disappointing progress. On the night of 7 July, 460 heavy bombers pounded Caen: after fighting in rubble-choked streets, British and Canadian troops advanced as far as the River Orne but left a substantial portion of the city in German hands.

Allied Difficulties
Failure to secure Caen highlighted two difficulties. The first was the cramped state of the bridgehead. By 30 June the Allies had landed 875 000 men, 150 000 vehicles and 570 000 tons (580 000 tonnes) of stores. There were thirteen American and fourteen British divisions ashore but, although the headquarters of both follow-up armies had landed, there was no room to deploy the armies themselves, and the Americans already had nine divisions waiting in England.

The second problem was specifically British. Put simply, the army was running out of men. The Americans had suffered 37 034 casualties and the British 24 698, but while the Americans were able to replace them the British, continuously engaged in one theatre or another since 1939, could not. In August Montgomery had to break up 59th Division. Battalions were split up to provide drafts, and an NCO in 2/Hertfordshire recorded that he was 'very sorry that our Bn is being broken up in this way ... I hate leaving comrades with whom I have been for so long ... It hardly seems possible that we are all breaking up and may never see each other again.'

The problem went deeper. Three British divisions, 50th Northumbrian, 51st Highland and 7th Armoured, were veterans of the desert.

Many of their officers and men thought that they had done their bit. Brigadier James Hargest, an experienced New Zealander, said of 50th Division that 'there was a strong feeling amongst the men while in England that the Div. should *not* be asked to do the assault on D-Day ...' When Major Martin Lindsay joined 2/Gordon Highlanders in Normandy he observed 'the way in which the men's feelings are considered in this division. Twice in two days I have heard, "The Jocks don't like raids".' Major-General G.L. Verney, who took over 7th Armoured Division after its commander was sacked, was uncomfortably penetrating in his analysis:

There is no doubt that familiarity with war does not make one more courageous. One becomes cunning, and from cunning to cowardice is but a short step. The infantryman who does not want to 'have a go' and can find opportunities for lying low at the critical moment; the tank man can easily find a fault in his engine or his wireless, and thus miss taking part in the battle ... two of the three divisions that came back from Italy ... were extremely 'swollen-headed'. They were a law unto themselves; they thought that they need only obey those orders that suited them.

Brigadier Hargest argued that 'the high percentage of officer casualties is due to the necessity of them being *always* in the front to direct advances in difficult country.' Lindsay realized that 'nearly every operation nowadays is a succession of company battles' and Major-General 'Pip' Roberts of 11th Armoured Division agreed that 'casualties in Company Commanders and their equivalent were probably the most serious loss that units suffered in this phase of the war.' Brigadier Bill Williams, Montgomery's chief intelligence officer, summed up the prevailing view: 'We were always well aware of the doctrine "let metal do it rather than flesh". The morale of our troops depended on this. We always said – "Waste all the ammunition you like, but not flesh."'

War at First Hand
Sometimes Normandy was more than flesh and blood could stand. Lieutenant Geoffrey Bishop of 23rd Hussars saw a friend's tank destroyed in their first action. He was buried in an orchard: 'Suddenly and silently all the regiment is gathered round. They have all known and loved Bob, and this simple tribute brings a choking feeling to my throat.' Bishop soon discovered that death had uglier faces. He watched a self-propelled gun burn while men tried to remove ammunition: 'In a flash there are two blinding reports – I have my glasses on them and can see quite clearly – a body shoots high into the air; the others disappear

in a cloud of black smoke ... That night ... there is a lurid glow from the gun and the smell of a burnt offering to the God of War.' Trooper Ken Tout of 1/Northamptonshire Yeomanry saw that a fellow gunner had failed to escape from a blazing tank, but: 'The explosions of ammunition ... served as a humane killer before the furnace began to grill him where he sat. Something in my being revolts more against the slow grilling of my flesh after death than against the sudden swift shattering of mind and body in a massive explosion.'

Noise wore men down. The German 'Moaning Minnie' multi-barrelled rocket launcher was especially frightening. 'The actual destruction is less than would be caused by the same weight of shells,' thought Lindsay, 'but the noise, and therefore the moral effect, is much greater.' There was the buzz-saw sound of the German MG 42 machine-gun and the slower rattle of the Bren; the 'feathery shuffle' audible in the split second before a mortar bomb burst with its 'flat, grating, guttural crash'; the railway-train rumble of 25-pdr shells going one way and the sharper whiz-bang of a high-velocity shell coming the other. A barrage could be almost soporific. Ken Tout tells how 'the continuous sporadic traffic of shells overhead and the fitful jazz beat of explosions behind us have merged into our consciousness until we disregard them.' There was no disregarding the SLAM-CRASH of an 88mm, the sound of the shell's impact and the weapon's firing arriving almost together. Perhaps the most telling accompaniment to tank battle was the smack of armour-piercing shot on armour plate, like the clang of bodkin point on breastplate, obscenely amplified.

There were yells of agony and tortured desperation. The commander of a stricken American Sherman groaned that he was in the most indescribable anguish, his plight relayed to his comrades because his radio was switched to 'send'. Radios, more numerous and reliable than in 1940, gave the crews of armoured vehicles an ability to communicate which soldiers had not known since orders, exhortation and banter reverberated round squares at Waterloo. British radio procedure could snap from hunting field – '3 Baker. Good show. Move back a bit and let the hounds see the foxes ...' – to hospital: 'Oboe 4 Able. Now 4 Charlie has brewed. I think there is a nasty about ten o'clock. Can't see ... all gone dark ... all gone cold ... somebody please, please, ple ...' And yet for the infantry, the battlefield was often empty and impersonal. Lieutenant Geoffrey Picot, mortar officer of 1/Hampshires, warned that:

Those who get their picture of a battle from films where seemingly hundreds of rival soldiers are packed into a few hundred square yards may have difficulty in imagining a real battlefield. You and a couple of pals can be hundreds of yards away from anybody else; you may not have much idea where friend or foe are. You fire from a concealed position on to a hidden target.

Smells laced the landscape. There was the sickly sweet stink of corpses, human and animal: bloated cattle in fields and strafed transport horses in lanes upset some soldiers more than the sprawl of khaki or grey. Crushed apples gave platoon positions, and sometimes tank turrets, a cidery tang. Tank crews relieved themselves into empty ammunition boxes or shell-cases. Ken Tout caught the real whiff of battle inside his Sherman tank 'Stony Stratford':

The August sun beats down. The tank engine is running. Our own guns are reeking hot to the touch. Each of us is sweating from fear and exertion. We can fairly feel the heat from the burning fields and the brewing tanks. Combined with the mounting heat there is the smell of roasting flesh outside as well as the animal smells and cordite fumes from within Stony Stratford's own grimy bowels.

As the fighting dragged on the strain increased, for men could see that the odds against them lengthened by the day. Major-General Hubert Essame and Eversley Belfield affirmed: 'When judging any lack of enthusiasm displayed in action, especially by veterans of the 8th Army, it must be remembered that, for most front line soldiers, the bleak rule was that you normally continued to fight on; either until you were killed, or so severely wounded as to be unfit for further active service in the line.' An experienced infantry officer thought that: 'Everybody cracks up in the end, of course, but you hope something will have happened by then.' Nearly three-quarters of a sample of 3500 British battle casualties came from the infantry, which made up less than one-quarter of the army.

The weight of battle bore down on the Germans too. The thirty-two-year-old Major Hans von Luck had recently arrived in Normandy to command 125th Panzer Grenadier Regiment in 21st Panzer Division when the Allies landed. 'The morale of the men was still surprisingly good,' he wrote, 'although all realized that Allied success in the west meant the end.' There was a glimmer of optimism: 'The announcement of new "miracle-weapons" gave men some hope of a turn for the better.' The ever-present risk of air attack and the weight of shells delivered by Allied gunners were a constant ordeal. In July the outgoing commander of 2nd Panzer Division told his successor that the division was hit by 4000 artillery and 5000 mortar rounds a day and in the last four weeks a total of six German aircraft had been seen over the divisional area.

Yet the Germans fought well. When Martin van Creveld sought to explain why the German army consistently inflicted casualties at about a

50 per cent higher rate than it incurred, he considered that 'indoctrination with National Socialist ideas, the exalted social status of the military, and (even) some odd quirks of national character may have contributed to this result.' A study of cohesion in the *Wehrmacht*, published shortly after the war, concluded that 'the unity of the German army was in fact sustained only to a very slight extent by National Socialism.' However, when Omer Bartov examined German performance on the Eastern Front he noted that turnover amongst personnel was so rapid that there was no time for small-group loyalty to take hold. He argued that the German army in the east underwent 'a fundamental process of barbarization' in which ideology had a key role.

Although ideology was far less of a bond in Normandy, largely because Anglo-American and Russian enemies were horses of very different colours, indoctrination played its part. A good case in point is 12th SS Panzer Division 'Hitler Youth', under its thirty-three-year-old commander Kurt 'Panzer' Meyer, which enjoyed a reputation for hard combat tempered by atrocity. A British medical officer described its wounded as: 'A tough and dirty bunch – some had been snipers up trees for days – one young Nazi had a broken jaw and was near death but before he fainted he rolled his head over and murmured "Heil Hitler".' At the other extreme was a prisoner captured by 7/Somerset Light Infantry, an 'old chap of forty [who] empties his pockets including his photos of wife and kiddy and his old pipe'.

Allied and German Firepower

'The German army …' noted van Creveld, 'regarded itself as a fighting organization above all … So strong was the grip in which the organization held its personnel that the latter simply did not care where they fought, against whom, and why. They were soldiers and did their duty …' Allied demands for unconditional surrender stiffened resolve: for some soldiers, death in Normandy was the lesser of many evils. Until the losses of mid-1944 destroyed the replacement system, German reinforcements were better trained than their Allied counterparts and introduced to battle with more careful preparation. The regiments within panzer and panzer grenadier divisions rarely fought as such, but were divided into *ad hoc* battle-groups containing a mixture of infantry and armour, a system which worked well in the German army but generally ran less smoothly in the British. Major Robert Kiln of the Hertfordshire Yeomanry doubted if any of his comrades 'had anything but admiration for the fighting ability of the German soldiers whether or not they hated them. In my view, as professional soldiers,

General Sir Bernard
Montgomery *(left)* com-
manded Allied ground
forces from a caravan in
the grounds of the Château
de Creullet. Most of his
tanks were Shermans.
Cromwells, seen here
(below) waiting east of the
Orne on 18 July, were used
by 7th Armoured Division
and the armoured recon-
naissance regiments of the
Guards and 11th
Armoured Divisions.

they were superior to any but the very best troops in the Allied Forces.'

Some German equipment was still superior to Allied. The Panzer IV remained effective, and the Panzer V Panther with its 75mm gun was arguably the best medium tank used by either side. The angular features of the Panzer VI Tiger scowled malignantly over the battlefield. This monster weighed 54 tons (55 tonnes) and carried an 88mm gun. It was so hard to conceal and manoeuvre that its crews called it 'the furniture wagon', but it could destroy the Sherman, workhorse of British and American armoured divisions, at 2000 yards (1800 metres), long before even a Sherman Firefly, with a 17-pdr gun rather than the 75mm in most Shermans, could hope to touch it.

Allied armoured crewmen lived in the shadow of the 88mm. 'That gun will blast a shot through the co-driver's seat and through the lower turret and through my shins and through the rear of the turret on its way … into the engine space primed with fuel fumes,' imagined Ken Tout as his tank rumbled through an orchard. The Sherman had its virtues: it was cheap to produce, mechanically reliable and simple to maintain. But it caught fire easily: the Allies nicknamed it the Ronson because it always lit first time. The Germans permitted themselves a rare jest and called it the Tommy Cooker.

John Keegan defined the tank's dual nature as preserver and destroyer: Vishnu and Shiva in one. To its acolytes it was war-machine, talisman and home: they fought, and often lived, within its carapace. A Sherman had a crew of five. Its commander usually rode with his head and upper chest above the finger-chopping turret hatch. The gunner sat on his right, head close to the telescopic gunsight with its rubber eye-pad, one hand on the pistol-grip of the electrically powered turret traverse and the other on the gun's elevation handwheel, foot ready to stamp on firing buttons for the main armament and coaxial machine-gun. The loader/operator was responsible for 'netting in' the radio set to the correct frequency and keeping on net despite buffetings which would shake it off. He thrust brass-cased shells into the gun's breech, selecting armour-piercing or high explosive as required, and jettisoned empty cases, automatically ejected from the breech as it slammed backwards on recoil, through the 'pistol port' in the turret's side. In the bow, below the turret crew, sat the driver, looking through periscopes if the tank was closed down, or sitting higher, with his head above his hatch, if it was safe to do so. His co-driver, who also manned the hull-mounted machine-gun, sat beside him.

The state of the tank's interior depended on many factors, not least the pace of action and the squadron sergeant-major's zeal. Its exterior was a reflection of a unit's style and experience. Some tolerated stowage of personal belongings outside, making room in the turret but increasing the risk of fire, and others favoured the attachment of spare wheels, track-links and even sandbags, to increase protection against armour-piercing rounds or the shaped-charge projectiles fired, often at suicidally close range, from the bazooka-like *Panzerfaust*.

Crewmen might sleep beneath their tank if the ground was hard and no rain was expected – most regiments had horror stories of men stifled beneath sinking hulls – or would wrap themselves in sleeping bags or the tarpaulin covers for the engine hatches and curl up beside the tank. They were always ready for a brew, usually tea unless coffee could be scrounged from nearby Americans, its water heated on a solid-fuel

OPERATION GOODWOOD

The attack of the British 8 Corps
18 July 1944

→ Allied troop movements

—×××— Corps boundary

≍ Bridge

⊦⊦⊦⊦⊦⊦ Railway

| 0 | 1 | 2 | 3 | 4 | 5 Miles |

| 0 | 1 | 2 | 3 | 4 | 5 | 6 | 7 | 8 Kms |

```
                    ┌─────────────────┐
                    │    8 Corps      │
                    │ Lt Gen O'Connor │
                    └─────────────────┘
```

GDS ARMD DIV	7 ARMD DIV	11 ARMD
Maj Gen Adair	Maj Gen Erskine	Maj Gen Ro

| 5 GDS ARMD BDE | 22 ARMD BDE | 29 ARMD |

| 32 GDS BDE | 131 INF BDE | 159 INF B |

Caen

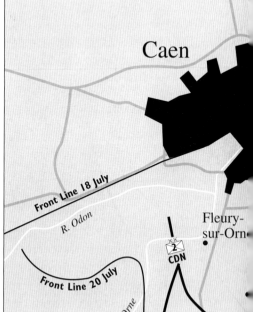

Front Line 18 July

R. Odon

Fleury-
sur-Orne

Front Line 20 July

R. Orne

2
CDN

St-André-sur-l'Orne •

St-Martin-
de-Fontenay

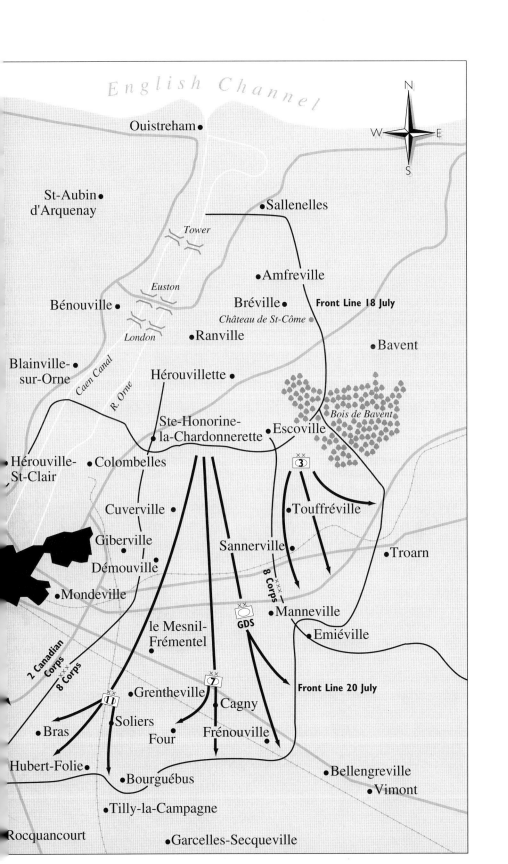

English Channel

N
W E
S

Ouistreham

St-Aubin d'Arquenay

Sallenelles

Tower

Amfreville

Euston

Bréville

Front Line 18 July

Bénouville

Château de St-Côme

Bavent

London

Ranville

Blainville-sur-Orne

Hérouvillette

Ste-Honorine-la-Chardonnerette

Bois de Bavent

Escoville

Hérouville-St-Clair

Colombelles

3

Cuverville

Touffréville

Giberville

Sannerville

Troarn

Démouville

8 Corps

Mondeville

Manneville

le Mesnil-Frémentel

GDS

Emiéville

2 Canadian Corps

8 Corps

7

Front Line 20 July

Grentheville

11

Cagny

Bras

Soliers

Four

Frénouville

Hubert-Folie

Bourguébus

Bellengreville

Vimont

Tilly-la-Campagne

Rocquancourt

Garcelles-Secqueville

cooker, primus stove or a tin of petrol-soaked sand. Tinned rations, such
as Irish stew, steak and kidney pudding, corned beef and currant duff,
were bulked out by hard-tack biscuits and supplemented from food
bought or foraged from farms.

The Start of the Break-out

On 10 July, Montgomery outlined his plan for the final break-out. Operation Cobra would launch the Americans towards Avranches, where they
would divide to plunge westwards into Brittany and eastwards towards
Le Mans and Alençon. The British would mount an offensive east of
Caen: Operation Goodwood. Time slippage, caused by bad weather and
the American need to secure St Lô, meant that Goodwood eventually
began on 18 July and Cobra on the 25th. Goodwood was always scheduled to precede Cobra, forcing the Germans to bring threadbare
armoured divisions – the crack Panzer Lehr was down to 40 tanks and
2200 men – to meet it, and give Bradley's American troops a clear run.

Some hoped for much more. Lieutenant-General Sir Miles Dempsey
of the British 2nd Army initially ordered Lieutenant-General Sir Richard
O'Connor's 8 Corps to send an armoured division to Falaise. Major-General Roberts thought that 'Falaise was in everyone's mind as a point to be
aimed for' and O'Connor discussed 'the best formation in which three
armoured divisions should move once they had broken through into open
country'. Eisenhower's headquarters, delighted to see Falaise mentioned,
hoped for a breakthrough. Dempsey thought it 'more than possible that
the Huns will break' and exploitation would ensue. Montgomery was
inwardly more cautious, but encouraged high hopes in others. On 14 July
he told Sir Alan Brooke, chief of the imperial general staff: 'I have
decided that the time has come to have a real showdown and to loose
[three armoured divisions] into the open country about the Caen–Falaise
road.'

Goodwood was Dempsey's brainchild, and showed fair appreciation
of those age-old determinants of battle: men, weapons and the ground.
The British were short of men but had plenty of tanks, for there were
now three armoured divisions, the Guards, 7th and 11th, together with
five independent armoured and three independent tank brigades in the
bridgehead, with some 2250 medium and 400 light tanks. Dempsey
hoped to 'utilize that surplus of tanks and economize infantry'. He proposed to use the air-power that had devastated Caen to clear the way for
his armoured divisions, which would advance, not into the boxy fields
west of Caen, but across the rolling countryside to the east.

A crescent of jurassic limestone curves down from the landing beaches towards Alençon and Le Mans. It is topped with an open, windswept landscape of big fields dotted with woods and pierced by quarries from which pale Caen stone is still cut. Dempsey's attention was focused on the area between Caen and Falaise, bordered to its west by the River Orne and its tributary the Laize, and to its east by the marshy Dives. It was approached though a bottleneck. On its western side were the Orne, its canal, and the industrial suburb of Colombelles, marked by tall factory chimneys. To the east stood a high German-held ridge surmounted by the Bois de Bavent. Only one armoured division could form up east of the Orne and, because the Germans could observe this area from Colombelles, concentration had to be delayed until the last possible moment.

An advantage of attacking east of Caen was that it was 'good tank country'. Three years later an official publication described it as 'very much in favour of the defence and ideal for the siting of the enemy's artillery, both field and anti-tank', and observed that only after a long advance on a narrow front could 'a real break-out ... be achieved'. Although the British had ample artillery, ammunition was in short supply and most guns would be sited west of the Orne until Cagny and the southern suburbs of Caen were cleared. Montgomery and Dempsey intended to use air-power as a substitute for artillery, and the former sold the operation hard to persuade Eisenhower to extract aircraft from the bomber barons.

Between 5.45 a.m. and 6.30 a.m. on 18 July 1944, 1056 RAF heavy bombers were to drop 6000 tons (6100 tonnes) of explosive on Colombelles, a 2-mile (3-km) belt running north–south through Sannerville, and Cagny. At 7 a.m., a wave of 482 American medium bombers would hit Démouville and the surrounding villages, and from 8.30 a.m. until 9 a.m., 539 US heavy bombers were to take on the southern slopes of the Bavent feature, the ridge south of Frénouville and the Bourguébus–Bras–Soliers area. Fighter-bombers would deal with gun areas, strongpoints, and furnish 'impromptu direct air support'. Bombs were to be fitted with delayed-action fuses in areas where craters would not obstruct movement of British tanks, but in the central corridor, where cratering was unacceptable, fragmentation bombs were to be used.

O'Connor's 8 Corps was to attack on the heels of this bombardment, its left flank protected by 1 Corps, which was to hold a hard shoulder facing the Bois de Bavent and push down to Troarn, while on its right 2 Canadian Corps was to clear Colombelles and Giberville, and then move up the Orne valley. It is easy to write about 8 Corps 'driving its armoured divisions through the bottleneck' as if this was a domestic task demanding rolled-up sleeves and manual dexterity. Each division contained 2745 vehicles, which had to cross three pairs of bridges over the Orne and its canal, following routes which kept wheeled and tracked vehicles apart. They then had to move along a corridor less than 2 miles (3 km) wide, past headquarters, field ambulances and gun-lines, and through 51st Highland Division's positions before they reached the front line. This had been protected by British mines, many laid during bad weather and enemy interference, often in standing crops. Details had been indifferently recorded, shelling had moved or buried many, and clearance had to be done by night. Eighteen gaps were made through the minefield, their approaches marked with wire and white tape, but there were still many mines about. When the attack was over it took three engineer field companies, working in daylight, five days to clear the remaining mines.

As 11th Armoured Division passed through its three allocated minefield gaps its troubles were only beginning. So narrow was the front that it had to advance with 29th Armoured Brigade leading, and this in turn had to lead with 3/Royal Tank Regiment for the first 2500 yards (2300 metres), after which 2/Fife and Forfar Yeomanry could edge up into line. They would be followed up by 159th Infantry Brigade, taking Cuverville and Démouville with the help of 2/Northamptonshire Yeomanry, the division's armoured reconnaissance regiment. The division was to finish up on the right of 8 Corps' sector, on the line Bras–Verrières–Rocquancourt, with a force covering Cagny. With 11th Armoured safely through the bottleneck, the Guards Armoured Division would follow, masking Emiéville on the left, and capturing Vimont and Cagny. When the first two divisions had secured their objectives, 7th Armoured Division would advance on the line Four–La Hogue to seize Secqueville and the high ground about Cramesnil.

Early on 18 July, a grenadier, waiting with the Guards Armoured west of the Orne, was awakened by what he called 'a distant thunder in the air'. A nearby Welsh guardsman heard a 'faint and steady hum – growing into an insistent throbbing roar until the whole northern sky was filled with aeroplanes as far as the eye could see.' Some aircraft found the target area obscured by smoke and dust, but 6000 100-lb and 9600 500-lb bombs were dropped on 16th Luftwaffe Field Division, in the bottleneck, and the battle groups of 21st Panzer Division behind it.

It is no exaggeration to call the Germans' experience hellish, and that was precisely the comparison used by Lieutenant von Rosen, company commander in the Tiger-equipped 503rd Heavy Tank Battalion.

It was like hell and I am still astonished that I ever survived it … It was so nerve-shattering that we could not even think. All the tanks were completely covered with earth and the gun turrets had been torn completely out of adjustment by the shock effect. Fifty men in the company were dead, two soldiers had committed suicide during the bombardment, another had to be sent to a mental hospital for observation.

Werner Kortenhaus, a tank commander in 22nd Panzer Regiment of 21st Panzer Division, saw 'little dots' detach themselves from the aircraft. There were:

… so many of them that the crazy thought occurred to us; are those leaflets? We could hardly believe that they could all be bombs. Then began the most terrifying hour of our lives. It was a bomb carpet, regularly ploughing up the ground. Among the thunder of the explosions we could hear the wounded scream and the insane howling of men who had been driven mad.

The *Luftwaffe* division had endured the bombing of Caen ten days before, and was reduced to a handful of shaking survivors, some shocked into incontinence. In particular, 21st Panzer was hard hit: part of 1/125th Panzer Grenadier Regiment had disappeared, and a battery of 200th Assault Gun Battalion had been destroyed in Démouville. These guns were the invention of Major Becker, a German reserve officer and factory owner, who had married German 75mm and 105mm guns to French Hotchkiss tank chassis. Luck tells us that his men laughed at Becker's ungainly guns when they first saw them, but 'the assault gun companies

Shermans of the 23rd Hussars, moving up past the factory chimneys of Colombelles, on 18 July. The regiment suffered severely on the Bourguébus ridge that afternoon.

were trained to work closely with the grenadiers, and this was later a decisive aid to our defence forces.'

'"MOVE NOW." These words echoed round throughout the regiment and tanks slowly surged forward,' wrote Captain Lemon of 3/RTR. 'Then suddenly about a hundred yards [91 metres] in front of the leading tanks the earth started "boiling" all along the front as the rolling barrage from the 25-pdrs began.' His regiment and the Fife and Forfars had passed through the minefield before the bombing stopped, and Lance-Corporal Ron Cox of the Yeomanry remembered 'opening a new tin of jam and spreading it thickly on innumerable biscuits and passing them round the crew. We exchanged banter: I think the humour was a bit forced and had a slight hysterical touch to it as we were all aware that this was going to be something big … My own emotion was a kind of numbed fatalism.'

The first railway line presented few problems. Tanks zigzagged across it to avoid exposing their bellies, and on the far side the yeomanry closed up on 3/RTR to form three waves of sixty-four tanks apiece. The infantry of 159th Brigade, Territorials from the Welsh borders, occupied Cuverville without mishap, but had to launch a formal attack on Démouville which was not cleared until mid-afternoon. The task of mopping up prisoners and pockets of resistance on the ground crossed by the armour consequently fell to the division's motor battalion, 8/Rifle Brigade, which should have had a company, mounted in half-tracks, with each of the armoured regiments. These companies were too weak to clear the villages in the centre of the battlefield, and this had unfortunate consequences.

The two leading armoured regiments, unaware of the delays behind them, found it easy going at first. Captain Lemon tells us that: 'There was very little opposition and one had a wonderful feeling of superiority as many Germans, shaken by the preliminary bombing and shelling, gave themselves up. As time passed they grew more aggressive, having overcome the effect of the bombs and shells …' The tanks were nearing the Caen–Vimont railway line, just beyond the limit of fire support afforded by the 25-pdrs, when the plan, developing so promisingly, began to come unstitched.

The German Response
Hans von Luck's battle group comprised 503rd Heavy Tank Battalion, 200th Assault Gun Battalion, a battalion of 22nd Panzer Regiment, a rocket-launcher detachment, a battalion of 16th *Luftwaffe* Field Division and 1 and 2/125th Panzer Grenadier Regiment. Luck had established 'a graduated defence about 15 kilometres [9 miles] in depth', with his

Panzer Grenadier battalions in blocking positions behind the *Luftwaffe*, the assault guns in villages and the tanks further back. He had enjoyed a few days' leave in Paris and reached his headquarters shortly after 9 a.m. on 18 July. It was immediately clear that all was not well, and his deputy told him that the bombardment had stopped barely half an hour before and there was no radio contact with units. Luck climbed into a Panzer IV and set off down the Vimont–Caen road, telling his adjutant to pass the news to the division and to send an officer forward to the tanks. 'Slowly and without interference,' he wrote:

I approached the village of Cagny which lay exactly in the middle of my sector and was not occupied by us. The eastern part as far as the church was undamaged; the western part had been flattened. When I came to the western edge of the village, I saw to my dismay about twenty-five to thirty British tanks, which had already passed southward over the main road to Caen … A glance to the north where my 1 Battalion ought to be, or had been, in combat positions. The whole area was dotted with British tanks, which were slowly rolling south, against no opposition.

Luck set off back down the road and was passing Cagny church when he saw four 88mms, barrels pointing skywards. Their young captain told Luck that he was part of the air-defence ring round Caen, and refused to take on the tanks, saying: 'Major, my concern is enemy planes, fighting tanks is your job. I'm *Luftwaffe*.' Luck drew his pistol and told the officer that he could 'either die now on my responsibility or win a decoration on his own'. 'I bow to force,' answered the captain. 'What must I do?' Luck ran out with him to the northern edge of the village and showed him where to post his guns, firing from an orchard across standing corn which concealed them well. Then he returned to his headquarters where he briefed Major Becker, who had a battery at Grentheville, west of Cagny and behind the railway line, and two in le Mesnil-Frémentel.

The 88mms in Cagny caught the Fife and Forfars in the flank. Ron Cox saw the tanks of his squadron leader and second-in-command hit. 'Other tanks I could see were stationary and some were beginning to brew,' he remembered. 'Dust and smoke were combining with heat-haze to make visibility more and more difficult. There were no targets. Nothing intelligible was coming over the radio. I watched through the periscope, fascinated, as though it was a film I was seeing.' His tank reversed, then there was a crash and shudder as it was hit. Sergeant Wally Herd shouted 'Bale out!' and as the crew ran, crouching, through the corn, the tank was hit again and smoke began to billow from it.

Luck's intervention destroyed sixteen of the Fife and Forfars' tanks but did not stop the regiment, and 3/RTR was already past by the time the German guns opened fire. It had lost only one tank to Major Becker's gunners in le Mesnil-Frémentel but, as it crossed the angle between the Caen–Vimont and Caen–Falaise railway lines, the battery in Grentheville hit it squarely. Major Bill Close, A Squadron's commander, saw:

Several anti-tank guns amongst the trees … the gunners frantically swinging their guns round towards us. In the cornfields around us were many multi-barrel mortar positions, which were already firing over our heads. They were quickly dealt with, in some cases simply by running over them with the tank. But the anti-tank guns were a different matter. Opening fire at point-blank range, they hit three of my tanks which burst into flames; and I could see that the squadron on my left also had several tanks blazing furiously.

After this, 3/RTR moved west of the village and advanced on Soliers, with Bras and Hubert-Folie prominent on the ridge behind it.

The Advance on Bourguébus Ridge

At 11 a.m. the battle seemed to be going well enough for the British. 11th Armoured Division was clear of the bottleneck, the Guards Armoured Division had passed through the minefield and begun to take over the eastern flank of the corridor, and 7th Armoured Division was on its way over the River Orne. A counter-attack from Frénouville had been attempted by 21st Panzer with its handful of surviving Mk IVs but they were quickly knocked out. The leading British regiments were across the Caen–Vimont railway line and had begun to ascend the ridge towards their objective.

The set-backs seemed minor. The Fife and Forfars and 3/RTR had each lost about a squadron. On the German side, Rosen's Tiger company had managed to get eight tanks into running order and had clawed the flank of the Guards Armoured around Emiéville, helping to prevent penetration between that village and Cagny. The Guards had been told that Cagny was strongly held, and had begun to swing west of it in their efforts to reach Vimont. And while 7th Armoured was indeed crossing the bridges, it was crossing them slowly. It took two hours for 1/RTR to cross, and there was a solid traffic jam between the bridges and the minefield.

Major-General Edgar Feuchtinger, commander of 21st Panzer, lacked armoured experience and was best known as organizer of the military element of Nazi party rallies. But the sternest *Kriegsakademie* instructor could not have faulted his division's response to Goodwood. The Germans were good at patching together improvised forces to meet potential breakthroughs, and by late morning the villages on the Bourguébus ridge were held by the divisional engineer battalion, stiffened by motor cyclists and scout cars from the reconnaissance battalion. The German artillery, intact behind the ridge, was out of range of batteries across the Orne, and those 88mms which had escaped the morning's calamities were ready to rake the long slopes with their fire.

Worse still, from the British point of view, Panzer Group West had been alerted by air photographs of the Orne bridges taken the previous night. The commander of 1st SS Panzer Corps, Obergruppenführer Sepp Dietrich (an ex-NCO described by the chilly Rundstedt as 'decent but stupid'), claimed to have learned just as much by putting his ear to the ground to hear the rumbling of hundreds of tanks. Panzer Group West issued a general warning to units around Caen, shuffled a battle-group of 12th SS Panzer Division to Lisieux as a backstop and ordered 1st SS Panzer Division to move from its position east of Caen against 11th Armoured Division. 1st SS Panzer Division *Liebstandarte Adolf Hitler* had served in Poland, France, Russia and Italy, and although it now had less than fifty Panthers and Panzer IVs these were crewed by men who blended long experience with the sternest resolve. The division scuttled round the southern outskirts of Caen, profiting from the scattered cover in the Odon and Orne valleys, to nudge its assault guns up on to the Bourguébus Ridge while its tanks growled around Bras, Hubert-Folie and Bourguébus itself.

'It is not ... altogether fanciful,' observed John Keegan, 'to compare the situation at Bourguébus ridge in the early afternoon of July 18th, 1944, with that at Waterloo at the same time of day 129 years and one month earlier.' The battered defenders still retained strongpoints ahead of their main position, which itself was sited on admirable defensive terrain with a reverse slope to shield reserves. O'Connor should have been able to look on to the other side of the hill, but the tank carrying the leading forward controller had been knocked out and links between ground and air were tenuous. Nor is comparison with Agincourt unreasonable. British tank crews resembled French men-at-arms: unquestionably brave; well (but not well enough) armoured; out-ranged by their most deadly opponents; and peering into periscopes as knights squinted through their visors.

'It was just as the leading tanks were level with Hubert-Folie that the fun began,' said an officer of 3/RTR. 'I saw Sherman after Sherman go up in flames and it got to such a pitch that I thought that in another few minutes there would be nothing left of the regiment.' Bill Close lost two of his squadron's tanks, and then his own. Desperate to get back into the battle, he commandeered a sergeant's tank at pistol-point, and saw 'the rest of the regiment heavily engaged, at least seven tanks blazing, and baled out crews making their way back to the embankment.' Further east, the Fife and Forfars were also in trouble, and as the 23rd Hussars approached the Caen–Vimont railway they saw pillars of greasy black smoke above this tank crematorium and were greeted by a yeomanry officer who reported, with understandable exaggeration, that his regiment had lost all but four of its tanks.

'It was no good sitting where we were,' admitted Geoffrey Bishop of the 23rd, and his C Squadron was ordered to advance on the village of Four. The squadron leader gave radio orders 'in an excited voice, but they were perfectly clear. They were to be his last.' Within minutes, five tanks were burning and another three were immobilized, and B Squadron, on the right, was losing tanks as quickly. Bishop saw that the medical officer had set up a dressing station in a signal box, 'and casualties started streaming back from the burnt-out tanks. The chaps were all blackened, their clothes burnt, and most of them had lost their berets. A tank which had survived came roaring back with a lot of wounded lying on the back of it.' The remnants of the regiment moved back behind the railway line, 'quite convinced that nothing could have been a greater failure, and everyone had seen the last of some of his best friends.' The attack fizzled out with a last charge by the Northamptonshire Yeomanry, which left sixteen of its Cromwell tanks below Bras.

The battle went on, although without the saturation bombing of Bourguébus which O'Connor had called for. He hoped to use 7th Armoured Division to join 29th Armoured Brigade in a two-pronged attack on Hubert-Folie and Bourguébus, but it was so badly delayed crossing the Orne and percolating its way through rear areas raided by the *Luftwaffe*, which threw its remaining strength into the battle, that it was not clear of the bridges until dawn on the 19th. Private Robert Boulton, in a Brengun carrier platoon of the Queen's Regiment, remembered that:

When we did get across, tanks and trucks were on fire all over the place. The dust was absolutely choking … There was a poor lad who had had most of the bottom of his back blown away. There was nothing to be done for him so he was just put outside on a stretcher. That poor devil screamed for about two hours; morphine seemed to have no effect. He was pleading for someone to finish him off. Our sergeant had been in the war from the start, and even he was white and shaken.

When the battle closed under cloudy skies on 20 July the charnel villages of Cagny, Bourguébus, Bras and Hubert-Folie had been taken. British penetration was at the best 7 miles (11 km) deep, and losses were great – 8 Corps alone lost over 400 tanks and 2000 men. When the losses of the flanking corps are included, 2nd Army had suffered some 6000 casualties, most of them already-scarce infantrymen. Montgomery had sent Brooke a wildly over-optimistic account of the action on the afternoon of 18 July, and over the days that followed he was assailed by a 'blue as indigo' Eisenhower and by air chiefs who accused him of having claimed their help on false pretences.

After the war Montgomery acknowledged that criticism was 'partly my own fault, for I was too exultant at the Press conference I gave during the Goodwood battle,' but went on to claim that he could not tell the press his 'true strategy' which had been to tie down German armour rather than break out. The tide of reproach was to be turned by two dramatic pieces of news. On 20 July there was an abortive attempt on Hitler's life, and five days later Bradley's American troops began Operation Cobra. Exactly a month later, all four Allied armies were level with the Seine, and the French 2nd Armoured Division liberated Paris: the battle for Normandy was over at last.

A View of the Field

The long connection between England and Normandy is summed up on the Memorial to the Missing, which stands on the Boulevard Fabian Ware, named after the founder of the Commonwealth War Graves Commission, on the western edge of Bayeux. 'We, once conquered by William,' reads the Latin inscription on its colonnaded front, 'have now set free the Conqueror's native land.' The memorial commemorates the 1537 British, 270 Canadians and one South African who fell in Normandy and have no known graves. Across the road is Bayeux War Cemetery, the largest British Second World War cemetery in France, which contains 4648 graves, including that of Corporal Bates of the Royal Norfolks, the only holder of the VC to be buried in Normandy. His headstone tells us that he was a Camberwell lad, a useful reminder that, by the end of a long war, the regimental system was not quite what it seemed to be.

Two Military Museums
Although Bayeux is off the Goodwood battlefield and a good half-hour by car from Caen, it is a sensible place to start a study of the battle because the Musée de la Bataille de Normandie, a stone's throw from the Memorial on the Boulevard Fabian Ware, is devoted to the break-out. Amongst the vehicles outside are a Sherman, an armoured vehicle Royal

Engineers on a Churchill tank chassis, and a German Hetzer self-pro-pelled anti-tank gun. The recommended route through the museum takes the visitor past cases displaying uniforms, weapons, newspapers and photographs, and a large room at the end of the circuit houses guns, one of them the powerful German 88mm that inflicted so much damage on the Allies.

The Musée-Memorial off the northern edge of the Caen ring-road (N13) is altogether different. Opened in 1988, it is a symbol of peace and takes a longer view of history. Its deals with occupation, resistance, liber-ation and reconstruction, and its concern for human rights reflects a cen-tury which seemed to offer many Frenchmen the choice between Verdun and Auschwitz.

Exploring Caen

Caen is the capital of Lower Normandy and houses the *préfecture* of the Calvados region. The town stands at the confluence of the Orne and the Odon rivers, and was fortified by the Viking leader Rollo, who secured a tract of territory from Charles the Simple of France by agreeing to con-vert to Christianity and to become Charles's vassal. In the eleventh cen-tury the Duchy of Normandy was a powerful independent state, and Norman adventurers travelled widely. The descendants of Tancrede de Hauteville established a kingdom in Sicily, and other Normans played a leading part in the crusades, ruling the Middle Eastern principalities of Antioch and Edessa.

Caen owed its rise to William the Conqueror, bastard son of Duke Robert, born to a tanner's daughter from Falaise in 1027. Its massive castle was begun by William in 1060 and improved by his youngest son Henry I. The Conqueror died at Rouen in 1087 and was buried in the Church of St-Etienne in the Abbaye aux Hommes at Caen, but his bones were scattered when the Huguenots sacked the church in the sixteenth century. A femur survives, and lies beneath the altar. In 1346, during the Hundred Years War, Edward III's men passed through Caen on their way to Crécy. They respected the Conqueror's tomb but little else: Caen was pillaged and its goods sent off to England down the Orne.

The bombing of July 1944, in the run-up to Operation Goodwood, did terrible damage to Caen. Three-quarters of the city was destroyed, thou-sands of its citizens were killed, many buried, dead or alive, beneath the rubble of their homes. When British and Canadian troops entered Caen on 9 July they were greeted with kindness but not wild enthusiasm. 'The women kissed them, the men saluted them, but with dignity, without mad exaggeration,' remembered the deputy mayor. 'We have all suffered too

The armoured divisions were withdrawn on 20 July. The weather broke, turning the ground into mud: here British soldiers struggle with a bogged motor-cycle combination.

much for our dearest ones to acclaim excessively those who have been forced by the necessity of war to do us so much harm.'

Operation Goodwood

To reach the Goodwood battlefield take the D515 northwards towards the ferry port of Ouistreham, turning westwards to Bénouville 3 miles (5 km) from the edge of Caen. Pegasus Bridge, which crosses the Caen Canal on the eastern edge of the village, was the site of the first Allied landing on D-Day and, with Orne Bridge just to the east, was secured in a brilliant *coup de main* by Major John Howard's D Company 2/Oxfordshire and Buckinghamshire Light Infantry. The original Pegasus Bridge was replaced in 1995, but markers show where Major Howard's gliders landed. The two bridges captured by the Oxfordshire and Buckinghamshire were used by divisions moving up for Goodwood and code-named Euston Bridges. Crossings to the south, opposite the centre of Bénouville, were code-named London Bridges, and crossings further north, approached through St-Aubin d'Arquenay, were known as Tower Bridges. Marked routes took vehicles towards the front line through Ranville and Le Bas de Ranville. For an excellent overview of the bottleneck, proceed through Ranville to the western edge of Bréville, on the ridge which bears the Bois de Bavent. This area was captured on the night of 12 June by 12/Para and 12/Devons, assisted by a troop of the 13/18th Hussars, attacking from Amfreville.

Looking south from Bréville one gets a cork's eye view of the bottle-neck. Pegasus Bridge and Ranville in the British 11th Armoured Division's concentration area are easily visible, as are Colombelles on the right and the Bois de Bavent on the left. In July 1944 the low ground beneath you was strewn with gliders used to fly in the Airlanding Brigade of the British 6th Airborne Division on D-Day: Geoffrey Bishop thought that they looked like the massed skeletons of prehistoric beasts. To reach the front line, take the D37b south as far as the D513. To your left, just outside Bréville, is the Château de St-Côme, unsuccessfully attacked on 19 June by 5/Black Watch of 51st Highland Division with the loss of 200 men. Turn right on the D513, go through Hérouvillette and swing south for Escoville on the far side of the village. The minefield ran along the southern edge of Escoville: gap 14 was where the houses peter out as the road leaves the village to the south. Look westwards across the field towards Ste-Honorine-la-Chardonnerette: the front line curled north-wards between the two villages, almost touching the D513, before swing-ing back to keep Ste-Honorine as a British-held salient.

To follow the advance of the British 29th Armoured Brigade one can drive through Cuverville and Démouville, where the absence of old houses testifies to the ferocity of the bombing, as far as the northern edge of Cagny, where a track strikes south-east towards Ferme du Château and a minor road runs south-west past new industrial buildings towards the main N13. The same spot can be reached after a good hour's walk down the track which neatly bisects the angle of the D228 and D227 where they fork south of Escoville, heading due south and edging south-west for the last mile or so. The narrow-gauge railway ran between Démou-ville and Sannerville just north of the N175, and its route can still be made out. The Autoroute de Normandie, which runs parallel with it is, of course, a modern addition.

Looking west from the junction of roads and track north of Cagny we can see the farm complex of le Mesnil-Frémentel from, very roughly, the position of the four *Luftwaffe* 88mms. 3/RTR had already passed through this gap heading south, and the rear elements of the Fife and Forfars were caught in it. To understand the difficulties of 3/RTR as it crossed the Caen–Vimont railway, proceed to Grentheville by way of the N13 and the D230. The tanks went over the first railway line and then, after fighting their way past Grentheville, jinked under the second, many using the tunnel on the minor road due west of the village. They then shook out to attack Bras and Hubert-Folie, west of the railway line, and were engaged by the German tanks and assault guns of 1st SS Panzer Division as they did so.

Finally, to look at the British advance from the German viewpoint, go on through Soliers into Bourguébus, and turn right for Hubert-Folie. Stop just over the railway bridge and look north-north-east. On a clear day one can see all the way back to Bréville, with Colombelles and the Bois de Bavent defining the bottleneck as clearly from the southern end of the battlefield as they did from the north. Most of the villages have been rebuilt although some older buildings, such as the stud at Manneville, north-east of Cagny, miraculously survived. It is easy to see why this was such a killing-ground, but hard to imagine the sights reported by one British officer:

It was a scene of utter desolation. I have never seen such bomb craters. Trees were uprooted, roads were impassable. There were bodies in half; crumpled men. A tank lay upside down, another was still burning with a row of feet sticking out from underneath. In one crater a man's head and shoulders appeared sticking out from the side. The place stank.

Over 2000 British, Canadian, Australian, New Zealand and Polish soldiers, many of them killed in Goodwood, are buried in the CWGC cemetery at Banneville-la-Campagne, on the N175 south-west of Sannerville. Amongst them is the artist Rex Whistler, a lieutenant in 2/Welsh Guards, the reconnaissance regiment of the Guards Armoured Division. When his regiment was probing Emiéville he left his tank to confer with his squadron leader and was killed. Many of Ken Tout's comrades of the Northamptonshire Yeomanry also rest in this beautiful place, and the regiment's white horse runs lightly across their headstones.

Further Reading

I have strong views about 'television history.' As a medium, television is complementary to, not in competition with, the written word. What television gains in immediacy it can so easily lose in detail: but in contrast, some academic prose seems designed to be impenetrable to all but the most committed. What follows is a personal recommendation on further reading for those who have enjoyed my TV programmes and the chapters in this book, and now wish to dig deeper. This is not a full bibliography, and certainly reflects favouritism on my part.

Hastings
Stephen Pollington, *The English Warrior: From the Earliest Times to 1066* (London, 1996) is a valuable study. Christopher Gravett, *The Norman Knight* (London, 1993) in the Osprey Warrior series is more constrained by its format but has some striking colour plates. Stephen Morillo (ed.), *The Battle of Hastings* (Woodbridge, Suffolk, 1996) is packed with major sources and scholarly interpretations, while Christopher Gravett, *Hastings 1066* (London, 1992), part of the Osprey Military campaign series, is an accessible popular history. Denis Butler, *1066: The Story of a Year* (London, 1966) now shows its age but still gives a wonderful feel for this decisive year.

Agincourt
Anne Curry and Michael Hughes (eds.), *Arms, Armies and Fortifications in the Hundred Years War* (Woodbridge, 1993) provides a scholarly assessment of military aspects of the war. Jonathan Sumption, *The Hundred Years War* (London, 1990) and Christopher Allmand, *The Hundred Years War* are the best overall histories. For the battle itself see Anne Curry, *The Battle of Agincourt* (London, 2000) and Matthew Bennett, *Agincourt 1415* (London, 1991).

Bosworth

Modern literature on the battle is overshadowed by the debate over its location. For the Wars of the Roses generally, see John Gillingham, *The Wars of the Roses: Peace and Conflict in Fifteenth Century England* (London, 1981) and A. J. Pollard, *The Wars of the Roses* (London, 1988). In *Battles in Britain 1066–1746* (London, 1994), Glenn Lyndon Dodds reviews the possible sites. He concludes that Peter J. Foss is right in *The Field of Redemore* (London, 1990) to challenge the traditional site. D. T. Williams disagrees in *The Battle of Bosworth*, a pamphlet published by Leicestershire County Council. Matthew Bennett is always worth reading on medieval warfare. The first edition of his *Battle of Bosworth* (Stroud, 1985) plumps for the traditional site, but there is a useful addition to the 1993 edition. Michael K. Jones recently entered the fray with *Bosworth 1485* (London, 2002), proposing yet another location.

Naseby

Glenn Foard, *Naseby: The Decisive Campaign* (Whitstable, 1995) is essential reading, not least because of its author's use of archaeological evidence and deep understanding of the terrain: another book by this author is scheduled for publication by Cassell in 2004. Martin Marix Evans, *English Civil War: Naseby, June 1645* (London, 2002) is a good popular study. I am a fan of Charles Carlton, *Going to the Wars: The Experience of the British Civil Wars 1638–1651* (London, 1992). Christopher Hibbert, *Cavaliers and Roundheads* (London, 1993) is an easily read history.

The Boyne

J. G. Simms, *Jacobite Ireland* (London, 1969) provides essential background, and Richard Dougherty, *The Williamite War in Ireland* (Dublin, 1998) is the best overall history of the war. The war's two major battles are the subject of John Kinross, *The Battle of the Boyne and Aughrim* (London, 1997). Visitors will find Edna O'Boyle's pamphlet *The Battle of the Boyne* (Duleek Historical Society, 1990) useful. *The Irish Sword*, journal of the Military History Society of Ireland, has several illuminating articles in its Winter 1990 edition.

Waterloo

This is one of history's most written-about battles: studying it is like sipping from a fire hydrant. Mark Adkin, *The Waterloo Companion* (London, 2001) is a comprehensive survey with particularly useful graphics. Waterloo was one of the case studies in John Keegan's elegant and seminal *The Face of Battle* (many editions, most recently London, 1991). David Chandler, *Waterloo: The Hundred Days* (London, 2001) and Christopher Hibbert, *Waterloo* (London, 1998) are excellent studies. The diligent Peter Hofschröer argues in two volumes of *1815: The Waterloo Campaign* that the German contribution to the battle has been underestimated by Anglophone historians and, more contentiously, that Wellington did not behave fairly towards Blucher, the Prussian commander.

Mons and Le Cateau

My own *Riding the Retreat: Mons to the Marne 1914 Revisited* (London, 1995) is part military history and part an account of following the campaign on horseback. John Terraine, *Mons: The Retreat to Victory* (London, 1960) is old but wears its years lightly. Keith Simpson, *The Old Contemptibles* (London, 1981) is good on the British military background. E. L. Spears, *Liaison 1914* (reprinted London, 2000), Frank Richards, *Old Soldiers Never Die* (London, 1933) and John Lucy, *There's a Devil in the Drum* (London, 1939) shine out amongst the many personal accounts.

The Somme

Martin Middlebrook, *The First Day on the Somme* (London, 1971) is a towering achievement. Martin and Mary Middlebrook, *The Somme Battlefields* (London, 1991) is a detailed guide and required reading for enthusiasts. Gary Sheffield, *Somme* (London, 2003) is a good study by a historian with a deservedly growing reputation in this field. Malcolm Brown, *The Imperial War Museum Book of the Somme* (London, 1996) is based on research in the museum's archive. For a (sanguine) view of the Somme's impact on British tactics see Paddy Griffith, *Battle Tactics of the Western Front* (London, 1994). Robin Prior and Trevor Wilson, *Command on the Western Front* is an archive-based study of the tactical methods of General Sir Henry Rawlinson, army commander on the Somme.

Arras

There is a chapter on Arras in my *Army Battlefield Guide* (London, 1990), which reproduces Rommel's situation maps, showing how he overestimated the threat posed by the attack. The best overall account of the campaign is Brian Bond, *The Battle of France and Flanders 1940* (London, 2001), although Alistair Horne, *To Lose A Battle: France 1940* (London, 1975) remains wonderfully atmospheric. Kenneth Macksey, *The Shadow of Vimy Ridge* (London, 1965) looks at this piece of France in three wars.

Dunkirk

Brian Bond, *The Battle of France and Flanders 1940* and the official history, L. F. Ellis, *The War in France and Flanders 1939–40* (London, 1953) are a good start. Dunkirk itself suffers from being over-mythologized or debunked, and readers need to keep their critical faculties well honed. See particularly David Divine, *The Nine Days of Dunkirk* (London, 1959) and Walter Lord, *The Miracle of Dunkirk* (London, 1982). For striking personal accounts see John Horsfall, *Say Not the Struggle* (Kineton, 1977) and Airey Neave, *The Flames of Calais* (London, 1972).

The Blitz

I wish that the atmospheric *The Blitz: The Diary of Edie Benson* (London, 2001) had been about when I was writing this book. The official history is Basil Collier, *The Defence of the United Kingdom* (London, 1975). Winston G. Ramsey (ed.), *The Blitz: Then and Now* (London, 1988) is a detailed, three-volume account of the air attack on the UK: Volume 2 deals with London in September 1940–May 1941. Tom Harrison, *Living Through the Blitz* is based on the government's mass-observation reports, and Robert Westall, *Children of the Blitz* (London, 1985) is an illustrated compendium of children's accounts.

Operation Goodwood

There is no single good book on this battle, but the 'Yeomen of England' chapter in John Keegan, *Six Armies in Normandy* (London, 1982) is wonderfully atmospheric. Carlo d'Este, *Decision in Normandy* (London, 1983) remains the best overall account of the campaign, and Max Hastings is characteristically sound in *Overlord: D-Day and the Battle for Normandy* (London, 1984). For the feel of armoured battle in Normandy one cannot do better than read Ken Tout, *Tank: 40 Hours of Battle, August 1944* (London, 2002). There will doubtless be a rush of new books to mark the 2004 anniversary.

Acknowledgements

A lifetime's fascination with battlefields means that I often spend more time in France than I do at home. My wife Lizzie, and my daughters Jessica and Corinna, deserve the reader's sympathy – and my heartfelt thanks.

Index

Picture Credits

BBC Books would like to thank the following for providing photographs and for permission to reproduce copyright material. While every effort has been made to trace and acknowledge all copyright holders, we would like to apologize should there be any errors or omissions.

Aviation Picture Library p. 333 (above, Imperial War Museum © Austin J. Brown); Bankfield Museum p. 195 (above, Calderdale Leisure Services); Bridgeman Art Library pp. 66, 78-9, 113, 132 (Alnwick Castle, Northumberland), 136 (Forbes Magazine Collection, New York), 177 (Scottish National Portrait Gallery); © British Museum p. 21 (below); Collections pp. 51 (© David Bowie), 120-1 (both, © David M Hughes); Crown Copyright Reserved, Public Record Office p. 71; Dover Museum p. 349; Estate of Rex Whistler 1996 Dacs/photo supplied by the National Army Museum London pp. 206-7, 406, 407; E.T. Archive pp. 52, 70, 74-5, 195 (below), 217 (above), 87 (below), 96-7 (centre), 186 (National Army Museum), 333 (centre, Imperial War Museum), 334-5 (Imperial War Museum), 391 (© Imperial War Museum), 395; The Fotomas Index pp. 127 (main picture), 156-7, 163 (left); Hulton Getty pp. 333 (below), 371 (both), 375 (right); Imperial War Museum pp. 232-3 (cut-out), 240 (both), 246, 247, 253, 256, 261, 275 (both; below, courtesy E. Shephard copyright holders), 280-1, 283 (both), 296, 299 (centre), 308 (right), 317, 319, 322-3, 328, 414 (below), 421, 429, 343, 357, 359, 375 (left), 377 (both), 389, 391; Kunsthistorisches Museum, Vienna p. 27 (below); Liddle Collection, University of Leeds p. 233 (above and centre); Mary Evans Picture Library pp. 163 (right), 189; © Michael Holford, pp. 21, 33, 46 (both); MOD Pattern Room, Nottingham pp. 195 (below), 400-1 (cut-out); National Portrait Gallery pp. 53 (above), 112, 139, 140; © Pacemaker Press International p. 193; Robert Hunt Picture Library p. 414 (above); The Royal Armouries, Leeds pp. 27 (above), 87 (above), 96-7 (above & below), 126-7 (cut-out), 137 (both), 170-1 (both); The Royal Collection © Her Majesty The Queen pp. 198-9; The Tank Museum pp. 299 (cut-outs, above and below), 308 (left), 326; © Times Newspapers Ltd p. 365; William Turner pp. 265 (above, courtesy Mr Marshall), 265 (centre), 265 (below, courtesy Mrs Hargreaves), 292 (courtesy Hyndburn Tourist Office); Ulster Museum, Belfast p. 176; The University of Ghent p. 108; Victoria and Albert Museum p. 217 (below); Wallace Collection p. 53 (below); Welsh Guards pp. 401, 407 (courtesy Colonel of the Regiment).